"Old Testament violence continues to be a [...] issue for many Christians today. Among the voices attempting to address the questions, one of the most prominent is that of Paul Copan. We can expect anything that comes from his desk to be serious, rigorous, and honest. *Is God a Vindictive Bully?* is no exception. It will be helpful—even redemptive—for many who wrestle with these questions. And while not all will wholly agree with him, it will be one of the go-to books on the subject for years to come."

—**Helen Paynter**, Centre for the Study of Bible and Violence, Bristol Baptist College

"Serious criticisms are often made of the Old Testament in general and of its portrayal of God in particular. These criticisms come both from within the church and from without. Copan here subjects these criticisms to careful scrutiny, testing them against the claims of the Old Testament. He finds that when we read the Old Testament with attention to its time and context, these criticisms are misplaced. Rather, the Old Testament is consistent with the New in revealing a God who is prepared to get involved with the mess of life and bring redemption. A careful and reflective work, this is important reading for thinking Christians who want to understand why the Old Testament matters for their faith."

—**David G. Firth**, Trinity College, Bristol

"In this very important and much-needed volume, Copan does a marvelous job of dealing with arguments that would introduce a separation between the God of the Old Testament and the God of the New Testament. With erudition he skillfully answers 'critics from without' and, unfortunately, 'critics from within' who advocate for this harmful dichotomy. I am extremely grateful for this faithful defense of the repeated affirmation in the New Testament that the God portrayed in the Old Testament is, indeed, 'the God and Father of our Lord Jesus Christ.'"

—**Jerry E. Shepherd**, Taylor Seminary, Edmonton, Alberta (emeritus)

"Can a God of love command an adulterer's execution? Copan explores this and many other objections to biblical texts. By careful reading he shows how biblical writings consistently present a single God, gracious and just. Questions and doubts current today are often superficial and unbalanced. Here are clear, well-founded answers for Christian believers."

—**Alan Millard**, University of Liverpool (emeritus)

"Many recent studies on the Bible's portrayal of divine violence attempt to resolve the canon's dissonances with categorical templates or through hermeneutical sleight of hand. Copan, however, refuses the path of least interpretive resistance and opts instead to take the tensive thickness of the Bible's testimony head on. Informed by careful reading and with due attention to contexts and nuances, he offers a study on the topic that is both encyclopedic in scope and thorough in its treatment of particularly problematic texts. Readers will find much to ponder in this important contribution to an urgent conversation."

—**L. Daniel Hawk**, Ashland Theological Seminary

"At a time when the credibility of the Bible and the character of God are being questioned by critics outside of the Christian community and by some within it, this book offers thoughtful, biblically credible, and theologically convincing answers. Furthermore, Copan exposes the fallacies of the Bible's detractors, as well as the flaws of their readings of the Bible and the ignorance of their conclusions."

—**James K. Hoffmeier**, Trinity Evangelical Divinity School (emeritus)

"Do you have a problem with something, or a lot of things, in the Old Testament? Copan has provided a virtual encyclopedia of helpful answers to frequently asked questions that trouble many readers. He tackles a whole range of objections that arise both from those who claim broad Christian allegiance to the Bible as a whole and from those who make no such claim whatsoever and use the Old Testament as a major reason for their hostility. This is a thoroughly detailed reference work that those of us who teach or preach the Old Testament will turn to frequently, or point others to, when such questions are aired. An excellent resource indeed!"

—**Christopher J. H. Wright**, Langham Partnership;
author of *Old Testament Ethics for the People of God*

"Copan's work speaks to current voices that assert the Old Testament's depiction of God is highly problematic or at odds with the New Testament. He engages critics from outside the faith who with vindictive glee mischaracterize the Old Testament's presentation of God. He addresses critics from within who jettison the hard parts of the Old Testament or assert its depiction of God is in error. God's people are often confused by and suspicious of the Old Testament, wondering how it aligns with Jesus; these conversations are pressing for my seminary students and for local pastors and congregations. Copan provides a valuable resource in accessible language that speaks with informed conviction and with grace. In a time when the Old Testament's necessary role in Christian faith is attacked and undermined, Copan's work serves the good of the church. I highly recommend it for all whose faith seeks understanding."

—**Lissa M. Wray Beal**, Providence Theological Seminary, Otterburne, Manitoba

Is GOD A VINDICTIVE BULLY?

Is GOD A VINDICTIVE BULLY?

Reconciling PORTRAYALS *of* GOD *in the* OLD *and* NEW TESTAMENTS

PAUL COPAN

Baker Academic
a division of Baker Publishing Group
Grand Rapids, Michigan

Published by Baker Academic
a division of Baker Publishing Group
PO Box 6287, Grand Rapids, MI 49516-6287
www.bakeracademic.com

Printed in the United States of America

Library of Congress Cataloging-in-Publication Data
Names: Copan, Paul, author.
Title: Is God a vindictive bully? : reconciling portrayals of God in the Old and New Testaments / Paul Copan.
Description: Grand Rapids, Michigan : Baker Academic, a division of Baker Publishing Group, [2022] | Includes bibliographical references and index.
Identifiers: LCCN 2021062173 | ISBN 9781540964557 (paperback) | ISBN 9781540966070 (casebound) | ISBN 9781493438006 (pdf) | ISBN 9781493437993 (ebook)
Subjects: LCSH: God—Biblical teaching. | Bible. New Testament—Relation to the Old Testament.
Classification: LCC BS544 .C655 2022 | DDC 231—dc23/eng/20220203
LC record available at https://lccn.loc.gov/2021062173

22   23   24   25   26   27   28   7   6   5   4   3   2   1

To William Lane Craig and J. P. Moreland,
whose friendship, scholarship,
dedication, and collaboration
have inspired, encouraged,
and strengthened me over the years.

"Remember those who led you, who spoke the word of God to you; and considering the result of their conduct, imitate their faith."

—*Hebrews 13:7*

Contents

Part 3 | Crime and Punishment
Violations and Penalties in Old Testament Law

Part 4 | For Whom the Bell Tolls
Harsh Texts and Difficult Old Testament Questions

Part 5 | Of Human Bondage
Women and Servants in Israelite Society

Part 6 | War and Peace

Warfare and Violence in the Old Testament (and the New)

Part 7 | The Heart of the Matter

The Summing Up of All Things in Christ

Preface

This book is a companion volume to my 2011 Baker book, *Is God a Moral Monster?* (hereafter, *Moral Monster*).[1] It is the natural overflow of my earlier work—including my coauthored book with Matthew Flannagan, *Did God Really Command Genocide?* (hereafter, *Genocide*).[2] Given the strong interest in these books, their translation into a number of languages, the ongoing opportunities I've had to speak on Old Testament topics, and the steady stream of *Moral Monster–* and *Genocide*-related questions, this follow-up book seemed fitting. It not only addresses *additional* challenging Old Testament topics. It also *fills in gaps* and makes some *tweaks*. That said, *Genocide* in its own right provides a wide-ranging, in-depth, cross-disciplinary treatment of Old Testament warfare.

This book's structure and content center on the Old Testament's relationship to the New. In light of God's revelation in Jesus Christ, how should we understand troubling texts from the Hebrew Scriptures? Does the New Testament reject all violence, wrath, and severity now that Jesus has come on the scene? How do "turning the other cheek" and "loving your enemies" square with commands to drive out the Canaanites or the Old Testament's harsh punishments and pronouncements? Did God *truly* command capital punishment and order the dispossession of the Canaanites? Or was that just the *misrepresentation* of God's message by fallen, violence-prone prophets or biblical narrators?

In the present work, I'll be addressing these new questions, in addition to others:

- Should the Old Testament be "unhinged" from the New?
- How should we think about certain contemporary, theologically "revisionist" claims that Moses, Joshua, and other prophets were seriously misguided and even issuing "demonic" commands?

xiii

- Did Moses borrow legislation from other ancient Near Eastern law collections? And if he did, does this suggest that the Mosaic law is "just another ancient law collection"?

- Does the law of Moses express significant worldview differences from other ancient Near Eastern law collections, or are they roughly approximate?

- Are the harsh punishments in Israelite legislation (e.g., stoning and burning to death) intended to be followed literally? What do the actual history of Israel and the ancient Near Eastern setting reveal?

- Why would God harden Pharaoh's heart?

- How could David be "a man after God's own heart"?

- How do we make sense of the "vindictive" imprecatory (prayer-curse) psalms?

- Is divinely approved coercive physical force ("violence")[3] found in the New Testament too?

- Were Israelite soldiers allowed to engage in battlefield rape?

In addition to tackling these new issues, I clarify, expand on, and—in some places—modify previous *Moral Monster* material:

- Does the term "patriarchal" adequately describe Israelite society? How much power did women in Israel really have?

- Are modern versions accurate in using the term "slave" and "slavery" in the Old Testament?

- Does Leviticus 25 support the treatment of foreign "slaves" as mere property?

- When it comes to the Canaanites, is the rendering "utterly destroy" (*haram*) an accurate or a potentially misleading translation? What about women, children, and the elderly?

- How much overlap do we have between the Old and New Testament portrayals of God?

In all of this, the goal is to add fresh material without significant overlap in content. Some overlap and recapping of themes will be necessary, though, to provide proper context. Thus, this book is a companion volume to *Moral Monster* and *Genocide*, all of which attempt to present a unified portrayal of the kind and severe God of both testaments.

By popular request, I've included subject and Scripture indexes in this volume—something not included in *Moral Monster*. However, thanks to Peter J. Vorster Sr., the Scripture index for *Moral Monster* is available at my website (www.paul copan.com).

Unless otherwise indicated, I use the New American Standard Bible 1995. Italics that appear in biblical quotations are my additions for emphasis. When citing a Hebrew poetic text, I use lowercase letters rather than the NASB's capi-talizations at the start of each line. In addition, I use textual forms in my Greek transliterations, though I stick primarily with the lexical forms of Hebrew words.

Heartfelt thanks to my longtime Baker editor Robert Hosack, whose friend-ship and encouragement I have appreciated over the years. I am very grateful to Tremper Longman III and Jerry Shepherd for their very helpful comments. Thanks to Professor Alan Millard, who offered detailed and immensely helpful insights to my previous *Genocide* book and this book as well. Thanks also to my Baker support team—James Korsmo and freelancer Kathy Noftsinger, who are stellar editors, as well as Sarah Gombis, Shelly MacNaughton, Lydia Koning, Anna English, and Rayce Patterson—for the labors behind the scenes. Thanks, too, to Old Testament scholars Claude Mariottini and Charlie Trimm, who kindly sent me prepublication copies of their books on Old Testament violence and the character of God, which I cite in this volume.

My beloved wife, Jacqueline, deserves special thanks for her thorough support and partnership through this and so many other book endeavors.

I dedicate this book with heartfelt gratitude to my decades-long philosophical mentors and partners in ministry, William Lane Craig and J. P. Moreland.

PART 1

The Great Divorce

*How Wide the Divide between
the Old and New Testaments?*

1

The Old Testament God

Critics from Without and from Within

Critics from Without: From A. A. Milne to Richard Dawkins

"Yahweh" or "Jehovah"—the God of the Old Testament—has plenty of critics. One such was A. A. Milne, creator of the Winnie the Pooh stories. He claimed: "The Old Testament is responsible for more atheism, agnosticism, disbelief—call it what you will—than any book ever written."[1]

What are their criticisms? The world's most outspoken atheist, Oxford's Richard Dawkins, gives them to us in a nutshell: "The God of the Old Testament is arguably the most unpleasant character in all fiction: jealous and proud of it; a petty, unjust, unforgiving control-freak; a vindictive, bloodthirsty ethnic cleanser; a misogynistic, homophobic, racist, infanticidal, genocidal, filicidal, pestilential, megalomaniacal, sadomasochistic, capriciously malevolent bully."[2] No wonder Dawkins advises parents not to use the Old Testament to teach morals to our children.

Dawkins is one of several "New Atheists" who rose to prominence in the wake of the September 11 attacks. They lashed out in condemnation not just of Islam but of *all* religion as poisonous and evil. Actually, my *Moral Monster* book uses these atheists' descriptions of the Old Testament God (Yahweh) as chapter headings. And the titles of that previous book and of this one are taken from Dawkins.

These particular atheists created a negative reputation for themselves, even among secular academics. They were utterly tone-deaf to widespread criticisms

3

of their rhetoric, caricatures, and arguments.[3] One former New Atheist, P. Z. Myers, called this movement a "train wreck."[4]

Even so, the bold challenge New Atheists presented has prompted many Christians to take a closer look at Scripture and reexamine texts that seemed much less troublesome to earlier generations of believers. Those are some of the critics from *without*.

Critics from Within: Not the "Textual" God but the "Actual" God

The Old Testament's portrayal of God has critics from *within* the Christian community as well. These include theologian and pastor Greg Boyd, Old Testament scholars Eric Seibert and Peter Enns, and others. On the one hand, *they would largely agree* with Dawkins's description of "the God of the Old Testament" as "genocidal," "vindictive," and so on. On the other hand, these critics from within don't think the *true* God is like this. The portrayal of "the most unpleasant character in all fiction" is not the *actual* God but the *textual* God.[5]

So, what's the difference between the "actual" God and the "textual" God? As these scholars see it, when Scripture says that *God* gave David the victory over Goliath (1 Sam. 17:45–47) or that *God* promised to "drive out" the Canaanites from the promised land (Josh. 13:6), that wasn't the *actual* God. The actual God is nonviolent, enemy-loving, self-sacrificing, and forgiving—especially as revealed in Jesus on the cross: "Father, forgive them" (Luke 23:34).

So the 415 mentions of "Thus says the LORD" often *don't* come from the *actual* God—as you might think—but come from just the *textual* God. Who or what is this *textual* God? This is *the literary depiction of God by a fallen, violence-prone, culturally conditioned ancient Near Eastern biblical narrator or prophet*. That is, the *textual* God is just a *fictitious* and *flawed* representation.

According to Boyd, in the cross of Christ the *actual* God exposes and repudiates the false, idolatrous, blasphemous falsehoods of this textual God.[6] The enemy-loving Jesus reveals a God who could never command or engage in "violence." The true God "hides" behind an ugly mask of violence and genocide.

Some of these critics from within also reject the doctrine of penal substitution. Often behind this critique are popular but outrageous caricatures and misrepresentations that no notable theologian defending this doctrine would endorse.

Table 1.1. The "Actual" God versus the "Textual" God

Actual God	Textual God
The *true* portrayal of God as nonviolent, enemy-loving, forgiving, as exemplified by Jesus on the cross.	A *fictitious* portrayal of God that originates from the fallen, violence-prone, culturally conditioned biblical author's or prophet's ancient Near Eastern worldview.

For example, a train switchman allows a train full of passengers to run over his young son playing on the track so that they won't be killed by an oncoming train on the other set of tracks. Such phony analogies tend to present *three* parties in this drama: an angry, wrathful God the Father; a loving but hapless Jesus forced onto the cross ("cosmic child abuse"); and sinful humanity. Rather than "sinners in the hands of an angry God," they think we should see the atonement only in terms of "sinners in the hands of a loving God."[7]

Why not both? A proper understanding of penal substitution has two parties in view—the loving and just triune God, and sinful humanity. Furthermore, God *loves* the world (John 3:16), and Jesus himself is *also* wrathful against sin (Rev. 6:16). Yet Jesus *voluntarily* lays down his life for lost human beings (John 10:17). The *triune God's* wrath against our sinful record is averted because the righteous Christ's accomplishment is *legally* imputed to our record if we receive this gift.

Consider how innocent, guilt-free parents legally represent their teenager, who has been the responsible party in an auto accident. They take care of the legal responsibility, paying the insurance costs (the legal penalty or "punishment") for their guilty teenager, thus allaying the potential "wrath" of the law. Though we can't get into this topic here, the doctrine of penal substitution is both robustly biblical and philosophically defensible.[8]

We're getting somewhat sidetracked, though. These critics from within claim that Old Testament prophets and narrators were simply "wrong" in much of what they said and did. After all, this was "inevitable" given all of the baggage of their ancient Near Eastern worldview.[9]

God's Kindness, God's Severity, and Human Honesty

The apostle Paul writes, "Behold then the kindness and severity of God" (Rom. 11:22). As we'll see in this book, severity, toughness, or harshness is a theme in *both* Old Testament and New alike. That is, severity is a description not just of the *textual* God but of the *actual* God. That doesn't mean, though, that severity or wrath is central to the triune God's nature. As we'll see, *love* is God's central attribute, and God's severity *flows out of* his love. God desires the ultimate well-being of humans, but he will sometimes have to say, "Enough is enough." He will have to act in judgment to stop dehumanization and other evils that undermine human flourishing.

Biblical scholar N. T. Wright declares that to deny God's wrath is to deny his love:

> Face it: to deny God's wrath is, at bottom, to deny God's love. When God sees humans being enslaved . . . if God doesn't hate it, he is not a loving God. . . . When God sees innocent people being bombed because of someone's political agenda, if God doesn't hate it, he isn't a loving God. When God sees people lying and cheating and abusing one another, exploiting and grifting and preying on one another, if God were to say, "Never mind, I love you all anyway," he is neither good nor loving. The

Bible doesn't speak of a God of generalized benevolence. It speaks of the God who made the world and loves it so passionately that he must and does hate everything that distorts and defaces the world and particularly his human creatures.[10]

We should expect this of the loving Cosmic Authority, whose severity cuts across the testaments.

The Old Testament as a Friend

Charitability and the Golden Rule of Interpretation

As biblical scholar Bruce Birch wrote, Old Testament texts "are rooted in a cultural context utterly unlike our own" with an outlook that is often "alien and in some cases repugnant to our modern sensibilities."[11] In light of such concerns, author Mathew Richard Schlimm asks: *What if we approached the Old Testament's laws and historical narratives with charity rather than suspicion?* That is, we show a willingness to understand them in their historical context and allow them to speak. It's like wanting to learn from an old friend who is introducing a different culture and country to us.[12] What if we sought first to give the benefit of the doubt?

Consider a "golden rule" of interpretation: *treat another's writing as you yourself would want your own writing to be treated.* This doesn't mean being naive or uncritical; it does mean being charitable and fair as we honestly examine challenges in the text.

As traditional, Bible-believing Christians, one problem we readily see with some of our critics from without—who may be non-Christians, but particularly those of the New Atheist variety—is that they tend to *pounce* on any biblical text that strikes them as harsh or wrathful or strange. They aren't too concerned about nuance or context, nor are they very open to reasoned explanation or discussion. For example, they may ignore references to God's patience with stubborn Israelites or his sorrow at human sin. Or they latch on to the word "slave" in the Old Testament—an unfortunate rendering, as we'll see—and they automatically assume this is identical to "Southern slavery."

On the other side, critics from within—that is, within the church—may recoil at biblical references to God's severity and forcefulness ("violence"); they emphasize God's kindness and love, as displayed in Jesus on the cross. These insider critics consider this Old Testament severity to be a mistaken portrayal of God by fallen, violence-prone biblical authors and prophets. Yet we'll see that New Testament authorities—and even Jesus himself—carry on the severity that most people restrict to the Old Testament. Jesus viewed himself as carrying on the calling and task of those prophets.

In light of the dual biblical affirmation of God's kindness and severity (Rom. 11:22), for our critics from *without*, we want to emphasize that *God is far more loving, kind, patient, tender, and merciful* than we could ever know. Throughout the Old Testament we see language of God attempting to woo his people back to himself (Hosea 2:14), being hurt by their rebellious hearts (Ezek. 6:9), longing to show mercy (Isa. 30:18) and to provide for them (Ps. 81:10–16), and pleading with them to return to him (2 Chron. 36:16). He patiently waits half a millennium (from the time of Abraham to the time of Joshua) to bring judgment on the "disobedient" Canaanites (Gen. 15:16; Heb. 11:31), and he is willing to relent in judgment if *any* people turn from their wickedness (Jer. 18:7–8; Jon. 4:2).

And for our critics from *within*, we emphasize that *God is more severe and harsh and unsafe* than they suggest. For those who oppress, dehumanize, defraud, mislead, and live hypocritically, divine wrath is the appropriate, just response, as it is to other objective moral evils. Thankfully, the God-created world we inhabit is one that guarantees cosmic justice will be done.

The theologian Stanley Hauerwas has offered this critique of someone's unorthodox view of God: "One of the things that bothers me about [his] God is that she is just too damned nice!"[13] Putting it another way, Garret Keizer writes, "The Lord my God is a jealous God and an angry God, as well as a loving God and a merciful God. I am unable to imagine one without the other. I am unable to commit to any messiah who doesn't knock over tables."[14]

The former nun Karen Armstrong wrote rather simplistically: "It is wonderful not to have to cower before a vengeful deity, who threatens us with eternal damnation if we do not abide by his rules."[15] Conor Cunningham—a religious scholar—responded: "Imagine if Hitler rather than an ex-nun had written those words."[16] To stress either divine kindness or divine severity at the expense of the other results in a skewed moral picture. Neither the critic from without (like Armstrong) nor the critic from within strikes the right balance.

Not that I myself presume to have attained the perfect balance with all moral questions tidily resolved. But as we look especially at the critics from within, I find too many inconsistencies and a good deal of selectivity to affirm the direction they take. I wish things were as easily resolved as they suggest!

EXCURSUS:
A Quick Word on God and Violence

Before getting further underway, we should note that the Old Testament does not ascribe "violence" (*hamas*) to God or to righteous humans or nations using physical force in a righteous cause. Rather, that word is associated with wicked, law-breaking, oppressive human beings; they injure, wrong, or harm physically or nonphysically. Without creaturely sin and violence, divine wrath and judgment wouldn't occur.

We could say that God uses *just coercive physical force* in response to human violence and oppression.[17] So even though we make reference to *divine violence* or *divine counterviolence* in response to human sin, keep in mind that such language is a concession to a conventional way of speaking. Scripture itself doesn't refer to God as *violent*.

Table 1.2. Responding to Critics from Without and Within

To critics from *without*	To critics from *within*
God is more loving, kind, patient, tender, and merciful than we could imagine.	God is more severe, harsh, and unsafe than they suggest.

Ragged Edges and Rough Pathways

In this book, we walk with the Old Testament as a friend—but over rough terrain and through slime pits. It reveals both an *idealism* of hoped-for peace and order and a *realism* about its ancient Near Eastern setting.[18] Thus, some of these Old Testament laws will "push society as far as it could go at that time without creating more damage than good," even if it "can and should ultimately go further."[19]

Another matter: *we shouldn't be surprised if some people may simply disagree about certain moral assumptions about what a good God once commanded under certain conditions and at a certain time and for certain reasons perhaps known only to him.* This doesn't mean reversing good and evil altogether. It does mean a divine command from a good God may still be *very difficult* and severe even if it isn't *intrinsically evil.* To command intrinsic evil would be impossible for God (Jer. 19:5).

Some critics from within may hold that certain divine commands are merely *difficult*, not *impossible*—while others may consider those commands just plain *impossible.* Kenton Sparks admits that *he's not sure* if God really commanded Abraham to sacrifice Isaac.[20] Greg Boyd says God *did* issue this command, even if the command seems troubling when taken on its own without any additional historical context.[21] Randal Rauser says God *couldn't* have done so,[22] even though the New Testament itself takes for granted that this was God's command (Heb. 11:17–18; James 2:21–23).

EXCURSUS:
Moral Intuitions and Harsh Divine Commands

Let's briefly examine Rauser's denial that God issued this command to Abraham. Rauser appeals to our basic moral intuitions to justify this claim: we just have this basic instinct that such a command is immoral. Although Matthew Flannagan and I deal with this objection in detail elsewhere,[23] I would say here that I readily agree that, *in general*, we ought to pay attention to these intuitions. However, *a good, wise God may make rare, highly specified, authorized exceptions for morally justifiable reasons.* Such exceptions don't imply that good and evil are utterly reversed or that we should therefore abandon those basic intuitions.

Rauser appeals to the Christian legal philosopher J. Budziszewski's fine work on conscience and moral intuitions to support his claim.[24] However, even Budziszewski makes room for certain divinely authorized exceptions, including both the sacrifice of Isaac and the driving out the

Canaanites. If a supremely good God, who is the author of life, has morally sufficient reasons for issuing this unusual, difficult command to Abraham, then "God is not commanding Abraham to commit murder."[25] This God is the *source* of moral duties, but he himself doesn't *have* duties. Further, he can make certain exceptions concerning the laws of human nature that don't destroy the integrity of the larger truth that he has ordained—namely, the created order. That is, God can issue these commands without acting contrary to his own nature or overturning the created natural order. In addition, Budziszewski, following Thomas Aquinas, recognizes overriding exceptions to these general operations *must be based on clear divine revelation*, which is what we indeed have in Scripture.[26]

Isaiah notes that God, in his severity, rises up "to do his deed—strange is his deed! and to work his work—alien is his work!" (Isa. 28:21 ESV). God will sometimes resort to strange and alien things—deviations from his heart's desire and from how things normally operate. And as the Christian novelist Flannery O'Connor maintained, such divine severity turns out to be a subversive means of redemption.[27]

In the midst of all of these questions, remember that ultimately God will do what is good and just. He will not do otherwise. A perfectly good, all-wise Cosmic Authority will have justifiable reasons for commanding or permitting certain actions—reasons for which we don't always have access.

A Brief Postscript on the Critic from Without

Through social media, a Christian asked me if atheists had been convinced by previous arguments in *Moral Monster* and *Genocide*. I replied that, speaking anecdotally, I've found that various atheists have indeed been persuaded to see that Old Testament laws on "slavery" were a far cry from what was practiced in the antebellum South and that Old Testament warfare texts utilize exaggeration or hyperbole and can't in any way be considered "genocide" or "ethnic cleansing." At any rate, those books—and this one too—are the type of book that may at least give helpful perspective to critics and questioners outside the Christian faith. They can help one put difficult Old Testament texts into a more understandable context, as well as minimize a number of common misunderstandings and barriers to belief.

The main thing is to keep the main thing the main thing. We should begin with the clear and then move to the unclear—rather than the other way around. Though I've written about this elsewhere,[28] in brief, begin with the Big Bang, which implies *theism*, and go to the historicity of Jesus's bodily resurrection, which confirms the truth of the *Christian faith*—and then work out any of the difficulties or murky details from there. I'll come back to these themes in the last couple of chapters.

2

Is the God of the Old Testament the Same as the God of the New? (1)

Marcion versus Moses

Paul writes that Christians are no longer under the law of Moses but "under grace" (Rom. 6:14–15). That *doesn't* mean that Old Testament saints were saved by following the law. No, they were still *saved by God's grace through faith*. That includes Abraham, who lived *well before* the Mosaic law was even given. He *believed* God's promise (faith), and he was declared righteous by God's grace (Gen. 15:6). And *that* was before he was even circumcised (Gen. 17; cf. Rom. 4:1–14).

In fact, Genesis 26:5 uses the "Mosaic law" language of Deuteronomy, affirming that "Abraham obeyed Me and kept My charge, My commandments, My statutes and My laws." To be saved by grace enables you to keep God's law—to live an obedient life that's pleasing to God. Hebrews 11 emphasizes the centrality of faith—trust in and allegiance to God—throughout the Old Testament.

This raises questions: Does the Christian then disregard the law of Moses and the rest of the Old Testament's ethical demands? What is the carryover to the New Testament?

This and the following chapters will examine the specific theme of the identity of the Old Testament portrayal of God compared to that of the New Testament. The present chapter looks at the ancient heretic Marcion's attempt to discredit Moses and the God of Israel. It concludes that he was seriously mistaken. What's more, the moral themes in the law of Moses—and the larger story of Israel—are woven into the New Testament's moral picture.

The next two chapters compare Moses and Jesus. Some of our critics from within will pit Moses against Jesus to create a wide moral gap between them. This is a misrepresentation. Moses and Jesus actually have much in common with each other, and the New Testament refers to Moses in highly approving terms.

"Unhitching" the Old Testament from the New?

Pastor and author Andy Stanley's book *Irresistible* claims that the New Testament must be "unhitched" from the Old. After all, the Old advocates misogyny (hatred of women) and treating women as property ("commodities"). It portrays God as "angry" while the New portrays him as "brokenhearted." In the Old you could hate your enemy, but Jesus tells us to love our enemies. So if we don't "unhitch" the Old, this will lead to all kinds of terrible things such as the "prosperity gospel, the crusades, anti-Semitism, legalism, exclusivism, judgmentalism," and so on.[1] The Old Testament is the "culprit" here—a stumbling block to faith because people have used it to justify all kinds of abuses.[2] The solution Stanley advocates is basic: disregard all Old Testament commands, and stick with Jesus's command to love. If we had followed Jesus's Sermon on the Mount (Matt. 5–7), this hornet's nest of Old Testament problems wouldn't have arisen within Christendom.

Well, that's both a sweeping and inaccurate statement. Consider, for instance, the Crusades and the various modern myths associated with them. (In *Genocide*, we mention five of them.)[3] Contrary to Stanley's assumption, the Crusades were largely a defensive *just* war—a protective response to long-standing and ongoing Islamic aggression. What's more, it was in fact *Jesus's* own words—loving your neighbor, laying down your life for a friend—most often quoted to rally the troops to fight. It *wasn't* Old Testament war texts.

What about anti-Semitism? The late distinguished Yale historian of theology Jaroslav Pelikan claims the opposite: anti-Semitism in the West is the result of "unhitching" the New Testament from its very Jewish roots.[4] Author and pastor Fleming Rutledge offers a similar counterpoint: "Many Christians continue, unthinkingly, to speak of 'the God of the Old Testament' as though this supposedly wrathful and judgmental God had been supplanted by an endlessly tolerant and indulgent Jesus. This ill-formed attitude is not exactly anti-Semitic, but it can be called into the service of anti-Semitism."[5]

Paul tells us that "all Scripture"—by which he means *the Old Testament*—is "profitable for teaching, for reproof, for correction, for training in righteousness" so that the godly believer "may be adequate, equipped for every good work" (2 Tim. 3:16–17). And for Jesus, to love God and others *expresses* the heartbeat of the Mosaic law and the Prophets (Matt. 22:37; cf. 7:12). Jesus and other New Testament authorities are regularly drawing on and applying that same moral heartbeat for the new covenant community. Love doesn't run contrary to their message—and that includes expressions of wrath.

Marcion Makes a Comeback

Marcion: Two Testaments, Two Gods

What's the relationship of the Old Testament to the New? And how does the New Testament itself treat challenging, severe-sounding Old Testament passages? The Christian theologian Origen of Alexandria (ca. 184–ca. 253) *allegorized* some tough or harsh-sounding texts. Now, he did take the Noahic flood as literal and historical, but he is known for emphasizing the "deeper" moral or spiritual meaning in the Canaanite texts as a picture of spiritual warfare. In like manner, the Cappadocian church father Gregory of Nyssa (ca. 335–ca. 395) maintained that Jericho represented one's former way of life, which needed to be overthrown. But even so, these men believed in these Scriptures—along with the New Testament—as inspired by one and the same God.

By contrast, the heretic Marcion (85–ca. 160) interpreted these harsh texts in a more straightforward, nonallegorical manner. He concluded that texts about the wrathful, punishing God of the Israelite nation *couldn't* be inspired Scripture. That God seemed so unlike the good, enemy-loving heavenly Father whom Jesus proclaimed. Marcion created a chasm between the Old and New Testaments. He came up with his own anti-Judaistic "Bible" drawn from Luke and some of Paul's Letters.

Neo-Marcionism Today? The "Textual" and "Actual" Gods and the Chasm Between

Has the long shadow of Marcion fallen across today's Christian landscape? A number of contemporary Christians like Andy Stanley, Greg Boyd, Peter Enns, Eric Seibert, Brian Zahnd, and others in the ballpark have been called "practical Marcionites"—as Old Testament scholar Tremper Longman puts it.[6]

On the one hand, we can commend such modern-day authors for wrestling with difficult passages that we all find perplexing and troubling. And we should all wrestle honestly with the biblical text and also try to remove as many *unnecessary* stumbling blocks as possible so that others may understand and embrace the good news of the gospel. We also want to be careful about using labels carelessly or superficially.

On the other hand, we must not create stumbling blocks that remove the sting of divine severity and just retribution by minimizing and explaining away harsh texts and difficult commands issued by a good and just God himself. I am concerned with a rising number of thinkers within the church who have greatly reduced what counts as authoritative Old Testament Scripture—and even portions of the New Testament. *They have formed their own narrower canon* (i.e., authoritative Scripture)—a canon *within* the biblical canon. This certainly moves in the direction of Marcionism.

For Seibert, violent Old Testament Scriptures—and even New Testament ones—should be rejected as merely human; they are not authoritative or inspired. They can't be from God. For Boyd, severe ("violent") and other harsh texts may technically be Scripture, and even historically true, but they are solely the product of mere fallen, violence-prone humans: "Thus says *Moses*" or "Thus says *Joshua*"—but not "Thus says *the [actual]* LORD."

Boyd's "actual God" canon is purportedly shaped primarily by the "cruciformity" criterion: *the character of God is most clearly expressed when Jesus cries from the cross, "Father, forgive them."* While this enemy-love does indeed express the heart of God, Boyd would have us think that divine harshness can't be connected to God because this isn't the "heart" of God's character. This is a false dichotomy (cf. Rom. 11:22). Though not his "heart language," God claims that "vengeance" belongs to him when humans defy him and dehumanize others. This too moves in the direction of Marcion.

Now the term "cruciformity" does remind us of Paul's guiding principle of knowing nothing but Christ and him crucified (1 Cor. 2:2). But when Paul hopes for assistance from the Roman military to physically protect him from a mob seeking to kill him (Acts 23:16–33), surely this wasn't a violation of cruciformity. In any event, we'll see that Boyd presents a *one-sided, narrow* slice of what the New Testament teaches about Jesus.[7] After all, *Jesus* engaged in coercive force when driving money changers from the temple (John 2:15); "*Jesus* . . . destroyed" unbelieving Israelites in the wilderness (Jude 5); and *Jesus* threatened to "strike dead" the followers of the false prophetess Jezebel (Rev. 2:23 NIV). These severe acts by Jesus are more than "Father, forgive them" on the cross; they look like the violence Boyd repudiates.

His fourteen-hundred-page book claiming God can't act "violently" gives no actual definition of "violence." He just assumes that "you know violence when you see it."[8] Yet Boyd would consider "violent" the act of a police officer who moves—with potential lethal force—to stop an assault on a woman or to prevent a terrorist attack against innocent civilians. But many of us consider such responses to be right and appropriate—acts of neighbor-love . . . but more on this in the next chapter.

Putting Moses in His Place

Moses—a Demonically Inspired Prophet?

According to Boyd and other critics from within, Moses was a misguided, fallen, violence-prone prophet who often *misheard* and *misrepresented* God's message.[9] Moses was more like a *demonically* influenced prophet when he commanded the Israelites to drive out and—if need be—fight against the Canaanites. After all, "what was regarded as heroic and God-glorifying in one epoch may turn out to be regarded as closer to demonic . . . in a later one."[10] To drive this point home, the critic, Boyd, claims that Moses's command to drive out the Canaanites violates the message of the cross and cruciformity. Because this runs contrary to Paul's gospel (1 Cor. 1:18; Gal. 1:8–9) the only conclusion we can draw is that we should place Moses's command "under God's curse."[11]

Despite this accusation, *nowhere* does Scripture indicate or imply that Moses was so utterly misguided. Indeed, a prophet who led Israel into immorality should be considered a *false* prophet, not a true one (Deut. 13:1–5). By contrast, *Moses was unlike any other prophet*; he knew God "face to face" (Num. 12:7–8; Deut. 34:10 NIV), and God repeatedly reminded Israel to listen to him (e.g., Num. 12:8; 16:28–40, 41–50). And Jesus and various New Testament writers confirm this. They speak with unqualified praise about Moses: "Moses was faithful in all [God's] house as a servant" (Heb. 3:5; cf. Matt. 8:4; 23:2–3; Luke 16:31; John 5:45–46; 7:19). These authorities assumed that when Moses said "thus says the LORD," this was the *actual* God. It wasn't some *textual* God—a deity that was the product of a culturally conditioned, violence-prone, sinful prophet.

Following Jesus faithfully includes adopting his authoritative approach to the Old Testament. But get this: Boyd and other critics from within will even *reject*—or *ignore*—authoritative-sounding statements in the New Testament if these conflict with their narrowed version of cruciformity.

Like Jesus, Paul was aware that the law of Moses was not ideal. Nevertheless, he—like Jesus—still uses affirmative language about the Mosaic law: it is "spiritual" (Rom. 7:14) and "holy and righteous and good" (Rom. 7:12; cf. 1 Tim. 1:8). Yet *the version of Moses we get from our critics from within makes it difficult to distinguish him—or Joshua or Samuel—from a false, demonically inspired prophet leading Israel to engage in wicked behavior in the name of the Lord.* But Old Testament prophets warned against those who just followed some imagined ("textual") deity of their own making: "Do not listen to the words of the prophets who prophesy to you, filling you with vain hopes. They speak visions of their own minds, not from the mouth of the LORD" (Jer. 23:16 ESV).

The Mosaic Law as a Booster Rocket

So what does Jesus mean when he says that Moses *permitted* certain laws because of human hard-heartedness (Matt. 19:8)? Here are a couple of implications:

Implication 1: Hard-hearted Israelites, not hard-hearted Moses. Jesus viewed not *Moses* as hard-hearted and morally compromised but rather the *Israelites*, to whom God gave the law.

Implication 2: Less-than-ideal laws. Though the Mosaic law was *not intrinsically immoral, this wasn't the perfect legislation for God's people for all times.* This law expresses God's tolerance for—and accommodation to—certain inferior moral conditions such as warfare, servitude, monarchy, and (many biblical scholars argue) polygamy.

Let's explore the role of the Mosaic law a bit more.

First, *the law of Moses helped regulate and put a restraint on certain flawed conditions and institutions to keep them from getting out of control.* After all, laws present *the behavioral floor* rather than *the lofty moral ceiling*. Laws express *the limits of tolerance rather than the ideal.* As Gordon Wenham puts it: "A study of the legal codes within the Bible is unlikely to disclose the ideals of the lawgivers, but only the limits of their tolerance: if you do such and such, you will be punished. The laws thus tend to express the limits of socially acceptable behavior: they do not describe ideal behavior."[12] John Goldingay puts it this way: "Legislation by its very nature is a compromise between what may be ethically desirable and what is actually feasible given the relativities of social and political life."[13] What is the ideal? To love God and others, find joy in God's presence, imitate his character, and live humbly (e.g., Ps. 51:16–17; Amos 5:21–27). Mere law keeping isn't the ideal.

Second, *the law, though imperfect, had an important preparatory place in Israel's history.* Paul spoke of the law as a "tutor"—a schoolmaster—until Christ came (Gal. 3:24–25). N. T. Wright compares the law to a *booster rocket*, whose thrust is needed to take a spacecraft outside the earth's atmosphere; when its task is accomplished, it is dropped off.[14] Likewise, the Mosaic law was necessary to establish ancient Israel in its nationhood, theology, institutions, and moral practices, but once Christ and the new covenant came in the fullness of time (Gal. 4:4), the Mosaic covenant had completed its preparatory task (Rom. 10:4). Now new identity markers would characterize the interethnic people of God—the new Israel (Rom. 2:29–30; Phil. 3:3; 1 Pet. 2:9).

Third, *the church as the "new Israel" is not "replacement theology" but "fulfillment theology."* The church *does not replace* the Old Testament people of God but rather includes them. The uniting of Jew and Gentile in Christ is the *fulfillment* of God's promise to Abraham to bless all nations through him.

Back to the booster-rocket image: once the law's purpose had been accomplished, it was set aside as the covenantal identity marker of God's people. We are under the new covenant ushered in by Christ. But this includes *much moral carryover* from the Old to the New. The same moral and spiritual fuel supply for the Mosaic booster rocket continues to fuel the new people of God by the same Spirit; he was necessary to sanctify and transform Old Testament saints as he does today. But instead of the bestowal of the Spirit on select individuals among God's people, he is God's mark and seal of *all* who belong to Christ (Rom. 8:9; cf. Acts 2:17–18). In addition, priestly mediators are no longer necessary since all believers are themselves priests before God, offering various spiritual sacrifices (1 Pet. 2:5, 9). Through Christ, each believer has complete cleansing and forgiveness (Heb. 9:13–14), a deep personal knowledge of God (Jer. 31:34; Heb. 8:11), and direct access to him (Heb. 4:16).

Moving from Moses's Covenant to Jesus's Covenant

Behind these less-than-ideal Sinai laws is the assumption that humans sin and are enmeshed within fallen, sinful social structures. As a result, various Israelite laws fell short of God's creational ideals rooted in Genesis 1–2:

- *male-female equality* (no patriarchy)
- *equal human dignity* (no classism, racism, master-slave, caste system, or other hierarchies)
- *permanent monogamous marriage* (no polygamy or sexual relations outside marriage)

While the Mosaic law wasn't given *to* us, it is still important *for* us as the new Israel. As we'll see, the new covenant brings with it a good deal of moral carryover for the Christian community.

So, what does this shift from Moses to Jesus look like?

A Creation-Recovered Ethic

Through Christ, the new covenant *recovers the creational ethic* of Genesis 1–2 (cf. Matt. 19:4–6; 1 Tim. 4:3–5). Through his resurrection, a new creation has begun (2 Cor. 5:17). Jesus is the *second Adam—the "new man"* (Eph. 2:15; 4:24; Col. 3:10) and the founder of a new, redeemed humanity.

A Christ-Shaped Ethic

As the descendant of Abraham, Jesus lived out ancient Israel's story as a faithful Israelite. He isn't only the second Adam, but he is the true Son that ancient Israel was not (Matt. 3:17). He came out of Egypt (Matt. 2:15), passed through the waters of the Jordan River in baptism (a second exodus), faithfully endured testing in the wilderness for forty days, and called a new Israel to himself (the twelve disciples).

The new covenant he inaugurated through his self-sacrificial death *informs the people of God to model their lives both on the incarnate Christ's exemplary life and service, his demanding teaching, and his self-giving death, and in light of the confident hope of the future bodily resurrection* (e.g., 2 Cor. 8:1–9; Phil. 2:5–11). We must follow not only the "old commandment" to love our neighbor but also the "new commandment"—to love one another *as Christ has loved us* (John 13:34; 1 John 2:7).

A Covenant-Identity Ethic

The old covenant was directed to *national Israel.* Its *ritual* laws such as circumcision and food laws served as typical boundary markers or marks of identification to distinguish Israel from the surrounding nations. By contrast, the new covenant is for *Jews and Gentiles in Christ.* Circumcision is no longer the mark of God's covenant people. Rather, it is God's Spirit who now indwells *all* of God's people, not just some of them, as under the old covenant (Rom. 8:9). And, as we've seen, each believer will have complete forgiveness, direct access to God's presence, and a personal knowledge of God: "All will know Me" (Heb. 8:11).

In terms of practices, instead of old covenant circumcision, *baptism* becomes the public initiatory rite and indicator of belonging to the Christian community. Instead of civil penalties, churches are to exercise *church discipline* (e.g., Matt. 18:15–17; 1 Cor. 5:1–13). Instead of a select order of priests, *all* of God's people are now priests with direct access to God, offering an array of spiritual sacrifices (e.g., Rom. 12:1; 15:16; Phil. 4:19; Heb. 13:14–15). Instead of the Mosaic distinction between clean (kosher) and unclean foods, Jesus declared all foods clean (Mark 7:19).

A Continuationist Ethic

The new covenant *reflects and extends the moral heartbeat of the old Mosaic covenant.* Some theologians have made this threefold ("tripartite") distinction within Israel's laws: *civil, ceremonial,* and *moral.* There's something to it. But remember that even though national Israel's *ceremonial* and *civil* laws were temporary, they were still *moral* matters: for Israelites to eat nonkosher foods or go uncircumcised was *immoral.*

That said, the old covenant ceremonial and civil laws don't carry over to the new covenant people. Yet the general moral fabric woven through the Mosaic law and Israel's story continues into the new covenant—especially the theme of loving God and loving others (Mark 12:30–31). In fact, the moral teaching of Jesus and Paul draws on the moral pulse of the Old Testament.

For example, nine of the Ten Commandments apply to Christ's followers (e.g., Mark 10:19; Rom. 13:8–11; 1 Tim. 1:8–10).[15] The exception is the Sabbath law, which was rooted in the first creation (Exod. 20:9–11); it was fulfilled in God's new creation, which began with Jesus's resurrection (Rom. 14:5; Col. 2:16).[16]

To get even more specific, consider a passage like Leviticus 19:2–18: its moral themes are carried over in James 2:1–13; 5:4; and 1 Peter 1:15–22.[17] For example, when James warns employers against withholding payment from those who have worked in their fields, lest their cries ascend to the Lord (5:4), he is harking back to Leviticus 19:13 and Deuteronomy 24:15.

The Christian philosopher-theologian Gordon Graham argues that there is "no such thing as *Christian* ethics."[18] One reason for this is that Jesus commanded and condemned the same sorts of things that Moses and the Old Testament prophets did. Furthermore, Jesus wasn't saying something highly original or unique about loving God and loving others, including one's enemies. In fact, Jesus didn't so much add *content* to morality, but he *embodied* it and gave it *fuller meaning* through his unique identity—including his life, teaching, death, resurrection, and the kingdom he inaugurated.[19] Scholar Millar Burrows likewise notes: "Essentially. . . what Jesus taught was the ethics of the Old Testament, with some shift of emphasis but with no change of substance."[20]

Likewise, C. S. Lewis claimed that the notion that the Christian faith "brought an entirely new ethical code into the world is a grave error" since "its Founder,

His precursor (the Baptist), [and] His apostles came demanding repentance and offering forgiveness, a demand and offer both meaningless except on the assumption of a moral law already known and broken."[21]

Also, because sin and evil persist within societies, the emphasis on the just use of coercive physical force continues into the New Testament, though this emphasis is diminished. Just force is a means of maintaining the public good (e.g., Acts 23:12–25; Rom. 13:1–8; 1 Tim. 2:1–2). This comes not through the church but through government officials who are commanded by God to preserve the peace, protect the innocent, and punish the guilty. This comes through just policing, a righteous judiciary, law enforcement that breaks up drug cartels and prostitution rings, and even just wars to protect innocent civilians and stop dehumanization and keep tyranny and terrorism at bay. Even if these officials don't live up to their God-given duties, the alternative is not to abandon them but to improve and reform them for the public good.

In sum, we have begun to see that the Marcion-like language and categories in recent scholarship don't reflect what either testament affirms. Nor do New Testament authorities—including Jesus—give us any reason to assert that Moses mishandled many of God's messages and that he seriously misrepresented God's intention for his people. In the next chapter, we look more closely at this theme—especially in our comparison of Moses and Jesus.

3

Is the God of the Old Testament the Same as the God of the New? (2)

Moses versus Jesus?

No Leeway on the Textual God versus the Actual God?

A Modern-Day Gap Factory?

Perhaps you know of the "straw-man fallacy." This is a logical misstep in which one attempts to construct or portray an opposing position in the worst possible light so that one can easily tear it down.

At least some who move in a Marcionite direction are doing this with Moses (see chap. 2). That is, they (a) take pains to *create as wide a gap as possible between the "textual" and the "actual" God* (effectively creating two "gods"), and thus (b) *construct airtight discontinuous and nonoverlapping compartments into which those two gods fit*. This produces dichotomies like hating enemies versus loving enemies, women as commodities versus women as equals, and so on. Creating these gaps without any stitch of nuance, however, renders the position all the more challengeable.

We can certainly commend our critics from within for trying to present God's character in as *good* and *loving* a light as possible. Indeed, this is something I myself am undertaking in this book! But they keep divine severity and coercive force at arm's length, as though Jesus's death on a cross clearly eliminates that severity or the use of divine coercive force. However tidy that solution appears at first, this gap-creation and dichotomizing are straw men. It's a lot easier to dismantle divine severity if you are selective in your treatment of New Testament texts[1] and you dismiss a lot of "thus says the LORD" talk as the product of human fallenness.

Slight Alterations?

In the spirit of Andy Stanley's call for "unhitching" the two testaments, theologian Greg Boyd claims that Jesus was *repudiating* the Mosaic law in the Sermon on the Mount: "You have heard that it was said . . . But I say to you . . ."?[2] Boyd claims Jesus "refuted" or "rejected" a number of Mosaic laws as intrinsically wrong and as too "harsh" or "meticulous," in violation of God's goodness.[3] Note a couple of concerns, however.

First, *Boyd allows no leeway in bridging the textual and actual God.* It's either one or the other—but this distorts and overstates. More accurate is that Jesus, followed by Paul, *relaxed* certain Mosaic laws pertaining to the Sabbath, food laws, or circumcision; after all, the Abrahamic promise to Jew and Gentile alike (Gen. 12:3; 18:18; etc.) was fulfilled in Christ. Jesus-followers have new identity markers, different from those of God's old-covenant people.

Second, part of the problem is that the critic from within (Boyd) turns Jesus's *correcting* the religious leaders' *misuse* of the Mosaic law into Jesus's *rejection* of that law. Even if these laws prove to be "harsh" or "meticulous," *Jesus gave no hint that these laws opposed divine goodness.* He routinely assumed they were divinely given by the *actual* God to national Israel for its own identity formation in preparation for the Messiah's coming. The Messiah would fulfill and make fuller sense of those laws for his new covenant people.

Third, *Jesus adapted and modified these laws*, but he himself got pretty *meticulous*: "Whoever then annuls one of the least of these commandments, and teaches others to do the same, shall be called least in the kingdom of heaven; but whoever keeps and teaches them, he shall be called great in the kingdom of heaven" (Matt. 5:19).

But let's now examine the claim by Boyd—that swearing or oath-taking, calling for "an eye for an eye," and God's taking "vengeance" are refuted or contradicted by Jesus in the Sermon on the Mount.[4] We'll see more clearly a certain selectivity, the creation of various straw men and of an unfortunate and inaccurate gap between Moses and Jesus.

"You Have Heard That It Was Said . . . ; But I Say to You . . ."

Clumsy Oaths? To Swear or Not to Swear?

Is it true that Jesus absolutely disavows vowing? Does Jesus tell his disciples to forswear swearing? Was *Moses's* word to the Israelites—"fulfill your vows [*tous horkous*] to the Lord" (Matt. 5:33)—contrary to *Christ's* command not to "swear [*omosai*] at all" (5:34 NIV)? Is it literally true that *anything* that goes beyond "yes" and "no" is from the evil one (5:37)? Does that mean believers shouldn't swear to tell the whole truth, "so help me God," in a court of law?

Boyd claims that *any* vowing or swearing commanded by the Mosaic law is immoral: for example, "you shall . . . swear by His name" (Deut. 6:13). Allegedly, when God allowed this practice in Israel, he was only "stooping" to bear the sin of his fallen, hard-hearted people.[5]

Is that really the proper explanation? No. For one thing, *Jesus opposed casuistry—sophisticated oath-taking practices that, ironically, were mere escape hatches from truth telling.* A cultural equivalent would be a child's crossing her fingers while lying to her parents; deception is justifiable with fingers crossed. What did Jesus have in mind? He expands on this truth-evasion charade in Matthew 23:16–22: swearing by the gold of the temple is a binding oath, but not if you swear by the temple alone—and so on.

Second, *in the New Testament, God, Jesus, and other authorities appropriate oaths, using the same language from the Sermon on the Mount.* For example, the New Testament reveals that the "actual" God swore to Abraham and David. And there's more:

- Zechariah referred to "the oath which [God] swore [*horkon hon ōmosen*]" to our father Abraham (Luke 1:73).
- God "had sworn . . . with an oath" (*horkō ōmosen*) to David (Acts 2:30).
- God confirmed his word with "an oath" (*horkō*) (Heb. 6:17; also, "vow" [*euchē*] in Acts 18:18; 21:23; "oath" [*horkōmosia*] in Heb. 7:21, 28).
- Paul used oaths repeatedly, appealing to God as "my witness" (e.g., Rom. 1:9; 9:1; 1 Thess. 2:5), or solemnly declaring that he was telling the truth and not lying and that God/Christ was his witness (Rom. 1:9; 9:1; 1 Tim. 2:7).
- James referred to his brother Jesus's oath prohibition (James 5:12), but James nevertheless urged Paul to join Jewish believers in making vows, which Paul did (Acts 21:23–26; cf. 18:18).
- Unfallen angelic beings even swore by God (Rev. 10:6).
- Jesus placed himself under oath at his trial (Matt. 26:63–64 NIV: "I charge you under oath by the living God: Tell us if you are the Messiah, the Son of God").

The biblical evidence clearly reveals that not *all* swearing is "from the evil one"— only the kind that attempts to evade truth telling. God's own oaths and swearing by his name are not demonic. *Correcting misuse is not repudiation.*

"An Eye for an Eye": Judicial Punishment or Personal Vendetta?

Our critics from within claim that Jesus repudiated Mosaic judicial punishments—"an eye for an eye." That means the actual God could *not* have commanded capital punishment in the Mosaic law.[6] Instead, Jesus calls us to "turn the other cheek," "not resist" the evil person (Matt. 5:38–39), and love our enemies (5:43–44). God never commands harm, we're told, and God's judgment is never one of *retribution*; rather, it is *redemptive* and *restorative*.[7]

Yes, God's great desire is to redeem and restore, but retribution isn't off the table for those who persist in violating God's commands. God would rather show mercy than bring judgment. He doesn't afflict willingly (Lam. 3:33) but does so as a last resort. When we look at the example of Jesus himself, we see a number of important themes related to love, vengeance, and the use of coercive force.

1. *Jesus opposed a misuse of the law to justify personal vengeance.* Jesus wasn't denying appropriate judicial punishment. Divine vengeance in Scripture is simply *retribution* or *redress*.[8] As in *Moral Monster*,[9] we'll explore further how specific *eye-for-eye* references focus on monetary payments rather than bodily punishments (e.g., Exod. 21:22, 27). The *eye-for-eye* principle emphasizes *proportionality*. The punishment fits the crime. And divine justice is God rendering to all according to their deeds (Rom. 2:6; Rev. 16:5–6). If redemption beyond this is possible, wonderful, but this doesn't eradicate the minimum of just punishment.

2. *To "turn the other cheek" is the response not to violence but to an insult.* In biblical times, cheek-striking wasn't an act of violence; it was a shaming insult (Job 16:10; Ps. 35:15; Lam. 3:30; cf. Isa. 50:6). Jesus was essentially saying, "Don't return insult for insult"—a point Peter makes as well (1 Pet. 3:9).

3. *Jesus himself didn't literally "turn the other cheek" when struck, and he used force in the temple.* At his trial, Jesus asked, "Why do you strike Me?" (John 18:22–23). He also forcefully drove out money changers from the temple. Jesus's Sermon on the Mount must be read alongside the life and teaching of Jesus as well as his words and actions elsewhere in the New Testament (e.g., Jude 5; Rev. 2:20–23).

4. *"Do not resist an evil person" (Matt. 5:39) is better understood as not resisting by evil means.*[10] After all, Jesus resisted evil people all the time, and he frequently challenged his religious opponents. What Jesus had in mind is what Paul picks up on: *no personal retaliation or returning evil for evil* (Rom. 12:17, 21).

5. *The Old Testament teaches both enemy-love and just punishment.* We're familiar with Mosaic judicial punishments, but Moses also taught *love of one's personal enemy* (Exod. 23:4–5; Lev. 19:17–18; cf. Prov. 24:17–18; 25:21–22). Moses *nowhere* commanded hating enemies, as some critics from within claim. As with other "you have heard it said" misinterpretations, Jesus here addresses the *misuse* of Moses to justify *personal* retaliation and hostility.

So, *enemy-love wasn't original with Jesus.* Both testaments teach that (a) loving one's personal enemy and (b) punishing a criminal can be done without contradiction. In Romans 12, Paul rejects *personal vengeance*, but in Romans 13 he affirms the state's role as a "minister of God" and an official "avenger" (Rom. 13:4).

6. *The apostle Paul exhibited this personal-official distinction in Acts 23.* When a violent mob threatened the apostle Paul's life, official state action was necessary.

Paul told his nephew to inform the commanding Roman officer about this plot. Paul received a military escort out of Jerusalem to Caesarea. He didn't turn the other cheek with a *personal* enemy who insulted him. Rather, he made an *official* appeal to the Roman government to do its job and protect an innocent civilian from harm, even if this required lethal force. And because Paul was a Roman citizen, he insisted on the right to be treated like one (Acts 16:35–39; 22:23–29). Even so, whenever Paul was imprisoned, he used it as an opportunity to proclaim the gospel (e.g., Phil. 1:13).

7. *To claim that the "actual" God didn't command capital punishment through Moses is false.* Capital punishment was the maximum penalty under the Mosaic law, but, as we'll see, it was only mandatory in the case of murder; otherwise, monetary payment was possible. Nevertheless, Jesus confirmed *actual God*–issued capital punishments in the Old Testament: rebellious children who cursed their parents were to be put to death according to "the commandment of God" (Matt. 15:3) and the "word of God" (15:6). Boyd is simply incorrect in saying that the actual God didn't command capital punishment and that Jesus was just using irony in exposing the religious leaders' inconsistency.[11] That's incorrect for several reasons: (a) In this passage Jesus also included *honoring one's parents* as God's "word" and "commandment" alongside *putting to death*. (b) *Peter likewise assumed a divinely mandated death penalty in the Mosaic law*: the person who didn't listen to the God-sent messianic prophet would be "destroyed" (Acts 3:23). (c) *The author of Hebrews speaks of the Mosaic law in this way:* "Every transgression and disobedience [under Moses] received a just penalty" (Heb. 2:2–3). The author adds: "Anyone who has set aside the Law of Moses dies without mercy on the testimony of two or three witnesses" (10:28). Furthermore, God's judgment is even more fearful and severe than Mosaic capital punishment (10:29; 12:25).

8. *Jesus himself was involved in severe judgments and "violence" against the wicked.* We've seen that Jesus rejected *personal* retaliation but nevertheless resisted evil persons and actions. *Outside his Sermon, Jesus himself forcefully resisted evildoers:* (a) he made a whip, overturned tables, and drove out money changers from the temple, and "He would not permit anyone to carry merchandise through the temple" (Mark 11:16); (b) he, "*Jesus*"—yes, that's in our best Greek New Testament manuscripts—not only "[saved] a people out of the land of Egypt" but also "afterward *destroyed* those who did not believe" (Jude 5); (c) he forcefully confronted Saul, the persecutor of Christians, striking him blind as he was thrown from his horse (Acts 9:3–9); (d) he ("the hand of the Lord") struck Elymas blind (Acts 13:11); (e) he threatened to "strike . . . dead" (*apoktenō en thanatō*) Jezebel's followers after promising to cast the false prophetess on a sickbed (Rev. 2:20–23 NIV).

9. *Critics from within who attempt to evade actual-God judgments in the New Testament tend to be selective.* Some critics from within will try to wriggle out of particular New Testament divine-judgment texts by saying that God merely withdrew his life-sustaining power in the death of Ananias and Sapphira (Acts

5:1–11)—or that Peter misused his God-given power against them; the *actual* God didn't directly take their lives. They make similar claims regarding Corinthian believers who were sick or died because they abused the Lord's Supper (1 Cor. 11:30).[12]

However, *since Jesus elsewhere uses coercive force—and lethally so at times— why not in these other cases?* After all, "the hand of the Lord" that brought about early church conversions (Acts 11:21) was the *same* "hand of the Lord" that struck Elymas blind (Acts 13:11). And the *same* "angel of the Lord" who delivered Peter from prison (Acts 12:7) caused worms to bring about King Herod Agrippa's death—in that same chapter (Acts 12:20–23)!

The book of Revelation contrasts the evil "beast" with Jesus, the innocent slain "Lamb" (Rev. 5:6, 12; 13:8), but it refers to the severe "wrath of the Lamb" (6:16; cf. God's wrath in the presence of "the Lamb," 14:10). Just as Hebrews 2, 10, and 12 remind readers of a "terrifying expectation of judgment" for those who repudiate God's gift of salvation in Christ (10:27), Revelation portrays divine wrath in similar terms. Indeed, Jesus is connected to coercive force (e.g., Rev. 2:16, 23; 6:16–17; 14:10).

True, Revelation uses violent *metaphors*—plagues (15:1–8), bowls of divine wrath poured out (16:1–21), the winepress of God's great wrath (14:19; 19:15), the great supper of God (19:17). Some scholars suggest that these metaphors somehow make God's/Jesus's wrath *less* severe. However, *they don't show how this is so*: "Violent metaphors don't somehow become non-violent just because literal language isn't used."[13]

The next chapter continues the Moses-versus-Jesus discussion: vengeance, severity, and the difference between "it is written" and "you have heard it said." Then we'll draw some of these threads together.

4

Is the God of the Old Testament the Same as the God of the New? (3)

Moses versus Jesus? (Continued)

Vengeance Is God's—or Maybe Not?

The critics from within claim vengeance is ungodlike. After all, in Luke 4:18–19, Jesus quoted Isaiah 61:1–2 with one allegedly significant omission: Jesus had come to preach the gospel, give sight to the blind, and set captives free. But, we're told, he deliberately "stopped just before" Isaiah's mention of "the day of vengeance" (*hēmeran antapodoseōs*) (v. 2).[1] Why? Vengeance is utterly opposed to the actual God's character.

Boyd boldly chastises the apostle Paul for his statement that God will "repay with affliction" (*antapodounai . . . thlipsin*) those who have oppressed the Thessalonian Christians (2 Thess. 1:6–9): Paul "seems to be satisfying the Thessalonians' and/or his own fallen thirst for vengeance to come upon their enemies."[2] So, whom should we believe—the apostle Paul or Boyd? We're going with Paul, folks. Here are a few reasons why.

First, believe it or not, *Paul was familiar with Jesus's Sermon on the Mount*. Echoing Jesus, Paul told believers: "Never take your own revenge" (*mē heautous ekdikountes*) (Rom. 12:19) by returning evil for evil but rather overcome evil with good (12:19, 21). But Paul, quoting the Old Testament (Deut. 32:25), also knew God will avenge and "repay" (*antapodōsō*) (Rom. 12:19). The verb form of the word is used in Isaiah 61:2 in the Septuagint ("the day of vengeance"), and Boyd wrongly claims Jesus renounced divine vengeance in Luke 4:19 when citing Isaiah. Again, let's definitely go with the apostle Paul on this rather than Boyd.

Second, *Jesus's earthly mission to "save" and not "judge" (*krinē*) the world* (John 3:16–17) *does not eliminate eventual and assured divine "vengeance" or "judgment"* (e.g., Rev. 19:2). The actual God warns that "vengeance [*ekdikēsis*] is mine" (Rom. 12:19; Heb. 10:30). Indeed, redeemed martyrs in heaven *petition* God to "judge [*krineis*] and avenge [*ekdikeis*] our blood" (Rev. 6:10). Likewise, "heaven . . . and you saints and apostles and prophets" will be satisfied at God's just judgment: "Rejoice over her . . . because God has pronounced judgment [*ekrinen . . . to krima*] for you against her" (18:20).

Third, if we want to talk about what Jesus left out when quoting Isaiah 61, *he also omitted the phrase "to bind up the brokenhearted"* found in Isaiah 61:1. Why would he do that? That would perfectly fit with his mission, wouldn't it? It seems that *absence* is not *evidence*—whether about divine vengeance or ministering to the brokenhearted.

Fourth, *Jesus uses even stronger wording than Paul*. For example, it would be better to hang a millstone around the necks of those who lead Christ's followers astray in order to drown them in the depths of the sea (Matt. 18:6). Surely our critic from within won't accuse Jesus of "satisfying his own fallen thirst for vengeance."

Both Jesus and Paul repudiate *personal* vengeance. Both recognize *divine* vengeance. This is a theme anchored in both testaments and in Jesus himself.

Jesus's Harsh Portrayals of His Heavenly Father

Divine Violence in Jesus's Parables

In Hosea 6:5 (NIV), God threatened to "cut [Israel] in pieces"—to "tear" and "carry off" (ESV). Boyd claims that this text reflects the prophet Hosea's "fallen and culturally conditioned heart."[3] He further claims that this language is so "horrendously violent," and it "blatantly contradicts the revelation of God in the crucified Christ."[4] There's one major problem, though: Jesus used *strikingly similar* language in his own parables to portray his heavenly Father as severe. Here are a few examples:

- Matthew 18:34–35 describes the king who forgave the massive debt of his servant: "And his lord, moved with anger, handed him over to the torturers until he should repay all that was owed him. My heavenly Father will also do the same to you, if each of you does not forgive his brother from your heart." While Jesus's language of "torture" is exaggerated, he speaks plainly about the severity of his heavenly Father's wrath. Note Jesus is commenting on and applying the parable story itself. This comment is *outside* the story.
- Jesus portrays his heavenly Father as a king who invites guests to a wedding. Yet one guest fails to comply with protocol: "Tie him hand and foot, and throw him outside, into the darkness, where there will be weeping and gnashing of teeth" (Matt. 22:13 NIV).

- Jesus also portrays his heavenly Father as a severe master who says about his enemies who have refused God's rule: "Bring them here and slay them in my presence" (Luke 19:21–22, 26–27).
- Jesus portrays his heavenly Father as an angered vineyard owner (Matt. 21). In Isaiah 5, God planted Israel as a choice vine, but it produced only worthless grapes. In Matthew, God reacts to the tenants' mistreatment of his messenger and then to the death of his son. Jesus then asks: "'Therefore when the owner of the vineyard comes, what will he do to those vine-growers?' They said to Him, 'He will bring those wretches to a wretched end, and will rent out the vineyard to other vine-growers who will pay him the proceeds at the proper seasons'" (Matt. 21:40–41). In the parallel in Luke 20:16, Jesus puts it this way: "He will come and destroy these vine-growers and will give the vineyard to others."

  This looks like the divinely engineered temporal judgment against Israel in AD 70, using Rome as an instrument.[5] It is the clear signal of a dramatic theological shift: national Israel would be reconstituted. The new Israel (the church) would be the newly appointed "vine-growers" (cf. Matt. 21:43).
- Using Hosea's "horrendously violent" language that "blatantly contradicts the revelation of God in the crucified Christ," Jesus says regarding those who know the will of the Father yet do not act in accordance with his will that the master, who represents *his heavenly Father*, will act with severity— that is, "cut them in pieces" (Matt. 24:51; Luke 12:46).

Now, if Jesus was showing us the "gentleness" and "nonviolence" of his heavenly Father (cf. John 14:9)—the "actual" God—these parables certainly don't reveal it. These parables express the reality of divine severity in physical (*temporal*) judgment on Israel in AD 70 (Matt. 21:33–48; Mark 11:13–14). We could add other such temporal judgments (Acts 12:20–23; 1 Cor. 11:30). The parables also express divine severity *eschatologically*—at the end of all things (cf. Matt. 24:51; Luke 12:46).[6]

Of course, the heart of God is love. Our heavenly Father knows the number of hairs on our head and cares for us far more than humble sparrows (Matt. 10:29–31). Jesus the Messiah is gentle and welcomes the weary and the repentant who have been burdened by sin. As for all who acknowledge their sin and broken-ness, Jesus will not break such bruised reeds or snuff out these dimly burning wicks (Matt. 12:20). But, like C. S. Lewis's Christ-figure in Narnia, Aslan the Lion, Jesus is severe with—and terrifying to—those who defy and oppose him. He will "rule all the nations with a rod of iron" (Rev. 12:5; also 9:15; cf. Ps. 2:9; Rev. 2:26–27)—a picture of severity and punitive judgment. But Revelation reveals that Jesus—the Lamb—is also a gentle shepherd who guides his people to the springs of life (7:17).[7] And in the vineyard parable, the owner is both the *victim* of violence and the *perpetrator* of counterviolence.

So when the vineyard tenants show disrespect and dishonor to the owner (God the Father) by killing his son (Jesus), God doesn't merely withdraw his protective power and allow other agents to fill the vacuum. Jesus indicated that his heavenly Father had not only destroyed Jerusalem before; he would do it again. This is the consistent witness across both testaments.[8]

Whether judgment is temporal or eschatological, Jesus's parables sound very much like the Old Testament portrayal of retributive justice—that of the *actual* God's.

A Possible Interpretation?

Some will argue that we should interpret these parables differently because parables reveal an "is" and an "is not" quality in them.[9] For example, God "is not" an unjust judge (Luke 18:1–8), and God "is not" commending the dishonesty of the "unrighteous" steward (Luke 16:1–9). This qualification isn't enough to blunt divine severity, however.

First, *Jesus in these same parables qualifies his points by indicating that the steward is "unrighteous," and the judge is likewise "unrighteous."* He makes no such qualifications about divine severity.

Second, *Jesus actually makes follow-up comments that fall outside the parable stories* (e.g., "My heavenly Father will also do the same to you" [Matt. 18:35]); in this, Jesus is telling us about who the actual God "is," not who he "is not."

Third, in the other parabolic descriptions of his heavenly Father, *Jesus does not attempt to downplay or qualify his heavenly Father's severity or harshness in judgment. Indeed, the very fact that severity and harsh judgment run throughout these parables suggests that our critic from within isn't taking their message of fearsome divine wrath seriously enough.* The book of Hebrews (2:1–2; 10:28–31; 12:18–29)—along with Jesus himself (Matt. 11:22, 24)—reveals the "terrifying" severity against those who turn their backs on Christ. To use the terms of our critic, the fearsome displays associated with the "textual" God's presence at Mount Sinai and the penalties for disobeying the law of Moses are far less severe than the fearsome judgments of the "actual" God against those who trample Jesus underfoot and insult the Spirit of grace (Heb. 10:29).

Again, even if Jesus's parables of divine wrath (e.g., "cutting in pieces") speak *metaphorically*, we've seen that *this doesn't make God's wrath or counterviolence less severe.* As theologian Miroslav Volf writes: "There are things which only God may do. One of them is to use violence."[10] And Scripture makes clear that God does delegate the task of divine temporal judgment to governments to "bear the sword" justly (Rom. 13:4; cf. Acts 23:16–24). Sometimes even apostles were instruments of God's physical judgment against other human beings (e.g., Acts 5:1–10; 13:8–12).

"It Is Written" versus "You Have Heard It Said"

Rather than pitting Moses against Jesus, we should pit these statements against each other:

1. The *divinely authoritative* "it is written" (e.g., Matt. 4:1–11) or "[thus] says the Lord" (e.g., Heb. 8:8, 9, 10)
2. The Sermon on the Mount's mention of the *human distortion* in "you have heard it said"

Boyd and other critics from within create a *false* interpretation of Moses as a prophet issuing *immoral* legislation. One scholar correctly states: "To assert that Moses (for one) distorted or misunderstood what God communicated runs afoul of the Pentateuch's insistence on the unique status of Moses as one who had direct access to and spoke directly with God."[11] The New Testament is equally clear on this.

In his approach to the Old Testament, Jesus gave no evidence of an "actual God versus textual God" distinction. No wonder Jesus's story of the rich man and Lazarus reminded his audience that they had available to them the clear, authoritative voice of "Moses and the Prophets" for moral and spiritual direction: "Let them listen to them" (Luke 16:29–31 NIV). Jesus made no actual-versus-textual-God qualification here—or elsewhere. This is a modern invention. Our critics from within have made this dichotomy something of a cottage industry.

Old Testament scholar John Goldingay warns Christians who desire to pursue justice, love, and liberation in the name of Jesus. Some of them may run the risk of accepting and encouraging moral commitments largely "shaped by the culture we live in, by our social context," and so they assume they are broadly correct in doing so, but they don't allow themselves to be confronted by Jesus himself, whose message was largely shaped by the Old Testament.[12]

Continuity and Discontinuity: Drawing Some Strands Together

Even though the new covenant community operates on different priorities than what national Israel did, certain realities about human fallenness persist: "The Church today, like Israel of old, still . . . has to live in a world distorted by hardness of heart and not as it was in the beginning."[13]

Again, we're no longer under the Mosaic law *as a covenant*—as the identity marker and charter for the ancient Israelites (Rom. 6:14). Nevertheless, many of these laws give insight into the heart and character of God and the priority of rightly ordered human relationships. Loving God and neighbor—which sums up the old covenant—carries over into the new covenant, along with many other duties and moral ideals.

Here are a few other areas of carryover to consider.

Love and Wrath

As noted, both testaments amply attest to divine love as well as divine wrath. Wrath itself is an expression of God's love and concern. In the New Testament, *both divine love and divine wrath are intensified.* God's love is clearly manifested in Jesus of Nazareth, especially in his self-sacrificial death for the sins of humanity. Yet God's wrath is also heightened against those who knowingly repudiate God's final revelation in Jesus Christ.

Just Coercive Force (Counterviolence)

While God's association with national Israel brings him into a world of brokenness, sin, and violence, God utilizes coercive force (counterviolence) in judgment. Remember, the Old Testament associates "violence" (*hamas*) not with God but with wicked, corrupt human beings.

In the New Testament, God works from the margins, outside of the machinery of earthly power. Even so, God's association with coercive force doesn't disappear in the New Testament and with the formation of the interethnic church (Mark 11:15–16; Jude 5; Rev. 2:20–23; and many of Jesus's parables). In Acts, the "hand of the Lord" saves people but also strikes them blind; the "angel of the Lord" delivers apostles from prison but also strikes dead a proud ruler. The list goes on.

Cursing and Blessing

Though we will go into this in more detail later, the Old Testament includes divine "curses" and "woes" against those Israelites who disobeyed God's covenant (Lev. 26:1–46; Deut. 27:15–26). Though God used warring nations and harsh physical conditions in judgment, God included the nation of Israel—with its prophets and kings—in the advancement of his kingdom. And God promised to bless those who cooperated with those purposes, and to curse those who attempted to thwart them (Gen. 12:3).

While the language of "curse" and "woe" is *lessened* in the New Testament, it *still continues.* Even the imprecatory ("curse") psalms are quoted therein. Jesus pronounced woes (Matt. 11:20–24; 23:1–36; 26:24; etc.), and he cursed Israel ("May you never bear fruit again"; Mark 11:13–14, 20–21 NIV). Paul pronounced the curse of judgment on those who taught false doctrine, distorted the gospel, and opposed Christ (Gal. 1:8–9; 1 Cor. 16:22).

Conclusion: No Refutation of Moses

Boyd mistakenly appeals to biblical scholar Graeme Goldsworthy to "support" his point that Jesus "refuted" the Old Testament law and "radically and permanently altered the way that the early church interpreted the Old Testament."[14] However, we shouldn't follow the *textual* Goldsworthy of our fallen critic from within! Rather, look at what the *actual* Goldsworthy says: "There is no doubt that the case can be made that the New Testament assumes continuity of the ethical law of Israel and nowhere repudiates it but rather sharpens the application of it."[15] Just so.

Like other New Testament authorities, Jesus didn't shrink from mentioning just divine judgments such as the Noahic flood or the destruction of Sodom, Tyre, and Sidon; in fact, he connected those *past* events of divine judgment to warnings about divine judgment in the *future* (Matt. 11:23–24; 24:37–39; Luke 10:13–15). Furthermore, Jesus even chastised his contemporaries, whose forefathers killed the prophets (Matt. 23:29–35), but *unlike our critics from within,* Jesus *didn't* chastise those Old Testament prophets for being "violence prone," for issuing "demonic" commands, or for leading Israel into battle or threatening severe judgments against Israel and other nations.

So if we're going to read Scripture with a "Jesus lens," we can't be selective—a glaring problem with our critics from within. A more faithful reading of Scripture also emphasizes divine *severity*—with Jesus in the thick of it. Jesus's teaching and example about enemy-love and about blessing rather than cursing are crucially important. But we can't solely emphasize this constricted focus—the narrow vision of what is called "cruciformity." The "Jesus lens" of the critic from within is more like a "Jesus tea-strainer," as one scholar puts it: "The biblical Jesus cannot be squeezed [through] the fine mesh of the progressive Jesus tea-strainer. Given the choice, we're . . . better off with the biblical one."[16]

PART 2

Lex Rex
(the Law, the King)

*What Makes the Law of
Moses So Special?*

5

"From Heaven or from Human Origin?"

Is the Mosaic Law Just Another Ancient Law Code?

Borrowing from the Pagans?

I recently received an email from an anonymous critic who immediately launched into his argument: because the Mosaic law was "basically borrowed" from other ancient Near Eastern law collections, it was a merely human law collection, not a divine one. Likewise, an atheist friend of mine suggests this approach: Why not just begin by assuming that the Bible—or, for our purposes, the law of Moses—is merely a human document, and see where you get from there?

This either-or scenario reminds me of Jesus's critics who challenged his authority: "By what authority are You doing these things?" (Matt. 21:23). Jesus then pushed back by asking them about John's baptism—Was it "from heaven, or of human origin?" (Matt. 21:25 NIV). Caught on the horns of a dilemma, they didn't want to affirm either. They opted for "We do not know" (Matt. 21:27).

Perhaps you've been challenged with a seemingly similar dilemma: either the law of Moses came "from heaven" or "it's of human origin." If the law of Moses wasn't dropped from heaven at Mount Sinai, then it must have simply mimicked or borrowed heavily from other legislation like Babylon's Code of Hammurabi. If a biblical author or editor *borrowed* material, it must be of human origin.

We'll now look at some questions related to the Mosaic law in its ancient Near Eastern context. Can the Mosaic law *both* borrow from other law codes or other ancient wisdom *and* still be inspired by God? Do we have to choose between the earthly and the divine alternatives in this case?

Other Biblical Books Do It Too

Biblical scholars have recognized resemblances between the book of Proverbs and an Egyptian book of wisdom—the "Teaching of Amenemope" (cf. Prov. 22:22, 29; 23:4–5, 10–11). They share a similar father-to-son instruction—a common theme in ancient Near Eastern wisdom. Of course, Proverbs emphasizes how wisdom is anchored in the knowledge of Yahweh—in "the fear of the LORD" (1:7; cf. Ps. 111:10).[1]

Is biblical borrowing from an outside source a deal-breaker for biblical inspiration? Let's explore this. First, *drawing on extrabiblical wisdom is done elsewhere in Scripture*. Two Old Testament authors cite the poetic "book of Jashar" (Josh. 10:13; 2 Sam. 1:18). Luke himself "investigated carefully" other Jesus-related material since "many [had] undertaken to compile an account of the things accomplished among us"; as a result, he compiled his own account (Luke 1:1–4). Paul of Tarsus—born at a major center of Stoic philosophy—quoted Stoic thinkers like Epimenides and Aratus in his preaching and his letters (Acts 17:28; cf. also 1 Cor. 15:33; Titus 1:12). In the process of God's "breathing" or inspiring Scripture, he deputized or appointed certain human beings—apostles and prophets—as his representatives to communicate the truth he intended. Such a process could easily include quotations from "outside" sources.[2]

Second, *all truth is God's truth*, so we can expect to see glimmers of God's light appearing throughout history and across civilizations. God *generally* reveals himself to people through philosophical truths, epic stories, wise traditions, ethical axioms, and common human experience (e.g., Ps. 19:1–6; Isa. 28:23–29; Acts 14:15–17; 17:22–30). God also reveals himself *specially* and *savingly* through Christ and Scripture. Whether general or special, all truth is from God.

As C. S. Lewis rightly observed, many myths in the world express truths about, say, grace or redemption, and these shouldn't be rejected just because "pagans" were talking about them. Lewis saw Jesus of Nazareth as the historical embodiment of the world's great myths, stories, and ideals. They point to, and find their fulfillment in, Jesus, in whom "myth became fact." Lewis's Oxford companion J. R. R. Tolkien made a similar point about how the gospel is captured by our best "fairy stories": once human beings were at peace with their Creator and each other; then things went terribly wrong; curse and sorrow followed; but a champion stepped in to rescue a suffering, beleaguered, sin-drenched humanity; and, as a result, "they lived happily ever after."[3]

Third, *we should expect the different types of literature (genres) in the Bible to resemble and reflect the ancient culture in which they were written*. For example, the Gospels resemble Greco-Roman biographies, and Paul's Letters (Epistles) follow the common letter-writing style of the Mediterranean world of his day. And, not surprisingly, the law of Moses does its own bit of resembling.

Unlike the universe, the Mosaic law wasn't created *ex nihilo*—out of nothing. It came to the Israelites within the familiarity of their own ancient Near Eastern context—but also with plenty of distinctive marks as well.

The Extraordinary in the Ordinary[4]

Outside Sources, Mosaic Borrowing, and Divine Communication

So we can appreciate that Moses—who "was educated in all the learning of the Egyptians" (Acts 7:22)—was familiar with ancient Near Eastern law collections. They were mainly sources of wisdom, instruction, teaching, and examples of justice. So a term like "law," or "law code," or "ethical code" doesn't precisely capture what these "collections" intended to communicate, as we'll see later. For our purposes, though, we'll use terms like "law" and "code" since readers are more familiar with this terminology.

The earliest law codes and related documents are *earlier* than the Mosaic law. The key documents come from the following sources:

- Sumerians (2350–1750 BC)
- Hittites (1650–1500 BC, with revisions in subsequent centuries)
- Babylonians (Laws of Eshnunna [1770 BC]; the Code of Hammurabi [1750 BC])
- Assyrians (third-millennium BC fragments; Middle Assyrian Laws from the fourteenth century BC)[5]

The earliest legislation of Israel—the Covenant Code of Exodus 20–23—dates back to the Mosaic period, around the thirteenth or fourteenth century BC. Even the basic material in Deuteronomy can be placed within the period of Moses rather than (as many have assumed) the seventh century—the time of King Josiah's reforms (more on this in the next chapter).

The Mosaic law didn't start from scratch or reinvent the wheel. It appropriated sources apart from any direct divine revelation to Moses, who selected and adapted material resulting in a "special synthesis."[6] Here are a few examples of how this worked.

Other ancient law collections: One Mosaic law about the ox that gored (Exod. 21:35) is identical to a Mesopotamian (Eshnunna) law (§53). Another similarity is the "law of retaliation" (*lex talionis*)—"an eye for an eye" (Exod. 21:24; Lev. 24:20; Deut.19:21). The Babylonian Code of Hammurabi (1570 BC) puts it this way: "If a man put out the eye of another man, his eye shall be put out" (§196; "bone" and "tooth" are also used [§§197, 200]).[7] The Mosaic law utilizes this language from ancient Near Eastern legal collections. As noted, *monetary* payment was the general expectation for a host of legal offenses—not literal eyes and teeth. And by "monetary" payment, we mean, here and throughout the book, "in kind" goods like sheep or timber, although silver bullion could be weighed and used for payment in larger amounts. But ordinary coinage came into existence around 600 BC.[8]

Offerings and sacrifices: These were widespread, deeply meaningful practices in the ancient world, and the saints offered sacrifices well before the burnt-offering protocols of Leviticus 1 (cf. Gen. 8:20; Job. 1:5; 42:8). Like purification rites or cleansing ceremonies, *God wove together these readily understood practices, which expressed deep human longings, into the fabric of the Mosaic law.* And through the death of Christ, the Lamb of God, these practices would once for all be fulfilled "to put away sin" (Heb. 9:26).

Commonsensical observations: The daughters of Zelophehad broke with convention when their father died. They petitioned Moses so that they could inherit their father's property. Why should it be parceled out to a *male* relative? This no-nonsense idea met with divine approval, and Moses granted their request (Num. 27:1–4). At other times, Israel's new circumstances or failures led to certain modifications in the law.[9] Now, if such practical ideas could be incorporated in Israel's law, why not *other* ideas or known ancient practices?[10]

Who Borrowed from Whom?

The law of Moses isn't one solid chunk of legislation or legal collection. It contains a number of codes within it that developed in Israel's early history (see table 5.1). Now, ancient Near Eastern scholars commonly assume that Israel's Covenant Code (Exod. 20:22–23:33) drew on a common ancient legal tradition of pre-Mosaic laws. Some claim that any similarities between the Covenant Code and the Code of Hammurabi indicate direct borrowing—the former from the latter.[11] More likely, *both codes draw from a yet more ancient common legal tradition.* After all, some laws within the Covenant Code are similar or even identical to other codes around this time, as we saw with the goring ox.

Table 5.1. Codes within the Mosaic Law

The Ten Commandments or "Words" (Exod. 20:1–17; Deut. 5:6–21)	These are the stable "core" throughout the Old Testament; except for the Sabbath commandment (Rom. 14:5; Col. 2:16), these are all reaffirmed in the New (e.g., 1 Tim. 1:8–11).
The Covenant Code (Exod. 20:22–23:33)	The "book of the covenant" (Exod. 24:3, 7) was Israel's earliest set of laws.
The Priestly Code (Exod. 25–31; Exod. 35–Lev. 16)	This was directed to the priests.
The Holiness Code (Lev. 17:10–26:46)	This was directed to the people.
The Deuteronomic Code (Deut. 12–26)	This reworked or repurposed previous laws from the Covenant Code and other earlier legislation in Leviticus.

Examples could be multiplied, showing that the Covenant Code reflects an exposure to a wide range of ancient Near Eastern legal traditions.[12] Later, we'll observe the very significant worldview and ethical differences between biblical law and other ancient Near Eastern law collections. But next, we'll move into the second portion of our discussion on the origin and development of the Mosaic law.

6

Multiple Sources and Late Dates?

Does the Mosaic Law Have Multiple Authors?
Was Fighting the Canaanites a Fiction
from the Sixth Century BC?

Strata or Strategy? Does the Pentateuch Have Multiple Sources?

It's perfectly fine to speak of Moses as an editor of materials that preceded him. No doubt there were oral traditions from the patriarchs and perhaps materials written on tablets for him to use—so, yes, *sources*. But some scholars have asserted that certain strata or strands of material in the Pentateuch are clearly from multiple authors who lived well *after* Moses. This is a very different way of looking at source material.

The German biblical scholar Julius Wellhausen claimed to have discovered these strata in 1878, yielding his Documentary Hypothesis. Since then, numerous scholars have assumed four basic strata, layers, or sources for the Pentateuch: the "authors" or "traditions" represented by J, E, D, and P (see table 6.1).

As time has passed, there's been much scholarly *disagreement* about these strands; speculation and contradiction abound. Gordon Wenham indicates that many scholars reject this hypothesis in whole or in part, and "they often come to mutually contradictory conclusions."[1] For example, on the book of Genesis alone, a comparison of two Documentary Hypothesis advocates—the late S. R. Driver and Richard E. Friedman—reveals around *one hundred* conflicting attributions of sources (mostly J and E); the same could be said about Exodus and beyond. Such conflicts reveal the *subjectivity* and *lack of adequate criteria* to differentiate J from E.[2] According to Wenham, this hypothesis has largely been abandoned or at least questioned. In fact, a large number of current Old Testament scholars

Table 6.1. J, E, D, P

J: *Jahwistic* or *Yahwistic*	Early monarchy	From the Hebrew word for "LORD" (*Yahweh*); this material includes stories from Genesis to early Exodus.
E: *Elohistic*	Early monarchy	From the Hebrew word for "God" (*Elohim*); this source includes stories in Genesis 25–50, though split between E and J.
D: *Deuteronomic*	Late monarchy	Refers to observing the law, loving and obeying "the LORD your/our God," warnings against disobedience, and so on.
P: *Priestly*	Post-exilic	Includes material about worship and the priesthood with other content found in Genesis 1, 17, and 23.

Source: Gordon Wenham, *Exploring the Old Testament*, vol. 1, *A Guide to the Pentateuch* (Downers Grove, IL: InterVarsity, 2003), 165, 170.

propagate it, and their students continue to apply it in doctoral dissertations. The noted Old Testament scholar David Clines even ridicules the hypothesis. He applies the same methodology to Winnie the Pooh stories in order to "prove" it was written by a number of authors, not just one. For example, the "fact" that each source utilizes a particular name—"Pooh," "Pooh-the-Bear," and "Bear"—indicates distinct sources![3] And so it goes.

We are wiser to *focus on the final form of the Pentateuch as a literary and theological unity*, as scholars are increasingly doing. The late John Sailhamer would say in my Old Testament classes: "Concentrate on the *strategy* of the Pentateuch, not on its *strata*."[4]

Mosaic Laws: Set in Stone, Upgraded, Abrogated?

Modifications in the Law of Moses?

We've seen that the law of Moses presents one layer of legislation after another, but the Pentateuch is a textually unified whole. But we see another dynamic at work as well: though the Ten Commandments are fixed and firm in Exodus 20 and Deuteronomy 5, some other Israelite laws don't appear to be set in stone for the nation of Israel:[5]

- Exodus 20:24–26 refers to an altar made of uncut stones, but later legislation made provision for an altar made of acacia wood overlaid with gold (Exod. 27:1–2; Lev. 17:3–7; cf. Josh. 8:31).
- Exodus 21:2–5 mentions that a *male* servant can go free after six years of service; later legislation included—or at least specifically mentioned—the *female* servant as well (Deut. 15:12–15).

- Exodus 21 speaks of freeing indentured servants after six years, but then Leviticus 25 mentions freedom from servitude and debt cancellation every fifty years.
- Exodus 22:31 prohibits the eating of animals killed by other animals; Leviticus 17:15, however, permits this under certain circumstances.
- Leviticus 7:19 prohibits the ceremonially unclean from eating meat; later on, the unclean are allowed to eat it (Deut. 12:15, 22).
- Exodus 12 mentions that the Passover was to be celebrated in a home (Exod. 12:1–27), but later this was to be celebrated in the place where the Lord would choose to set his name (Deut. 16:16).
- In Numbers 9:6–10, some men are under the justifiable assumption that because they were ceremonially unclean due to coming in contact with a dead body, they were not allowed to celebrate the Passover. (Note a similar kind of restriction for Israelites when approaching Mount Sinai in Exod. 19:10, 14.) But upon their request followed by Moses's inquiry before the Lord, this petition was granted, and unclean persons were officially able to celebrate Passover.

Various commentaries will wrestle with how to view these shifts. While we can't go into detail here, perhaps we could examine how scholars have approached the matter.

Are Earlier Laws Superseded or Complemented?

During the twentieth century, a number of Old Testament (or Hebrew Bible) scholars took the position that some later Mosaic laws are more developed and thus *supersede* earlier laws.[6] This approach suggests that those particular laws are simply in conflict with each other, just sitting side by side, left without resolution. Apparently, the earlier laws were invalidated or replaced when applied in later situations. This view has been called the "supersessionist" view. To *supersede* would essentially be to *abolish* previous laws.

More recently, a growing number of scholars have claimed that even though some later laws are revisions of earlier laws, they *complement* earlier ones. One scholar writing on biblical servitude comments on Leviticus 25 (the Year of Jubilee) in light of earlier servitude legislation in Exodus 21: "My purpose is to show that the jubilee of Leviticus 25 does not supersede the earlier biblical legislation on slaves, but implies and completes it."[7] (See table 6.2.)

I can't go into detail, and this is an ongoing conversation, but I can present some positive aspects of the complementary view.

First, *later biblical authors like Jeremiah and Ezekiel drew on these different layers of allegedly contradictory material*, seemingly illustrating the complementary view at work. However, these prophets quoted this material *without thinking they were quoting something contradictory*. Nor do they give priority

Table 6.2. Supersessionist versus Complementary Approaches

Supersessionist	Later Mosaic laws are more developed and thus *supersede*—and effectively *abolish*—earlier laws, though leaving them without resolution.
Complementary	Though there may be revisions due to differing circumstances, times, or places of worship, these later Mosaic laws are *organically connected*. They *complement* and *complete* one another; they do not remain standing in contradiction to one another or pitted against each other.

to one layer over another.[8] For example, the servitude theme of Jeremiah 34:8–22 draws on earlier servitude texts like Leviticus 25:10, 39–46 and Deuteronomy 15:12–18. Jeremiah views these different strands as complementary rather than opposed to each other.

Second, *the fact that the law incorporates these different traditions without evidence of privileging one over the other suggests complementarity rather than supersession.* Perhaps we should give greater credit to the final editor of these collected laws in the Pentateuch. This person wasn't unsophisticated, as some have suggested, nor has he simply compiled a bunch of hopelessly contradictory texts, as some have also argued.

Third, *in the end we don't have conflicting collections or anthologies of laws or wisdom, but rather we have modified purposes for these additional layers of legislation.* Yes, we do have adjustments and adaptations in light of *new times, new places of worship, and changing circumstances.*[9] In addition, God was the primary initiator of these changes due to new or modified purposes for these additional layers of legislation.[10]

Fourth, *this complementary view is more organic than the supersessionist.* It has the advantage of avoiding the idea that one layer of legislation or wisdom is pitted against another—that we have competing visions of law within each layer that just sit there, unresolved.

Finally, *this view also makes sense of the repeated statement in Deuteronomy,* "*as I have commanded you*" (12:21; 24:8; see also 5:12, 16; and 18:2 ["promised" [*dabar*]). This would indicate that earlier Mosaic material is *not being rejected* but is being *incorporated* into the larger body of the Mosaic law.

Was Fighting Against the Canaanites a "Myth"? (Or, Were Deuteronomy and Joshua Written Six Hundred Years *after* Moses and Joshua?)

Some Background: Deuteronomic Theology

A common scholarly assumption—some would say fact—is that the writing of Deuteronomy came hundreds of years after the time of Moses. That is, it was

Table 6.3. A Summary of Deuteronomic Theology in the Book of Joshua

Yahweh wars	The Lord commanded the Israelites to "drive out" and fight against the Canaanites (Deut. 7:1–26; 20:1–20; cf. Josh. 1:1–9; etc.).
Distribution of the promised land	The land that God promised to the patriarchs in Genesis would be given to Israel and apportioned according to tribe (Deut. 1:7–8; 6:10, 18; 7:8; 34:1–4; cf. Josh. 19:51; 23:1–5).
The unity of Israel	Both books take for granted a united Israel—or "all Israel" (Deut. 1:1; 5:1; 11:6; cf. Josh. 3:7, 17; 4:14; 7:23; 8:21, 24; 23:2). It would be strange if both books had been written well after the two kingdoms—the northern (Israel) and southern (Judah)—had been divided or, worse still, after the Northern Kingdom had been overrun and eliminated as a political reality by the Assyrians in 722 BC.
The role of Joshua	Joshua succeeded Moses before entering Canaan. The Lord promised that just as he was with Moses, so he would be with Joshua (Deut. 1:37–38; 3:28; 31:7, 23; cf. Josh. 1:2–9, 17; 4:14).
The covenant and the Mosaic law	The phrase "the book of the law" (Deut. 31:26) is a technical term for the covenant document; it appears in Joshua too: "this book of the law" (1:8). Incidentally, without this document, God's treaty or covenant with Israel was not valid.

Source: Gordon J. Wenham, "The Deuteronomic Theology of the Book of Joshua," *Journal of Biblical Literature* 140, no. 2 (1971): 140–48.

written during the time of King Josiah's religious reforms (622 BC), and perhaps it was finalized during the Babylonian exile (sixth century BC). During those reforms, Josiah removed the high places used for worship in order to centralize worship in Jerusalem.

But the plot thickens. Some say Joshua must have been written sometime during Judah's exile in the sixth century BC. Why? Because Joshua (particularly, chapters 1–12) clearly made use of "Deuteronomic" theology and language (see table 6.3); therefore, the book of Joshua must have been written *even later* than Josiah's time.

What is the implication of a later date for Joshua? *It was written when the Canaanites were no longer an identifiable grouping of people in Israel.* So all of those warfare commands were merely anti-idolatry, pro-covenant-keeping rhetoric. Driving out the Canaanites was not necessary.

Joshua, History, and Chronology

In an effort to reinforce their point, a number of scholars claiming a late date for Joshua assert that *archaeological evidence for Joshua's conquest of Canaan is lacking.* This absence of evidence appears to clinch the case for a nonhistorical, "mythological," and rhetorical use of Joshua. For example, Randal Rauser appeals to archaeologists Israel Finkelstein and Neil Asher Silberman's book *The Bible*

Unearthed, which challenges the historicity of Old Testament accounts about the patriarchs, the exodus, and the conquest under Joshua.[11]

However, other scholars *defending* the historicity of Joshua present good reasons for the traditional position—that this book was written around the mid-thirteenth century BC. Noted British Egyptologist Kenneth Kitchen writes about Finkelstein and Silberman's book that "our two friends are utterly out of their depth, hopelessly misinformed, and totally misleading," and their treatment on the exodus is also "the most factually ignorant and misleading" material Kitchen has ever read.[12] As for warfare against the Canaanites, Kitchen himself makes the case that no such conflict exists between an early date for Joshua and archaeology.[13] Tremper Longman also argues that Joshua uses standard literary devices of exaggeration commonly found in ancient Near Eastern war texts, and that *the book reveals an effort to represent actual past events from the fourteenth century BC; it is not centuries-later, nonhistorical rhetorical device against idolatry.* For example, notice the frequent references of "to this day" (Josh. 4:9; 6:25; etc.).[14]

There are other considerations, but here I select three:

> *Gradual infiltration:* The Scriptures bear testimony to a *gradual* Israelite infiltration into the land of Canaan—not a sudden military incursion; this fits with the facts of archaeology. Judges 1 repeatedly affirms that the Israelites "could not drive them [i.e., the Canaanite populations] out," and they had lived within Israel for generations (e.g., 2 Sam. 24:7; 1 Kings 9:16).

> *Jericho and Ai:* Critics have claimed that we should have more archaeological evidence available for Jericho (along with Ai) if the fighting there can be considered historically grounded. But Jericho—then a relatively small fort—shows signs of significant erosion. And if it was made of mud brick, we rightly shouldn't expect much to remain. Likewise, the "city" of Ai, whose name means "ruin," wasn't large either, and only a small force of Israelites was needed to fight against it (Josh. 7:3–5).[15]

> *Twenty thousand out of Egypt:* Numbers 1:46 states that 603,550 Israelite men left Egypt, which could be about two million people overall. But there's no archaeological indication of such a massive population wandering the wilderness. As we'll see later, the Hebrew word translated "thousand" (*eleph*) is simply an undefined "unit" or "group." The number at the exodus would have been more like twenty thousand—a number that wouldn't conflict with what archaeologists have discovered.

The Implications of Deuteronomy's and Joshua's Very Late Dates— and Some Responses

So if Deuteronomy and Joshua had been written *well over half a millennium after the time of Moses and Joshua*, then, according to these scholars, what implications follow?

Implication 1: Rhetoric over history. The language of "driving out" and "destroying" Canaanites was *rhetorical* rather than *historical*. After all, the Canaanites as an identifiable group weren't around when Deuteronomy and Joshua were written.

Implication 2: Worship over warfare. Deuteronomy's war commands and Joshua's battle scenes are really just about *avoiding Canaanite-like idolatry and promoting covenant obedience.* Again, the Canaanites were no longer an issue in the land.[16] This sounds like some early Christian spiritualizers such as Gregory of Nyssa, whom we mentioned in chapter 2: We need to overthrow the Jericho in our lives—that is, put aside our former way of life.

Although we'll come back to the warfare question at the end of the book, here are a few preliminary responses:

Response 1: This rhetorical anti-idolatry "solution" won't persuade readers who consider the plainer reading of Deuteronomy and Joshua as basic descriptions of historical war-related events.[17] The attempted historical reconstructions to date these books to the seventh century BC are tenuous and debatable, and this approach marginalizes Scripture, making it an unstable starting point for interpretation.[18] What's more, the earlier books of Exodus and Numbers assume that living, breathing Canaanites presented a military challenge to Israel that required deep trust in the Lord (Exod. 23:27–33; 34:11–16; Num. 13:28–33; 14:4–9, 39–45)—just as Deuteronomy and Joshua assume. To reinforce this theme, divine assistance for Israel to defeat the two kings Sihon and Og in battle (Num. 21) is a theme repeated throughout the Old Testament (Num. 32:33; 1 Kings 4:19; Ps. 135:11; etc.).

Response 2: The New Testament authorities interpret these Canaanite events as historical (e.g., Acts 7:45; 13:19; Heb. 11:31–33), including Rahab as part of Jesus's lineage (Matt. 1:5; cf. Ruth 4:20).

Response 3: Scripture texts written both before and after Josiah's reforms and into Judah's exile also mention God's own role of coercive force to help Israel defeat its enemies and enter the land. Prior to Josiah's time, Amos, a prophet to the Northern Kingdom of Israel (eighth century BC), declares his involvement in Israel's military victory over Sihon and Og: "it was I who destroyed the Amorite before them" (Amos 2:9). After Josiah's time, we read about God's helping Israel drive out the Canaanites (e.g., Neh. 9:23–25; cf. Isa. 63:1–7).

Furthermore, this rhetorical approach seems strange since these two books assume the ongoing existence of Israel's twelve tribes. However, the Northern Kingdom of Israel (i.e., ten of Israel's tribes) was nonexistent after 722 BC. So it seems odd that both the "drive them out" and "destroy" commands as well as references to the northern ten tribes (e.g., Josh. 12:1–22:34) are nonhistorical rhetoric.

Reasons to Consider an Earlier Dating of Deuteronomy

For the sake of space, we'll note just a few arguments for an earlier dating of Deuteronomy, whose existence is so important within the book of Joshua before, during, and after battle (e.g., Josh. 1:8; 8:30–35; 23:6; 24:26: "the book of the law" / "law of Moses" / "law of God").

Deuteronomy's Hittite Treaty–like Structure

Deuteronomy's structure closely resembles *second*-millennium BC Hittite treaties from around 1400–1200 BC (see table 6.4). These treaties were between a ruler (a "suzerain") and a ruled people (his "vassals").

Rather than dating Deuteronomy in the seventh century, the commonsensical approach would be to follow the second-millennium date (fourteenth century BC), which seems to be staring us in the face. Consider the fact that earlier (second millennium BC) treaties have a *balance* of blessings and curses; in later (first millennium BC) treaties, curses appear *without blessings*. Furthermore, the *order*

Table 6.4. Ancient Second-Millennium BC Hittite Treaties
and Their Deuteronomic Parallels

Form of Ancient Near Eastern (Hittite) Treaties	Parallels in Deuteronomy
Preamble or title, identifying the author of the covenant and often beginning with "These are the words . . ."	1:1–5, which begins, "These are the words Moses spoke to all Israel."
Historical prologue or retrospect, mentioning previous relations between the two parties involved; past benevolences of the suzerain are the basis for the vassal's gratitude and obedience.	1:6–4:49, which reviews Israel's recent history.
General stipulations, which are laid upon the vassals by the suzerain.	5–11, which includes the Ten Commandments.
Specific stipulations	12–26, which concerns idolatry, helping the poor, the conduct of the king, warfare, marriage, divorce, and the like.
Blessings and curses—that is, lists of blessings if the vassal keeps the covenant and curses if he breaks it.	27–28, which lists twelve curses for disobedience and blessings for obedience.
Witnesses (usually deities) invoked to testify to the making of the covenant.	30:19: "I call heaven and earth as witnesses against you"; 31:19 (NIV): ". . . a witness for me against them"; 32:1–43 (NLT): "Listen, O heavens, . . . hear, O earth. . . ."

of second-millennium treaties is more consistent with Deuteronomy than what appears in first-millennium treaties.[19] Given such factors, the noted Egyptologist Kenneth Kitchen concludes that Deuteronomy would likely have been written during or shortly after the Mosaic era. This would fit nicely within that same Hittite time period.[20]

Concerning Joshua, we could add that this too fits within a second-millennium ancient Near Eastern literary setting. The reasons for this include stereotypical battle language, hyperbole, geographical descriptions, name usage (onomastics), the nature of battle accounts in Joshua 9–12, and the boundary lists in chapters 13–19, as K. Lawson Younger has shown.[21]

"The Place the LORD . . . Will Choose" as Ancient Language

A key reason for assuming the late dating of Deuteronomy is its mention of "the place which the Lord your God will choose" (12:5; cf. 12:11, 18; 31:11). This is presumably Jerusalem, and its location is established only later in Israel's history—under David's reign. So is this really sufficient reason to locate "the place the LORD will choose" within Josiah's day? No, it is not.

1. *This place-the-Lord-will-choose theme sounds very much like Exodus 15, which dates to Moses's time.* Scholars agree that Exodus 15 dates to the Mosaic era—the second millennium BC. This Song of Moses was sung after God's deliverance of Israel through the Red Sea (also called the "Reed Sea"), which also involved the drowning of Egypt's army. The song makes reference to God's guiding Israel "to [his] holy habitation" (v. 13) and planting them "in the mountain of [his] inheritance" and "[his] dwelling, the sanctuary" (v. 17).

2. If this "place" of Jerusalem was clearly known during Josiah's time and Deuteronomy had been written during that time, *it's strange that this specific location isn't actually stated.*[22]

3. *The attitude toward Jerusalem in Deuteronomy and Joshua is different from that in Kings.* Deuteronomy and Joshua mention Jerusalem only in passing, and it's an unconquered Jebusite city (Josh. 15:63). The central sanctuary is evidently located elsewhere. In contrast, the editor of Kings appears to regard all worship outside Jerusalem as sinful (2 Kings 17).

Josiah's Reforms as Inspired by Deuteronomy's Theology

The covenant curses that were so disconcerting to Josiah (2 Chron. 34:24) are found—along with blessings—in Deuteronomy 27–28. These were part of the "words of the law" (2 Chron. 34:19)—most likely drawn from material in Deuteronomy. Keep in mind the claim with which we are dealing: Deuteronomy was written during the time of Josiah's reforms. But the eighth and eighteenth years of his reign, Josiah was already destroying idols and altars associated with them in Judah (2 Chron. 34:3–7). Then in the eighteenth year of his reign, the "book of the law" (Deuteronomistic material) was discovered in the temple (34:8–35:19), Josiah's *initial* reforms—including the temple's renovation—were well underway. Despite King Josiah's godly initiative, he was distressed at the reading of the law and the divine curses threatened for disobeying it (vv. 19–21; cf. Deut. 28:20–68). So the discovery of the "book of the law" prompted *further* reforms, including a covenant-renewal ceremony in Israel, but Josiah was already in anti-idolatry mode well before then. Israel's own story had plenty of anti-idolatry content to promote Josiah's monotheistic reforms, even without the book of Deuteronomy.

Other Old Testament Material (Pre-Josiah) That Draws on Deuteronomy

Scholars have observed that Deuteronomy and the book of Hosea share strikingly similar and overlapping themes—including the "wilderness" image. *Yet Hosea was composed a century before Josiah.* Other good reasons exist for anchoring material from Deuteronomy to an earlier time in Israel's history—at least early enough for Hosea to draw upon its themes.[23]

We have some good reasons for an earlier dating of Deuteronomy, but it's not necessary to affirm that Deuteronomy's *final form* was written down before Moses died. After all, the account of Moses's death in Deuteronomy 34 was clearly *not* recorded by Moses. And Moses's own name doesn't appear in Deuteronomy 12–26. Some later editing of Deuteronomy, no doubt, took place, but we can suggest this: we have Moses's exact *voice* (*ipsissima vox*)—that is, his intentions and meaning—that form the basis of the book of Deuteronomy, even if we don't necessarily have Moses's exact *words* (*ipsissima verba*).[24] We could compare this to how Luke summarized Paul's (probably two-hour) speech at Athens (Acts 17:22–31). Luke gave us the exact *voice* of Paul, though not necessarily his exact *words*.[25]

Where does all of this leave us? We can say that historical reconstructions of biblical texts may be interesting and helpful up to a point. But *they can also become a highly speculative enterprise with conflicting opinions and scenarios.* Indeed, we have good reason to see the entire Pentateuch as a coherent, well-constructed literary document that basically tracks Israel's second-millennium history and on which Joshua draws—well before Josiah's reforms.[26]

7

Differences between the Law of Moses and Ancient Near Eastern Laws (1)

The Biblical Vision and Worldview

So keep and do [these statutes and judgments], for that is your wisdom and your understanding in the sight of the peoples who will hear all these statutes and say, "Surely this great nation is a wise and understanding people. For what great nation is there that has a god so near to it as is the LORD our God whenever we call on Him? Or what great nation is there that has statutes and judgments as righteous as this whole law which I am setting before you today?"

—Deuteronomy 4:6–8

[The Jews'] laws are different from those of all other people.

—Esther 3:8

In what ways did Israel's worldview differ from that of neighboring nations? Or *was* there any real difference? Our focus here is on Israel's law collection—the Mosaic law—and the key differences between Israel's "statutes and judgments" and those of their neighbors. Yes, Israel borrowed some laws from a preexisting ancient Near Eastern legal tradition. And behind some of Israel's laws is a presumed hard-heartedness and sinfulness (Matt. 19:8), which reflected the nonideal conditions of their ancient Near Eastern setting. Even so, in what way *could* the nations detect Israel's "wisdom" and "understanding" and see God's greatness and glory revealed? The two chapters after this one will explore that theme.

The "Instruction" of Moses: Merely Selected Illustrations of Wisdom?

When we think of "the law of Moses," terms like "legislation" and "comprehensive" or "systematic" may come to our minds. But this should be qualified somewhat.

First, *to some degree, the Mosaic "law" is more like "wise instruction" than a legal code.* The word *torah* is often translated "law," but it means "teaching" or "instruction." To a certain extent, the Mosaic law was like other ancient Near Eastern law collections. We could compare them to a kind of textbook that provides academic indicators of what wise rule should look like. These laws weren't immediately consulted for legal rulings. Unlike our modern Western legal system, ancient Near Eastern rulers and judges didn't refer to these collections as legal manuals.

Some scholars have argued that the law of Moses gives "wisdom" much like the book of Proverbs does. It doesn't so much furnish a list of commands or mandates but rather makes *observations* of what "works" in life and what doesn't.[1] One is wise—or it works—to keep away from a prostitute's seductions, to adopt relational skills, to avoid quick-tempered people and quarrelsome conversations. Likewise, the Mosaic law doesn't give rules or duties as a law code would. It tells us what a wise person would do. After all, wisdom can't be legislated. The Mosaic law's emphasis is "you will know" rather than "you ought."

According to a couple of scholars, God gave wisdom in the law, not commands: "If God did not give rules, . . . there are no rules to follow. If God did not provide legislation, there are no laws to obey"; furthermore, "the desire to take the teaching of the Bible seriously, whether the Old Testament or the New, does not entail an obligation to read the Torah, even the Decalogue [Ten Commandments], as moral instruction."[2] But does this "wisdom" emphasis really mean that we don't have actual commands in the Mosaic law? We'll respond to this below.

Second, in addition to the wisdom emphasis contained in these ancient collections, *they weren't comprehensive or systematic guidebooks that were strictly applied by judges in legal judgments.* Walton and Walton write: "Both Torah and the New Testament writings can perhaps inform our moral sensibilities, but they do not stand as a *comprehensive* system or provide an authoritative source for determining *all* behavior."[3] The Mosaic law, like other ancient collections, is a sampling of wisdom ("aspective"); it doesn't cover the full range or a panorama of human behavior.[4] For example, it devotes much space to kosher laws (Lev. 11; Deut. 14) but gives only a few short verses on divorce (Deut. 24:1–4; cf. 22:19, 29).

So is it true that because the Mosaic law is a sampling of wisdom, it's not a suitable moral guide for life? And is it the case that the law of Moses was bound up with God's covenant for the nation of Israel alone and that it didn't apply to those outside Israel? We explore these matters in the remainder of the chapter.

Yes, Illustrations of Wisdom—alongside Ethical Demands and Duties

Avoiding False Alternatives

Is the law of Moses *nothing more* than illustrations of proverbial wisdom—as it was with other ancient Near Eastern law collections? And does the law's lack of comprehensiveness undermine its potential for moral guidance? These are two questions we'll tackle. As we'll see, *while the law of Moses resembles an ancient Near Eastern law collection, it goes beyond that, and it's okay to speak of "law" and "legislation."*

In addressing the two questions above, we want to be careful not to create the following false alternatives:

> *False alternative 1: Either the law gives wisdom, or it has nothing to do with moral commands.* If wisdom is the skill for living, fulfilling certain *practical moral* duties will be required for living wisely. Parents begin with duties in teaching their children moral virtue and character formation. These aren't separate.[5] Even so, we can derive basic commands, ethical duties, and moral priorities from collections of wisdom—like "Honor your father and mother," or "You ought to get wise guidance for your life." Other scholars claim that the Mosaic law combines *law collection, wisdom material,* and *priestly prescriptions* together—materials that were independent collections in other ancient Near Eastern settings. Moral exhortations, legal prescriptions, and wise injunctions are interwoven therein.[6]

> *False alternative 2: Either the law is a comprehensive moral system, or it doesn't provide significant moral direction.* But so what if it's not comprehensive? Just as the New Testament epistles address specific ethical subjects without providing a comprehensive overview in each of them, we get significant moral guidance from them—and we can make sound judgments and draw correct inferences based on those epistles. We could say the same about the Gospels.

A Mosaic of Moral Implications

In what follows, we'll look at some reasons why the Mosaic law radiates moral or ethical implications.

First, *Israel's judges would more likely consult Israel's instructions than would judges in other ancient Near Eastern cultures.* The law was more than textbook or academic examples of wisdom. For example, priests were to teach the people

Israel's laws and statutes (Lev. 10:11; Deut. 33:10). Every seven years the "law"—probably material from Deuteronomy—was to be read to the people at the Feast of Booths (Deut. 31:9–13). And one role of the prophets was to be "covenant enforcers": they were to remind the people of their obligation to heed the Mosaic covenant (e.g., Jer. 34:8–17; Mal. 4:4). And even if, say, capital punishments for certain offenses weren't carried out literally (except for murder), the law would still remind the people: "This is a bad thing. Avoid it!"

Now, we're not always told *why* certain instructions or prohibitions were given. For example, what's the problem with cooking a kid goat in its mother's milk (Exod. 23:19; 34:26; Deut. 14:21)? Well, we can make plausible inferences: perhaps this was a Canaanite fertility ritual, or it presented a symbolic clash—*life* (mother's milk) and *death* (cooking a baby goat). Even so, the ancient Israelites were more likely to grasp their rationale than we are today.[7]

Second, *national Israel was to be a role model to surrounding nations, and that includes moral uprightness.* If Israel's law was merely a wisdom collection under God's covenant with Israel, *was it all culturally relative without any moral carryover?*[8] Of course not. True, the Mosaic law was directed to national Israel. However, Israel's being a model of wisdom to its ancient Gentile neighbors would certainly include being a moral example (Deut. 4:6–8). What's more, the surrounding nations were obligated to heed God's general moral law (e.g., Amos 1–2). And through the Israelite prophet Jonah, God warned the Ninevites—a noncovenant people—who listened and repented (Jon. 3:5–10). God didn't hold against them that Nineveh hadn't paid attention to the finer points of the Mosaic law given to Israel.

Third, *the New Testament authorities take the law to be speaking on moral matters.* Some will say that Jesus and the apostles were swimming in a different cultural river than ancient Israel. Jesus and the apostles interpreted "law" according to their own first-century understanding of it—as meaning "duty" or "moral obligation." So rather than reading the Mosaic law as illustrations of wisdom (i.e., as originally intended), they read the Mosaic law as a legal or moral code instead.

However, rabbis in Jesus's day and beyond likewise assumed a moral framework within the Mosaic law. And as we'll soon see, the Mosaic law from the very outset had clear moral undertones and implications. But for now, we can see how the moral heartbeat of the Old Testament carries over into the New and is applied as *duty* or *obligation.* Here are some examples:

- In chapter 2 we noted that James and 1 Peter pick up on moral themes found in Leviticus 19.
- Jesus tells his hearers to pay attention to what their religious leaders *say* about the Mosaic law, but *not to do what they do* (Matt. 23:2–3).
- Paul says that the law of Moses is "holy," "just," and "good" (Rom. 7:12 NRSV). Paul also makes clear that the second part of the Decalogue (Ten Commandments) has enduring value (1 Tim. 1:8–12).

• On the topic of homosexual *acts*, Paul not only follows the creational pattern of Genesis 1–2 (cf. Rom. 1:26–27). He also draws on the moral stance
and specific wording of the Torah. That is, the reason(s) such acts were
wrong in Leviticus 18:22 and 20:13 would be enduringly relevant.[9]

Yes, the Old Testament has a moral heartbeat that flows into the New Testament.
Christ and the apostles would take those "weightier matters of the law" (Matt.
23:23 ESV), filter them, and apply them to the new covenant community.

Fourth, *the Mosaic law is embedded within a larger narrative that assumes
a moral understanding and illustrates moral success and failure*. Unlike other
ancient Near Eastern law collections, the Mosaic law is part of a larger narrative
structure that is connected from Genesis through 2 Kings—though Ruth-less in
the Hebrew canon (there Ruth appears after Proverbs). These Old Testament
narrators presume a moral point of view and don't need to regularly remind us
with statements like "the thing that David had done displeased the LORD" (2 Sam.
11:27 ESV). They typically assume a morally informed readership.[10]

In describing many biblical actors, who are indeed a mixed bag, these narrators take for granted that we readers can detect their moral flaws. For example,
though trusting God's promises, Abraham regularly deceived others about his wife
(and half sister) Sarah. She recounted how Abraham told her, "*Everywhere* we
go, say of me, 'He is my brother'" (Gen. 20:13). Other patriarchs, David, Gideon,
Jephthah, and Samson did trust in God at crucial points and were commended
for their trust in God (see Heb. 11), but they *weren't* commended for sins like
sexual immorality or lapses into idolatry.

Consider the most morally compromised of the judges—Samson. Throughout
his career he made numerous misjudgments and took for granted his divinely
given physical strength. But trust in God would come through periodically. For
example, he depended on God's supernatural help when fighting Philistines with
nothing more than a humble donkey's jawbone (Judg. 15:15–18).[11] And he offered
a heartfelt cry—and last gasp of faith—to God to assist him just before he died
(Judg. 16:28).

The Israelite world—like our own—is one "where there are few perfect saints
and few unredeemable sinners: most of its heroes and heroines have both virtues
and vices; they mix obedience and unbelief."[12] Their "mixed ethical achievement"
reminds us that God desires moral integrity but still keeps his promises and remains loyal to his people despite their failures.[13] In 1 Corinthians 10:6–12, Paul
reminded his audience of the Israelites' *negative moral example* of disobedience
in the wilderness: engaging in idolatry, committing adultery, grumbling, and complaining. Generations of Israelites knew, as we know today, that these *narratives
instruct and shape our theological and moral understanding*. One scholar went
so far as to say that narrative *is* theology.[14]

Fifth, *the Sinai covenant had a stronger personal or relational—as well as
ethical—dimension as compared to other ancient Near Eastern law collections*.

In the next couple of chapters, we'll see how Israel's worldview expressed in the Mosaic law has a moral or ethical heartbeat. Though the law gives examples of wisdom and though the law isn't comprehensive for all aspects of Israelite life, it reveals a moral structure and a starting point for moral duties and behavior.

Harvard scholar Jon Levinson nicely sums up various themes for us. He notes that in ancient Near Eastern treaties, stipulations ("laws") tend to be few. But the Torah (the "law [instruction] of Moses"), which includes smaller collections of law, is momentous in that it covers "all manner of things" within a covenant framework: "Now the observance even of humdrum matters of law has become an expression of personal faithfulness and loyalty in covenant." He adds:

> Even when the commanding voice of the covenantal suzerain, namely God, is not explicit in their grammatical structure, laws have become commandments, and the Israelites' opportunities to demonstrate their love for the LORD have become correspondingly more numerous, effectively encompassing the whole of life. Good deeds become acts of personal fidelity to God: they are not simply the right things to do within some rational code of ethics (though they may be that as well). Conversely, bad deeds become acts of betrayal. They are not simply morally wrong in the abstract: they wrong the divine covenant partner who forbad them.[15]

8

Differences between the Law of Moses and Ancient Near Eastern Laws (2)

Human Dignity, Relationship, and Equality

Distinguishing Between the Broader "Biblical Vision" and Certain "Biblical Laws"

God "Dirties" His Hands?

One of our critics from within, Peter Enns, maintains that when we compare the Mosaic laws with those of other ancient Near Eastern law collections, the Mosaic laws appear to be "less special" and "less unique."[1] You may be familiar with the expression "not seeing the forest for the trees." That is, when we focus on certain details (the trees), we miss seeing the bigger picture (the forest). This is the mistake made by various critics—both within and without.

As noted, various Israelite laws reflect God's accommodation to human sin and hard-heartedness (Matt. 19:8); that means many of these laws don't reflect God's moral ideal. They are often *concessions* to human failure. They give us the moral floor rather than an ethical ceiling, often expressing *what God tolerates, not what he delights in.*

God meets his people partway between the *ideal* and *fallen reality*. He begins where they are but seeks to move them in a redemptive direction through moral formation and a restoration of the creational ideals. As John Goldingay writes, "God gets his hands dirty to a certain point" by working "within a fallen world though not the original product of his own pure hands."² Part of this accommodation is God's stepping into an already *violent* world and reluctantly responding with coercive force (counterviolence).

This all brings us to an important distinction—between *vision* and *laws*.³

The Biblical Vision

Someone has said that morality isn't *a system of rules* but rather *rules within a system* of designed or purposeful ends.⁴ In our case, specific Mosaic "rules" or "laws" take on greater clarity and coherence when we look at the larger biblical vision, which includes the ideals, goals, or ends for which humans have been created.

First of all, *these ideals are laid out in Genesis 1–2*: God wanted his people to look *backward* at those ideals in order to move *forward*, away from the broken, fallen structures of the ancient Near Eastern setting. These ideals include

- *God-given human dignity* or the capacity to co-rule (with God) in caring for creation and to relate to ("walk with") God (Gen. 1:26–28; 2:15; 3:8)—all humans as priest-kings;
- *male-female equality* as opposed to patriarchy and subordination (Gen. 1:26–27);
- *no intrinsic or essential class distinctions* as opposed to slavery/servitude, racism, classism (Gen. 1:26–27); and
- *monogamy*, or one man, one woman as one flesh for one lifetime—that is, exclusivity, complementarity (i.e., physical/physiological), conjugality, and permanency (Gen. 2:24; cf. Mark 10:6–9).

Job expresses this vision: both he and his servants came from the same place—the mother's womb (Job 31:13–15). They are equals! *Less-than-ideal*, "permitted" biblical servitude *laws* were given in a fallen situation to regulate against abuse, though these laws reflected a redemptive, humanizing direction.

Second, *ancient Near Eastern cultures had far different priorities from our own: community, stability, and maintaining order*. This is a different mindset from our own Western perspective, which values democracy, individuality, freedom, privacy. So we must appreciate this ancient context for what it is.

Third, *the larger moral vision of the Old Testament can't be reduced to particular laws in the Pentateuch*. This means treating the Mosaic law as a wisdom collection that is relative to Israel misses the larger worldview picture or vision being expressed. That notion ignores the moral undercurrent and historical narrative intended to shape and inform Israel's ethical understanding so that Israel might represent God's goodness and wisdom to the surrounding nations.

Fourth, *Israel's occasional borrowing of "laws" from surrounding nations doesn't mean that Israel's law is pretty much "just like other ancient law collections."* Observing borrowing and seeing similarities shouldn't blind us from noticing significant worldview differences. So, it's less helpful to compare Israel's code law-for-law with other ancient legislation than to compare and contrast their underlying theological and moral visions or worldviews.

So, we should focus more on Israel's overarching biblical *worldview*—its *vision* or *ideals*—and less on specific *laws* that assume human fallenness and sin, even though they still possess redemptive elements. That will be the more illuminating path to take.

Specific Worldview Comparisons between Israelite and Ancient Near Eastern Laws

Let's now look at broader thematic comparisons, which reveal significant worldview differences. The *manner* in which these laws are articulated—and the narrative structure or larger story that undergirds them—can potentially shape an ancient culture's imagination and moral formation. The potential was there to set Israel apart as a "wise" and "understanding" people.[5]

Intrinsic Human Dignity versus Selective Dignity

In the ancient Near East, the earthly *king* was associated with a god's "image"— an honor that didn't extend to ordinary human beings. By contrast, God created humans in his image as corulers with God (*kings*) and worshipers of God (*priests*). These priest-kings were made to care for creation alongside God (Gen. 1:26–28; cf. Ps. 8), and they were to relate to or walk with God (Gen. 3:8; cf. 5:22, 24; 6:9). God calls ancient Israel as a "kingdom of priests" (Exod. 19:6), and this is the calling of restored, redeemed humanity in Christ (1 Pet. 2:9; Rev. 1:6; 5:10). Walter Brueggemann states that "it is now generally agreed that the image of God reflected in human persons is after the manner of a king who establishes himself to assert his sovereign rule where the king himself cannot be present."[6]

Other ancient creation accounts present a degraded or diminished view of humanity. For example, the Mesopotamian Atrahasis myth presents humans as disdainfully created from a lower god's blood and the assembly of gods' spit. In the Enuma Elish account, the lower gods were griping about the work the higher gods made them do—digging irrigation canals for agriculture. So the higher gods made humans in order to do slave labor so that the lower gods could rest from that drudgery.

By contrast, Genesis 1–2 presents humans as possessing a sacred dignity. This unique "image of God" feature has at least two relevant implications:

> *Implication 1:* "*All* agents (e.g., slaves, captives, and criminals) are regarded as persons and should be treated accordingly."
> *Implication 2:* "All legal subjects are seen as *free, dignified*, and *self-determining* human beings."[7]

The fact is that other ancient Near Eastern nations *simply didn't* believe that all humans are created equal.

Relational versus Detached Covenant-Making

Another unique feature of the biblical God is *his desire to establish a relationship, dialogue, and interaction with his people*—just as he did with humanity at the very beginning (Gen. 3:8). Thus, God's laws were given to Israel to shape a relational moral outlook and their social identity.

Underlying this was *God's repeated reminder to Israel that they were once slaves in Egypt whom he rescued.* Thus, Israelites were to care for aliens and strangers (*gerim*) in their midst and to provide for servants when their service term was completed (e.g., Deut. 10:19; 15:10–15)—themes to which we will return later.

Likewise, God's *compassionate character* ("for I am compassionate") was to shape in Israel a *compassionate spirit* toward those in debt (Exod. 22:27 NIV). God's *just* character (God "does not show partiality nor take a bribe") and his delivering Israel from bondage in Egypt were to serve as Israel's basis for *pursuing justice* for the most vulnerable—widows, orphans, and aliens (Deut. 10:17–18).

By contrast, other ancient Near Eastern deities or kings *reveal no interest in such a relationship.* The voice behind the other "[ancient Near Eastern] laws provides almost no inspiration for morality shaping, providing no interpersonal relationship for the legal subjects" in order to "shape their brotherhood and peoplehood."[8]

Furthermore, *Israel's more personalized covenant-making—and thus morality-shaping—is reinforced by the fact of the common second-person prescriptions in the Mosaic law*: "you shall" / "you shall not." By contrast, this feature is rare or missing altogether in ancient Near Eastern codes. One scholar suggests that this fact may be connected to the didactic (instructional) dimension of the Mosaic law.[9]

Moral Monotheism versus Fragmented Polytheism

Israel's God, Yahweh, provided a morally coherent framework for the world—something that the plurality of ancient Near Eastern deities couldn't. Those deities were *part of* the earthly or *immanent* realm. They were not beyond it (*transcendent*). After all, they created humans to meet their needs of food, clothing, and care. They also engaged in acts like rape, incest, and bestiality. In one Canaanite poem—The Baal Cycle—the deity Baal has sex with a heifer "seventy times seven" and "eighty times eight," and she "bears a boy." He rapes his sister Anath while she is in the form of a calf—so, rape, incest, and bestiality all in one act. He even has sexual relations with his mother, Asherah—with the permission of his father, El—in order to humiliate her.[10]

By contrast, the good Creator in Genesis 1 is the Lord of Israel and Ruler of all the nations. The book of Exodus portrays Israel's God as no mere regional deity. He challenged the oppressive Pharaoh of Egypt—the superpower of that day—exerting his strong hand against that nation's deities in each of the plagues (Exod. 12:12).[11]

Self-Sufficient God versus Needy, Lazy Deities (The Great Symbiosis)

We noted above the fact that God created human beings in his image to be his *co-regents*, not his *slaves* to do a deity's "dirty work" in the world. The biblical God is self-sufficient, all-powerful, and free—and thus not in need of humanity:

- *Self-sufficient:* Without creation, God existed independently (self-sufficient). His divine existence depends on nothing outside himself. God is not a contingent (dependent) being.
- *All-powerful:* God spoke, and the world was created. He didn't need preexisting matter lying around so that he could shape the world into existence. If that were the case, then God's ability to create would have been the result of sheer luck: God just happened to have the proper creation materials lying around, without which he couldn't have created. No, the accurate picture is that the existence of matter itself—the "stuff" of physical creation— depends on God.
- *Free:* God created freely and graciously. He did not *have* to create anything (Ps. 50:10–12). He was free to create out of nothing rather than be hemmed in by whatever preexisting materials were available to him (Gen. 1:1; Ps. 33:6; John 1:1–3).

By contrast, the other ancient Near Eastern deities were *needy. They brought humans into being to do their work for them and to meet their needs.* How so? In their rituals, worshipers would awaken, feed, and clothe their gods, and at the end of the day the gods would be put to bed. In one account, the gods say, "Let them bring us our daily portions."[12] And, in return, the gods would (hopefully) cause crops to grow and grant fertility to humans and their livestock.

This has been called "the great symbiosis." That is, the gods and humans work closely with or depend on one another in a way that is mutually advantageous. Also, the gods were *concerned about themselves—not the humans they created.* And even if humans did what the gods expected, there were still no guarantees from the gods that humans would be treated favorably—unlike God's promised covenant blessings for Israel's obedience.[13]

Divine Direction versus Divination

The *Genocide* book notes another worldview difference that relates to discerning and validating divine guidance.[14] The Old Testament prohibits magical practices and divination (Lev. 19:26; Deut. 18:10; 1 Sam. 15:23; etc.). Yet within other ancient Near Eastern settings, discerning the will of the gods came through following impoverished, fuzzy, and easily manipulated divination methods. John Walton writes: "Divination produced the only divine revelation known in the ancient Near East. Through its mechanisms, the ancients believed not that they could know the deity, but that they could get a glimpse of the designs and will of the deity."[15]

How was this divining done? By consulting animal entrails or the movement of heavenly bodies—hardly a sturdy and sure form of guidance. And essentially, a priest could claim the authority of the gods who had whispered in his ear, but no one else could get in on the secret. There was no way of confirming the trustworthiness of the diviner.

Things were different in Israel. For Israelites, *miracles* were a standard, publicly accessible way of detecting God's mind on a matter during certain periods of Israel's history. For example, the Lord clearly favored Moses's prophetic vantage point over that of the rebellious Korah, who probably had some priestly role in Egypt and apparently wanted a share in Aaron's priestly privileges and access to the holy place.[16] He met with a very public and, as it were, groundbreaking end, which made plain whom God was promoting (Num. 16:28–29): "By this you shall know that the LORD has sent me" (cf. Jer. 28:1–17, esp. vv. 15–17).

In addition to validating signs and wonders, a simple, nondicey indicator of God's direction was *the casting of lots*. This method yielded an unambiguous binary answer—a clear *this* or *that*, *yes* or *no*. (This was practiced in other ancient Near Eastern settings along with the more common, but ambiguous, divining practices.) And the one who cast lots would be a publicly authorized and divinely validated person (e.g., Lev. 16:8; Josh. 18:6; 1 Sam. 10:20; cf. Acts 1:26).[17] In unusual cases, an idolatrous false prophet who might perform signs was to be kept in check by prior divine revelation (Deut. 13:1–5), and even pagan magicians attempting to mimic the true God's wonders would eventually be outdone by him (Exod. 7:22; 8:18; 9:11).

Sabbath Rest versus All Days Alike

The biblical Sabbath was also unique in the ancient Near East. Walton notes: "It is now widely acknowledged that no such observance has been found" outside of Israel's domain.[18] Ancient Near Eastern cultures utilized solar and lunar phases for reckoning time, and their creation accounts—as in Genesis 1–2—refer to seven days in a week (a 6 + 1 structure). But their seven-day cycle was not theologically based.[19]

By contrast, Israel's Sabbath law was based on God's command and was rooted in the structure of creation. Later, Jesus would reinforce the point that the Sabbath was made for humans, not humans for the Sabbath (Mark 2:27). This day was set aside for rest—to benefit *all* persons in society and within a given household, including servants and even animals (Deut. 5:14).

While other ancient Near Eastern cultures celebrated special days, none of them were legislated. The implication is this: "Without such legislation, it is likely that many poor people would have continued to work while the wealthy enjoyed their celebrations, perhaps taking a short break to watch or join processions."[20]

Persons versus Things

Another key worldview difference is that the Mosaic law promotes a "law of persons"—humans as corulers with God—which entails a strong humanitarian concern. By contrast, a "law of things" is presupposed in other ancient Near Eastern collections; even though occasional concern is expressed for the sick and vulnerable (e.g., Code of Hammurabi §§148, 185–86), the broader worldview picture is that humans aren't truly distinctive from the rest of creation.

The persons-versus-things contrast is reinforced by the fact that property rights in the Mosaic law are significantly more humane than in other codes. These Mosaic property rights "never involve mutilation, beating, or death."[21] If an Israelite stole something, that person had to make multiple restitution to the theft victim. Furthermore, the degree of punishment didn't depend on *whose* property was stolen, which was the case in neighboring nations. Also unlike other nations, the severity of punishment didn't depend on the gender or social status of the thief.[22]

Beyond this, the Mosaic law was also unique in its prohibition of even *thinking about* or *desiring to* deprive neighbors of what legitimately belonged to them: "You shall not covet" (Exod. 20:17; Deut. 5:21).[23]

Rights versus No Rights

The implication of biblical law is that all humans—whether war captives (Deut. 21:10–14), foreign runaway slaves (23:15–16), or the socially vulnerable (14:28–29; 26:12–13)—had rights and were to be treated as *free agents* (e.g., 30:19). They were not considered *things* or *objects*. In other parts of the ancient world, no such rights existed for, say, war captives, criminals, or slaves.[24]

Democratized versus Hierarchical Values

The biblical doctrine that all humans bear the divine image presupposes a "democratization" of value—that is, a fundamental equality of humans.[25] This meant that favoring the rich *or* the poor—the high *or* low—in society was *forbidden*: "Do not pervert justice; do not show partiality to the poor or favoritism to the great, but judge your neighbor fairly" (Lev. 19:15 NIV). The alien in the land was to be judged by the same laws as the Israelite citizen (Num. 15:15–16, 29; Lev. 24:22; cf. Exod. 12:48–49). Kings like David and Ahab were not above the law; they were called to account for their wicked acts (2 Sam. 12:1–23; 1 Kings 21:17–29).

By contrast, other ancient Near Eastern law collections ascribed value to persons according to their social status and issued judgments and punishments according to class ranking. These law collections differentiated between the freeman (a person) and the slave (a thing).[26]

The German scholar Norman Gottwald pointed out the huge divide between two social classes in ancient Near Eastern societies:

- *the dominant tribute-imposing class:* the political elite and those benefiting from state power
- *the dominated tribute-bearing class:* the peasants and others who were taxed, had to pay tribute, and so on[27]

In the Old Babylonian era (2000–1600 BC), during which the Code of Hammurabi was written, society consisted of a threefold structure:

- *elite citizens or freemen:* priests, nobility, merchants, and so on
- *subordinate citizens:* craftsmen, laborers, tenant farmers, and the like
- *chattel slaves:* considered the property of their owners, including foreign captives

By contrast, although Israel had marginalized people, Israelite law had no social stratification; *all Israelites were free.* The common term for "slave" or "servant" (*ebed*) literally means "worker."[28] David Baker writes: "It is characteristic of Old Testament law that the beneficiaries are not the elite but those at the margins of society."[29]

So although priests, prophets, kings, and judges existed in Israel, a fixed hierarchy or stratification is rejected in Israel's law; it favors a strong egalitarianism: "The Pentateuch [i.e., the book of Moses] articulates a new social, political, and religious order, whose core is a single, uniformly empowered, homogeneous class."[30] That's why, for example, the distinction between debt servant and the free citizen was not a sharp one, as in the cultures surrounding Israel.

The Hebrew Bible scholar Joshua Berman likewise observes this "more egalitarian order" of male and female, and humanity overall; this theme is rooted in Genesis 1. That text "stands in contrast to the creation myths of Mesopotamia," and it is "championing humans as rulers rather than servants."[31] Some critics argue that the biblical God created humans to enslave them;[32] however, that is actually the picture in the ancient nonbiblical creation stories. God created human beings to *rule over* the earth *with him:* "You have made [humans] a little lower than God" and "crown him with glory and majesty!" (Ps. 8:5; cf. Gen. 1:26–28).

These fundamental worldview contrasts are significant and come with wide-ranging moral implications for the Israelites. The next chapter discusses more contrasts.

9

Differences between the Law of Moses and Ancient Near Eastern Laws (3)

Poverty and Wealth

Land Use: The Right of People or of Kings?

... the land which the LORD our God is giving to us.
—Deuteronomy 2:29

Royal ownership of land was a common theme in ancient Near Eastern law collections. Ultimately, all land belonged to the king. Any personal holding of the land was temporary; it ultimately reverted back to the crown. In Israel, however, the land was a gift to God's people, and ancestral land was passed on to one's descendants as a sacred inheritance.[1]

For example, one unique feature of Israel's legislation was the assistance it offered foreigners enslaved against their will—and likely mistreated—who could flee to Israel for safety. Israelites were typically tied to their own tribal territories, but these oppressed foreigners had great flexibility about where to settle—namely, in any of Israel's cities (Deut. 23:15–16). We'll look at the topic of servitude—including the question of foreign servants—below.

Foreigners: Concern or Silence?

> So show your love for the alien, for you were aliens in the land of Egypt.
>
> —Deuteronomy 10:19

A theme that pervades the Mosaic law is concern for the alien. This humanitarian feature was reinforced by the reminder—thirty-six times—that the Israelites were once aliens in Egypt. As noted, Israel's own story was to have a morally shaping effect in their relationships with outsiders. By contrast, there appears to be "relatively little concern for resident aliens in ancient Near Eastern laws"; while occasional or sporadic protections or provisions are given to foreigners, these texts "do not mention resident aliens."[2] Within Israel, however, even a "resident alien could become prosperous, even more so than an Israelite (Lev. 25:47)."[3]

Bribes: Prohibition or Permission?

> You shall not take a bribe, for a bribe blinds the clear-sighted and subverts the cause of the just.
>
> —Exodus 23:8

While the law codes of Israel's neighbors frowned on the practice of bribery, judges were permitted to receive "payment of fees and gratuities." If this "transaction" were to be questioned, the judge and donor could simply refer to it as a "gift" rather than a bribe. By contrast, "Old Testament law is quite distinctive from the laws of neighboring countries in its categorical prohibition of all payments to judges by litigants" (e.g., Exod. 23:8; Deut. 10:17; 16:19; etc.).[4]

Employment Rights: Prominent or Absent?

> You shall give him his wages on his day before the sun sets, for he is poor and sets his heart on it; so that he will not cry against you to the LORD and it become sin in you.
>
> —Deuteronomy 24:15

Employment rights "do not feature in other ancient Near Eastern law collections."[5] Israel's laws, by contrast, emphasized two important aspects:[6]

1. *Sabbath rest for all.* Israel's law mandated Sabbath rest; this was to benefit Israel's entire society—including the employer, the employed, and even

work animals (Exod. 20:8–11)—as well as grant opportunity for corporate worship.[7]

2. *Prompt payment of wages.* Employees were to be paid promptly and fairly. Hired workers were to receive wages "before the sun sets" (cf. Lev. 19:13). If workers gave their cloaks as collateral, these had to be returned before nightfall (Exod. 22:26–27; Deut. 24:13).[8] We've noted in chapter 2 that James 5:4 picks up on this theme.

Provision for the Poor: Intentional or Unmentioned?

Nor shall you glean your vineyard, nor shall you gather the fallen fruit of your vineyard; you shall leave them for the needy and for the stranger. I am the LORD your God.

—Leviticus 19:10

When you reap the harvest of your land, moreover, you shall not reap to the very corners of your field nor gather the gleaning of your harvest; you are to leave them for the needy and the alien. I am the LORD your God.

—Leviticus 23:22

In these Leviticus texts—along with Deuteronomy 23:24–25—poor Israelites and resident aliens could freely glean grain and pick up fruit from another's orchard. This is beautifully illustrated in the book of Ruth, where this "woman of excellence" (Ruth 3:11) collected produce the harvesters had missed from a landowner's field or trees. Ruth actually belonged to three of the vulnerable groups in Israel—a resident alien (from Moab), an orphan, and a widow (cf. Deut. 24:19–21).[9] Unlike the scenario in Augustine's experience, gleaning and "scrumping" were the poor person's legal right—and the landowner's duty. Again, this provision "is unique in ancient Near Eastern law."[10]

These gleaning laws presuppose that *the poor had the privilege of working for their food*; it was up to them to take the initiative. The practice meant the landowner wasn't unduly burdened to make provisions available by exerting additional effort.

Also, another means of assisting the poor was the triennial tithe ("tenth"): "At the end of every third year you shall bring out all the tithe of your produce in that year, and shall deposit it in your town" so that "the Levite . . . and the alien, the orphan and the widow who are in your town, shall come and eat and be satisfied, in order that the Lord your God may bless you in all the work of your hand which you do" (Deut. 14:28–29; cf. 26:12–13).

Note that while tithes *were* a part of the larger ancient Near Eastern landscape, these were payable *to the palace or temple*. This particular tithe in Israel "becomes the first known tax instituted for the purpose of social welfare."[11]

Loans for the Poor: No Interest versus Interest?

You shall not give him your silver at interest, nor your food for gain. I am the LORD your God, who brought you out of the land of Egypt to give you the land of Canaan and to be your God.

—Leviticus 25:37–38

Israel's lending laws stand out in contrast to other ancient Near Eastern nations like the Babylonian and Akkadian codes (i.e., the Code of Hammurabi and the Laws of Eshnunna). In these settings, a lender had the right to charge interest rates of 20 percent, 33 ⅓ percent, or even 50 percent for loans of money or grain.[12]

By contrast, Israelites were not permitted to charge interest to their fellow Israelites—one of several laws to protect them from falling (further) into poverty and dependency—because the Israelites were once in bondage in Egypt (Lev. 25:35–38; Deut. 23:19–20). Not charging interest was the mark of a righteous person (Ps. 15:5). Unlike the "alien" (*ger*) who lived under Israelite law and could *not* be charged interest (Lev. 25:35–37), the "foreigner" (*nokri*) *who had no covenant obligations within Israel and was primarily interested in commerce*, could be charged interest (Deut. 23:20[21]).

Notice that I am *not* saying here that other ancient Near Eastern law collections expressed *no* concern for the poor, that debts were *never* wiped away, or that social reforms *never* took place. But Israel's *consistent, nonhaphazard* lending laws and debt-forgiveness still stand out as a steady reminder of legal restraints in Israel to protect against taking advantage of the poor.[13]

Debt Forgiveness: Predictable or Haphazard?

At the end of every seven years you shall grant a remission of debts.

—Deuteronomy 15:1

A poor Israelite's debts were to be canceled in the seventh year (Exod. 21:2; Deut. 15:1–2) and in the fiftieth "Year of Jubilee" (Lev. 25). All (indentured) Israelite servants were to be set free, with their debts canceled. Any land that the owner had been leased due to their poverty was returned without any remaining debt.[14]

· Now, some scholars have been impressed by the fact that occasionally in other ancient Near Eastern nations debt forgiveness might occur in a shorter period of time—or even that land might be given to a citizen by the king. This isn't all that earth-shattering, however, as such debt cancellation was typically the result of a royal decree.[15] Perhaps it came with a king's accession to the throne. But *it wasn't enshrined in the official legal codes or mandated as a regular occurrence*.[16] And while rulers may have wanted to appear desirous of helping the poor, they were also keen on reducing discontent and perhaps preventing certain persons from becoming too wealthy and powerful. Rather than debt relief being established and predictable, it could come without warning, which would make for an unstable economic situation. And, as mentioned, a portion of land given to a citizen by royal decree would *automatically revert back to the king after a given period of time*. It was understood that the land belonged to the king.

By contrast, Israelites didn't have to wait for royal orders or decrees, "which might never be issued unless there was a pious king on the throne or a politically opportune moment arose."[17] Of course, in Israel's system, unscrupulous people—in anticipation of the Year of Jubilee—could get a loan the year prior without the intention of paying it back. Such legislation, though, does assume honesty and integrity.[18]

Yes, Israel had some laws in common with their ancient Near Eastern neighbors,[19] and we've noted that various laws in Israel were permitted because of the hardness of human hearts (Matt. 19:8). And some of these humanizing laws were not always put into practice (e.g., the Jubilee Year in Leviticus 25). But keep in mind the overarching distinction between the *ideals* of the *biblical vision* or *worldview* as opposed to *particular laws* that sometimes expressed what was merely *tolerable*. The biblical vision reveals a marked contrast with that of Israel's neighbors. If Israel had focused on this vision, their neighbors would have realized, "Surely this great nation is a wise and understanding people" (Deut. 4:6 ESV; cf. 1 Kings 3:28).

PART 3

Crime and Punishment

*Violations and Penalties in
Old Testament Law*

10

A Bit of Ancient Near Eastern Context

Perhaps you've heard about purportedly outmoded laws in the United States that are still on the books. For example, you can't set a mousetrap in California without a hunting license. Nor can you sprinkle salt on railroad tracks or blow your nose in public in Waterville, Maine. Virtually all citizens in these jurisdictions are oblivious to those laws, and perhaps those laws were ignored from the very start.[1]

What about the Mosaic law and the sometimes-severe penalties included in it? The book of Leviticus states that those who engage in certain *incestuous relationships* must be burned to death (Lev. 20:14); the same goes for the daughter of a priest who turns to *harlotry* (Lev. 21:9). *Mediums* and *spiritists* are to be "stoned with stones" (Lev. 20:27). And whatever the method, the death penalty awaits those who *commit adultery*: "Both of them shall die" (Lev. 20:10; Deut. 22:22). But how were those penalties understood by the original hearers, and were they even carried out? Was body maiming a reality in ancient Israel?

Literal Death Penalty and Severe Punishments? Yes, Sometimes

Some of our critics from within reject the idea that God could have permitted the death penalty in ancient Israel.[2] But, as we've seen, the New Testament makes clear that the death penalty was divinely and justly permitted (Matt. 15:4; Mark 7:10; Acts 3:23; Heb. 10:28–29; 12:18–20; cf. Heb. 2:2–3). But what are we to make of those ancient references in which the guilty "shall be put to death"? Are these always literal?

Theoretically, the maximum penalty for sixteen different violations or crimes in Israel was death—including bestiality, adultery, kidnapping, incest, prostitution, false prophesying, and so on. *But all of these could be commuted to monetary payment ("ransom"), with one exception.* Murder demanded capital punishment; no ransom payment was permitted: "You shall accept no ransom for the life of a murderer, who is guilty of death, but he shall be put to death" (Num. 35:31 ESV). Walter Kaiser writes, "This has widely been interpreted to imply that in all the other fifteen cases the judges could commute the crimes deserving of capital punishment by designating a 'ransom' or 'substitute.' In that case the death penalty served to mark the seriousness of the crime."[3]

Were there times when capital punishment was carried out? At key moments in Israel's history, yes it was. For example, during Israel's fledgling nationhood, we are specifically told that an Israelite who flagrantly or knowingly *violated the Sabbath* (Num. 15:32–36) and one who *blasphemed* (i.e., slandered) God's name (Lev. 24:10–23) were capitally punished. These were with divine approval—"as the LORD had commanded Moses" (Num. 15:36; Lev. 24:23). But as we'll see, these appear to be *exemplary* and *unique* rather than the common practice or protocol in Israel—to put the fear of God into the Israelites.

The same is likely true about Achan, who stole a wedge of gold and a costly garment after the battle of Jericho—Israel's first battle in Canaan. He and his family were put to death—another powerful reminder to all Israel (Josh. 22:20). This was unusual—an exception to the principle that the perpetrator of a sin alone must be punished and not anyone else in his family (Deut. 24:16). Another possibility, according to biblical scholar Craig Keener, is that Achan's family was punished "because, obviously, [Achan] couldn't have hid[den] this [plunder] under the tent without them knowing and participating in the subterfuge." All family members were complicit, being well aware that Achan buried the loot underneath his tent.[4]

These punishments in Israel's early history are much like what happened in the earliest days of the Jerusalem church. God struck down Ananias and Sapphira, who lied about their "generosity" (Acts 5:1–11). As a result, "great fear came over the whole church, and over all who heard of these things" (v. 11). But such a dramatic event of deadly divine judgment was hardly a predictable occurrence. Of course, God could cause death or sickness when professing believers carry out moral or spiritual abuses (e.g., 1 Cor. 11:30). Jesus himself threatened to cast a false prophetess on a bed of sickness and even strike dead her followers (Rev. 2:22–23).

Nonliteral Punishments in the Ancient Near East

We have reason to suspect that, in general, these severe punishments were not to be literally carried out. For one thing, many of the stated punishments in ancient

Near Eastern law collections served as examples of wisdom that highlight certain worldview priorities and matters of importance. As we'll see, Israelites apparently viewed the "severe punishment" scenario in the same way.

Let's look at some examples. The Code of Hammurabi presents exaggerated or hyperbolic punishments.[5] One example is a builder's slipshod house construction, which results in its collapse and the owner's son's death. The punishment? The builder's son was to be put to death (§§229–30). In another instance, a physician whose patient died or was blinded during surgery was to have his hand cut off (§218).

One noted ancient Near Eastern scholar, J. J. Finkelstein, writes that such punishments can't possibly be taken literally. To do so would be absurd and even insane.[6] He wonders what reasonable person would enter the surgical profession if it meant the risk of having a hand amputated. And who would go into house-construction work if, in the event of the owner's son's death, his own son could be put to death?[7]

These brutal-sounding punishments are *exaggerations*, and they aren't making a *legal* point. When these laws were first drawn up, they were meant to serve as a *warning* or an *admonition*. To the construction worker, the caution is this: Woe to the slipshod builder who cuts corners to make a shekel. To the medical doctor, the message is similar: In your medical practice, don't be careless about your patient's life and her physical well-being. If these laws were literally enforced, they would be highly impractical and outrageous. From the beginning, these threats were meant to be hyperbolic, Finkelstein says.[8] So these laws—or samples of wisdom—were *designed to drive home certain worldview ideals or priorities*.

Second, *behind these laws is the assumption of a system of ransom or monetary payment*. As noted earlier, while provision for revenge (retaliatory mutilation) was included in ancient Near Eastern law collections, they commonly allowed for monetary payment (ransom) in its place.[9] Commenting on the Code of Hammurabi's penalties, Joe Sprinkle writes that "if a system of ransom were assumed where the life of the builder or his son could be redeemed and the hand of the physician could be redeemed by pecuniary [i.e., monetary] ransom," then these laws would (a) serve as a warning ("an admonitory function") for which "the more graphic statement of the penalty—execution or mutilation—is more effective" and (b) also be practical as law.[10]

The next chapter will address crime and punishment in Israel. It will examine specific laws on capital punishment, maiming, and ransom—and how Israel practiced this in periods beyond their stay at Mount Sinai.

11

Israel's Punishments as Nonliteral in the Pentateuch

We've seen that *ancient Near Eastern law collections were more a matter of worldview illumination—examples of wisdom—rather than meant for direct application*. As for Israel, we've seen that the Mosaic law and its surrounding narrative have *a relational and moral tone pulsing through it—with clear ethical implications*. The New Testament picks up on this tone. However, when it comes to literally applying the law of Moses in terms of punishments, ancient Israelites "did not assume the Torah was designed for literal implementing."[1] This chapter examines how the Mosaic law itself reveals this—and how Israel's Scriptures thereafter reflect this as well.

A Look at the Biblical Texts

> When an ox gores a man or a woman to death, the ox shall be stoned, and its flesh shall not be eaten, but the owner of the ox shall not be liable.
>
> —Exodus 21:28 ESV

The *lex talionis* (law of retaliation) has gotten much bad press. Some critics claim that the "eye for an eye" and "tooth for a tooth" law is barbaric and crude. After all, this primitive practice calls for bodily mutilation, doesn't it?

Actually, this law is *metaphorical*—except for "life for life," as we've seen. John Goldingay says that this formula is "almost poetic or parabolic."[2] As with Israel's contemporaries, Israel also treated punishments within these law collections in a fairly nonliteral fashion. Many of Sinai's threatened punishments weren't literally implemented, which was true of other ancient Near Eastern codes. And not only did the Israelites not carry out the death penalty for violations of potentially capital crimes; the biblical text also doesn't "suggest that Israel behaved wrongly in not implementing the Torah's sanctions. People did not assume the Torah was for literal implementing, and the narrative assumes they were not wrong to see things that way."[3] As we've seen, the exception for this was murder, with all other punishments typically commuted to payment. We see this in a number of instances in Israel's law.

Exodus 21:22–25: Tussling Men, Pregnant Woman

If men struggle and strike a pregnant woman who then gives birth prematurely—but without further injury—then the injuring party must pay a fine. If there is *further* injury, then a *heavier* penalty is to be paid. Of course, if the unborn child dies, this would be an *accidental* death, which is *not* a capital offense. This would be like the accidental killing of another person "without enmity," "without lying in wait," or without "seeking . . . injury" (Num. 35:22, 23). In that case, one could flee to a city of refuge for protection. So "life for life" would not be a suitable punishment (Num. 35:10–34).[4]

Of particular interest in the case of the injured pregnant woman is this: the formula "life for life, eye for eye" *wasn't* a literal "mutilation for mutilation" or "bodily injury for bodily injury." After all, the mention of "burn for burn" (v. 25) *doesn't fit* the scenario of striking a pregnant woman in a fight.[5] Indeed, "tooth for tooth" penalty doesn't fit either. Something *nonliteral* is in view.

Exodus 21:26–27: Gouging Out Eyes, Knocking Out Teeth

In this case, if an employer gouges out his indentured servant's eye, the employer's eye isn't literally gouged out in return. Rather, the servant can go free without any remaining debt to pay. The same applies to knocking out a servant's tooth. (Perhaps this is why this type of service is considered *indentured*!) Now if he strikes down and kills his servant, then the employer (master) is to be put to death ("avenged" [*naqam*]; Exod. 21:20 NET). This was an affirmation of the servant's rights and full humanity.

Also in Exodus, we read that if a servant who is struck by his employer doesn't immediately die but survives a day or two, then the employer isn't to be put to death (21:21). A common criticism is that the employer was at liberty to beat a servant to within an inch of his life without any penalty. But this is a strained and uncharitable reading of the text. And it just isn't true, for at least three reasons. First, *if a servant lost an eye or a tooth, his employer was to release him without any lingering debt* (vv. 25–26). Second, *the text doesn't say that the employer won't be punished.* He just won't be executed ("avenged") since this wasn't an act of intentional murder.[6] Third, as we'll see, *an abused servant within Israel*

could flee from an oppressive employer just as much as an abused foreign slave
could run away to Israel to find refuge.

Exodus 21:28–36: The Goring Ox

This passage contains various stipulations regarding a goring ox and the owner's responsibility to do something about it. These include a warning against negligence. This law could be compared to a person driving a car with defective brakes; if she knows this, she should get them fixed rather than continuing to drive. If she doesn't, she *will* be morally culpable if she drives anyway and ends up injuring or killing a pedestrian.[7]

Now, was this task of stoning an out-of-control ox literal? Even in this case, it seems not. Two reasons could be given for this. First, *this would have been a daunting, herculean task.* One commentator asks: "How does one stone a half-ton, aggressive, homicidal ox, whose testosterone is at flood level?" He advises, "He that is without fear, let him cast the first stone."[8]

Furthermore, while this case study of the goring ox may offer insight about neglect that is innocent and neglect that is culpable, *it is nevertheless highly theoretical and not based upon actual ox-goring occurrences.* This is the clear impression we get from the relevant cuneiform tablets—that is, tablets with "wedge-shaped" strokes of signs made by a stylus on wet clay, which was characteristic of early ancient Near Eastern writing. Finkelstein writes that "in all of the tens of thousands of cuneiform documents relating to legal matters which have thus far come down to us, there is hardly a single allusion to a real instance in which an ox killed or injured a person or another animal."[9] If such an event had occurred, it "would have been rare at best."[10]

As an aside, some raise a question about this text, which mentions the case of an ox that is known to be dangerous and kills a male or female servant: Why shouldn't the ox's owner pay with his life—as when a free person is killed (v. 29: "[The ox's] owner also shall be put to death")? Doesn't the fixed sum of thirty silver shekels as a ransom for a servant's death (v. 32) indicate intrinsically lower worth?

Keep in mind the following issues:

1. *The goring ox must still be put to death if it kills a servant,* and this would have been a heavy financial loss for the ox's owner.

2. *The capital case against the negligent ox owner could be commuted to payment.* Verse 29 states that the owner "shall be put to death." But this is immediately followed by a ransom option: "If a ransom is demanded of [the ox's owner], then he shall give for the redemption of his life whatever is demanded of him" (v. 30).

3. *The ransom amount in the case of a free person's death was not fixed, whereas it was fixed for a servant.* Verse 32 states that ransom payment

for the death of a servant is already set by law. In the case of a free person, the plaintiff, defendant, and judge would have to settle on a ransom price that was not established by law. Desmond Alexander writes: "The figure of thirty shekels is probably the minimum value that was to be placed upon a human life [for ransom]. . . . This suggests that for the author . . . there was little fundamental difference between a free person and a slave. The main distinction lay in the fact that it was easier to calculate the amount of the ransom to be paid for causing the death of a slave."[11]

Deuteronomy 19:15–21: False Witness and Proportional Punishment

Though bearing false witness *could* potentially be a capital crime, it all depended on harm the false witness intended to bring: it could be murderous or less than murderous. A false witness was to be *punished in accord with his intention* to harm a fellow Israelite: "You shall do to him *just as he had intended* to do to his brother" (v. 19). So the statement "life for life, eye for eye, tooth for tooth, hand for hand, foot for foot" (v. 21) suggests that "the punishment varies with the severity of the accusation"; so the demanded monetary penalty for injury should be proportioned according to the degree of harm done.[12]

Exodus 22:16–17 and Deuteronomy 22:28–29: Seducing an Unbetrothed Girl

If a man seduces a virgin who is not engaged, and lies with her, he must pay a dowry for her to be his wife. If her father absolutely refuses to give her to him, he shall pay money equal to the dowry for virgins.

—Exodus 22:16–17

If a man finds a girl who is a virgin, who is not engaged, and [catches (*tapas*)] her and lies with her and they are discovered, then the man who lay with her shall give to the girl's father fifty shekels of silver, and she shall become his wife because he has violated her; he cannot divorce her all his days.

—Deuteronomy 22:28–29

Seduction, Not Forcible Rape

The *Moral Monster* book addresses these parallel passages,[13] but I'll elaborate here.

The issue here is *seduction*; it is *not* forcible rape. The word "takes" or "catches" (*tapas*) in Deuteronomy 22:28 is a weaker verb than the one used for actual *forcible* rape in verse 25 ("forces" [*hazaq*]). Note too that *both* are found out: "They are discovered" (22:28)—not "*He* is found out." If anything, this was akin to what we today call "statutory rape"—when a minor is involved, but there is nevertheless *mutual consent.* Thus, the common argument from critics—"How terrible that this girl must marry her rapist"—is a false charge.

What's more, the Exodus passage indicates that if the father "absolutely" or "utterly" refuses to give his daughter to the seducer, the seducer then must pay the "dowry"—that is, the "bride price" (*mohar*) that provided financial security for the woman in case of divorce or the husband's death. Either way, the man must pay.[14] Without such protections, the man who seduces and has sex with a virgin does economic (and other) damage to her and her family. After all, another man who might want to marry this girl later on wouldn't pay the "bride-price" typically paid for virgins (Exod. 22:16–17).[15]

Proving Premarital Virginity

The Old Testament vision assumes that since sexual relations are to be preserved for marriage (e.g., Gen. 2:24), a spouse's expectation was that a previously unwed person entered into marriage as a virgin. Just prior to the above Deuteronomy 22 passage about rape and seduction, verses 13–22 present a scenario that brings together (a) *this premarital expectation of virginity* and (b) *a husband who proves to be a false witness against his wife.*

> If any man takes a wife and goes in to her and then turns against her, and charges her with shameful deeds and publicly defames her, and says, "I took this woman, but when I came near her, I did not find her a virgin," then the girl's father and her mother shall take and bring out the evidence of the girl's virginity to the elders of the city at the gate. The girl's father shall say to the elders, "I gave my daughter to this man for a wife, but he turned against her; and behold, he has charged her with shameful deeds, saying, 'I did not find your daughter a virgin.' But this is the evidence of my daughter's virginity." And they shall spread the garment before the elders of the city. So the elders of that city shall take the man and chastise him, and they shall fine him a hundred shekels of silver and give it to the girl's father, because he publicly defamed a virgin of Israel. And she shall remain his wife; he cannot divorce her all his days. (Deut. 22:13–19)

Premarital sex, though wrong, was viewed less severely than adultery. Now, if this woman had indeed been faithless *during engagement*, then this was tantamount to *adultery.* For instance, after Mary was "found to be with child from the Holy Spirit" while being betrothed to Joseph, he sought to "divorce her quietly" (Matt. 1:18, 19 ESV); as with the Old Testament, her perceived unfaithfulness was a breach of a marriage-like bond during her engagement.

So if the husband's charge turns out to be true, then the maximum penalty—capital punishment—could be implemented for adultery (v. 21). We've already seen, however, that such an offense could be commuted to a lesser penalty.

Now, what if the woman's parents can establish her innocence? How would this even be done? The parents would spread a "cloth" (*simlah*) (v. 17), which, according to one suggestion, would be a blood-stained sheet giving evidence of a prewedding menstruation showing she was not pregnant. Whatever the solution, it is likely that the full proceedings aren't described here and that the cloth was probably just one part of a larger complex of evidence; some suggest that even eyewitnesses could be included to substantiate the woman's innocence since a cloth by itself wouldn't be rock-solid proof.[16]

The Husband as a False Witness

So, what if her defense demonstrates the woman's innocence? Perhaps the husband claiming to have a "dud" wife is actually motivated by greed; maybe he is trying to rob his father-in-law of the bridal gift of fifty shekels and asserting that his father-in-law has stolen from him. While the crime of theft requires double restitution (Exod. 22:7), there is also the crime of being a false witness. And *since the wife, if guilty, would theoretically have to pay with her life, then the guilty husband's life should be on the line too.*

However, do we see an execution here? No. Rather, the accuser—the false witness who has "publicly defamed her" (v. 19) and "charged her with shameful deeds" (v. 16)—pays twice the bridal gift price, one hundred shekels (cf. v. 29). Here again, *we have a monetary payment, not a literal proportional capital punishment for adultery* (i.e., sexual relations with another man during engagement).[17]

Leviticus 24:16–23: Blasphemy, Murder, and Animal Killing

Moreover, the one who blasphemes the name of the LORD shall surely be put to death; all the congregation shall certainly stone him. . . . If a man takes the life of any human being, he shall surely be put to death. The one who takes the life of an animal shall make it good, life for life. If a man injures his neighbor, just as he has done, so it shall be done to him: fracture for fracture, eye for eye, tooth for tooth; just as he has injured a man, so it shall be inflicted on him.

—Leviticus 24:16–20

This passage begins with the question of *what to do with a blasphemer*—someone who slanders God. To make things a bit more complicated, the text weaves in other considerations—like killing a human and killing an animal (v. 18).

Then comes a fuller expression of the law of proportionality (*lex talionis*): "If a man injures his neighbor, just as he has done, so it shall be done to him: fracture for fracture, eye for eye, tooth for tooth; just as he has injured a man, so it shall be inflicted on him" (vv. 19–20).

In the fuller context, we begin with (a) *blaspheming* and then move to (b) *killing a human* and then to (c) *killing a domesticated animal*. So how does "life for life" apply here? For example, if "Israelite Aleph" kills an animal from the flock of "Israelite Beth," the punishment *isn't* that Israelite Beth then *gets to kill an animal* from Israelite Aleph's flock. No, the penalty would most likely be a monetary one (i.e., in kind—a live sheep for the dead one), which "surely would have been acceptable."[18]

Furthermore, the idea of literal body maiming here is challenged by two facts:

Fact 1: We have plenty of other examples where monetary payment will suffice (e.g., payment or freedom from debt in the case of eye or tooth injuries).

Fact 2: The larger context doesn't allow for a straightforward application of an exact replication of the injury ("life for life") since the passage begins and ends with the mention of a blasphemer, but includes within it a sequence of punishment for homicide and for killing a domestic beast (vv. 17–18, 21).[19]

So "life for life" need not be seen as literal for both humans and animals but as a ransom—a sufficient monetary substitution.

Some Preliminary Conclusions

As we think about severe-sounding punishments mentioning eyes, teeth, hands, and feet, we gain perspective by looking more closely at the three Pentateuchal references to injuries and maimed body parts: Exodus 21 (premature birth or possibly miscarriage); Leviticus 24 (blasphemy); and Deuteronomy 19 (false witness). As Raymond Westbrook and Bruce Wells have argued, these injuries and maimings don't seem to fit their contexts: "The overall impression is of an ancient maxim, applied wherever 'measure for measure' is to be the standard of justice, whether or not the case involves any of the physical injuries listed."[20] Furthermore, there "would have always been the allowing of a monetary punishment to take the place of physical punishment," and the eye-for-eye principle requires appropriate payment and no more.[21]

Another point here: Israel's "democratized" laws stand in contrast to ancient Near Eastern laws such as the Code of Hammurabi. In Babylon, the eye-for-eye principle applies to *equals*, not to those who are different in social ranking:

§200: If a man knock out the teeth of his equal, his teeth shall be knocked out.

§202: If any one strike the body of a man higher in rank than he, he shall receive sixty blows with an ox-whip in public.

§203: If a free-born man strike the body of another free-born man or equal rank, he shall pay one gold mina.

§203: If the slave of a freed man strike the body of a freed man, his ear shall be cut off.

These laws are strikingly different from the priorities of the Mosaic law. As Christopher Wright notes, Israel's "socially decentralized and non-hierarchical" worldview assumes the fundamental equality of each person regardless of rank, and this provided a good deal of social freedom.[22] The law repeatedly emphasizes the same treatment of each person before the law, whether Israelite or alien living in the land (e.g., Lev. 24:16; Num. 15:16)—or whether one is "poor" or "great" (Lev. 19:15). As Theodore Roosevelt purportedly said, "No man is above the law and no man is below it."

The next chapter looks at the support for nonliteral physical punishments from Old Testament biblical history.

12

Israel's Punishments as Nonliteral in Old Testament History

Revenge and Ransom

The late ancient Near East scholar Raymond Westbrook held that ancient Near Eastern and Israelite law alike assumed a "revenge-and-ransom system." That is, they allowed for either (a) physical *revenge*-type punishment (capital punishment, maiming a body part) or (b) *ransom*-type punishment (monetary payment). Monetary punishments were usually imposed. And if a person refused or was reluctant to pay up, then the physical-punishment threat could be implemented.[1]

As already noted, while other potentially capitally punishable offenses in Israel could be commuted to monetary payment, the penalty of capital punishment for murder was firm in Israel's law: "You shall accept no ransom for the life of a murderer, who is guilty of death, but he shall be put to death" (Num. 35:31 ESV).

However, *in Israel's recorded biblical history, no literal practice of bodily maiming is actually carried out. The same is true with the death penalty for offenses like committing adultery, cursing one's parents, and the like.* Even so, "life for life," which sounds like capital punishment, may still take the form of monetary payment. Consider an example from 1 Kings 20:39: A disguised prophet calls out to the king: "Guard this man; if for any reason he is missing, then your life shall be for his life, or else you shall pay a talent of silver." Notice that here, "life for life" is essentially monetary payment ("a talent of silver").[2]

The remainder of this chapter briefly engages in two case studies of potential capital offenses—adultery and cursing one's parents.

A Look at the Biblical Texts

Case Study 1: Adultery and Capital Punishment

The Mosaic law indicates that adultery is potentially capitally punishable. Deuteronomy 22:22 reads: "If a man is found lying with a married woman, then both of them shall die, the man who lay with the woman, and the woman; thus you shall purge the evil from Israel." Yet post–Mosaic law texts paint a different picture.

Proverbs 6:29–35, which warns against adultery, also assumes a *ransom payment* for such an act. Of course, the man "who commits adultery with a woman is lacking sense," and "he who would destroy himself" assumes that his act didn't result in his execution (v. 32). But the text continues: the man who sleeps with his neighbor's wife may even offer "ransom" and "many gifts"; however, the affronted, justifiably jealous husband would likely refuse any such offers (v. 35). So in the case of the husband's refusal, the death penalty could potentially be implemented. But the text is quite clear that the husband could be "bought off."[3]

Even so, the book of Proverbs emphasizes the shame, disgrace, and loss of reputation that adultery brings (e.g., 7:5–25; 9:13–18). *The death penalty is never brought in as an actual threat or deterrent—to either the man or the seductress.* The text just doesn't demand that consequence.

What about the question of the woman caught in adultery (John 8:3–11)? Boyd brings up this text, saying that Jesus "ingeniously" prevented her execution.[4] But consider the following:

1. Boyd doesn't acknowledge that this passage is missing in our best Greek manuscripts and thus not part of John's original Gospel. (We could add that this critic doesn't follow the *actual* text but follows the *inserted* text of a fallen, though well-meaning, copyist!)[5]

2. Jesus's audience knew the religious leaders had no authority to execute someone for such a crime. The only capital crime they could execute was when a foreigner entered into the temple's Court of Men, where a wall inscription warned about this (cf. Acts 21:27–29; also Ephesians 2:14, which mentions this "dividing wall").[6]

3. Where was the adulterer, without whom the woman alone was "caught"? His absence not only rendered the whole accusation highly suspect but absolutely removes any possibility of punishment (cf. Lev. 20:10).

4. The point is *not* that only sinless people can cast the first stone, as Boyd maintains. Jesus was simply exposing the accusers' hypocrisy and their selectivity in following the Mosaic law. Indeed, Jesus and other New Testament authorities took for granted the possibility of capital punishment based on divine command in ancient Israel (Matt. 15:1–9; Acts 3:23; Heb. 2:1–2; 10:28–31). Truly, the religious leaders had no intention of seeing the woman stoned.[7]

5. This chapter shows that the Mosaic law certainly didn't require the death penalty for adultery; rather, it permitted monetary payment for adultery. Indeed, such financial arrangements were the typical manner in which adultery was settled.

Let's get back to our original discussion, which underscores a couple things about adultery in Israel. First, *the stipulations in the Mosaic law were usually a last resort, as adultery was typically handled in a private manner*—according to the consciences of the sexual participants and "the unofficial action of offended husbands." Second, *the fact that Israel had laws prohibiting adultery revealed that fidelity in marriage was of great public importance*; thus adultery was much more than a private issue, as this act contributed to the destabilizing of families and Israelite society, yet "society's tolerance of the offence was not so extreme that it was willing often to apply the maximum penalty."[8]

EXCURSUS:
What About Premarital Sex (Fornication) with a Servant Girl?

We've noted earlier that premarital sex (fornication) in Israel was not as severe an offense as adultery. Even so, this act was wrong, and a penalty was to be paid. In Leviticus 19, we have the scenario of a man who sleeps with a servant girl:

> If a man sleeps with a female slave who is promised to another man but who has not been ransomed or given her freedom, there must be due punishment. Yet they are not to be put to death, because she had not been freed. The man, however, must bring a ram to the entrance to the tent of meeting for a guilt offering to the LORD. With the ram of the guilt offering the priest is to make atonement for him before the LORD for the sin he has committed, and his sin will be forgiven. (vv. 20–22 NIV)

What is going on here? First, *the employer's promise to another man was informal and not an official betrothal, which required a betrothal payment.* Though the employer (master)—who bore the responsibility of arranging for marriages within his household—promised her to another man, that man had not yet betrothed himself to her. That act would have involved a betrothal gift, which would have "freed" (ransomed) her to make the betrothal official (2 Sam. 3:14). As with the seducer in Deuteronomy 22:28–29, if this outsider slept with her, then he would have to marry her and take care of her.[9]

Second, *the standard penalty had to be paid for the employer's broken oath.* Because another man had interfered with the original arrangement and caused the employer's (master's) oath to be violated (a sacrilege), he had to pay the standard penalty for oath-breaking—a guilt offering (Lev. 6:2–3, 6).[10]

In sum, given Israel's history and its post-Sinai literature, how was adultery dealt with? One biblical scholar writes: "It is worth observing that there is no recorded instance, in the whole of Jewish narrative literature of the biblical period, of anyone actually being put to death for adultery. This may be an accident, though it is certainly not because adultery itself is infrequently mentioned."[11]

Case Study 2: Cursing Parents and Capital Punishment

Dishonorable acts such as cursing or striking one's parents had severe penalties attached to them (Exod. 21:15, 17; Lev. 20:9). Such acts were not merely private matters; they ruptured the family and larger community, and so they were of *great public importance*. Thus, the law court could carry out a severe punishment for the rebellious son who was a glutton and a drunkard (Deut. 21:18–21); the community that was being impacted was also placed in charge of disciplining him.[12]

In such a scenario, this is no small child casually insulting or saying "I hate you" to a parent.[13] Rather, this is a defiant middle-aged adult who persistently engages in "a serious breach of filial duty" and fails to take responsibility for himself and those around him.[14] This was a high-handed public act of repudiation, essentially declaring, "You are not my parents!"

The book of Proverbs reveals the same pattern as with adultery. Rather than the maximum sentence of a death penalty being carried out, the consequences of such an act are shame, dishonor, and ostracism from the community. The middle-aged son who "assaults" his father and "drives his mother away" is "a shameful and disgraceful son" (Prov. 19:26). Proverbs 20:20 presents a foreboding tone about cursing one's parents: "He who curses his father or his mother, his lamp will go out in time of darkness." Likewise, "The eye that mocks a father and scorns a mother, the ravens of the valley will pick it out, and the young eagles will eat it" (30:17). On the other hand, listening to parents and honoring them will bring their approval and cause them to rejoice (Prov. 23:22–25).

The point is this: Proverbs doesn't threaten a Mosaic death penalty. However, this doesn't rule out the death penalty if extreme measures need to be taken.[15]

Conclusions

The law of Moses sets limits, but this does not mean that the stiffest penalty was always administered. *Typically, financial payment (ransom) proved to be the resolution—not a literal eye-for-eye punishment.* In fact, we have no case in Israel's history where literal maiming took place as a punishment.

One scholar writes that "*it is likely that the death penalty was rarely utilized.*"[16] He adds: "This undoubtedly ensured that its use did not have the effect of devaluing human life, for frequent recourse to capital punishment may well suggest that human life is of little esteem, thus negating the very reason for adopting it."[17]

John Goldingay sums things up in these two statements:

> It's striking that the Old Testament tells quite a few stories about actions such as adultery to which the death penalty is attached, but it never speaks of someone

being judicially executed. It seems that Israel was no more literal about these rules than it was about the rules concerning an eye for an eye, which is the principle it illustrates. The death penalty was a theory, not a practice.[18]

So far as we know, no one ever treated [the eye-for-eye punishment] as if it were a literal law. . . . What it did was set limits to the compensation someone has a right to seek when one gets injured. Likewise, as far as we know no one was ever executed for offenses such as belittling one's parents, or most of the many "capital" offenses in Israel's rule of life. Saying "such a person should be put to death" is a way of saying, "This is a really wicked thing to do; terrible consequences may follow."[19]

Goldingay says elsewhere, "People did not assume the Torah was designed for literal implementing," and we "have virtually no information" on whether the death penalty—for idolatry, adultery, murder, and rebellion against parents—was actually carried out."[20]

PART 4

For Whom the Bell Tolls

Harsh Texts and Difficult Old Testament Questions

13

How Was David "a Man after God's Own Heart"?

In the last few chapters, we looked at issues related to severe-sounding penalties and punishments in the Mosaic law. We'll next look at challenging moral questions about David and Saul, God's hardening Pharaoh's heart, instances of divine "smiting," harsh-sounding psalms, and similar themes. In this chapter we consider difficult questions concerning David and Saul.

We're becoming increasingly familiar with stories of Christian leaders who have fallen through sexual immorality, financial impropriety, and arrogant untouchability. In our Western culture of megachurches and celebrityhood, we have witnessed failure after failure of popular Christian leaders who not only are unaccountable to others but also get angry when their status is challenged. Along the way, they appear to have lost touch with themselves, with God, and with others. In a sober warning about being a teacher, James writes that Christians in such positions of authority will be judged "with greater strictness" (James 3:1 ESV).

King David serves as just such an example from antiquity for our modern times. In this chapter we look a bit more into David's life and failures along the way. Of course, David replaced King Saul, whose heart was *not* after God's. But wasn't David a man who likewise failed *hugely*? Was David really all that different from Saul?

"A Man after God's Own Heart": What Does That Phrase Mean?

Pierre Bayle (1647–1706) was an influential French philosopher whose ideas served as a kind of arsenal for the Enlightenment or Age of Reason. This is particularly true of his *Historical and Critical Dictionary* (*Dictionnaire historique et critique*). In the first edition of his dictionary (1697), he listed David's failures and vices alongside the biblical affirmation that David was "a man after God's own heart" (cf. 1 Sam. 13:14). After offending many readers, Bayle toned down his statements in the second edition (1702).

Bayle affirmed, though David was one of the world's greatest men, "we should not consider him as a royal prophet, who was after God's own heart."[1] Bayle inferred "from the silence of the scripture" that certain negative actions of David's must have been done "of his own accord."[2] Thus "the grace of God very often directed him; but on several occasions, passion got the better; policy silenced religion."[3] Bayle concluded that "David is doubtless a sun of holiness in the church; . . . but that sun had its spots."[4]

Despite David's adultery, murder, and polygamy, how was he "a man after God's own heart"? As it turns out, two possible interpretations are on offer, though they are not necessarily mutually exclusive.[5] The first option is the commonly presumed, or received, view. The second, however, better or more consistently accords with the biblical narrative, although the first option overlaps with it.

Option 1: David aligned himself with God's aims. *David trusted God and ultimately sought to live in conformity with God's purposes.* In contrast to many other kings and leaders in Israel, David continually returned to God and acknowledged his sin and failures. This is exemplified in Psalm 32 ("I acknowledged my sin to you, and I did not cover my iniquity" [v. 5 ESV]) as well as in Psalm 51 ("The sacrifices of God are a broken spirit; a broken and contrite heart, O God, you will not despise" [v. 17 ESV]). And when confronted by the prophet Nathan, he immediately acknowledged his wrongdoing (2 Sam. 12:13), and the general course of his life moved in a Godward direction.

Though this first option is the best one, it nevertheless offers some secondary insight into why Saul's kingship ultimately failed and why David's didn't—and why David's kingship was more favorable than his son Solomon's: "When Solomon was old, his wives turned his heart away after other gods; and his heart was not wholly devoted to the LORD his God, as the heart of David his father had been" (1 Kings 11:4). Despite David's many failures, his life overall expressed allegiance to the one true God of Israel.

Option 2: *God* chose *David* to fulfill his aims: *God carried out his historical, redemptive purposes through David.* The phrase *doesn't* necessarily indicate that David's mindset was at one with God's. The expression more literally is "a man according to God's heart." So the emphasis *isn't* on David's *character*. Rather, *God had set his heart and mind on David.* The identical Hebrew phrase—the preposition *k* + *leb* = "according to [one's] heart"—is used in

1 Samuel 14:7, where Jonathan's armor bearer urges him to act "according to your desire [heart]."

The same phrase is also found in 2 Samuel 7:21 when David expresses gratitude to the Lord for revealing that Solomon was to build the temple: "For the sake of Your word, and according to Your own heart, You have done all this greatness to let Your servant know." (See also Ps. 20:4 ["your heart's desire"]; Jer. 3:15 ["shepherds after My own heart"].) So this phrase "never means what the popular understanding finds in the phrase's application to David."[6]

Even God's covenant with David in 2 Samuel 7 assumes David was flawed: "When he commits iniquity, I will correct him with the rod of men and the strokes of the sons of men" (v. 14). Yes, God chose David's house—not Saul's—to endure, but this wasn't due to superiority of character.

Given David's massive failures, the second option seems a better fit. As one commentator puts it, "The emphasis is more on the freedom of Yahweh's choice than on David's character."[7]

EXCURSUS:
Did the Lord or "Satan" Incite David?

Incidentally, one of our critics from within (Boyd) points to 2 Samuel 24:1 to support the distinction between the actual and textual God. There, *the Lord's anger* incited David to take a census that resulted in divine judgment. This, we're told, was the *textual* God; it wasn't the *actual* God. But the later book of Chronicles attributes this incitement to *Satan* (i.e., some adversarial being).

Boyd claims that the Chronicler was *more enlightened* than Samuel's author since God can't be the author of evil. The Chronicler *corrected* the distorted and mistaken ancient Near Eastern worldview of Samuel's author, who attributed anything—whether good or evil—to God. The Chronicler was in tune with the *actual* God's character and tried to keep God removed from this evil action.[8]

While we see repeated examples of what appears to be God *causing* an evil action, we recognize that this is merely *divine permission*. God isn't the author of evil, though he in his sovereignty permits evil and uses it in the outworking of his purposes (Gen. 50:20). Various theologians will distinguish between God's "preceptive" will (what God *commands*), his "permissive" will (what God *allows*—e.g., an adversary's testing of Job), and his "decretive" will (what God *decrees* and will happen—e.g., the second coming of Christ).

Let's focus on our critic's claim that the Chronicler is "more enlightened" than the Samuel author. This is false. We actually see *the opposite* in the account of Saul's death. The Chronicler there appears *less enlightened* than the author of Samuel. The Chronicler says that it was because of Saul's consulting a medium that "[The LORD] killed him and turned the kingdom to David the son of Jesse" (1 Chron. 10:14). That looks like the *textual-God* perspective that our critic from within dismisses. And the Samuel author sounds more like an *actual-God* spokesman when he writes that "*Saul* took his sword and fell on it" (1 Sam. 31:4).

To reinforce our point, Boyd critiques the textual God in 1 Kings 22:22–23. There, the Lord "has put a deceiving spirit into the mouth of all these your false prophets," who are promising King Ahab victory. By contrast, the true prophet of the Lord, Micaiah, announces Ahab's defeat in battle. Boyd declares that it's "challenging to absolve God" of deception here.[9]

Now, remember that Boyd believes that the Chronicler is more enlightened than the author of Samuel and Kings. And this "lying spirit" passage would be yet another opportunity to demonstrate this enlightenment: God's sending the "lying spirit" in 1 Kings 22:22–23 is a parallel phenomenon to God's provoking David to take a census (2 Sam. 24:1). But does the "illumined" Chronicler clarify things by saying that God was somehow removed from deception here? No, he uses the identical, word-for-word language as does the author of Kings (see 2 Chron. 18:21–22). Here too Boyd ignores this important parallel passage in his discussion.

Deuteronomy 17 and Kingly Failure

In Deuteronomy 17:14–23 (ESV), God warned future kings of Israel about three danger zones—*power, sex,* and *money*:

> *Power:* "He must not acquire many horses for himself" (v. 16)
>
> *Sex:* "He shall not acquire many wives for himself" (v. 17)
>
> *Money:* "Nor shall he acquire for himself excessive silver and gold" (v. 17)

The root of the danger is a heart or idolatry problem: "lest his heart turn away" (v. 17) and—if he disregarded God's law—"his heart [would] be lifted above his brothers" (v. 20). In their proper place, these three things—power, sex, and money—are gifts from God. When they become God-substitutes or idols and steal one's affections away from God, they lead to shipwrecked lives (e.g., 1 Tim. 6:9). Rather than being exceptions to the rule, Israel's kings were to *set the standard* in these areas of human vulnerability. However, David became ensnared by them (see table 13.1).

As noted in *Moral Monster*, David's son Solomon failed to an extreme.[10] The narrator of 1 Kings indicts Solomon for violating God's law in Deuteronomy 17. Solomon had accumulated *chariots and horses/horsemen* (4:26; 10:26), *women* (11:1–3), and *wealth* (10:21–29). Of course, wealth could be a gift from God and could be dedicated to God (e.g., Solomon's using wealth to build the temple). The problem comes with setting our hearts on wealth.

Deuteronomy 17 points out great spiritual dangers for kings, and Solomon proves to be Exhibit A, as his heart turned away from God (11:3–4). David escaped that disastrous outcome, though. But in both cases, these kings became enamored of what would bring personal and spiritual danger. And it is no wonder that David became easier prey to temptation due to unrestrained sexual urges.

What begins as a hairline crack can lead to a massive fault line. Thankfully, though David went astray, he returned to the grace of God and called out for mercy (Ps. 51). Indeed, he and the other mixed bag of "heroes of faith" in Hebrews 11 are commended because they looked to God and trusted him.

Table 13.1. David's Failures as King

Horses	"He must not acquire many horses for himself" (Deut. 17:16).	In David's day, horses were like tanks to be used in battle. Yes, he may have hamstrung horses to render them useless to his enemies, but he kept one hundred for himself (2 Sam. 8:4).
Wives and concubines	"He shall not acquire many wives for himself" (Deut. 17:17).	David accumulated eight wives: Saul's daughter Michal (1 Sam. 14:49; 18:27); Abigail, who brought a gift to David and used sweet (flattering?) words (1 Sam. 25:39–42); Ahinoam (1 Sam. 25:43—though not Saul's wife, who had the same name); Maacah; Haggith; Abital; Eglah (2 Sam. 3:2–5; 1 Chron. 3:1–3); and Bathsheba (2 Sam. 11:26–27). He took to himself concubines and would leave behind ten of them in Jerusalem during his son Absalom's insurrection (2 Sam. 5:13; 15:16).
Gold and silver	"Nor shall he acquire for himself excessive silver and gold" (Deut. 17:17).	David took shields of gold and "very much bronze" and brought them to Jerusalem (2 Sam. 8:7–8), and he also received articles of silver, gold, and bronze (v. 10). He then dedicated gold and silver from the nations he subdued (v. 11).

"Through No Fault of His Own"? Was Saul Really That Much Worse Than David?

This brings us to the question of "Saul versus David." Even though God had picked David to accomplish his purposes (God's "heart"), in what way was he different from Saul?

Some critics and certain biblical scholars have claimed that Saul's career as king was doomed by God from the outset.[11] By contrast, David did the same kinds of rash or foolish things that Saul did, but God apparently gave him a pass. Saul just couldn't please God or the prophet Samuel. For example, Saul had been waiting seven days for the prophet Samuel to come and offer a sacrifice before battling the Philistines. Their army massively outmatched Saul's in number and military "machinery" of chariots and horses—"like the sand which is on the seashore in abundance" (1 Sam. 13:5). Saul decided to go ahead and offer the burnt offering himself (vv. 8–15)—and then Samuel showed up. What else could Saul have done in such desperate circumstances?[12] So, did God "rig" things against Saul? Let's have a closer look.

First, *the prophet Samuel told Saul that an established kingly dynasty could have been his, had he obeyed* (1 Sam. 13:13). God's awareness of what Saul *would do* didn't change the fact that Saul himself was responsible for undermining his own future prospects. Even his son Jonathan admitted that Saul had brought trouble to the land (14:29). Saul first forfeited his claim to a lasting *dynasty* (13:14) and then later forfeited the legitimacy of his *kingship* (15:28).[13]

Second, *although Samuel failed to come promptly, Saul had historical precedent for trusting in God and waiting, even when facing a large army*. Gideon had already faced Midianites, Amalekites, and "all the sons of the east," who were "as numerous as locusts; and their camels were without number, as numerous as the sand on the seashore" (Judg. 7:12). Yet Gideon had defeated them with only a small band of men—three hundred of them (v. 7).

Third, Saul *engaged in partial obedience, rash behavior, and blame shifting, and he attempted to take God's glory from him*. We can list a few areas where Saul falls short of expectation:

1. Instead of waiting like his father Saul did, Jonathan took king-like initiative against the Philistines (1 Sam. 14:6); meanwhile, Saul made a rash vow, which jeopardized Jonathan's life (14:43–44).
2. Then, after the Amalekites had attacked Israel *yet again* (1 Sam. 14:48) and the prophet Samuel commanded Saul to fight against them (15:3), this king created problems for himself:
   a. *Saul displayed partial obedience:* He preserved animals from the limited localized battle against the Amalekites (v. 5: "the city of Amalek"); he also preserved the Amalekite king Agag as a trophy to honor himself (15:20).
   b. When Samuel exposed Saul's disobedience, *Saul blamed "the people" for this action* (15:15, 21)—unlike David, who immediately repented when Nathan the prophet confronted him (2 Sam. 12:13).
   c. *Saul also set up a monument to honor himself* (1 Sam. 15:12) rather than honoring God's name. In both preserving Agag and building a monument for himself, Saul revealed a spirit of independence from God and his treasonous attempt to make a name for himself. He "has effectively declared independence" from God as his covenant Lord ("suzerain") by "honoring himself in the place of the [divine] emperor and by taking a vassal [subject/servant] of his own."[14]

In Deuteronomy, God sought to establish his own "name" at a designated location (Jerusalem), but here Saul attempted to usurp God's covenantal role to establish his own name.[15] Thus it was an act akin to divination and idolatry (15:23): "These represent breaches of political loyalty to the divine sovereign. . . . The divine sovereign's retribution against Saul likewise follows standard procedure: the rebellious regent is dethroned and replaced."[16]

Fourth, *Saul violated Israel's treaty with the Gibeonites (under Joshua) by try-ing to get rid of them (2 Sam. 21:1–4).* Although the biblical text doesn't reveal this about Saul until David's reign, God had brought a three-year famine to Israel because of "Saul and his bloody house, because he put the Gibeonites to death" (2 Sam. 21:1). As Israel had entered Canaan, the fearful Gibeonites (Hivites) had made a treaty with Joshua under false pretenses (Josh. 9:1–27). When this was discovered, the Gibeonites were made "hewers of wood and drawers of water for the congregation and for the altar of the LORD, to this day, in the place which He would choose" (v. 27). But Saul violated this treaty when he "sought to kill them in his zeal for the sons of Israel and Judah" (2 Sam. 21:2). Here we have yet another grievous act of disobedience by Saul.

In sum, though David—"a man after God's own heart"—committed terrible sins of committing adultery with Bathsheba and murdering Uriah (2 Sam. 11), his confession was immediate when Nathan revealed this wrongdoing: "I have sinned against the LORD" (2 Sam. 12:13). By contrast, Saul failed to carry out God's commands fully (partial obedience), and when he was found out, he blamed others (1 Sam. 15:15, 21). What is worse, Saul was acting to usurp God's glory and covenant-making role with Israel to make a name for himself. As one scholar notes, "It would be difficult to argue that David . . . was morally better than Saul, but he did understand that Israel's king must reign under Yahweh and not as a king with final authority."[17]

14

Why Does God Harden People's Hearts?

Pharaoh's Hardened Heart

And the LORD hardened Pharaoh's heart, and he did not listen to them, just as the LORD had spoken to Moses.

—Exodus 9:12

How does God's hardening Pharaoh's heart seem at all fair? This verse appears to suggest that Pharaoh had no choice but to do what he did. He was doomed to remain unrepentant. But if, as some argue, God has the power to soften a person's heart, then it seems cruel that God doomed him to persist in refusing to let Israel go.

Is this *theological fatalism*—that humans are mere puppets since God is in charge of everything and his will is always accomplished? Was God *making* Pharaoh sin? Was Pharaoh really refused any opportunity for repentance or salvation?

What "Hardening" Means

Exodus uses three different verbs for "harden" (*hazaq, kabed, qashah*); they are roughly synonymous, and they express the idea of being "strengthened, resolute, determined, firm-hearted"—or, more negatively, "stubborn." "Hardened" means "having or being given the willpower to do what one has decided." So in a positive sense, it could mean "take courage" (expressed with a different verb, *amets* [Pss. 27:14; 31:24(25)]). But in the negative, it expresses "stubbornness."[1]

The first half of Exodus repeats the following "hardening" lines, using three different subjects:[2]

- *the Lord:* "And the LORD hardened Pharaoh's heart" (9:12; 10:20, 27; 11:10; etc.)
- *Pharaoh's heart:* "Pharaoh's heart was hardened" (7:13, 22; 8:19; 9:7; etc.)— a more neutral rendering
- *Pharaoh:* "He hardened his heart" (8:15, 32; 9:34)

We could also add that God hardened the hearts of Pharaoh's *officials—and* that they hardened *their own* hearts too (9:34–35; 10:1). And the New Testament refers back to this event: God "has mercy on whom He desires, and He hardens whom He desires" (Rom. 9:18).

Pharaoh: A Fairly Nasty Person from the Outset

Again, was Pharaoh a puppet whom God prevented from repenting? Not at all.

First, *Pharaoh wasn't exactly a tenderhearted ruler before God got to him, and he repeatedly hardened his heart against God.* For generations, the Egyptian pharaohs had a track record of oppressing the Israelites. This is the scenario we encounter in the early chapters of Exodus. God took note of Israel's bondage, their groaning, and their cry for help (Exod. 2:23–25). And even before the first plague, Pharaoh's heart was "stubborn" (7:13–14). And he only got worse throughout the narrative. When Moses showed up, Pharaoh utterly disregarded Moses's message from God to him (5:2). Pharaoh then punished the Israelites by making their strenuous labor even more difficult: they would now have to gather their own straw to make bricks (5:4–23).

Second, *God didn't harden Pharaoh's heart until near the end of the sixth plague* (Exod. 9:12). This is significant. When the apostle Paul declares that God "hardens whom He desires" (Rom. 9:18), he is quoting from the *latter portion* of the Israel-in-Egypt narrative. However, *by that point, Pharaoh had already hardened his own heart* against God (Exod. 9:16). Of course, early on before the plagues began, God had assured Moses that he was more powerful than the world's mightiest ruler, and his eventually hardening Pharaoh's heart would demonstrate this (4:21; 7:3).

Third, *throughout the plagues, Pharaoh was still able to harden—or soften—his own heart* (e.g., 9:34). The narrative makes clear that Pharaoh wasn't locked in by God to resist divine influences:

- *Pharaoh asked Moses to pray for him,* and so Moses did; God removed the plague, and then Pharaoh hardened his heart (8:15, 32; 9:34).
- *Moses used conditional language* ("if"), which implies Pharaoh's genuine (libertarian) free choice in this process: "If you refuse . . ." (8:2; 9:2; 10:4); "If you do not let my people go . . ." (8:21). Moses relayed God's question to Pharaoh: "How long will you refuse to humble yourself before Me?" (10:3). This question doesn't at all suggest a fatalistic inevitability.

- *Pharaoh repeatedly "did not listen"* (7:13, 22; 8:15, 19; 9:12).
- *Throughout the narrative, God exerted gracious influences so that Pharaoh would soften his heart or humble himself:* Moses prayed for Pharaoh (8:8, 28; 9:28; 10:17); his magicians and courtiers tried to persuade him (8:19; 10:7); God spared the Hebrews from the latter plagues; Pharaoh resorted to partial obedience (8:8, 25–28; 10:24); and he was partially repentant (9:27; 10:16).[3]

Challenging the Egyptian Superpower: Who Is Really in Charge?

The repeated *goal* of this divine hardening was so that "you [i.e., Israelites and Egyptians alike] will know that I am the LORD" (Exod. 6:2, 7, 8, 29; 7:5, 17; 8:10, 22; 9:16, 29; 10:2; 14:4, 18; cf. 14:31). As noted, Israel's God—the God of slaves—stepped into earthly affairs to rescue his people. He challenged and overwhelmed this ancient superpower and its gods on "foreign" turf. While he could show his greatness through soft-hearted rulers, he also did so through a hard-hearted earthly ruler—the *anti-God* figure, Pharaoh.[4]

One of the Hebrew words for "harden"—*kabed*—often means "make heavy"; it is related to the noun for "glory" (*kabod*). Early on in Exodus, Moses said he was "slow"—"heavy" (*kabed*)—in speech and tongue (4:10). And though Pharaoh "made heavy" Israel's brick-making load (5:9), God sent the Egyptians "heavy" plagues—a "heavy" swarm (8:24[20]), "heavy" pestilence (9:3), "heavy" hail (9:18), "numerous" (literally, "heavy") locusts (10:14). And in this "heaviness," God would be glorified or "honored" (*kabed*) before Pharaoh (14:4, 17–18). Indeed, this is what happened in the final climactic scene of hardening his heart at the Red Sea, when the Egyptian chariot wheels "became heavy" (*kabed*; 14:25).

In all of this, the point isn't that God overrode Pharaoh's will to prevent repentance—nor did that happen. Rather, *God's supremacy* is the focus: God entered the earthly geopolitical scene to undermine an arrogant earthly ruler who was dismissive of Israel's God.[5]

EXCURSUS:
A Brief Glimpse of the Heart-Hardened Canaanite Kings

For it was of the LORD to harden their hearts, to meet Israel in battle in order that he might utterly destroy them.

—Joshua 11:20

In this context of God's supremacy displayed in his hardening hearts, it might be helpful to note this phenomenon in Joshua, as this also anticipates our discussion of Old Testament warfare later in the book. Joshua's parallel use of "hardening" language connecting God's dominion to Canaan's geopolitics harks back to Exodus. As we'll see, Israel's God had displayed his mighty power through the plagues in Egypt, the Red Sea crossing, and other wonders. The Canaanites knew this well and should have heeded these warning signs (cf. Josh. 2:10–11; 5:1; 9:9–10).

Now, as Israel had crossed the Jordan River on dry ground (4:22–24), these self-hardened Canaanite "kings" (i.e., military leaders or chieftains) continued to resist God anyway. According to commentator Lissa Wray Beal, the fact that there "was not a city which made peace with the sons of Israel" except the Gibeonites (Josh. 11:19) suggests that "other groups besides the Gibeonites could have negotiated peace with Israel."[6] Clearly, making covenants with other nations was forbidden *if it meant forsaking Yahweh* (e.g., Num. 25:1–2; Deut. 7:2). But as Joshua 11 implies, this was different from agreeing to terms of peace. Rahab, Canaanite "strangers," and—by trickery—the Gibeonites did so as well (Josh. 2; 8:33, 35; 9:15). Because *already-resistant* Canaanites repudiated acknowledgment of the sovereignty of Yahweh, he gave them over to their desire, hardening their hearts (cf. 11:20). In the end, all the land—and Israel too—would know that Yahweh was God over all (4:24)—even though he would receive any Canaanite who was responsive to his initiating grace.

A Special, Temporary Case of Divine Hardening?

Some have argued that the biblical narrative suggests that God's hardening action may be temporary and not absolute.[7] Why not consider the possibility that God's hardening of Pharaoh's heart was both *special* and *temporary*? It was *special* in that, in this unique moment of salvation history, God took the opportunity to challenge the arrogance of the world's most powerful leader of the day. God's hardening Pharaoh's heart revealed that the God of the oppressed Hebrews was in charge, not Pharaoh. Along with the hardening of the hearts of the Canaanite kings, this action could be viewed as an exceptional situation—not the norm for how God generally operates.[8]

Though this hardening wasn't necessarily permanent, Pharaoh was stubborn before God got to him (cf. Exod. 8:15, 32). And *God foreknew what the Egyptian plagues would do to harden Pharaoh's spirit against letting Israel go*. But none of this necessitates that Pharaoh's hardening was permanent. There's nothing in the narrative to suggest this. Pharaoh could potentially have humbled himself before the God of Israel after the plagues were through—much like the wicked king Manasseh did at the end of his days while in prison (2 Chron. 33:12–13). Pharaoh's state of "double-stubbornness" was limited to God's humiliating this haughty ruler and the false gods propping him up.[9] Even so, God never overrode Pharaoh's will. God doesn't harden a (potentially) soft, humble heart.

Divine Hardening in Both Testaments

We've looked at the unique context of divine hardening of Pharaoh, whose hardening may not be the norm. But we still do see the theme of divine hardening in other places in Scripture. Is there a wider application of God's hardening people's

Table 14.1. Two Stages: Divine Hardening Follows Human Self-Hardening

Stage 1: *Human* hardening: "Do not harden your hearts" (Ps. 95:8).	*Humans harden their own hearts* by rejecting God and resisting his gracious initiatives. For example, God commands all people to repent (Acts 17:30)—that is, all without *exception*, not just the elect. This implies that he gives sufficient grace for *everyone* to carry out this command, although it can be resisted (e.g., Acts 7:51).
Stage 2: *Divine* hardening: "It was of the LORD to harden their hearts" (Josh. 11:20).	*God may further harden the hearts of the hardened* if he chooses to do so; that is, God "gives them over" to their ways, withdrawing grace so that, at least for a time, repentance seems further out of reach. This is like the parents of rebellious adult children: they withdraw their influence after having attempted to assist them. Doing so will perhaps enable those children to see what it's like to live with the full consequences of their actions.

hearts across both testaments? Perhaps we can make some general observations about divine hardening.

Hardening in Two Stages

The biblical evidence suggests a two-stage heart-hardening process. First, *humans harden themselves against God's initiating grace.* Second, *if God chooses to do so*—as in the case of Pharaoh—*he may further harden people's hearts by releasing them to their own desires, while scaling back gracious divine influences toward them.* God will "give [people] over" to their willfulness and evil desires (cf. Rom. 1:24, 26, 28).[10] (See table 14.1.)

Two-Stage Hardening in Biblical Texts

Let's examine a few texts related to human and then divine hardening, should God choose that route.

Psalm 81:10–16

God invited Israel to "open your mouth wide, and I will fill it" (v. 10). But Israel refused this gracious offer (stage one). So in stage two, God "gave them over to the stubbornness of their heart" so that they might "walk in their own devices" (v. 12).

Jeremiah 5:21–25

Although the "stubborn and rebellious" Israelites "have eyes but do not see" and "ears but do not hear" (v. 21), repentance is not impossible. God expects them to respond to his initiating grace: "They do not say in their heart, 'Let us now fear the LORD our God.'" God is not to blame: "Your sins have withheld good from you" (v. 25). That is why they had become "foolish and senseless" (v. 21).

Mark 4:12 (Citing Isa. 6:10)

Jesus told parables so that those outside the kingdom "may indeed see but not perceive, and may indeed hear but not understand, lest they should turn and be forgiven" (ESV). But is God *preventing the salvation* of Jesus's opponents, as some have argued? No, divine hardening is stage two: God hardened the hearts of Jesus's already-resistant opponents. After all, earlier, in Mark 3:5, Jesus had looked on the religious leaders with anger, "grieved at their hardness of heart" (ESV). *That* was stage one—the human self-hardening process. And why would Jesus be grieved, if God the Father had made repentance impossible?

John 12:37–41 (Also Citing Isa. 6:10)

Here God is said to have "blinded their eyes" and "hardened their heart" lest these religious leaders understand and "be converted and I heal them" (v. 40). Again that divine hardening is stage two.

Stage one *immediately precedes* the divine-hardening verses. These leaders *have already hardened their own hearts, despite Jesus's words that things could have been otherwise.* Jesus had just been exhorting them: "For a little while longer the Light is among you. *Walk while you have the Light,* so that darkness will not overtake you; he who walks in the darkness does not know where he goes. *While you have the Light, believe in the Light, so that you may become sons of Light*" (vv. 35–36).

Even earlier in John, *these leaders had genuine opportunity to become sons of light rather than remaining in darkness*: Jesus spoke to his opponents "that [they] may be saved" (John 5:34), but they were "unwilling to come to [Him], so that [they] may have life" (5:40). His religious enemies would increasingly cut themselves off from salvation through their own self-hardening (stage one). Jesus later *urged them at least to believe because of the signs he had performed* so that they would understand that Jesus was approved by the Father (10:38).

By contrast, consider the brothers of Jesus. Before his resurrection, when they weren't believing in him, they were part of "the world" (John 7:5; cf. 1:10). Jesus even rebuked them: "The world cannot hate you" (7:7). But after the first Easter, his brothers came to believe in him and were no longer part of the Jesus-rejecting "world" (Acts 1:14).

Vessels of Wrath and Dishonor?

As Paul makes the connection to Pharaoh in Romans 9, perhaps we should take the next step by looking at the related perplexing mention of "vessels of wrath" and "vessels of mercy"; these are also called "vessels for honorable use"—for "glory"—and "dishonorable vessels" that are "prepared for destruction" (vv. 21–23). Does this text imply that the fate of certain persons is *divinely fixed without any genuine opportunity to freely respond to God's initiating grace*? Some argue this way. But as with Pharaoh's hardened heart, this language does not imply that "dishonorable" vessels are inevitably doomed to separation from God, that they have no say in the matter.

First, *Paul wasn't referring to their condition as a permanent, unalterable state of separation fixed by God*. Keep in mind that in this Romans 9 context, the "dishonorable" vessels are unbelieving ethnic Jews. But salvation is available to *any* Jew—or Gentile—who trusts in Jesus the Messiah so that they are no longer under God's judgment (Rom. 10:17). In fact, part of Paul's mission was to "save" Jews (Rom. 11:14; cf. 1 Cor. 9:20), and Paul was even willing to be condemned for their sakes (Rom. 9:3).

The "vessels" imagery of Romans 9 harks back to Jeremiah 18:1–10, where God is portrayed as the sovereign *potter*; along with other nations, Israel is portrayed as the *clay*. There, God says that if he wanted to make "another vessel" out of a "spoiled" one, he could do as he pleases. What is critical to note is that *the destruction or preservation of the vessel (Israel or any nation) was conditioned upon their repentance*: "*If* that nation against which I have spoken turns from its evil, [then] I will relent [repent] concerning the calamity I planned to bring on it" (v. 8). Or if a nation *fails* to obey God's voice, "then I will think better of the good with which I had promised to bless it" (v. 10). Notice God's desire is to bless, not destroy. God doesn't desire the death of the wicked (Ezek. 18:33; 33:11).

Now compare the similar language of Romans 9 and 2 Timothy 2:20–21, which bears out this conditionality:

> Or does not the potter have a right over the clay, to make from the same lump one vessel for honorable use and another for common use [*ho men eis timēn skeuos ho de eis atimian*]? What if God . . . endured with much patience vessels [*skeuē*] of wrath prepared for destruction? And He did so to make known the riches of His glory upon vessels [*skeuē*] of mercy, which He prepared beforehand [*proētoimasen*] for glory. (Rom. 9:21–23)

> Now in a large house there are not only gold and silver vessels [*skeuē*], but also vessels of wood and of earthenware, and some to honor and some to dishonor [*ha men eis timēn ha de eis atimian*]. Therefore, if anyone cleanses himself from these things, he will be a vessel for honor [*skeuos eis timēn*], sanctified, useful to the Master, prepared [*ētoimasmenon*] for every good work. (2 Tim. 2:20–21)

There are vessels of "honor" and "dishonor" in a large house. Some are used for elevated purposes while others have a more dishonorable use (think: chamber pots). Notice the conditionality here: "If a man cleanses himself from these things, he will be a vessel of honor, sanctified, useful to the Master, prepared for every good work."

As long as people rebel and disobey God, then they are appointed to doom (1 Pet. 2:8). But if they turn and respond to God's grace, then they become part of God's elect people in God's elect Son, Jesus Christ (Eph. 1:4). Remember that just as Jesus's brothers were once part of "the world" (John 7:5), they were not "stuck" there. They would come to the "light" and become followers of Christ (John 8:12); as a result, they were no longer part of "the world." If we respond to God's initiating grace by faith and don't resist it (Acts 7:51), we will be incorporated into Christ by his Spirit and become vessels of honor.

Divine hardening in both testaments doesn't indicate necessary or inevitable condemnation. God may choose to give people over to their own desires by *withdrawing* his gracious influences in their lives (hardening whom he desires), or he may *continue* to exert those influences (showing mercy on whom he desires). But those whom God hardens were already self-hardened.[11]

15

Divine Smitings (1)

Noah's Flood, Egypt's Firstborn, Uzzah's Death

Hitting the "Smite" Key?

I have two favorite cartoon strips. One of them is Bill Watterson's magical *Calvin and Hobbes*—about an impish, imaginative, adventuresome young boy and his toy tiger, which comes to life and engages in conversation when others are not around. The second is *The Far Side* by Gary Larson. It's full of hilariously imaginative scenarios, such as standing, talking cows that suddenly start grazing and mooing when human beings pass by.

One *Far Side* cartoon shows God at his computer. Here we have the stereotypical caricature of a bearded, white-haired, white-robed being looking at a computer screen. He is viewing a hapless, unthinking person walking down the sidewalk, stepping just underneath a piano being lowered out of a window by a rope. And "God" has his index finger pointing to the keyboard, ready to press the key labeled "Smite." This is how some people think of "the Old Testament God." He is not "slow to anger" (Exod. 34:6). Rather, he is "eager to smite."

In this chapter, we want to look at three acts of divine "smiting" that many people find troubling: the flood of Noah (Gen. 6–8), the killing of the firstborn of the Egyptians (Exod. 11–12), and the death of Uzzah after he touched the ark of the covenant (2 Sam. 6).

The Flood of Noah (Gen. 6–8)

The story of Noah in Genesis 6–9 is well known to many of us. It is a commonly told story in children's Sunday school classes and in Bible readings at bedtime. Many sentimentalized pictures portray Noah with pairs of cute animals with their heads sticking out of the ark. Even in one *Far Side* cartoon, Noah is on the ark. In front of him are a couple of dead animals, whose legs and hoofs are visible. He is a bit exasperated and mildly scolds two pairs of meat-eaters: "Well, so much for the unicorns. . . . But from now on, all carnivores will be confined to 'C' deck." However, the actual biblical story of Noah and the ark is far more sobering, and some might say horrifyingly violent and cruel.

This book isn't the place to discuss the many questions related to the flood story, including

- the extent of the flood (e.g., was it regional, though affecting all humanity?),
- the seemingly exaggerated language of the ark's gargantuan size (450 feet long, 75 feet wide, and 45 feet high),
- the apparently hyperbolic descriptions of the flood's magnitude (covering the highest mountains; waters from springs of the great deep), and
- the end of the underlying historicity of the account and the beginning of the symbolic, literary, and theological aspects.

Delving into such questions here isn't our objective.[1] Gordon Wenham insists that "the theological significance of the flood is more important than its date or extent."[2] So here we are simply observing key themes that put this story into clearer perspective. Perhaps this may clarify some murkiness and smooth down some of the jagged edges of this story.

First, *the flood account expresses God's deep grief and sorrow.* Genesis moves from Cain's murder of his brother Abel (Gen. 4) to the violence preceding Noah's flood (Gen. 6). God's response to the earth's "violence" and "wickedness" is that of *great distress* (Gen. 6:5, 11). *He is more deeply grieved than angry* (6:6–7: "grieved in his heart"). One scholar observes: "Divine anger . . . must be understood against the backdrop of divine sorrow."[3] And no wonder: at the creation, God looked upon ("saw" [*raah*]) it and pronounced it "very good" (1:31). Now God "saw" (*raah*) that it was *ruined* (*shahath*; 6:12).[4] The Lord's "heart was filled with pain" (6:6 NIV) because of the evil in the "heart" of human beings (6:5). That is, *wickedness in the human heart affects the heart of God.*[5]

Also, this reason for sending the flood (human violence and wickedness) is far different from other ancient flood accounts. In some cases, *no* reason is given (e.g., the Sumerian Iridu Genesis account and the Babylonian Epic of Gilgamesh). In another case, the flood comes because humans make too much noise (the Akkadian Athrahasis account). But the theme of God's grief even after he reluctantly judges is a constant theme in Scripture. For example, God tells Israel, "If you stay in this land, I will build you up and not tear you down; I will plant you and not uproot you, for I am grieved over the disaster I have inflicted on you" (Jer. 42:10 NIV; cf. Isa. 47:6; 54:7–8; Zech. 1:15).

Second, *God simply finished off the ruination and disintegration that humans began.* So, the earth was *ruined* (*shahath*; 6:12) due to murderous and violent human beings (6:5, 11–12); terrible evils abounded in this human self-destruction. Thus, God used the flood to complete the well-advanced *ruination* (*shahath*; 6:13).[6]

As the earth was overwhelmed with violence and ruin, the language here speaks of "de-creation"—an undoing of what God had made (6:11–13). The parable of the vineyard (Isa. 5) tells a similar story of God's interaction with Israel (i.e., the vineyard). God did all he could have done by planting a choice vine in optimal conditions. Yet he lamented, "What more was there to do for My vineyard that I have not done in it?" (v. 4). The vineyard produced only worthless fruit of violence, distress, and injustice; God had to bring judgment, as a last resort. Likewise, in Genesis 6–8, God *finished the job that his defiant creatures had begun—and he was grieved by it.*

Third, *God graciously restored his creation.* The flood story prepares the way for a type of "new creation" story in the wake of the human disruption of God's moral and creational order and the harm brought to his image-bearers. God persisted with humanity rather than giving up. Despite human rebellion and ruin, God had a plan for re-creation, which parallels the original creation story:

- Like Adam (3:8), Noah "walked with God" (6:9).
- God "plants" a garden (2:8), and Noah "plants" a vineyard (9:20).
- The Spirit hovers over the waters (1:2), and the dove "hovers" over the waters (8:11).
- Both the original creation and this renewal of creation involve a blessing to "be fruitful and multiply" (1:28; 8:17; 9:7) as well as the image-of-God theme (1:26–27; 9:6).
- Through humans' misusing of the fruit, sin entered both the garden (Gen. 3) and Noah's vineyard (9:22–23). In their wake came the covering of nakedness (3:7; 9:22–23) and an ensuing curse (3:14–19; 9:25).

Fourth, *God further addressed the problem of a mutually murderous humanity by instituting capital punishment to help prevent the downward spiral of such activity.* Echoing the theme of humans as God's image-bearers (Gen. 1:26–28), this post-flood mandate passage presents a corrective to violence toward other human beings: "Whoever sheds the blood of a human, by a human shall that person's blood be shed; for in his own image God made humankind" (9:6 NRSV).

Finally, *a good God—the gracious giver and sustainer of life—has certain claims on us, unlike that of fellow human beings.* One philosopher points out this divine prerogative: "God as the author of our being would have rights over us that we do not have over our fellow humans."[7] Just like parents have a unique claim on their own children and not on their neighbors' children, so God has a particular, unique authority over us that is qualitatively different from human authority. God our creator does not owe us life or longevity of days.

Amid the questions about divine judgment, remember first human wickedness, God's profound grief, humanity's well-advanced disintegration, God's dedication to renew his creation, and God's putting in place new measures to address the deep human problem of murder and violence. On top of this, God as the author of life has a certain claim on us that fellow humans do not.

The Killing of the Egyptian Firstborn (Exod. 11–12)

Now it came about at midnight that the LORD struck all the firstborn in the land of Egypt, from the firstborn of Pharaoh who sat on his throne to the firstborn of the captive who was in the dungeon, and all the firstborn of cattle.

—Exodus 12:29

By faith [Moses] kept the Passover and the sprinkling of the blood, so that he who destroyed the firstborn would not touch them.

—Hebrews 11:28

Myth and History

The first Passover in Egypt was the night that the Egyptian firstborn were also slain by "the destroyer"—an agent commissioned by "the LORD"—the "I AM WHO I AM" (Exod. 3:14). This was the final plague against Egypt and its gods (12:23, 29; cf. v. 12). That event finally brought a hard-hearted Pharaoh to his knees so that he would finally let Israel leave Egypt.

Prior to the time of Moses, there existed an Egyptian literary tradition—a "mythological tale"—that looks uncannily like what Exodus describes:

- "It is the king who will be judged with Him-whose-name-is-hidden on the day of slaying the first-born" (Cannibal Hymn, in the Pyramid Texts)
- "I am he who will be judged with 'Him-whose-name-is-hidden' on the night of slaying the first-born" (Coffin Text VI).
- ". . . on that night of slaying the first-born, on the day of slaying the first-born" (Coffin Text II).[8]

One scholar observes "These passages are strong evidence that a mythological tale once circulated in which some or all of the first-born in Egypt—whether gods, mortals or animals, were slain on a certain day or night. Such a myth may very likely lie in the background of the biblical account."[9] Egyptians—and Israelites—who were aware of this tradition would have further confirmation of the superiority of Israel's God.

Now, this connection is certainly an interesting one. However, what is more foundational is the *actual* historicity of Israel's presence in Egypt and its exodus from this land of bondage. Some skeptics—including some of our critics from within (e.g., Eric Seibert)—may call these historical claims into question;[10] other scholars, though, have defended the general reliability of the Scriptures on this matter. Their arguments include

- evidence of Semitic peoples living in Egypt prior to the time of the exodus;
- an abundance of Egyptian loanwords ("Egyptianisms") used by the Hebrews;
- the Egyptian origin of various Israelite names (e.g., Phineas, Hur, Korah); and
- the Pentateuch's abundant, plausible references to Israel's firsthand experience of life in Egypt (e.g., Exod. 1:14; 2:11, 23; 5:4–19; 12:37; Num. 11:5; 33:5).[11]

There is more, but let's skip to our examination of this troubling event.

God's Firstborn, Egypt's Firstborn—and Moses's Firstborn

The early portion of Exodus involves a confrontation of two "firstborns" belonging to two powers: *Israel's God*, who was also the creator and sovereign over the nations, and *Egypt's gods, represented by the earthly ruler Pharaoh*.

Exodus 4 reveals that if Egypt was going to oppress God's firstborn, then God was going to bring judgment on Egypt's firstborn. Notice the connections:

- God was preparing Moses to issue the command to Pharaoh to free Israel— God's "son, My firstborn" (4:22).
- Because of Pharaoh's anticipated refusal, God threatened to take the life of *Pharaoh's* firstborn, as the representative of those in Egyptian households: "So I said to you, 'Let My son [Israel] go that he may serve Me'; but you have refused to let him go. Behold, I will kill your [Pharaoh's] son, your firstborn'" (4:23)—that is, at the Passover.
- *Life/death* and *firstborn* are also connected to *circumcision* (4:24–26). Moses had failed to circumcise his own *firstborn* son Gershom (2:22). This needed to be done if Moses was to lead God's firstborn, Israel, out of Egypt. He had to serve as a model of obedience to the Abrahamic covenant with its sign of circumcision (Gen. 17:14). If Moses failed in his duty, Gershom would be excluded from the benefits of the covenant community. Thus God would

smite Moses if the situation were not remedied.[12] As with the Passover, here the shedding of blood (Gershom's circumcision) preserved life (Moses's).[13]

The Passover and the Plague

Given this context, we can make a few observations about the final plague on Passover evening.

First, *God rendered to Egypt what Egypt had done to Israel.* Death coming to Egypt's firstborn was an example of God's repaying the Egyptians according to what they did to Israel. God called Israel "My firstborn son" (Exod. 4:22). Earlier, a brutal pharaoh commanded that the newborn boys in every *Israelite* family be put to death (1:16, 22). The oppressed Israelites' "outcry" (*tseaqah*) arose to God because of the Egyptians' oppression (3:7, 9). In like manner, under another brutal pharaoh, the *Egyptians'* "outcry" arose after the death of *their* firstborn at Passover (12:30). So, God's responsiveness to one "outcry" brought on another. *God treated Egypt as Egypt treated Israel.*

Second, *the enslavement of the Israelites would have required the involvement of a large population of Egyptians, and Egypt prospered because of their enslavement of Israelites.* The households of Egypt were extended families that lived together—not mere "nuclear families" composed of mother, father, and children.[14] But the severity of divine judgment on Egypt for oppressing the Lord's firstborn is clear enough, as every level of Egyptian society was affected.

Third, *the already-nasty Pharaoh compounded the misery of Israel's enslavement, which rendered judgment on Egypt all the more fitting.* On top of long-standing oppression, Pharaoh doubled Israel's workload: in addition to making bricks, the Israelites themselves now had to gather their own straw for bricks (straw helped reinforce the durability of the bricks).[15] This decree from Pharaoh fueled Israelite resentment against Moses (Exod. 5:1–21). The slaying of the firstborn would be the plague to finally break Pharoah's stranglehold on God's firstborn, Israel.

Fourth, as with the flood, *God took last-resort action against Egypt.* As we just noted, the last plague against Egypt's firstborn *finally* prompted Pharaoh to relent, despite the severity of the nine previous plagues. So even though God hardened Pharaoh's heart, the effect was not so overpowering as to completely prevent Pharaoh from giving in.

Fifth, as we'll see with the Canaanites, *God's taking on the deities of Egypt is a picture of spiritual warfare* (Exod. 12:12)—a theme that is more fully developed in the New Testament. This and other threats against Israel's mission and identity loomed large. Israel's ongoing presence in Egypt, in bondage, without any exodus, *threatened the eventual blessing to the nations of the earth: no exodus, no Israel, no Messiah, no salvation.*

Finally, as we saw with the flood, *God is the giver—and taker—of life.* He is under no obligation to bestow life or sustain it for seventy or eighty years.

The Death of Uzzah (2 Sam. 6)

But when they came to the threshing floor of Nacon, Uzzah reached out toward the ark of God and took hold of it, for the oxen nearly upset it. And the anger of the LORD burned against Uzzah, and God struck him down there for his irreverence; and he died there by the ark of God. David became angry because of the LORD's outburst against Uzzah, and that place is called Perez-uzzah to this day.

—2 Samuel 6:6–8

This event of God's striking down Uzzah troubles not only modern-day readers. King David himself was angry at God for this divine "outburst." Uzzah was well-intentioned: he tried to steady the toppling ark that sat atop an ox-drawn cart heading toward Jerusalem (2 Sam. 6:2). As a result, David became fearful, wondering, "How can the ark of the LORD come to me?" (6:9). Boyd concludes that this smiting was ultimately "demonic," as the ark had come to be idolatrously misused by Israel as a kind of good luck charm for blessing and success in battle. However, claims Boyd, God was willing to stoop to identify with Israel even though they attributed demonic power to God, who would never strike a person down.[16]

How should we approach this story? What is actually happening here?

First, *the events surrounding the ark's transport were a setup for disaster.* When it came to moving the ark, Israel had a kind of "warning label" in the Mosaic law: *Follow these two fundamental rules for transporting this sacred ark:*

Rule 1: Use the ark's rings and poles. "You shall put the poles into the rings on the sides of the ark, to carry the ark" (Exod. 25:14).

Rule 2: The Kohathites must carry the ark. Only the Kohathite family members (from Levi's tribe) were allowed to carry the ark (Exod. 25:12–14; Num. 7:9).

These regulations clearly rule out ox carts. So David, who actually commissioned moving the ark (2 Sam. 6:2), should have followed directions.

On top of this, Uzzah had been staying where the ark was temporarily housed (1 Sam. 7:1; 2 Sam. 6:3–4). So perhaps we have another relevant circumstantial factor: *Uzzah had gotten used to the ark's presence and had lost sight of its sacred significance.* It's like in the film *Raiders of the Lost Ark.* Archaeologist Indiana Jones (Harrison Ford) captured the lost ark of the covenant, but government bureaucrats ("top men") had this "relic" crated, stored away, and ultimately buried in a massive warehouse. Jones commented, "They don't know what they've got."[17]

Second, *the Israelites already knew the severe consequences of mishandling the ark.* Back in 1 Samuel 6, the Philistines were in possession of the ark, which they had captured after battling the Israelites, who treated the ark like a lucky charm, hoping its presence in battle would ensure victory (1 Sam. 4:1–11). The text indicates the danger into which Israel was stepping as they misused this holy object: "They carried the ark of the covenant of the LORD of hosts who sits above the cherubim" (4:4).

The ark in the wrong hands brought only plague and trouble. An outbreak of deadly tumors afflicted Philistine cities and villages (1 Sam. 5:6, 9, 12). When some Philistines were curious enough to open the ark to look into it, God struck them down with "a great slaughter." The Philistines eventually got rid of the ark, sending it back on a "cart" (*agalah*) led by two cows that made their way back to Israelite territory (6:7–8).

While the Philistines didn't know any better, David should have. He ordered the ark to be brought to Jerusalem, and those doing so likewise put it on a "cart" (*agalah*) (2 Sam. 6:3). As before Israel's battle with the Philistines, here come *the same somber words* just before the ark was improperly used again: "And David arose and went with all the people . . . to bring up from there the ark of God which is called by the Name, the very name of the LORD of hosts who is enthroned above the cherubim" (6:2). And then came Uzzah's instant death.

Third, *letting the ark fall to the dirt would not have desecrated it*. The ground wasn't considered inherently unclean or defiling. So its falling to the ground wouldn't have created a serious problem.

Fourth, *the Israelites had already known that when one gets closer to God and to sacred items, the more prepared one has to be*. When Aaron's high priestly sons Nadab and Abihu "offered strange fire" (Lev. 10:1)—an idolatrous act—fire came from the Lord's presence and consumed them (v. 2). God left Aaron with the warning, "By those who come near Me I will be treated as holy, and before all the people I will be honored" (v. 3).

Final Comments

Various contextual and literary considerations bring clarity to these three acts of divine "smiting." They reveal the following realities:

1. *The flood:* God's grief and reluctance when judging sin
2. *Egypt's firstborn:* God's judgment as proportional ("As you have done to others, so it will be done to you")
3. *Uzzah:* God's punishment after ample warning and historical precedent

The next chapter likewise examines another sampling of difficult texts.

Now, some of our critics from within deny that the "actual" God had anything to do with this destructive flood, the death of the firstborn, or the slaying of Uzzah. God simply withdraws his presence and his influence, and so evil cosmic forces rush in to wreak their destructive power on human beings.[18] But it is hard to square this with the evidence.

Regarding the flood of Noah, the New Testament witness reveals that a grieved *God* "brought a flood upon the world of the ungodly" (2 Pet. 2:5). Regarding Egypt's firstborn, God declared that "when *I* see the blood *I* will pass over you" (Exod. 12:13). In remembrance of this event, future generations of Israelites were to engage in the Passover rite and explain its meaning. "It is a Passover sacrifice to *the* LORD who passed over the houses of the sons of Israel in Egypt when *He* smote the Egyptians, but spared our homes" (Exod. 12:27). Though the agent in this event is called "the destroyer" (12:23) and "he who destroyed the firstborn" (Heb. 11:28), this is clearly *God's* agent. The *agent's* actions are portrayed as *God's* in both testaments (see also Pss. 78:51; 105:36; 136:10).

Even *Jesus himself* engaged in coercive force against the money changers (Luke 19:45 ESV: "He . . . began to drive out those who sold"). More sobering is Jesus's action in destroying Israelites: "*Jesus*, who saved a people out of the land of Egypt, afterward destroyed [*apōlesen*] those who did not believe" (Jude 5 ESV). Once again, we see continuity between the testaments and the carryover of both the kindness and severity of God/Jesus.

16

Divine Smitings (2)

Elisha and the Bears, and Punishing Children to the Third and Fourth Generations

Getting Our Bearings on Elisha and the Mauled "Children"

He went up from there to Bethel, and while he was going up on the way, some small boys came out of the city and jeered at him, saying, "Go up, you baldhead! Go up, you baldhead!" And he turned around, and when he saw them, he cursed them in the name of the LORD. And two she-bears came out of the woods and tore forty-two of the boys.

—2 Kings 2:23–24 ESV

As the story goes, the newly commissioned prophet Elisha cursed a group of "young lads" or "young children" after they had mocked him; Elisha's action brought out of the woods two female bears that mauled forty-two of them. One could perhaps envision this news headline based on a story in 2 Kings 2: "Israelite Prophet Summons She-Bears to Maul Kids."

This story is commonly blasted by critics from without and from within. One critic from within (Boyd) says that if we read this story in light of the cross of Christ, then Elisha's calling down a curse and bringing harm to these boys was sinful and a "misuse of divine power."[1] All of this "cursing" stuff is part of the "pre-Christian perspective of the author,"[2] and Jesus wouldn't call down fire from heaven to "incinerate enemies," would he?[3]

The junior prophet Elisha parted and crossed the waters of the Jordan River. The narrator depicts him as a "new Joshua" who succeeded his mentor. He used his departed mentor Elijah's mantle to part the waters (2 Kings 2:13). And like Joshua, he challenged Canaanite-like idolatry in the Northern Kingdom of Israel. In a final mission before his ascent to heaven, his mentor Elijah had just gone to Samaria, Bethel, and then Jericho (1:1–2:4). Elisha then retraced these steps but in reverse order—Jericho, Bethel, and then Samaria (2 Kings 2).

Elijah "went up" (*alah*) to heaven (2:11). Then Elisha was mocked by "young lads" or "young children" (*nearim qetannim*) in Bethel—the major center for Israel's idolatry. They were telling this "baldhead" to "go up" (*alah*) as well (2:23). This "baldy" insult was probably intended to contrast Elisha with his "hairy" mentor, Elijah (1:8). In response, Elisha called down a curse on them, and forty-two of these "lads" (*yeladim*) (2:24) were mauled by two female bears.

"But They're Just Kids!"

The narrator uses two words for "youths": *nearim* (2 Kings 2:23) and *yeladim* (v. 24). Without much more context, we might get the impression that they were like little kids on the playground calling someone names. But are these just a bunch of small kids saying insulting things?

First, *these terms can—and here do—refer to young adults, not simply elementary-school-aged children.* The book of Kings emphasizes this. Earlier in 1 Kings 12:8, King Rehoboam foolishly listened to the advice of his contemporaries (*yeladim*) rather than the wise, experienced elders. The term *nearim* is also used in 1 Kings 20:13–15, where it refers to young men *capable of fighting in battle*. In fact, various translations render this word as "young men" (NASB), "junior officers" (NIV), and "servants" (ESV).

Second, *one of these same words is used of David.* He was the "youngest" (*naar qaton*) of his family (1 Sam. 16:11). Indeed, when seeking to anoint a new king, the prophet Samuel looked at Jesse's other "children" (*hannearim*), among whom was the strong, warrior-like Eliab (vv. 6–7). And later in that chapter David is called a "mighty man of valor, a warrior" (v. 18). In fact, this "young man" had already killed a lion and a bear before he killed Goliath (cf. 1 Sam. 17:37). The term *naar* is also used of Joseph as a seventeen-year-old (Gen. 37:2). Basically, this term can refer to *an unmarried male who is not yet head of a household.*[4]

Third, *not only can the term* yelad *refer to young adult (unmarried) males, but it may have an additional connection to a young man belonging to a royal house.* This is the sole term used in 1 Kings 12 to refer to King Rehoboam's young advisors (vv. 8, 10)—that is, "young adult males, usually with royal associations."[5] In 2 Kings 2, these young royals confronted Elisha. They, "far from being little children, are young men of the royal and perhaps priestly establishment at Bethel."[6]

Fourth, *the same number of young men killed—forty-two—appears in 2 Kings 10*: there are forty-two young men from the royal house of Omri whom Jehu slaughters (10:14). This number is *symbolically connected* to the concept of potential blessing or curse from God. That is, this connection indicates that this two-bear attack was the result not of a cranky prophet's curses but rather of divine intent.[7]

Covenant, Curses, and Carnivores

This raises the matter of promised blessings and threatened curses in the Mosaic covenant. Just a cursory glance at the biblical narrative indicates that God *longed to bless* and only *reluctantly* carried out judgments against Israel. He bore patiently with disobedient generations of Israel by prophetic warnings and punishing only when there was "no remedy" (2 Chron. 36:16). That's where these youths come in.

First, *these youths mocked Elisha and showed disdain for his prophetic status.* As Bethel was a center of idolatry, these young men represented treasonous covenant-breaking and a refusal to listen to God's prophets. Note the contrast here with the earlier grateful reception of Elisha at Jericho.[8] There, the school of prophets bowed themselves before Elisha and declared of him, "The spirit of Elijah rests on Elisha" (2 Kings 2:15). As a result, he brought healing to them (v. 21). Compare this to the harm that came to these young men of Bethel.

Second, *the covenant blessings and curses explicitly mention the calamity these youths encountered.* In his criticism of Elisha's actions here, Boyd doesn't mention Leviticus 26:22, which warns of this curse for covenant-breaking: "I will let loose among you the beasts of the field, which will bereave [*shakal*] you of your children . . . and reduce your number." And here is a similar threatened judgment: "I will send the teeth of beasts against them" (Deut. 32:24). Other prophets picked up on this specific judgment as well: wild beasts would "bereave" (*shakal*) Israelites of their children (Ezek. 5:17; cf. Amos 5:18–19).[9]

This very language is found in this Elisha narrative. At Jericho, Elisha brought "healing" to poisoned waters, which had earlier brought death and bereavement (NASB "unfruitfulness" [*shakal*]; 2 Kings 2:21). By contrast, at Bethel, because the young men mocked God's prophet, Israel was "bereft" (*shakal*) of its children—in this case "rendered *un*fruitful." Listening to the prophet means blessing and fruitfulness; refusing to listen brings curse and unfruitfulness or bereavement. Unlike the blessing of creation of being fruitful and ruling over the animals (Gen. 1:28), in this instance, Israelites were cursed with unfruitfulness (bereaved of children) and were ruled by beasts.

Now, it appears that an enigmatic passage of Ezekiel 20:25 also refers to these curses: "I [God] also gave them statutes that were not good and ordinances by which they could not live." As there are at least half a dozen interpretations concerning what "not good" means,[10] we should be careful about being unnecessarily dogmatic here.[11] Though I discuss this unusual passage in *Moral Monster* in the context of infant sacrifice and its prohibition,[12] we here can add another dimension to the discussion. John Walton and Harvey Walton suggest that these "not good" commands are likely the "judicial decisions" that God makes against unfaithful Israelites. They were not for Israel's good because Israel had not chosen the path of life God commanded (Deut. 30:19). God's judgments against them brought disorder rather than order. Thus God "decreed war, drought and exile rather than blessing."[13]

Smiting in New Testament Perspective

Prior to the "smiting" event with Elisha, his mentor Elijah had called down fire from heaven (2 Kings 1). One critic from within (Boyd) denounces Elijah's (alleged) misuse of divinely given power. He appeals to Luke 9:51–55,[14] where a village of Samaritans "did not receive" Jesus: "When his disciples James and John saw it, they said, 'Lord, do you want us to tell fire to come down from heaven and consume them?' But [Jesus] turned and rebuked them" (ESV).

True, Jesus refused to act as Elijah did in this instance, and he didn't call twelve legions of angels to protect him from death (Matt. 26:53). But Jesus wasn't thereby declaring such prophetic actions "demonic" either. As one theologian remarks: "This is not necessarily to condemn what Elijah said and did in a different space and time. It is to declare that it is not the way of God for Jesus and his disciples in this day and hour."[15] Furthermore, the disciples wanted to take matters into their own hands in bringing judgment ("Do you want us to tell fire to come . . . ?").

As we've seen, Jesus and other New Testament authorities affirm that God commanded the death penalty in ancient Israel (e.g., Matt. 15:3–6; Mark 7:10; Acts 3:23; Heb. 2:2–3; 10:28–29). This doesn't carry over to how the new Israel (i.e., the church) deals with its rebellious members. If our critics from within think that the divine judgment in the Old Testament was severe, it is far more so for those who turn away from the gospel (Heb. 2:2–3; 10:28–29; 12:18–29).

The Old Testament prophets who pled with Israel to return to a merciful God also exhibited a holy ferocity in light of their vocation. They were tasked with opposing idolatry, covenant-breaking, and moral compromise that undermined Israel's national and missional identity. What may look like prophetic mean-spiritedness to some of our critics from within actually is very much like Jesus's driving money changers from the temple; denouncing with "woes" the religious hypocrites or Israelite cities of his day (Chorazin, Bethsaida, and Capernaum); cursing the fig tree (Israel) so that it would no longer produce fruit, promising the destruction of Jerusalem (Mark 11:21); threatening to "strike dead" the false prophetess Jezebel's followers (Rev. 2:20–23); and, yes, "destroy[ing] [Israelites] who did not believe" (Jude 5). Behold, the kindness and severity of God.

The Doctrine of Intergenerational Punishment: Not Readily Apparent

I the LORD your God am a jealous God, visiting the iniquity of the fathers on the children to the third and the fourth generation of those who hate me, but showing steadfast love to thousands of those who love me and keep my commandments.

—Exodus 20:5–6 ESV

The LORD passed before him and proclaimed, "The LORD, the LORD, a God merciful and gracious, slow to anger, and abounding in steadfast love and faithfulness, keeping steadfast love for thousands, forgiving iniquity and transgression and sin, but who will by no means clear the guilty, visiting the iniquity of the fathers on the children and the children's children, to the third and the fourth generation."

—Exodus 34:6–7 ESV

How do these texts square with Ezekiel 18:19–20? There, God *doesn't* punish children for the sins of their parents: "The soul who sins shall die. The son shall not suffer for the iniquity of the father, nor the father suffer for the iniquity of the son," adding that "the wickedness of the wicked shall be upon himself" (v. 20 ESV; cf. 33:10–20). And didn't Jesus himself reject the notion of intergenerational punishment when asked about the man born blind (John 9:2–3)?

Once again, we have the two-sided coin of divine love and divine wrath. The Exodus 34 text reflects Exodus 20 and is echoed throughout the Old Testament.[16] But what about intergenerational punishment?

One of our critics from within (Boyd) asserts that this Ezekiel text is a *correction*—indeed a *repudiation*—of Moses's notion that God punishes successive generations: "Ezekiel specifically taught that children are never punished for their parent's sin (Ezekiel 18). This insight arguably corrects the earlier Israelite conception of Yahweh 'punishing the children for the sin of the parents to the third and fourth generation' (Exod 20:5)."[17] But here are a few reflections in response.

First, *if Ezekiel were "correcting" or "repudiating" Moses's teaching hundreds of years later, why didn't other contemporary prophets "correct" Exodus 20:5?* Around a century before Ezekiel, the prophet Nahum mentioned divine wrath alongside God's grace: "The LORD is slow to anger," but he is also "avenging" and "takes vengeance" "and . . . will by no means leave the guilty unpunished" (Nah. 1:2–3). Beyond this, Ezekiel's contemporary Jeremiah also harked back to Exodus 20:5 and 34:6–7: the Lord "shows lovingkindness to thousands," but also "repays the iniquity of fathers into the bosom of their children after them" (Jer. 32:18). *Here we see no shift from the "textual" God of Moses to the "actual" God of Ezekiel (or Jeremiah or Nahum) after all. This is the same theological pattern throughout Israel's history.*

Lest the critic from within think that Jeremiah needs correcting about the "actual" God, we point out that *in the preceding chapter*, Jeremiah mentioned that "everyone will die for his own iniquity" (31:30). But that same idea is *already found way back in Deuteronomy 24:16*. God made clear that children weren't to be punished for the sins of their fathers—and vice versa: "Everyone shall be put to death for his own sin." The notion that Ezekiel was "correcting" Moses conflicts with the facts.

Second, *God's punishing (literally, "visiting" [paqad]) is against "those who hate Me"—that is, those who break from God's covenant to worship other gods and thus declare enmity with God (Exod. 20:5)*. Interestingly, Boyd doesn't mention that it is the third and fourth generation "*of those who hate Me.*" Those "haters" are *covenant-breakers—disloyal Israelites* aligned with foreign gods and the immoral practices associated with them. Being covenant-breakers puts them under the potential threat of capital punishment—that is, the divine judgment of the curses. These were terms included in ancient Near Eastern treaties, including Israel's.

This is why God described himself as "jealous" (Exod. 20:5). The Lord delivered Israel from bondage in Egypt (cf. 20:2–3), and he covenantally and graciously bound himself to them in "steadfast love" (*hesed*). In this marriage-like covenant, God was thus passionate or *zealous* to preserve that relational loyalty. Any right-thinking spouse would become passionate about any third party who threatens to undermine the marriage.

Old Testament scholar Claude Mariottini comments on Exodus 20:5:

> The visiting of the sins of the fathers comes upon the third and the fourth generation of those who reject God. These words clearly say that not all the descendants of an individual are punished for his sins. Thus, it is not the children and the grand-children of an individual who are punished, but only those who reject God or those who reject the demands of the covenant. The expression "those who reject me" is not found in Exodus 34:6–7 and in Numbers 14:18. The reason for its presence in the second commandment is because the statement deals with the breach of the covenant, that is, the rejection of Yahweh to follow other gods.[18]

Third, *the term "visit" isn't exactly "punish"—as most translations put it—but rather means "visiting the iniquities"* (cf. Jer. 11:23; Amos 3:14). This term involves a *close examination* that then results in a judge's decision.[19] This isn't a rash or capricious judgment; it is measured. This is because God is "slow to anger."

Fourth, *the exaggerated contrast between two extremes—"the third and the fourth generation" and "thousands" of generations—emphasizes the abundant blessing of obedience, not the negative aspect of judging future generations. God is more ready to forgive than he is to "visit."* Carol Meyers comments: "We can only wonder if this is the language of hyperbole, meant to emphasize the importance of obeying this stricture, rather than an expression of belief that the innocent descendants of someone who disobeyed would have to pay the consequences. . . . Blessings will come to the 'thousandth generation' (20:6) of those whose love for God means that they obey all God's teachings. Such blessings will last, in a sense, forever."[20] If an actual generation is more like twenty-five years (or perhaps even twenty), then *the "third and fourth" generation essentially amounts to roughly the span of a lifetime.* The negative consequences of sinful patterns and actions of parents often hang over the heads of their children and children's children, especially while those parents are alive: "The prolongation of divine punishment is limited to the generations who might be born within the lifetime of the offender."[21]

The expression "third and fourth" emphasizes *limitation on judgment*; *it undermines a spirit of hopelessness and despair in the face of divine judgment.* This is in contrast to *no limits* set on the extremity of God's mercy. So it's thousands of generations versus a lifetime. Or on a smaller scale, compare God's anger lasting for a moment to his favor for a lifetime (Ps. 30:5).

Yes, God's great desire is to abundantly bless—to show "steadfast love" or "covenant loyalty" to a thousand generations. As we see in the New Testament, God prefers blessing over cursing—but some will be "accursed" by their own resistance to the initiating grace of God (Matt. 25:41; Acts 7:51).

Fifth, *God's concern isn't to blame the innocent for another's sins but to not let subsequent generations off the hook for continuing the same sinful patterns.* According to Douglas Stuart, this text has been "widely misunderstood."[22] No, successive generations don't incur *guilt* from the deeds of previous generations. Rather, *God won't give a pass to the third and fourth generations on the alleged basis that they learned those practices from their parents.* Rather, "God will indeed punish generation after generation . . . if they keep doing the same sorts of sins that prior generations did. If the children continue to do the sins their parents did ["those who hate Me"], they will receive the same punishments as their parents."[23]

Sixth, *parental sins will have negative consequences for the next generation, though a future corporate national judgment may come due to general covenantal disobedience.* While transference of parental guilt onto children is problematic, the *consequences* of parental sin—or righteous living—is obvious.

Thus, we can make some important distinctions at this point:

1. *The Old Testament expresses general legal and moral accountability of individuals before the law* (cf. Exod. 23:7: "I will not acquit the guilty"). To any Israelites who complained because God was punishing them for their parents' sins, God basically says, "Well, I tell you what. Let's forget your fathers' sins. I'll just judge you for own behavior. Let's see if that actually changes anything."[24]

2. *Sinful choices by parents will predictably bring harmful consequences to children.* Just think of parents who are engaged in substance abuse. That said, children will also benefit from wise parental decisions.

3. *At a national level, God's patience and longsuffering end, and the long-threatened judgment falls on a particular generation.* Generations of covenantal disobedience may give rise to God's saying, "Okay, that's it!"—and national judgment finally falls: "Our fathers sinned, and are no more; it is we who have borne their iniquities" (Lam. 5:7). This happened to Israel under the Assyrian Empire (eighth century BC) and to Judah under the Babylonian Empire (sixth century BC).

Jesus himself threatened judgment on Israel, which came via the Romans in AD 70. He warned: "Woe to those who are pregnant and to those who are nursing babies in those days! But pray that your flight will not be in the winter, or on a Sabbath" (Matt. 24:19–20). Divine judgment meant hardship for those who were on hand when it eventually fell. And in the face of judgment, Jesus wept over Jerusalem, desiring her repentance rather than judgment, but she refused (Matt. 23:37).

In both testaments are indications of individual personal responsibility for one's own actions without denying the corporate responsibility as well as an eventual national judgment that falls after generations of covenantal disobedience.

Delighting in Smiting? Does God Take Pleasure in Punishing?

It shall come about that as the LORD *delighted* over you to prosper you, and multiply you, so the LORD will *delight* over you to make you perish and destroy you; and you will be torn from the land where you are entering to possess it.

—Deuteronomy 28:63

Wrath is an expression of God's love and care; God longs to show compassion (Isa. 30:18) and doesn't desire the death of the wicked (Ezek. 18:23; 33:11). He doesn't "afflict willingly" (Lam. 3:33). How then do we make sense of this verse quoted above? Does God *really* have equal pleasure in both *blessing* Israel and *judging* it? Boyd writes, "It seems apparent that Moses believed Yahweh would be just as happy bringing destruction on his people as he would be bestowing blessings."[25]

Our critic, however, engages in a flat reading of the text, failing to appreciate that this is a *rhetorical device* to send a sober warning and to get Israel's attention. To God's mind, it's not a toss-up between his desiring to bless or judge. Deuteronomy itself makes clear that *God cares about Israel's obedience and its flourishing*: "Choose life in order that you may live" (Deut. 30:19). Indeed, even after judgment, "the LORD will again take delight in prospering you, as he took delight in your fathers" (v. 9 ESV). In a similar vein, after God's renewed covenant with his people (Jer. 32:40), God announces his *ultimate desire*: "I will rejoice over them to do them good and will faithfully plant them in this land with all My heart and with all My soul" (v. 41).

When humans defy God and there is no alternative, God's "delight" in severity merely *indicates the fittingness of divine judgment and putting the world in proper moral order*. But for our critic from within, let's go to the New Testament itself. In God's final judgment on the false, idolatrous city of Babylon, there is a righteous call to *rejoice* in the victory of God, who has vindicated his oppressed, persecuted people: "Rejoice over her, O heaven, and you saints and apostles and prophets, because God has pronounced judgment for you against her" (Rev. 18:20).

Keep in mind N. T. Wright's reminder that denying God's wrath means denying God's love.[26] God is not indifferent. Rather, he hates all that distorts and defaces his creation.

17

"Bashing Babies against the Rock"?

Imprecatory Psalms in the Old Testament

The Imprecations Are Staggering

Introducing the Imprecatory Psalms

When I was a boy, I would occasionally hear this Middle Eastern–sounding "curse": "May the fleas of a thousand camels infest your armpits!" Now, *that* was playful. The imprecations from Psalm 137 are *not*. A mourning, mocked, traumatized, and displaced psalmist wrote this while in exile by "the rivers of Babylon":

> Remember, O LORD, against the sons of Edom
> the day of Jerusalem,
> who said, "Raze it, raze it
> to its very foundation."
> O daughter of Babylon, you devastated one,
> how blessed will be the one who repays you
> with the recompense with which you have repaid us.
> How blessed will be the one who seizes and dashes your little ones
> against the rock. (vv. 7–9)

The psalmist appears to treat a ruthless, evil action as a blessing.

Welcome to the imprecatory psalms! These vengeance prayers or curse prayers are found throughout the Psalms (Pss. 7, 12, 35, 55, 58, 59, 69, 79, 83, 109, 139). Imprecations have two features: (a) *a prayer or call to God* and (b) *a request for God to bring vengeance, calamity, and judgment upon the enemies of the psalmist/God.*[1]

Even the term "woe" (*hoy*)—found throughout the prophetic literature—overlaps with imprecation. Notice the woe-imprecation parallel in Zechariah 11:17 (ESV):

Woe: "Woe to my worthless shepherd, who deserts the flock!"
Imprecation: "May the sword strike his arm and his right eye! Let his arm be wholly withered, his right eye utterly blinded!"

"Curse" and "woe" are used similarly in two comparable passages:

Curse: "Cursed be anyone who strikes down his neighbor in secret" (Deut. 27:24 ESV).
Woe: "Woe to him who builds a city with bloodshed and founds a town with violence!" (Hab. 2:12).

In addition, curses and woes are often found in a series (e.g., Deut. 27:15–26 with Isa. 5:8–23; 28:1–33:1; Hab. 2:6–19).[2] Repeatedly in the Gospels, Jesus himself carries on that prophetic "woe" tradition, most notably when he denounces Israel's hostile religious leaders in Matthew 23 and chastises cities that rejected his teaching and accompanying signs (Matt. 11:23–24; 24:37–39; Luke 10:13–15).

The Imprecatory Psalms and Their Critics

In addition to dashing little ones on the rocks, another psalm seems to endorse hatred: "Do I not hate those who hate You, O LORD? And do I not loathe those who rise up against You?" (Ps. 139:21). What's more, God himself "hates" evildoers (5:5; 11:5). But doesn't God *love* the world (John 3:16)?

One critic from within (Boyd) says that such psalms are in "direct contradiction to Jesus."[3] After all, Jesus commands *enemy-love* and *prayer* for persecutors (Matt. 5:43–48). One biblical scholar claims that using the imprecatory psalms for devotional purposes or as a model of prayer "runs the risk of infecting religious people with harmful attitudes. Do the prayers for vengeance against personal enemies sacralize violence?"[4] That is, do these psalms legitimize or bless violence or harm to others?

Indeed, the imprecatory psalms shock us Westerners. In his *Reflections on the Psalms*, C. S. Lewis calls them "terrible or (dare we say?) contemptible" prayers; they are "devilish," "profoundly wrong," and "sinful." He views Psalm 109, which appears to get deeply personal, as "perhaps the worst."[5] It is "as unabashed a hymn of hate as was ever written."[6] Here is a sampling from that psalm: "May his days be few" (v. 8 ESV); "May his children wander about and beg" (v. 10 ESV); "May his posterity be cut off" (v. 13 ESV).

Along similar lines, consider the German theologian Dietrich Bonhoeffer, who was killed under Hitler's orders for his faithful opposition to the idolatrous Nazi ideology. He asked about one imprecatory psalm (Ps. 58): "Is this frightful Psalm of vengeance our prayer? Are we actually allowed to pray in such a manner?" His response was clear: "No, we are certainly not permitted to pray like that. . . . Only he who is totally without sin can pray like that. This Psalm of vengeance is the prayer of the innocent."[7]

What are we to make of these angry psalms? Are they just expressions of a fallen, sinful ancient Near Eastern writer? Do we have any indication about what Jesus and other New Testament authorities thought about these harsh psalms?

The Imprecatory Psalms through Ancient Near Eastern Eyes

The Ancient Near East

Lewis got some things wrong about Israel and their ancient Near Eastern neighbors. He said that such imprecatory prayers were unique to Israel, who had "sinned in this matter worse than the Pagans" in that they "cursed more bitterly than the Pagans."[8] If anything, it's the other way around. There are remarkably bitter ancient Near Eastern pagans. The (Babylonian) Curse of Akkad (2400 BC) expresses these wishes: "May the cattle slaughterer slaughter his wife" and "May your sheep butcher butcher his child." An Assyrian text (from 672 BC) wishes leprosy and death followed by the feasting of vultures and jackals on enemies' corpses.[9] Such examples could be multiplied.

Curse and God's Covenant with Israel

In addition, the curses of the surrounding ancient Near Eastern nations were *incorporated into their magical practices and enacted by their deities*.[10] The "success" of a curse or blessing was due to the whim of some ancient Near Eastern deity whose "message" was interpreted by a priest's scrutinizing an animal's entrails or the movements of heavenly bodies.

The imprecatory psalms weren't like this. The "success" or "fulfillment" of any curse had to be anchored in the will and purposes of a good, just, compassionate, covenant-keeping God. Moreover, the psalmists' curses reflected God's covenant promise to Israel. These anguished writers located their blessing and curse language in God's promise to Abraham that God would bless those who bless Abraham's offspring—and curse those who cursed his people (Gen. 12:1–3)—and that God rewarded persons and nations according to their deeds, as we shall see.

Psalm 137

A Little Background

A bit of historical context helps us to understand this psalm. The psalmist appears to be exiled in Babylon. The exile itself came in three waves—under

Jehoiakim (2 Kings 23:34–24:6; Dan. 1:1–4), then Jehoiachin (2 Kings 24:6–16), and finally Zedekiah in 586 BC (24:17–25:21). This lasted until 535 BC, when the first of three waves of exiled Jews returned to Jerusalem. The destruction of Jerusalem in the third wave was a trauma and a devastation. Jews believed their beloved Jerusalem couldn't be moved (Ps. 46:5), and now here it was, ransacked and ruined.

On top of this, the Babylonian captors *taunted* the Israelites, *forcing* them to sing "songs of Zion" (Ps. 137:3). And to add insult to injury, Israel's Edomite brothers—the descendants of Esau—joined in Babylon's cruelty. They not only aided the Babylonians in the destructive rampage and pillaging at Babylon's destruction of Jerusalem and the temple; they even blocked fleeing Israelites from escaping. Indeed, they engaged in treachery by handing their "cousins," as it were, into Babylonian hands (Obad. 11–14).

Symbolism and Graphic Imagery: Who Are These "Little Ones"?

As we think about "little ones" dashed against the rock in the setting of intense, emotional Hebrew poetry, consider several interpretive options that scholars have offered. Maybe this harsh-sounding language ought to be interpreted with a bit more nuance than many suppose.

Option 1: "Little Ones" as Babylon's Royal House

One noted scholar on the Psalms—Erich Zenger—says that Psalm 137 is actually a political poem—and those "little ones" *aren't* infants: "[This] deals with the end of Babylon's reign of terror. This is also important with respect to the image of the children of the daughter Babylon, who are to be smashed against the stone pavements of the capital city. 'The children' are those of the royal house, that is, of the dynasty (cf. Isa. 7:14–16; 9:1–6). The horrible image means to say that this dynasty of terror ought to be exterminated completely ('root and branch')."[11] He translates the final verse, "Happy is the one who seizes you and puts an end to your rule forever."[12] While such translations risk losing the literary or poetic imagery, it's helpful to keep that political dimension in mind.[13]

Option 2: "Little Ones" as Babylonian Soldiers

Scholar Knut Heim observes that the "little ones" symbolize "a destructive brutal army":

> The entire psalm is constructed on a specific kind of metaphor, called personification. Jerusalem and Babylon are treated as if they are female human beings with emotions and other human characteristics. Arising from this . . . [the] "daughter Babylon" is not a young, vulnerable female with small children, but the symbol of a destructive and brutal army. Consequently, the "little ones" to be killed are not innocent infants; rather, the "children" of the personified army represent adult

soldiers, the very people who taunt, threaten, and humiliate the poet and his or her compatriots in the earlier verses of the psalm.[14]

The major point in these first two interpretations is *the wish that Babylonian oppression and tyranny would end.* This view is held by an array of biblical scholars. We've already seen how one of them renders Psalm 137's final verse: "Happy is the one who seizes you and puts an end to your rule forever."[15] Here is scholar Othmar Keel's translation: "Happy is he who puts an end to your self-renewing domination."[16]

From a historical point of view, the Babylonian people *themselves* considered their rulers to be tyrants. When the Medo-Persian ruler Cyrus invaded Babylon (539 BC), he not only brought an end to Babylonian tyranny, but he also gave the Babylonian people reason to celebrate! Ancient Near East scholar Edwin Yamauchi writes: "The inhabitants of Babylon greeted Cyrus not as a conqueror but as a liberator, and spread green branches before him."[17]

The metaphorical language called for an end to future Babylonian kings, soldiers, and other oppressors to prevent such a threat from ever happening again. Isaiah 14:21 has this in mind: it calls for killing the sons of cruel, merciless fathers "lest they rise and possess the earth, and fill the face of the world with cities." Isaiah predicts this end of Babylon (cf. 13:16), and Psalm 137 is simply asking God to fulfill this prophecy—to bring an end to the devastating influence of Babylon.

Option 3: Hyperbole

While some see the "little ones" as symbolic—Babylon's royal house, terror-inspiring soldiers, perpetuators of torment and oppression—others say Psalm 137 is *hyperbolic.* It simply employs a typical element of Hebrew poetry—namely, vivid and striking imagery: "Biblical poetry, like most poetry, employs graphic imagery to portray and express its ideas. . . . This imagery [in Psalm 137:8–9] is no more intended to be taken literally than elsewhere in the psalms where the psalmists speak of rivers clapping their hands [Ps. 98:8] and mountains singing for joy [Ps. 148; cf. Isa. 49:13]."[18]

The late biblical scholar G. B. Caird wrote about the function of hyperbole in the Hebrew Bible: "Hyperbole or overstatement is a figure of speech common to all languages. But among the Semitic peoples its frequent use arises out of a habitual cast of mind, which I have called absoluteness—a tendency to think in extremes without qualification, in black and white, without intervening shades of grey."[19] So whether it's loving Jacob and hating Esau, leaving no survivors, utterly destroying or expressing strong emotion here in the imprecatory psalms, hyperbole is a common thread throughout.

Overstatement or exaggeration could also apply to Psalm 109—that text C. S. Lewis found most reprehensible. There the psalmist prays that the oppressor's children become orphans and his wife a widow, that no one show kindness to them, and that their belongings be seized by creditors (vv. 9–10). Lewis isn't alone in his view that this imprecatory psalm sounds utterly unchristian and has no part of the Christian faith.[20]

Once again, we should remember *how psalmists are frequently given to exaggeration and overstatement in their deep emotion.* Just imagine your reaction to a neighbor who tries to give drugs to your child or tries to seduce your teenage daughter. You'd be more than outraged; you'd want to inflict bodily harm. Deep anger is a sign that we care.[21]

Many of these imprecatory psalms *present the psalmists' thoughts not in their cooler moments but when their emotions are white-hot or raw.*[22] Yet even with the call for judgment against Babylon and its tyranny, God's exiled people must also "pray for the welfare of the [Babylonian] city" where they now reside; they are to "pray to the LORD on its behalf" (Jer. 29:7). This isn't a contradiction. The ultimate longing and prayer for Babylon's peace is good and God-like, but if Babylon continues with oppression and injustice, then asking for divine judgment on Babylon is warranted.

So yes, the poetry here uses "picturesque, even graphic, language"[23] that shouldn't be taken literally—no more so than when the psalmist claims his heart is wounded within him (Ps. 109:22) and that he is fading away like an evening shadow (v. 23).

Option 4: The Call for Just Recompense

Psalm 109 presents another angle on interpreting certain harsh-sounding psalms—namely, *asking God to render to all people according to their deeds.* The psalmist pours out his heart to God about his persecutors, using the third-person plural (vv. 1–5). For example, "*They* have spoken against me with a lying tongue" (v. 2). Then the psalmist presents to God the list of nasty things his enemies wish upon him, using the third-person singular (vv. 6–19)—such as this: "Appoint a wicked man against *him.* . . . When *he* is tried, let *him* come forth guilty; let *his* prayer be counted as sin!" (vv. 6–7 ESV). So in verse 20 the psalmist prays for God to turn these things against them.[24]

Typically, these imprecatory psalmists aren't expressing a desire for *personal vengeance*, but they call on *God* to bring justice—to render to each person what is due.[25] So what is happening in Psalm 109, where the afflicted, traumatized psalmist asks God to make the oppressor's wife a widow and his children orphans (v. 9)? There is a logic to the request for God to judge the wicked. If God brings an end to a wicked oppressor (think of nasty Haman in Esther), then his death means that his wife will be a widow and his children fatherless. This just states the obvious—and this is exactly what God threatens in the Mosaic law (Exod. 22:22–24; cf. Prov. 22:22–23). Such are the natural, realistic consequences that come from God's defending his people. The implication is the same for the heavenly martyrs who call on God to avenge their blood (Rev. 6:9–10); if their murderers are divinely removed from the scene, then their wives will be spouseless and their children fatherless. The psalmist is simply calling on God, who is concerned about the most vulnerable, to help the afflicted.

Table 17.1. "Dashing Your Little Ones": Four Options

Babylon's Royal House	Babylon's Soldiers	Hyperbole	Just Recompense
"Bring an end to the line of oppressors and tyrants."	"Bring an end to those armies that tyrannize and destroy."	Extreme or heightened imagery not intended to be taken literally.	"Just as they have treated others, so may they be treated."

Let's not forget, too, that the psalmist's enemies are malicious. They are bent on destroying the Lord's servant "by all means of the magical effect of curses" (Ps. 109:28).[26] The psalmist calls on God against them. This reflects what the law of Moses calls for: when there is false accusation, priests and judges are to investigate the "malicious witness" and then they "shall do to him just as he had intended to do to his brother" (Deut. 19:16–19).

Emotion and the Lack of Theological Precision?

If psalmists express what is in their anguished hearts, they will often use exaggeration and extreme language. So we could expect some theologically imprecise language at times.[27] One commentator notes that the psalms "allow God's people to vent their feelings" even though we may not give those occasional statements "complete theological endorsement or legitimacy."[28]

Here are some examples of this theological imprecision expressed to God in emotional anguish:

My God, My God, why have you forsaken me? (Ps. 22:1)

You [God] have rejected us. (Ps. 44:9)

O God, You have rejected us. (Ps. 60:1)

You have . . . rejected . . . Your anointed. You have spurned the covenant of Your servant. (Ps. 89:38–39)

You have deceived me, and I was deceived. (Jer. 20:7)

So if someone presses the point about the psalmist's wanting to have literal children dashed against rocks, a *fifth* option is to include a category of theological imprecision due to expression in the midst of outrage and trauma.

Conclusions about Imprecatory Psalms

Psalm 137 and other imprecatory psalms are honest cries from the depths of despair, calling on God to rectify matters. The psalmists have experienced varying

Table 17.2. Three Principles of Imprecation

PRINCIPLE 1: RETRIBUTION *God is a just Judge and Redeemer who takes "vengeance" against tyrants and oppressors.*	This repeated theme is found in the earliest song that Moses and the people sang after the exodus from Egypt (Exod. 15:1–19), followed by Deuteronomy's Song of Moses (31:30–32:43, esp. 32:25–26). This is echoed in the Song of Moses in Revelation 15:3–4 (cf. 6:9–11).
PRINCIPLE 2: PROPORTIONALITY *God will render to each person according to what he has done.*	This *eye-for-eye* principle (*lex talionis*) is repeated in the Mosaic law and throughout the Scriptures (e.g., Prov. 24:29; Rev. 22:12). God will give to each according to his deeds (Rom. 2:6; cf. 1:32: "deserve to die" [ESV] / "worthy of death").
PRINCIPLE 3: COVENANT *The covenant-making God will curse those who curse his own people.*	God will stand against those who oppose his covenant people in defiance of his kingdom and the outworking of his purposes in this world (Gen. 12:3; Ps. 2:1–12; cf. Luke 18:7–8; Acts 9:3).

degrees of traumatization, and they are asking God to step in. We can draw some strands together at the end of this preliminary chapter on these harsh psalms.

First, *these curses are invoked in extreme conditions*—where power is abused, where the helpless are oppressed, and where unthinkable evils are committed. Despite the psalmists' attempt at kindness and generosity to others, these writers were treated cruelly and vindictively in return (e.g., Ps. 41:9).

Second, *rather than taking matters into their own hands, these angry psalmists call on a holy, just God to take vengeance on their behalf.* It is God—not they—who must repay (Deut. 32:35). With no other alternatives, they call on God to act against profound injustice and the oppression of these obstinate persons.

Third, *critics from without should be careful about dismissing pleas for divine judgment as fallen, culturally conditioned, violence-prone requests.* One psalm of David is placed in 2 Samuel 22, where it mentions God's deliverance from David's strong enemy (vv. 18, 49) and how God equips David and gives him victory over his foes (vv. 30, 35–46), and executes vengeance (v. 48). After this psalm, David is described as the "sweet psalmist of Israel" (23:1)—an affirmation followed by his claim to divine inspiration: "The Spirit of the LORD spoke by me, and His word was on my tongue. The God of Israel said, the Rock of Israel spoke to me, . . ." (vv. 2–3). This plain, bold claim serves as a caution against critics from within who frequently dismiss such Old Testament prophetic assertions.

Fourth, *these imprecations are rooted in three primary ideas, which span both testaments.* The "curses" and "woes" of the imprecatory psalms are grounded in principles of *retribution, proportionality,* and *covenant* (see table 17.2).[29]

So contrary to Lewis, we have seen that the imprecatory psalms have a proper moral and theological place in Israelite liturgy and worship. What then about theologian Dietrich Bonhoeffer's claim that only the perfectly innocent Jesus could utter these prayers?

The next chapter examines the New Testament's understanding of these psalms and whether or not the Christian can pray them. Then the chapter thereafter will explore the notion of divine "hatred" and how to make proper sense of it.

18

"Let His Homestead Be Made Desolate"

Imprecatory Psalms in the New Testament

Are Christians Allowed to Pray the Imprecatory Psalms?

You've probably not heard of a procedure called a "psalmectomy."[1] It happens when church authorities or editors at "religious" publishing houses remove offensive-sounding psalms from "Christian" prayer books. For example, Pope Paul VI called for the removal of three imprecatory psalms (Pss. 58, 83, 109) from the Liturgy of Hours. On the Protestant side, the 1979 Episcopal Book of Common Prayer placed some of these psalms in brackets, suggesting they be omitted in worship.

However, all of the psalms—including the "imprecatories"—had been central to Jewish spiritual life and liturgy. (We could add that the ancient Jews didn't edit out warfare texts and other severe passages that were part of Jesus's Bible—the Old Testament—to make it "nicer.") So we must ask: Does the gospel permit us to use them all? Was Bonhoeffer, whom we cited in the last chapter, *in*correct about saying that we dare not pray such prayers?[2] Does the New Testament itself give any indication that they may at times be used by Christians? The answer to all of these questions is yes—but with guarded hearts and self-scrutinizing care.

Blessing and Cursing in the New Testament

"From the Same Mouth Come Both Blessing and Cursing"?

Both testaments express that God prefers to show *kindness*, but *severity* also cuts across *both* testaments. *Both* testaments call for *loving* one's neighbor,

131

including one's own personal enemy, but they also express divine *vengeance* (i.e., just retribution). The New Testament portrays *Jesus himself* as the one who exacts vengeance even though the purpose of his earthly mission was to bring life (John 3:16; 10:10). And in *both* testaments, the overlapping themes of "curse" and "woe" exist—directed at those who defy God's purposes, oppress the saints, and dehumanize others—though this "woe" theme *isn't as pronounced* as in the Old Testament, as we have noted in the last chapter and explore further below.[3]

In *both* testaments, a tension exists. Both Jesus and Paul alike command their hearers to *bless* their personal enemies rather than *curse* them (*kataraomai*: Luke 6:28; Rom. 12:14; James 3:9–10). Yet a closer look at some of the severe things they say reveals that both blessing and cursing are coming from the same mouth (James 3:10)!

Jesus's Severe Words

As we've seen, Jesus spoke harsh words in response to Israel's leaders' hypocrisy and exclusionary nationalism; he pronounced woes on cities that refused to believe in him and the supporting miracles he furnished to vindicate his claims. Even though the Lord rained fire and brimstone down on Sodom and Gomorrah, Jesus said that judgment on Capernaum would be more severe (Gen. 19:14; Matt. 11:23–24; cf. Luke 17:29). So Jesus's rebuke to his disciples who wanted to rain down fire on Jesus-rejecting Samaritan cities (Luke 9:54) was due to the fact that (1) this judgment was premature (Jesus's *first* mission was to save and not condemn or destroy), but worse-than-Sodom-like judgment would eventually fall on such cities of Jesus's day; and (2) the disciples wanted to take matters of judgment into their own hands. But it's not as though such cities didn't have severe judgment awaiting them.

In a parabolic act, Jesus himself "cursed" (*katērasō*) the fig tree, declaring that it would no longer bear any fruit (Mark 11:21; cf. vv. 13–14). Jesus told the religious leaders of his day that "the kingdom of God will be taken away from you and given to a people producing its fruits" (Matt. 21:43 ESV). The fig tree that Jesus cursed represented national Israel, and Jesus was warning that divine judgment would fall on Jerusalem in "this generation" (Matt. 24:34)—that is, with the Roman invasion in AD 70.

At the final judgment Jesus will tell his "accursed" (*katēramenoi*) opponents to depart from him (Matt. 25:41). *Who* curses them? It is God/Jesus, as this verb expresses what scholars call "the divine passive." That is, the unstated subject is *a divine person*. This reflects what the Old Testament says: *the same word is used in the Greek Old Testament*, where God promises to *curse* (Heb. *qalal*) those who curse the offspring of Abraham (Gen. 12:3). Yes, Jesus prohibits malicious *personal* labeling (Matt. 5:22: "fool" [*mōre*]), yet he uses *identical language* for those who are false teachers and stumbling blocks to *others* (Matt. 23:17: "fools" [*mōroi*]). The curse language brings with it a concern for divine protection of the vulnerable or powerless, who could be harmed or led astray.

Jesus's same harsh language against his opponents occurs elsewhere, *primarily related to false teachers and hypocrites, for whom he saved his strongest words of rebuke*:

"swine," "dogs" (Matt. 7:6)

"fools," "brood of vipers" (Matt. 23:17, 33; cf. 3:7, where John the Baptist uses the same "brood of vipers" language)

"your father the devil" (John 8:44)

The "righteous" of Jesus's day not only refused to humble themselves before God made incarnate, but they misled and corrupted others in the process (Matt. 23:15). For those stumbling blocks, Jesus said it would be better for them to have a millstone fastened around their neck and be "drowned in the depth of the sea" (Matt. 18:6). And those who refuse to believe in Jesus are "judged already" (John 3:18). All of this sounds very much like the imprecatory psalms.

Paul's—and Other Apostles'—Severe Words

Just as Jesus directed his most forceful language against religious leaders who misused their authority, Paul too calls false teachers "enemies of the cross" (Phil. 3:18); he calls them "accursed" because they taught a false, distorted gospel that required circumcision and other Jewish identity markers before a person could become a Christian (Gal. 1:8–9). But "neither circumcision nor uncircumcision" ultimately mattered under the new covenant (Gal. 5:6). Christ fulfilled the Abrahamic promise to bring blessing to all the nations; one did not have to become Jewish in order to find acceptance before God.

Elsewhere, Paul writes: "If anyone does not love the Lord, he is to be accursed [*anathema*]" (1 Cor. 16:22). And Paul uses the language of God's "curse" that hangs over Jews attempting to gain righteousness by the law (Gal. 3:10–13). This was not personal, as Paul wished he himself could be "accursed" (*anathema*) for the sake of his fellow ethnic Jews (Rom. 9:3), and he wept for those Judaizers who promoted false teaching (Phil. 3:2–3, 18–19). And this curse that hangs over unbelieving Jews applies to Gentiles too: all of us rebels against God and violators of his law and his righteous character are under God's curse and in need of redemption. Those who are "accursed"—that is, *all* of us without God's saving grace—simply receive just divine judgment; "curse" is simply getting what we deserve from God if we refuse to repent.

Since Paul commands Christians to bless others, he no doubt tried to be kind and prayed for his enemy "Alexander the coppersmith," who "did me much harm." Even so, Paul also plainly states that "the Lord will repay him according to his deeds" (2 Tim. 4:14). And for those mobs who afflicted the Thessalonians?

Paul says it was "just for God to repay [them] with affliction" (2 Thess. 1:6); this was the law of just recompense mentioned in the Old Testament. It wasn't to satisfy a "fallen thirst for vengeance,"[4] despite Boyd's claims. It is instructive to note that, when Paul was in Athens, he was angered when "observing" (*theōrountos*) the idols there, but, even so, he graciously and respectfully engaged in conversation with the Athenians: "I observe [*theōrō*] that you are very religious in all respects" (Acts 17:16, 22). Clearly, there was no personal animus against idolaters.

In addition to Jesus and Paul, we could add a couple other voices. When Simon the magician tries to buy "the gift of God with money," Peter tells him severely, "May your silver perish with you" (Acts 8:20)—a kind of curse.

As we've seen in Revelation, redeemed martyrs in heaven plead for divine justice; they ask God to *judge* and *avenge* their blood (Rev. 6:9–11). And when the wicked city of Babylon will be destroyed, the redeemed can rightly rejoice that cosmic justice has been done (Rev. 18:20).

Interestingly, Boyd gives Jesus a pass on his harsh language of "dogs," "swine," and "fools" because Jesus's harsh words were "motivated by love."[5] But no such leeway is given to the apostles who use the same harsh language (2 Pet. 2:22; Rev. 22:15).[6] Of course, Paul wept for the enemies of the cross whom he called "dogs" (Phil. 3:2, 18). Isn't his harsh language motivated by love too? This is, of course, a *selective* reading of the New Testament. Whether from Jesus or the apostles—let alone the Old Testament—those who *defy* God's kingdom, *distort* the gospel, and *dehumanize* others are "cursed." They stand under God's judgment unless they humble themselves before God and repent—like the persecutor Saul/Paul on the Damascus road.

The New Testament's Use of Imprecatory Psalms

Paul's Use of the Imprecatory Psalms

Boyd denounces David's attitude in Psalm 69:23, where he calls on God to *blind* and *disable* those who are attempting to bring him harm. Because the psalmist aligns himself with God's purposes, these evildoers are reproachful and hostile toward him (vv. 6–9), and the psalmist calls on God to deal with them.

As we've seen, *imprecatory psalmists commonly call on God to do to his enemies what they are plotting against the psalmists*: to fall into the pit that they've dug for the psalmist or to become ensnared in the net they set for him (Pss. 7:14–16; 35:7–8; 57:6). So, logically speaking, *if these opponents are blinded or otherwise physically afflicted, they can't carry out their evil deeds*. Yet our critic from within says that this stands in "direct contradiction to Jesus," who healed the blind and disabled.[7]

As we'll now see, *several New Testament authorities quote various imprecatory psalms*. Indeed, the apostle Paul cites this allegedly mean-spirited Psalm

69 passage in Romans 11:8–10, applying it to hard-hearted Israelites: "Let their table become a snare and a trap, a stumbling block and a retribution for them; let their eyes be darkened so that they cannot see, and bend their backs forever" (ESV). John Goldingay points out with amusement how, even though the New Testament carries on the Old Testament tradition of imprecations, "Western Christians think that people who believe in Jesus should not pray the way these psalms do."[8]

In living demonstration, Paul—while "filled with the Holy Spirit" (Acts 13:9)—not only called Elymas a "son of the devil"; he struck Elymas blind "by the hand of the Lord" (v. 11). This wasn't a *personal* attack. Rather, Elymas had tried to "turn the proconsul away from the faith" (v. 8)—a stumbling block seeking to undermine another's reception of the gospel and the kind of action Jesus considered damnable (Matt. 18:6). This "smiting" passage parallels Peter's actions against Ananias and Sapphira, who were struck dead for lying (Acts 5:5, 10).

As we've seen, that "hand of the Lord" that struck Elymas is the *same* "hand of the Lord" involved in evangelism, with the result that "a large number who believed turned to the Lord" (Acts 11:21). And that "angel of the Lord" who directed Philip to the spiritually searching Ethiopian eunuch (8:26) and also delivered apostles from prison (5:19; 12:7) is the *same* "angel of the Lord" who struck dead the boastful Herod (12:23).

The Ministry of Jesus and the Imprecatory Psalms

In addition to Paul, Jesus himself *twice* quoted imprecatory psalms. He cited Psalms 25 and 69, respectively:

Zeal for Your house will consume Me. (John 2:17)

They hated Me without a cause. (John 15:25)

Then, just after Jesus's ascension, the apostle Peter himself quoted two imprecatory psalms, directed at Judas the traitor (Acts 1:20). As another apostle would need to fill Judas's place, Peter drew from Psalm 69:25: "Let his homestead be made desolate." He then quoted from Psalm 109—"Let another man take his office" (v. 8)—the "worst" of the psalms, according to C. S. Lewis![9]

But didn't Jesus come to give life rather than to "steal and kill and destroy" (John 10:10)? But we've seen that Jesus himself threatened to "throw [Jezebel] on a sickbed" and to "strike [her followers] dead" (Rev. 2:20–23). And in Jude 5, Jesus's half brother directly connects *Jesus* to lethal judgment: "Jesus, who saved a people out of the land of Egypt, afterward destroyed those who did not believe" (ESV). Yes, Jesus heals and saves, but he can also strike dead those who lead his people astray—or judge the rebellious Israelites of old. So in certain contexts of judgment, Jesus *does* indeed physically *kill* and *destroy*—though not steal!

The Old Testament encourages loving one's personal enemies and praying for persecutors. Jesus does so too, but he approves of believers' prayers "day and night" for God to "bring about justice" (Luke 18:7–8; cf. Rev. 6:9–11). Revelation 18:4–6 calls for this same justice: "Pay her back even as she has paid, and give back to her double according to her deeds; in the cup which she has mixed, mix twice as much for her." Some of our critics from within might say that this cry sounds like a voice *from hell*. But John tells us that this is a voice *from heaven* denouncing the wicked city of Babylon.

Imprecatory Psalms in an International Context

What does a Pakistani Christian do when his daughter is kidnapped at gunpoint and then is forced to marry a Muslim against her wishes? What about Coptic Christians in the Sinai Peninsula being systematically forced to convert to Islam or be shot?[10] How should we react when Nigerian Christian girls are kidnapped, raped, and enslaved by the terrorist group Boko Haram—not to mention this group's displacing entire communities, slaughtering as these terrorizers roam the "Christianized" countryside?[11]

And there's Elizabeth—a young Christian girl who was kidnapped and forced into prostitution in southeast Asia. In her anguish, she wrote these verses of hope on the wall of her "crib": "The LORD is my light and my salvation—whom shall I fear? The LORD is the stronghold of my life—of whom shall I be afraid? When evil men advance against me to devour my flesh, when my enemies and my foes attack me, they will stumble and fall" (Ps. 27:1–2). Thankfully, she was rescued by members of the International Justice Mission, and she would go on to college and eventually graduate.[12] Just coercive force to rescue or prevent such evils is an act of loving one's neighbor; indeed, it is necessary to rescue those being dragged away to death and slaughter (Prov. 24:11).

Given these kinds of stories, those imprecatory psalms start to sound all the more appropriate. Yes, *we desire the salvation of terrorists and kidnappers and murderers in hopes that they, like the former persecutor Saul, might be converted.* But if they persist in their ways, we pray for divine justice to be done: "Pay them back" (cf. Rev. 18:6).

Goldingay reminds often-comfortable Western Christians that these psalms shouldn't be an embarrassment to us, who often don't have any *true* enemies compared to the truly persecuted and oppressed believers in other parts of the world.[13] In their case, they "may not find [such psalms] incongenial."[14] African Christians have faced pernicious accusations of witchcraft, which bring them devastation, harm, and shame.[15] Indeed, in places "where enemies will use spiritual forces to bring harm to others through charms and recitations, Christians have come to see the imprecatory psalms as psalms of protection and defense."[16]

Praying for God to vindicate his name and to bring justice for his people and deal with their enemies—however he chooses—is exactly the point of Jesus's story of the persistent widow. Indeed, the New Testament has its share of imprecatory prayers and requests for divine vengeance (Acts 8:20; 2 Tim. 4:14; Rev. 6:9–11; 11:17–18; 15:2–4; 16:5–7; 18:1–8). God is an avenger (1 Thess. 4:6),[17] and imprecations from both testaments are a call for the "public vindication of God's truth" in that they express a willingness to make God's enemies our enemies.[18]

As biblical scholar N. T. Wright comments on the imprecatory psalms, "If there is injustice, if the poor are being oppressed, then it is right to pray that God will rid the world of that. Part of our reaction to the so-called 'cursing Psalms' is that we think the modern world basically has the problem of evil solved. The Psalms bring us up short and say, 'No, evil is real, and some people are so wicked that we simply must wish judgment upon them.'"[19]

Real Enemies, Real Wickedness, Real Anguish

As we've seen, with some modification for hyperbole or metaphor, the imprecatory psalms don't seem so far-fetched after all. These psalms express a concern to counter the false conclusion of the wicked—that "God does not care, is powerless, or even may not exist."[20]

So, what are some major takeaways here?

Marcionite dangers? The scholar Erich Zenger boldly suggests that those who reject wholesale the imprecatory psalms reflect a Marcionite perspective. These psalms capture the spirit of justice and reward throughout Scripture, but Marcionism, he claims, ultimately rejected the fundamental theme of "a dramatic conflict between the righteous and wicked."[21] While we must be careful about using labels of "heresy," we should also compare certain family resemblances and ask whether the same tendencies Marcion exhibited are resurfacing today.

God's action. Certain acts are "worthy of death" (Rom. 1:32). The imprecatory psalms reveal that it's better to pray for *God* to punish the wicked than to personally take matters into *our own hands* and attempt to retaliate out of vengeance. This may not necessarily mean God's taking their lives, but it may involve one step short of this—namely, God's thwarting their plans (e.g., Ps. 35:4–6).

Hope in God's justice. And if the wicked refuse to repent for their shedding innocent blood and their acts of dehumanization, it is right to pray in hope that God will bring about cosmic justice, honoring his holy name and reputation.

Persecuted Christians. There are an estimated 340 million Christians living in areas of high-level persecution. To pray these imprecatory prayers is an attempt to stand with these brothers and sisters in Christ.[22] The same is true *wherever* people are dehumanized and traumatized through rape, sexual enslavement, and other forms of oppression.[23] These psalms awaken us and shake us out of our passivity to resist a world of profound suffering and oppression. We Westernized Christians have largely lost sight of two things:

1. *The suffering of others* (How often do we pray for the persecuted church?)
2. *The final judgment* that awaits those who think they are getting away with oppression, violence, and tyranny (Rev. 18:20)

Indeed, the book of Revelation—along with the imprecatory psalms—reminds us of these realities, and they serve as great comfort to Christians in non-Western settings.

Taking up the imprecatory psalms—with care. In praying the imprecatory psalms, *we may see ourselves within them*—perhaps *not* even as the suffering psalmist, but as those who may somehow contribute to the oppression of others, or at best, who ignore the plight of the oppressed. So when the author of Psalm 139 speaks out strongly against God's enemies (vv. 19–22), he also shows spiritual sensitivity by asking God to search him and test his thoughts (vv. 23–24).

Concluding Thoughts

Zenger observes how these "psalms of zeal" are no longer a part of the modern Western church's prayer life, with our cushioned, self-satisfied living. This is why we often find them odd and bewildering. He argues that to remove these stinging, harsh psalms—or portions of them—from our Psalters and prayer books reflects a residual Marcionism but could even reflect an anti-Semitic ideology. We can be too quick with our "nice" Christianized clichés and comebacks without properly understanding the psalmists in their ancient Near Eastern as well as individual contexts.

Beyond this, *these psalms awaken us and shake us out of our passivity to resist a world of profound suffering and oppression.* Since we Westernized Christians have largely lost sight of the suffering of others and of the final judgment that awaits, these psalmists remind us of that day to come.

True, the New Testament *more strongly emphasizes love and blessing and kindness*—even of one's enemies—than the Old. But *the New Testament doesn't suddenly drop the theme of curse and woe.* The Old Testament emphasizes temporal, physical judgments against Israel and other nations, but the New Testament does too, if to a lessened degree—for example, Jesus's pronouncements against Jerusalem (Matt. 24; Mark 13; Luke 21) and his other temporal judgments as well (Rev. 2:15–16, 20–23; cf. Acts 13:11; 1 Cor. 11:29–30).

Scholar John Day puts it this way: "The [spirit] of the Imprecatory Psalms, in the face of sustained injustice, hardened enmity, and gross oppression, is consistent with the ethics both of the Old and New Testaments, while at the same time recognizing that the New Testament evidences a certain progress in the outworking of that essentially equivalent ethic."[24]

The imprecatory psalms provide a rich resource for disempowered, marginalized, and oppressed Christians. The entire church needs to pay closer attention to the imprecatory psalmists' spirit, which is ultimately in line with the full-orbed gospel. We need look no further than to those redeemed martyred saints in heaven who call on a "holy and true" God to "judge" and to "avenge" their blood (Rev. 6:9–11). The *martyrs'* cruciform and Christ-centered theological stance reminds all believers that God is the great Defender and Avenger, upon whom we may call with humility and fear.

19

Loving Jacob, Hating Esau?

Putting Divine and Human Hatred in Perspective

"I Have Loved Jacob; but I Have Hated Esau"

"I have loved you," says the LORD. But you say, "How have You loved us?" "Was not Esau Jacob's brother?" declares the LORD. "Yet I have loved Jacob; but I have hated Esau, and I have made his mountains a desolation and appointed his inheritance for the jackals of the wilderness." Though Edom says, "We have been beaten down, but we will return and build up the ruins"; thus says the LORD of hosts, "They may build, but I will tear down; and men will call them the wicked territory, and the people toward whom the LORD is indignant forever."

—Malachi 1:2–4

This passage has troubled many readers. And it's not just an Old Testament thing. Paul quoted this passage in Romans 9:13. He said that before Rebecca gave birth to Jacob and Esau—they were womb-mates—and before they could do anything good or bad, God had determined: "The older will serve the younger" (v. 12). Was God's "loving" Jacob and "hating" Esau unjust? Paul insists that it was not (v. 14).

If God is a God of love, how can he *hate*? And isn't it arbitrary for God to love one people (or person) and to hate another without any basis? A closer look at this text brings some illumination and clarity.

First, *the original context of Malachi refers to God's prerogative to choose one nation over another*. In the original context of Malachi, the Israelites ask God, "How have You loved *us*?" (1:2)—that is, the *nation* of Israel. The text continues in this vein, speaking of God's judgment on the nation of Edom, Esau's offspring:

140

"*We* have been beaten down. . . . *They* may build . . ." (1:4). Indeed, God had told Rebecca that there were "two nations" in her womb (Gen. 25:23). A good, just God has complete authority to choose *any* nation to be his particular channel of blessing. This, however, is a selection not to *salvation* but to *mission*, as we'll soon see.

Second, *Romans 9 reminds us that a sovereign God can select not only a nation (Israel over Edom) but also individuals (Jacob over Esau) to accomplish a certain task or mission.* Think of the somewhat fictitious film *Amadeus* (1984): the lesser but hard-working composer Salieri felt justified in rejecting Christ, symbolized by burning a crucifix in the fire; after all, how could Jesus bypass him and pour out such exquisite musical talents on an impious scoundrel like Mozart, who could compose final, polished musical scores on the very first attempt? But God is beholden to no one. We have no claim on him. All is of grace.

Likewise, in choosing Jacob over Esau, God's free choice is independent of either person's good or bad deeds. This is why Jesus told his disciples, including Judas Iscariot: "Have I not chosen you, the Twelve? Yet one of you is a devil!" (John 6:70 NIV).

Third, *these texts don't indicate that Esau as a person was somehow divinely blocked from finding salvation.* Esau's problem was his own immorality and godlessness—not God's damning him before he was born (Heb. 12:16). Though God didn't choose Esau (Edom), this fact by itself wouldn't prevent him from experiencing personal salvation. And God's choosing this or that person—or nation—for a task or mission doesn't thereby guarantee their salvation. Though they could overlap, *salvation* and *mission* are distinct, much like God's choosing Judah over Joseph to establish the *messianic* line (Gen. 49:8–12), which was independent of the question of salvation. Paul had been chosen to be a messenger to the Gentiles, but he still had a choice to respond to that commission. He reported that he had not been *disobedient* to the heavenly vision (Acts 26:19).

Fourth, *"love" and "hate" in Scripture are often comparative terms.* "Hate" can merely mean "love less." For example, Jesus spoke about a disciple's being so devoted to him that his follower's relationship to parents may appear as "hate" (Luke 14:26). However, the parallel passage makes clear that Jesus warned against *loving* one's father and mother *more than* Christ (Matt. 10:37).

Fifth, *God's choosing Jacob/Israel wasn't a guarantee of salvation for most Israelites.* Early on, most Israelites perished in unbelief in the wilderness (Heb. 3:7–19)—the generation with whom God made a covenant at Mount Sinai. By contrast, Jesus preached to the descendants of Esau (Edom): those from the region of Idumea (Edomites) came to hear him (Mark 3:8). Of course, Amos anticipated a day of restoration of "the fallen booth of David," when the Gentiles would be gathered into the people of God (Amos 9:10–12). That includes "the remnant of Edom" and "all the nations who are called by My name"—an event that was being fulfilled in the first century as the gospel went to the Gentiles (Acts 15:16–18). Even back in Deuteronomy, the Israelites were commanded: "You shall not detest an Edomite, for he is your brother" (Deut. 23:7). God didn't literally "hate" Edom, as we commonly think of that word (we'll look at the word "hate" in the next section).

Sixth, *even nations God had not originally chosen would be incorporated into the people of God.*[1] The Old Testament mentions nations hostile to Israel that would one day be included as part of the fulfillment of God's promise to bless the nations through Abraham (Gen. 12:1–3)—a promise ultimately fulfilled in Jesus Christ (Gal. 3:26–29).

> I will record Rahab [Egypt] and Babylon
>   among those who acknowledge me—
> Philistia too, and Tyre, along with Cush [Ethiopia]—
>   and will say, "This one was born in Zion."
> Indeed, of Zion it will be said,
>   "This one and that one were born in her,
>   and the Most High himself will establish her."
> The LORD will write in the register of the peoples:
>   "This one was born in Zion." (Ps. 87:4–6 NIV)

> In that day there will be a highway from Egypt to Assyria, and the Assyrians will come into Egypt and the Egyptians into Assyria, and the Egyptians will worship with the Assyrians. In that day Israel will be the third party with Egypt and Assyria, a blessing in the midst of the earth, whom the LORD of hosts has blessed, saying, "Blessed is Egypt My people, and Assyria the work of My hands, and Israel My inheritance." (Isa. 19:23–25)

Isaiah 19 uses language from Exodus 3:7–12: the Lord heard the cry of "My people" in Egypt, and he promised to deliver them using signs and bringing them to the land he promised. In a future redemptive turn, Egypt along with Assyria will also be called "My people." As Christopher Wright has put it, those enemy nations hostile to Israel would be moved from God's "hit list" of judgment to his "home list" of redemption.[2] That is, *the plans he had for Israel are the plans he has for Egypt (and Assyria) as well.* These nations have the same "chosen" status.[3]

So God's choice of Israel (whom he "loved") was not an injustice to other nations. Jon Levinson points out: "The fact that you love your husband or wife in a very special sense does not imply an injustice towards other men and women. Nor does it imply that, by objective criteria, those other individuals do not surpass your beloved in various respects."[4]

In addition, God did not enter into a covenant with Israel due to this people's moral credentials (Deut. 6:10–15; 9:4–6). God's choosing Israel and delivering this people out of bondage in Egypt was a gracious gift. *This gracious act—* rather than God's sheer power or sovereignty—called for Israel's gratitude. This excludes any spirit of complacence or a sense of entitlement—of "mistaking gifts for possessions"—for which God often rebuked Israel.[5]

"Loving the Sinner, Hating the Sin"?

> The boastful shall not stand before your eyes;
>   you hate all evildoers.
>
> —Psalm 5:5 ESV

> The LORD tests the righteous,
>   but his soul hates the wicked and the one who loves violence.
>
> —Psalm 11:5 ESV

> Do I not hate those who hate You, O LORD?
>   And do I not loathe those who rise up against You?
>
> —Psalm 139:21 ESV

Those who have been in Christian circles a long time have likely heard the statement "We should love the sinner but hate the sin." After all, Jesus commanded his disciples to love their enemies—and not follow the common claim of his day to "hate your enemy" (Matt. 5:43).

But what do we do with these quotations from Psalms 5 and 11? They speak of divine hatred. David uses this "hatred" language in Psalm 139:21–22—toward those who rise up against God. Should we *imitate* this inspired author's hatred? What is even meant by the terms "hate" or "hatred" (*sane/sinah*)? *Can* we really separate sin from sinner? How can we righteously, safely pray to God against certain persons? We briefly explore these questions below.

For starters, *this hatred isn't personal.* Rather, "hatred" refers to *standing against or opposing such persons—taking a "zero-tolerance" stance toward those who oppose ("hate") God.*[6] In Psalm 139, David was angered by those who would oppose or "rise up against" God. In response, he set himself up in opposition to them as well.[7] He essentially declares, "I stand with God over against the wicked."[8]

God "hated" Esau (Edom) by siding with—making a covenant with—Israel. And when Edom acted treacherously against Israel, God set himself in opposition to Edom for this (Obad. 10; Mal. 1:4). We've seen that Jesus used this strong language of allegiance to him, which can look like hatred toward one's parents, even though, as Jesus makes clear, loving or honoring parents is divinely commanded (Mark 7:9–13).

Can We Separate the Sin from the Sinner?

We *can't* tidily separate or abstract the *sinner* (e.g., an adulterer) from the *sin* (committing adultery)—or from sin's *consequences* (e.g., ravaged marriages and families, out-of-wedlock births). Or think about those who make their livelihood by kidnapping girls and selling them into sexual slavery.⁹ To oppose their evil *deeds* is to oppose *them*.

God *can love sinners (John 3:16) while at the same time his wrath remains on them (3:36).* Likewise, when we see oppression, some of that indignation ("hatred") should rise up within us as we align ourselves with God's purposes and call on God to resist or even stop ("hold . . . back") those who oppress (Prov. 24:11–12). God's standing against sinners themselves makes sense because of the damage sinners are doing to themselves and to others. *To oppose the sin will involve opposing the sinner.* After all, God himself will judge *the sinner*, not *sin* in the abstract.

Examining Our Hearts

Just after David spoke about opposing ("hating") those who oppose God, *he acknowledged the potential danger that lurks in every heart that cries out for justice:* "Search me, O God, and know my heart; try me and know my anxious thoughts; and see if there be any hurtful way in me, and lead me in the everlasting way" (Ps. 139:23–24).

A fine line exists here. Just as God desires the repentance of the terrorist, serial killer, and tyrant, who destroy or dehumanize others (2 Pet. 3:9), we rightly ask for God to intervene—drastically, if necessary—*if they do not repent*, so that their oppression would cease. Paul *wept* for those who led others astray with false doctrine (Phil. 3:18–19), but he *called for just judgment* on them if they didn't repent (Gal. 1:8–9; 5:12).

We've seen that the wicked king Manasseh humbled himself before God after having done "more evil than the nations whom the LORD destroyed before the sons of Israel" (2 Chron. 33:9). We should always be open to—and rejoice in—God's mercy on repentant sinners. But God will also judge even his own people—just as he had done to the Canaanites: "As I plan to do to them, so I will do to you" (Num. 33:56).

Such texts serve as a warning for us: we must be on guard against *our own* evil hearts lest we stand in God's way and thwart his purposes. As the late Christian statesman John Stott wisely wrote about those who are hostile to God: "We cannot desire their salvation in defiance of their own unwillingness to receive it. This is the heart of the matter."¹⁰ He added: "We should earnestly desire the salvation of sinners if they would repent and equally, earnestly desire their (and our) destruction if they (or we) will not."¹¹ So perhaps we could modify the psalmist's words about those who defy God: *"Work in their heart—or stop their heart—but examine my heart."*

The New Testament verifies the appropriateness of praying against *defiant, unrepentant* evildoers who oppress and lead astray (Matt. 23:32–36; Luke 18:7–8; 1 Cor. 16:22; Gal. 1:8–9; 2 Thess. 1:6–10; 1 Tim. 1:20; Rev. 6:9–11; 18:20). These prayers, along with the imprecatory psalms, are ultimately an act of *surrender*, leaving the prerogative of vengeance to Yahweh in acknowledgment that justice belongs to him. He must bring resolution. The pattern in the imprecatory psalms can be summarized thus: "This act of surrender is central. Justice is something that only Yahweh can bring about, and it must be left to him."[12]

We've seen that God's "hatred" of Esau (Edom) means choosing Jacob (Israel) over him to be a vehicle of blessing to the nations. In general, divine hatred against the wicked means God opposes or sets himself against them and their agenda. But this opposition doesn't exclude divine love toward all sinners (John 3:16). And when it comes to separating "loving the sinner" from "hating the sin," this seems like a theologically tidy division, but it is ultimately problematic. In the end God will judge sinners, not merely their sin. And while we should pray against those who harm and oppress or distort the gospel that God would obstruct their purposes or deal justly with them in his own way, we do so with a grieved spirit, as our ultimate hope is that they repent and find salvation.

PART 5

Of Human Bondage

*Women and Servants in
Israelite Society*

20

Is the Old Testament Really
Misogynistic and Patriarchal?

Oppressed Women in a "Male-Dominated" Israelite Society?

Andy Stanley asserts that, unlike the New Testament, the Mosaic law promotes "misogyny" and views women as "commodities" rather than "partners."[1] Likewise, the liberal feminist theologian Rosemary Ruether claims that the Old Testament endorses the "enslavement of persons within the Hebrew family itself: namely, women and children."[2] *Misogyny* (hatred of women) and *commodities* and *enslavement* (females as property) are strong declarations, but are they accurate?

On closer examination, the picture is far different. Though less-than-ideal in many ways, the role of women in Israelite culture was significantly more nuanced than many "anti-patriarchy" critics proclaim. Indeed, the term "patriarchy" gets thrown around quite a bit in scholarly literature, and I've used it myself in the past.[3]

Now, there *were* less-than-ideal cultural conditions affecting male-female relations. The father/husband in a household had a presumed legal priority over others. He served as the official point person of the home and thus the buffer between the household and broader Israelite society. Perhaps some might call this a "soft patriarchy."

However, many critics use "patriarchy" in a very *vague, negative sense*; they mean something like "male dominance" or "pyramidal hierarchy."[4] But a good portion of recent scholarship has called into question this very ill-fitting category for ancient Israel. That is, even if Israelite males overall had greater cultural or legal sway in certain areas, to use the label "patriarchy" might be misleading.

149

Carol Meyers of Duke University and former president of the prestigious Society of Biblical Literature raised the question in her 2013 presidential address: "Was Ancient Israel a Patriarchal Society?"[5] Her response was "No, ancient Israel should not be called a patriarchal society, for the term 'patriarchy' is an inadequate and misleading designation of the social reality of ancient Israel."[6] She added that patriarchy is a "modern construct."[7] Even if a perfect "gender equality" wasn't present in Israelite society, it was a far cry from being "male-dominated."

How Patriarchal Was Ancient Israel?

Down with Patriarchy! Up with Heterarchy!

The term "patriarchy"—a seventeenth-century term—is problematic and needs serious overhauling. It conjures up inaccurate notions: absolute male domination and authority in society and within a household; intrinsic male superiority because of physical strength and intelligence; the exclusion of women from social influence; the status of women as victims to male-dominated social forces; and the treatment of women as property.

Over the past 150 years or so, much critical biblical scholarship has assumed a strong patriarchal (male-dominated) outlook in Israel. This scholarship has drawn on disciplines such as anthropology and sociology, which have themselves been strongly influenced by—among other factors—Marxism, Darwinian (naturalistic) evolutionism, and feminism.

This perspective has not held up well. The landscape is actually changing, thanks to a cluster of scholars—including a new wave of feminist theorists—who have rejected previous misrepresentations of the woman's status in ancient Israel.[8]

Meyers has not only asserted that Israel was not patriarchal, but she has elsewhere urged readers of the Old Testament to rethink such "constructed" categories: "It is time for us to acknowledge that patriarchy is a Western, constructed concept, not a 'social law' or an immutable feature of all societies. As a constructed model, it is essentially an oversimplification and systematization of data used for comparative purposes. And as for all such models, new information can and should mean that it has outlived its usefulness."[9] In other words, the term "patriarchy" is difficult to define and is often used far too loosely or misapplied. For example, does "patriarchy" refer to male sexual or reproductive dominance, to the father's power in the household, or to male-based power structures that oppress women?

Another problem is that the term is *anachronistic*—namely, it's of a more recent vintage based on Marxist ideology and more modern sociological categories.[10] Yet this label has been simplistically slapped onto ancient Israel in a one-size-fits-all fashion. However, it actually doesn't apply to the much more nuanced and complex setting of ancient Israelites living in the Iron Age (1200–600 BC). While there was a certain male dominance in Israel, it was only *fragmentary*—not at all sweeping, absolute, or totalistic.[11]

For example, in Genesis and elsewhere men like Abraham and Jacob hardly exhibit "male dominance" and "pyramidal hierarchy."[12] They are at times dominated or overruled by their wives (e.g., Gen. 21:10–13; 30:14–17). Or consider how inheritance was *patrilineal* (i.e., passed on to succeeding generations through the male line). But when the daughters of Zelophehad challenged this, God approved of their request and affirmed their right to the inheritance (Num. 27:1–11).

John Goldingay acknowledges that Israel was "less patriarchal" than we might think. He goes so far as to say that it was "relatively egalitarian."[13] So instead of patriarchy, Meyers suggests the much more flexible concept of *heterarchy*. This concept recognizes the existence of multiple, complex hierarchies of "power dynamics" that involved both independence and mutual dependence: "Israelite women were not dominated in all aspects of Israelite society but rather were autonomous actors in multiple aspects of household and community life."[14]

The Unkosher Treatment of Women?

Moral Monster looked in detail at the symbolic significance of Israel's kosher laws (Lev. 11; Deut. 14).[15] One reason for kosher foods was that they marked Israel's set-apartness among the nations; Israel's food was to be an identity marker for God's people. Of course, later on Jesus would declare all foods clean (Mark 7:19), indicating that what disciples in the new covenant community ate was no longer a mark of belonging or identity. Paul too acknowledged that no food is inherently unclean since all that God has created is good (1 Tim. 4:1–5; cf. Gen. 1:31).[16]

As it turns out, the Mosaic law's discussion of kosher food prompted one author to bring gender and power relations into the conversation. How so? To focus on kosher food is to focus on *meat*. Yet doing so ignores the proper place of *grain* in Israelite life. The alleged implication is that this emphasis overlooks the role of women, who devoted so much time to preparing grains for food: "The trend of privileging meat eating with sacred practices (as in Lev. 11) while giving no 'textual space' to those parts of the diet that women produced and prepared effectively marginalizes what women bring to the table and the hard work behind it."[17]

What should we make of this? Is there a kernel of truth to this charge that discussion of kosher foods marginalized women in ancient Israel? Not at all. The average Israelite's diet was much more plant-based (grains, fruit, olives), and meat wasn't typically on the menu. So for practical purposes, kosher laws would largely have been irrelevant in Israel.[18] Wealthy Israelites would have meat in their diet, but the average Israelite would have meat at Passover and on other special occasions.[19]

Furthermore, Old Testament texts devote plenty of space to the place of life-sustaining grain—from the latter chapters of Genesis (buying grain in Egypt, Joseph's managing grain production and distribution), to grain harvesting in

Ruth, to prophetic texts that mention the stages of planting, harvesting, threshing, and grinding grain and producing food from grains (e.g., Isa. 28:24–29;
Ezek. 4:9).

Truly, grain in the home was primarily under the control of women, and their
role was "essential for household survival": "Senior women functioned as the
COOs (Chief Operating Officers) of their households. They were hardly oppressed and powerless. Nor were they subordinate to male control in all aspects
of household life. Rather, in subsistence households in traditional societies comparable to ancient Israel, when women and men both make significant economic
contributions to household life, female–male relationships are marked by inter-
dependence or mutual dependence."[20] In these male-female partnerships, "men
dominated some aspects, women others."[21] That is, male domination in Israel
was *fragmentary*, not totalistic or absolute. Again, "Israelite women were not
dominated in all aspects of Israelite society but rather were autonomous actors
in multiple aspects of household and community life"—that is, *heterarchy* rather
than *patriarchy*.[22]

Ancient Israelite Women and "Rosie the Riveter"

You are probably familiar with the iconic World War II poster featuring "Rosie
the Riveter." She was the tough- and determined-looking woman sporting a red
bandana and flexing her muscles. This image inspired many women to enter the
industrial workforce vacated by men in order to support the war effort. In the
poster, she tells women, "We can do it!"

Ancient Israel had its share of women with that can-do spirit, often operating
independently of men. As we saw, recent scholarship is increasingly recognizing
just how empowered and involved Israelite women—those ancient "Rosies"—
really were.

Consider how these strong women could rise to positions of leadership and
exert great influence:

- Miriam the prophetess (Exod. 15:20), who was part of the leadership team
  "sent" by God to go before Israel in the wilderness (Mic. 6:4)
- Deborah the prophetess and judge in Israel (Judg. 4:4–5)
- Huldah the prophetess (2 Kings 22:14)
- Esther the queen (Esther 2:17), who courageously risked her life to deliver
  her people from extermination
- the "strong" or "capable" (*hayil*) woman of Proverbs 31:10–31, who is
  clearly the manager of her home, is industrious, engages in trade and
  commerce (vv. 14, 24), purchases property from her earnings (v. 16), and
  makes decisions quite independent of her husband, who fully trusts her
  (v. 11)

- Ruth, likewise called a "strong" or "capable" woman (Ruth 3:11), who was a foreigner who came to live in Israel
- Ruth's mother-in-law Naomi, who knew what was happening around her, took her own initiative, and worked behind the scenes to help Ruth (3:1–6, 18)
- the "wise woman" of Tekoa, with whom the military commander Joab consulted (2 Sam. 14:2)
- the female sage of Abel Beth-maacah (2 Sam. 20:14–22)

This female independent decision-making was evident elsewhere in various places in the Old Testament:

- Abigail, who apportioned a large number of foodstuffs without consulting her husband (1 Sam. 25)
- Micah's mother, who had access to two hundred pieces of silver, which she used to build a household shrine (Judg. 17)
- the Shunammite woman, who was called a "prominent [*gedolah*] woman" in Shunem (2 Kings 4:8), wielded much influence, and even ended up persuading the king to restore her property rights after her property had been taken over by squatters (2 Kings 8:1–6)[23]

In addition to upright women, there were some influential female "baddies" as well:

- Jezebel, the queen and wife of Ahab (1 Kings 18–19, 21; 2 Kings 9)
- Athaliah, the queen mother of Ahaziah (2 Kings 11)
- Noadiah, the false prophetess who attempted to intimidate Nehemiah (Neh. 6:14)

The Old Testament reveals how prominent women were leaders and influencers in Israel.[24]

Israel's "Guilded" Age

The United States experienced the "gilded age" of industrialization and economic growth from around 1870 to 1900. In the ancient Near East, Israelite women lived in a "*guilded* age." That is, they were quite involved in various vocational guilds—groups or associations for females who were experts in certain fields. These included crafts as well as trades. Women were what we could call "professional" singers or musicians (1 Chron. 25:5–6; Ezra 2:65). They were also hired as mourners and served as prophetesses. This could also take on a dark side— for example, they could be soothsayers or witches (e.g., 1 Sam. 28:7). They also engaged in psychological care, counseling, midwifery, and health care.[25] The result was that women could "achieve status and recognition that [are] not dependent on the parameters set by male-oriented kinship patterns."[26]

True, Israelite women didn't serve as priestesses—but the vast majority of Israelite men also did not serve as priests. And only Aaron's descendants within the tribe of Levi could serve as high priests. However, women could serve in an informal capacity at the house of God—"at the doorway of the tent of meeting" (Exod. 38:8; cf. 1 Sam. 2:22). By contrast, in other ancient Near Eastern cultures, women could officially serve as cult prostitutes (Deut. 23:17), and priestesses represented the female consort of the national deity. So when God's "covenant wife," Israel (cf. Ezek. 16; Hosea), turned the pagan goddess Asherah into Yahweh's consort, this was a treasonous covenantal violation (Deut. 16:21; 2 Kings 21:7).[27]

In the continuum between the ideals of Genesis 1–2 and total male domination, Israel's situation is still nonideal. We've seen that although the term "patriarchy" is anachronistic and carries too much ideological baggage, males in Israel tended to have greater legal and official roles than females; even so, a growing number of scholars believe that a term like "heterarchy" is more accurate than "patriarchy" as a description of Israelite society. The social dynamic in ancient Israel included empowered, influential women and female professionals. They were regularly appreciated in marriage partnership, in running households, and in guilds and associations in the broader Israelite society. Even if not the ideal of Eden, the situation in Israel was certainly a far cry from the "misogynistic" or "women as commodities" claim.

21

Espousing Multiple Wives?

Revisiting the Matter of Polygamy

Engendering Confusion

> For this reason a man shall leave his father and his mother, and be joined to his wife; and they shall become one flesh.
>
> —Genesis 2:24

A critic from without, Jennifer Wright Knust, says in her book *Unprotected Texts* that the Bible endorses premarital sex, prostitution, and same-sex sexual relations.[1] The subtitle of her book is *The Bible's Surprising Contradictions about Sex and Desire*. She asks what happens when we read marriage texts in the Bible "literally" or "seriously." Well, "we might have polygamy again. We might have not only polygamy with wives" but "with concubines and slaves." She adds that the New Testament presents marriage as a waste of time and a distraction, according to Paul (1 Cor. 7). Overall, the Bible offers us zero guidance when it comes to marriage.[2]

While we can't address all of the confusions here,[3] we can offer a few responses. First, *certain biblical contexts or distinct emphases by biblical authors may raise certain tensions or questions about various issues, and we may have to let these questions "sit" without any further information available to resolve them*. In other cases, we can see more clearly what is going on. For instance, biblical authors will leave or include material in accordance with the theological emphasis they want to present. Samuel and Kings present the "warts and all" of Israel's kings— David's adultery, Solomon's idolatry, Manasseh's deep apostasy. By contrast,

Chronicles highlights God's blessings on Judah's kings when they trust in him (cf. 2 Chron. 20:20), but it doesn't mention David's adultery or Solomon's idolatry, and it adds mention of the imprisoned Manasseh's repentance after his long-standing apostasy (2 Chron. 33:12–13). But the reader of Chronicles would have been well aware of those kingly failures as part of the backdrop of Israel's royal history.

Second, *actions that are described in the Old Testament aren't necessarily mean prescribed.* Is shouldn't be confused with *ought.* The fact that (a) God doesn't directly judge a deviant action or (b) a biblical narrator doesn't "call out" human beings who act sinfully doesn't equal "approval." Biblical *testimonials* are not necessarily *templates.*[4] So even if polygamy is permitted in the Old Testament, that doesn't mean it is on par with the marital ideal of monogamy in Genesis 2:24.

Third, *a number of biblical narratives are particularly geared to help us empathize with people in difficult circumstances.* The desperate woman Tamar had been wronged by her father-in-law, Judah, prompting her to act as a prostitute. Because he had broken his promise to give his son Shelah to Tamar in marriage, she enticed Judah into a sexual encounter so he would at least give her offspring, even if it wasn't through Shelah (Gen. 38:11, 21–22). Yes, the Bible condemns prostitution (Deut. 23:17), but the narrator paints a sympathetic picture of Tamar in a difficult situation created by Judah. Tamar was a desperate woman and Judah a promise-breaker. Other narratives defending women against men could be included here.

Fourth, *even if the Old Testament incidentally mentions multiple wives or prostitution or premarital sex, its standard operating procedure regarding marriage and sexuality is the creational pattern.* The norm or ideal is spelled out in Genesis 2:24—reinforced by Jesus (Matt. 19:3–6): *one man and one woman as one flesh for one lifetime.*[5] In Matthew 19, Jesus presented the essence of marriage:

- *exclusivity:* "A man shall leave his father and his mother and be joined to his wife" (v. 5)
- *complementarity:* "male and female"; "a man . . . his wife" (vv. 4, 5)
- *conjugality:* "The two shall become one flesh" (v. 5)
- *permanency:* "What therefore God has joined together, let no man separate" (v. 6)

Fifth, *in addition to the general sexual-marital ideal laid out in Genesis, Israel's own covenantal context was critical.* At the heart of ancient Near Eastern law collections is the emphasis on preserving order and promoting stability. This is quite distinct from Western values like individual rights, democracy, free markets, and personal privacy.[6] In ancient Israel, *stability* and *well-ordered family life* were crucial for the nation's ongoing social and religious function. And as noted in *Moral Monster,* laws regarding women that at first glance seem harsh turn out to be aimed at protecting women from certain vulnerable situations or outcomes.[7]

Revisiting the Topic of Polygamy

And you shall not take a woman as a rival wife to her sister, uncovering her nakedness while her sister is still alive.

—Leviticus 18:18 ESV

Thus says the LORD God of Israel, "It is I who anointed you king over Israel and it is
I who delivered you from the hand of Saul. I also gave you your master's house and
your master's wives into your care, and I gave you the house of Israel and Judah; and
if that had been too little, I would have added to you many more things like these!"

—2 Samuel 12:7–8

In *Moral Monster*, I took the position that Leviticus 18:18 *prohibits* polygamy
(two or more wives).[8] I still find this view the most plausible one,[9] but I should
mention here another view a number of evangelical Old Testament scholars take—
the "nonideal-but-permitted" view.

View 1: Nonideal but Legally Permitted (Tolerated)

A number of evangelical scholars would say God or Scripture *tolerates* polygamy.[10] It isn't ideal but isn't viewed as inherently immoral. The Old Testament
permits polygamy, which was practiced in the ancient Near East.

In addition to the cultural shame of not having children, the labor of children
was important for sustaining households, and they provided a kind of "social
security" for aging parents. So for this reason, a man might take a *secondary* wife
(e.g., Abraham married Hagar) because the *primary* wife (e.g., Sarah) could not
produce children.

Nevertheless, the laws God gave Israel were designed to protect women. David
Lamb writes, "God set up the ideal for marriage in Genesis, but in a non-ideal
world, he gave laws to protect everyone involved: wives, husbands, slaves, widows,
concubines, and prisoners."[11]

View 2: Legally Prohibited Though Periodically Ignored

Some scholars hold that Leviticus 18:18 does indeed prohibit polygamy—even
if its violation wasn't penalized by the Mosaic law or in Israelite practice.[12]

After the introduction of prohibitions of sexual relations with "any . . . close
relatives" (*kol-sheer*) (v. 6 ESV), the *incest* laws are covered in 18:7–17. Each of
those verses begins with "the nakedness of" (*ervath*) and then adds "you shall
not uncover" (*lo thegalleh*). Then verse 17 again mentions the "close relative"
(*shaarah*) to round out this section on incest.

Verse 18 *brings a shift in structure and content.* Among other things, verses
18–23 cover *nonincestuous* sexual relationships (polygamy, adultery, same-sex

sexual relationships, etc.). Verses 18–23 reveal a *different structural pattern* than the preceding verses, suggesting a new (nonincest) section.[13] So 18:18 isn't *incest* (that is, focusing on the marriage of a man to a woman and her biological sister). Rather, despite standard objections, a more plausible case can be made that we have here basic *polygamy*—a man married to two Israelites (two female fellow citizens).[14] Also, the Qumran community (the Dead Sea Scrolls folks) would understand Leviticus 18:18 to be referring to a prohibition of polygamy.[15]

Certain marriage relationships that were permitted in patriarchal times (e.g., Abraham marrying his half sister Sarah) would later be prohibited in Leviticus 18. Polygamy appears to be another such prohibition in 18:18. That said, perhaps this ancient Near Eastern practice wasn't enforceable or didn't rise to the level of strong moral and social unacceptability and thus could be more easily ignored.[16]

On the first view, polygamy is *regulated* but not *endorsed*. The Mosaic law doesn't *endorse* polygamy but merely tells Israelites what to do when this happens. The second view claims that polygamy is *prohibited*. In either case, actual Old Testament narratives involving polygamy are cast in a negative light and are fraught with practical difficulties.

A Third View?

A *third—and more problematic—view* on polygamy comes from some of our critics from within. They would maintain that the *textual* God of the fallen biblical narrator *endorsed* polygamy—as in the 2 Samuel 12 passage cited above.[17] On this "textual God" view, many wives were viewed as a blessing and a gift from God. This is Proverbs 18:22 with a twist: "He who finds [*many wives*] finds a good thing and obtains favor from the LORD" (ESV).

A Few Comments on Polygamy and 2 Samuel 12

A Poor Advertising Campaign for Polygamy

Consider Old Testament stories involving polygamy: Abraham with Sarah and Hagar (Gen. 16 and 21), Jacob with his two primary wives and two secondary wives (Gen. 29–35), or Elkanah with his wives Peninah and Hannah (1 Sam. 1). Polygamous practice in the Old Testament was bound up with jealousy, division, rivalry, and tension. In chapter 7 we noted the instructional moral value narratives can provide (e.g., 1 Cor. 10), and narrative can teach us something here—namely, by giving bad publicity for the practice of polygamy.

Textual Indicators Undermining Polygamy

Though Hagar was humanly viewed as Abraham's wife (Gen. 16:3), she was referred to as "Sarai's maid" (Gen. 16:8–9; cf. 21:12). Also, God regularly referred to Sarah as Abraham's "wife" (e.g., Gen. 17:15, 19; 18:9–10). And, even though

Ishmael—Abraham's son through Hagar—would become a great nation (Gen. 17:20), Isaac was referred to as Abraham's "only son" (Gen. 22:2).

In addition, after Jacob's conversionary wrestling match with the angel and his name change to "Israel," he would call only Rachel "my wife" (Gen. 44:27)—even though he had earlier referred to Rachel, Leah, and their maids as "my wives" (Gen. 30:26; cf. 31:50). And, significantly, the Genesis 46 genealogy refers to Leah, Zilpah, and Bilhah as the women who "bore to Jacob" children; however, Rachel *alone* was classified as "Jacob's wife" (Gen. 46:15, 18, 19, 25).[18]

Could it be that these textual distinctions tell us something negative about polygamy?

God's "Giving" Gifts to David Doesn't Involve Adultery and Incest

Second Samuel 12's reference to God's *giving* David all the things belonging to Saul must be interpreted as general. After all, if we went along with the third, "textual God" view mentioned above, God's "giving" lots of wives as a divinely approved gift would pose another problem: it would look like God was endorsing both adultery and incest—clearly prohibited in the Mosaic law—and that would be taking the "textual" God to outrageous limits, even for our critic from within.

Approving of Adultery?

We're told that God "gave" (*nathan*) to David Saul's wives (2 Sam. 12:8). Yet God threatened to bring judgment on David in that God would eventually "give" (*nathan*) to David's rebellious son Absalom *those same wives*. That is, Absalom would *commit adultery* with them (12:11). But surely this kind of "giving" has the broad sense of permission—not divine blessing and approval.

Approving of Incest?

To add to the problem, David was King Saul's son-in-law (1 Sam. 18:27), and Saul's wife was *Ahinoam* (1 Sam. 14:50)—though not the same Ahinoam David had previously taken on as an additional wife (1 Sam. 25:43). But if our critic from within is correct, then the "gift" of *Saul's wife* Ahinoam would be another violation of the Mosaic law: "Cursed be anyone who lies with his mother-in-law" (Lev. 18:8; Deut. 27:23 ESV).

God's Willingness to Give David "Many More Things" as General

According to the prophet Nathan, what did God do for David? In this list (2 Sam. 12:7–8), God

1. anointed him king;
2. rescued him from Saul;

3. gave him all that belonged to Saul ("your master's house and your master's wives"); and

4. gave him the house of Israel and Judah.

This list is something of an official transaction that took place when David assumed kingship in Israel. *All that belonged to Saul was automatically transferred to David's household.* One commentator writes: "It was a common practice for a new ruler to take over the wives of the previous ruler as a sign of supremacy and control. Although this was not permitted under the law of Moses, it happened in Israel as elsewhere. Thus Absalom, for example, made a major political statement when he openly slept with his father's concubines ([2 Sam.] 16:21–22)."[19]

Old Testament scholar David Lamb summarizes things for us here: "While it seems like more wives are implied, it's possible that God is just saying he would have been willing to give him other things, perhaps like what he does to Solomon in 1 Kings 3—wisdom, riches, long life, etc."[20]

Deuteronomy 17's Warnings to Kings

Solomon's many wives and concubines (1 Kings 11:3–4) proved to be a pitfall, and this problem applied to David as well: "Many wives is a bad thing, even for kings."[21] Israel's kings were to set the example for the nation, but both David and Solomon failed to follow the injunctions of Deuteronomy 17.

The main point about David's wives is this: God had given David everything that once belonged to Saul—his household and his kingdom. God wasn't making a statement about the blessings of polygamy. Indeed, we've seen that actual cases of polygamy in the Old Testament demonstrate the opposite—that it's *not* a blessed estate. Rather, in the language of the prophet Nathan's lamb parable (2 Sam. 12:1–5), David had everything—including a "flock" of women—but he nevertheless forcibly took another's "lamb" (Bathsheba).

In this chapter, we have seen that we have good reason to hold that polygamy was prohibited in the Mosaic law (Lev. 18:18), even though other evangelical scholars hold that polygamy was nonideal but tolerated. In addition, Old Testament historical narratives portray polygamy in a negative light—a very poor advertising campaign for its practice. However, the view of the critic from within that the textual God "blessed" David and others with multiple wives reads too much into the biblical text.

22

Other Troubling Texts about Women

The Nameless Concubine, the Question of War Rape

Two major criticisms related to the status of women in the Old Testament concern the nameless concubine of Judges 19 and the question of Israelite soldiers engaging in war rape—a common practice of soldiers in Gentile nations surrounding Israel. This chapter tackles both of those issues.

The Nameless "Concubine" of Judges 19

The Narrative

During the time of the judges, Israelites "did what was right in their own eyes" (Judg. 17:6; 18:1; 19:1; 21:25 NRSV). Judges 19:1 mentions this terrible condition, and then the text goes on to illustrate just how low Israel had descended—into a horrific, traumatic story of abuse.

A married woman left her Levite husband, and headed back to her father's house in Bethlehem. After several months, her husband came to win her affections—to "speak tenderly to her in order to bring her back" (v. 3). After the "son-in-law" (*hatan*) left his "father-in-law" (*hoten*) (vv. 4, 5), he lodged at Gibeah in the tribal territory of Benjamin (v. 14)—where the horror began.

While in Gibeah, local men surrounded the house, demanding to "have relations with [lit. "know"] him" (v. 22). The host instead offered his own "virgin daughter" and his visitor's "concubine" to them (v. 24). In the end, the visitor "seized his concubine and brought her out to them; and they raped and abused her all night until morning" (v. 25). After this brutal gang rape ended, this tortured, brutalized woman crawled to the threshold of the house and died. When the husband was ready to leave, he callously said, "'Get up and let us go,' but there was no answer" (v. 28). He then took her body home, cut it up into twelve pieces, and sent it to each Israelite tribe (v. 29). The tribes were shocked, and when the tribe of Benjamin refused to give up the perpetrators of this abuse (20:13), a civil war against the Benjaminites ensued.

Understanding the Story

Critics of the story *rightly* claim that the Levite showed no regard for the humanity of his wife; he simply used her in a self-protective way. And after the night-long trauma of gang rape, he looked out of the door entrance at her lifeless body and told her to get up. Only afterward did he appear heroic and publicly demand that the perpetrators be called to account. But why didn't the narrator condemn this man? Wasn't the narrator being complicit in this act by keeping silent?[1]

In response, first, *this narrative comes at the tail end of a story of Israel's moral and spiritual decline*—a period when all Israelites did as they pleased. The narrator was illustrating this very point. As we've seen, *is* does not equal *ought*; *description* is not *prescription*. This story is part of that decline.

Second, *in some parts of the narrative, this woman was more of an agent than we may realize*. For one thing, she decided to leave her husband, departing to her father's home—something we *wouldn't* necessarily expect in this culture. And the husband followed her to persuade her to come back to him, which also affirms her agency and personhood. When they were staying with the woman's father, she was referred to as a "*girl*" (*naarah*) rather than a "concubine" (*pilegesh*)—a term often used to indicate a "second-tier" wife like Keturah, whom Abraham married after his "primary" wife died (Gen. 25:1–4). And while this woman was at *her* father's house (v. 3)—not at *her husband's* or *her father-in-law's* house—the text indicates that *she again takes initiative and exerts agency*. As for her husband, she even "brought him in" to the house (v. 3). But when her husband took charge of her afterward, she became a voiceless, agentless "concubine."

Third, *the text does not make the Levite look good at all*. He appears to display narcissistic characteristics:

1. After having tried to sweet-talk his way back into his wife's life, he failed to repair the breach with his wife and simply returned to his old ways.
2. He made a huge mistake by dismissing his father-in-law's concern about safety, and he undertook the risky journey anyway.
3. The Levite repeatedly diminished his wife's status and dignity.
4. The textual problem in verse 2 is important. The Hebrew text says that the woman "played the harlot against him." However, the Greek translation states that she "became angry with him." The "angry" alternative—found in

the RSV, NET, and NLT—makes more sense: *the Levite would not have run after a woman who had gone into prostitution, thus humiliating himself.* If she engaged in prostitution, he would have sought to punish her somehow (cf. Gen. 38:24). But the father's joyful attitude at his son-in-law's visit indicates that no serious breach had taken place.

Fourth, *the narrator himself makes a moral judgment, condemning this vile act against this poor woman.* He refers to the gang rapists as "wicked men"—literally, "sons of Belial" (19:22; cf. 20:13). The narrator's voice has a tone of indignation. Truly, he blames *men: the men of Gibeah, the Levite, and the host.* The woman was a victim of their evil acts. Those who love God don't act in this way. In fact, *the entire community* responded in outrage to such a vile act: "Nothing like this has ever happened or been seen" (Judg. 19:30 TLV); and again, "What is this wickedness that has taken place among you?" (Judg. 20:12). *Both the narrator and the community of Israelites stood up for the woman to express outrage at what happened to her.*

Despite the horrors of this account, the narrator did not gloss over the wickedness of this event. The text indicates—both implicitly and explicitly—a strong antagonism toward the actions of these men. So the claim that this nameless concubine was not defended by the narrator is simply not true. We have textual indicators that reinforce her personhood and dignity as well as the wickedness of the various men who were complicit in this act.

Sexual Slavery and War Rape?

A critic from without might claim that after a war, Israelite soldiers could freely "rape" women.[2] And after battle, women could be preserved as "sex slaves" for Israelite men.[3] If warriors could take plunder such as animals or material goods, why not rape women as well?

This practice was carried out by Israel's ancient Near Eastern neighbors. And later in history, the taking of sex slaves would be permitted by Muhammad as well (e.g., the Qur'anic phrase "those whom your right hands possess" refers to this). But this does not at all fit the worldview and values of ancient Israel.

First, we've noted that *the Old Testament law assumes that sexual relations were to be within the bond of a marriage between husband and wife* (Gen. 2:24; Deut. 22:13–18)—*as reinforced by Jesus himself* (Mark 10:7–9). Contrary to Jennifer Wright Knust's book *Unprotected Texts,*[4] the biblical sexual standard is *not* a great variety of sexual activities and marital practices, as we've indicated in the last couple chapters.

Second, *the critics simply utilize an argument from silence, as we're not told what Israelite men specifically did with prisoner-of-war women.* For a number of reasons, comparison between Israel and other ancient Near Eastern nations reveals an elevated, redemptive moral picture for what God expected of Israel before, during, and after battle.[5]

Third, *Deuteronomy 21:10–14 presents a postbattlefield scenario that addresses this issue.* This passage demands that compassion and honor be shown the female prisoner of war who is a prospective wife of an Israelite man. Whether the marriage came off or not, she was not to be humiliated. Here are *five redemptive elements* from this passage:

- a month-long waiting period
- mourning/assimilation rituals: cutting hair, clipping nails, and discarding former clothing
- marriage covenant before sex
- command to let the woman go free (no servitude) if he changes his mind about marrying her
- concern voiced for the woman's honor

Fourth, *divine commands pertaining to Israelite soldiers involved ritual purity and sexual abstinence as they went into battle.* Israel's "Yahweh battles"—fighting for the Lord—involved ritual preparation. Thus, sexual abstinence was assumed, which would rule out any kind of rape. Of course, adultery laws already ruled that out.

Yes, Israel's *neighbors* engaged in ritual sex—"sacred acts" involving prostitution in their temples. This Gentile practice carried into intertestamental literature—for example, when the temple was overtaken by "the gentiles, who took their pleasure with prostitutes and had intercourse with women in the sacred precincts" (2 Macc. 6:4 NJB). Though Israelites at times imitated the surrounding nations in this ceremonial sex (e.g., 2 Kings 23:7), God condemned it. Such ceremonial sex was forbidden for Israelites (Lev. 21:7, 9; Num. 15:39; 25:1–4; Deut. 23:17–18; 1 Kings 14:24; 15:12; 22:46; Hosea 4:4).

For example, when the Israelites approached Mount Sinai leading up to the sacred covenant-making ceremony, they were prohibited from engaging in sexual intercourse (Exod. 19:14–15). In their sacred service, priests were to avoid exposing their nakedness (Exod. 20:26; 28:42). Even in everyday life in Israel, certain sexual boundaries were still in place—such as not having sexual relations during a woman's menstruation period (Lev. 15:24–25; Ezek. 18:5–6; 22:10), a law that, according to some scholars, was issued to prevent a man from taking sexual advantage of a woman. In *worship*, ritual sex was prohibited; when *fighting* for the Lord, war rape would be as well. After all, Israel's Yahweh-approved battles were spiritual in nature, and in the nation's earliest battles, the ark of the covenant was present (Num. 10:35–36; Josh. 6:7–13; 2 Sam. 11:11; cf. 1 Sam 4:1–11). It was a sacred object associated with God's presence (1 Chron. 28:2: "the footstool of our God").

Not only was the *ark* specially set apart. The same was true of *soldiers*, including removing themselves from any sexual activity before and on the battlefield.

Think of how David's soldiers could eat the loaves of consecrated bread—reserved for priests alone (Lev. 24:5–9)—only on the condition that they had "kept themselves from women" (1 Sam. 21:4). Indeed, David emphasized that this was standard procedure for his soldiers: "Truly women have been kept from us as always when I go on an expedition" (21:5 ESV; cf. Josh. 3:5).

This makes all the more startling and vile the act of King David's adultery with Bathsheba while her husband Uriah was in battle. And when called from battle, Uriah refused to be with Bathsheba while his fellow soldiers fought. As Uriah told David: "The ark and Israel and Judah dwell in booths, and my lord Joab and the servants of my lord are camping in the open field. Shall I then go to my house, to eat and to drink and to lie with my wife? As you live, and as your soul lives, I will not do this thing" (2 Sam. 11:11 ESV). *Uriah would not engage in sexual pleasure while his comrades could not.*

The just-married Israelite male was not to fight in battle but to stay at home and be happy with his new wife (Deut. 24:5). This may also suggest the special place that sexual pleasure has within marriage. The battlefield was not the place.

So when Moses allowed virgins to be taken as brides for Israelite soldiers (Num. 31:18), Israel's specific Israelite postbattle policy—not to mention the creational ethic (Gen. 2:24) and the Mosaic law in general—ruled out rape (e.g., Deut. 21:10–14).

Again, such arrangements weren't ideal. But compared to the practices of other ancient Near Eastern nations, such a measure was a protective one and a significant, redemptive moral advance over these other cultures.[6]

Fifth, *war rape was a point of pride for other ancient Near Eastern nations (as well as the Greeks and Romans).* The rulers of these nations depicted such scenes on coins, city walls, statues, paintings, columns—and in their annals. By contrast, the Israelites never celebrated the rape of enemy women.[7]

Sixth, *unlike Israel, nations such as Mesopotamia, Egypt, and Assyria commonly took war captives (including children) as slaves to serve as sexual objects (ritual prostitutes) in their temple worship—a process that left these slaves vulnerable to the whims of those managing the temples.* Worshipers would pay for this sexual activity, which in turn helped fund the temple service. The Akkadian piece Ishtar Will Not Tire invites men to come with their sexual powers to find gratification with her—in this case, through debt-slave prostitutes.[8]

The second half of this chapter presents quite a contrast that existed between Israel's approach to the postwar treatment of women and that of other ancient Near Eastern nations. Clearly, Israel's worldview rendered war rape off-limits.

On both these topics—the nameless "concubine" and war rape—we see that women are not to be understood as "commodities" or objects to be used. They are made in God's image, and they are to receive the rightful honor and care as those possessing dignity and worth.

23

"Servants" in Israel

Persons or Property?

> If I have rejected the cause of my manservant or my maidservant,
>   when they brought a complaint against me,
> what then shall I do when God rises up?
>   When he makes inquiry, what shall I answer him?
> Did not he who made me in the womb make him?
> And did not one fashion us in the womb?
>
> —Job 31:13–15 ESV

The Mosaic Law: Rejecting the Ancient Near Eastern Divide

As we've seen, the biblical vision and worldview are often at odds with the outlook found in other ancient Near Eastern law collections. All humans—not just kings—are God's image-bearers; they are fundamentally equal in dignity and status, in contrast to the social hierarchies in neighboring countries with corresponding punishments based on where one stood on the social ladder.

Along came the Greeks and Romans with an outlook similar to that of the ancient Near East. Plato (427–347 BC) took a negative view of manual labor. His pupil Aristotle (384–322 BC) assumed some humans are born to rule, others to serve. Some are slaves *by nature*.[1] Using a slave was no different from using an animal.[2] Aristotle wrote that a slave is an animated or living tool and that a tool is an inanimate or lifeless slave.[3] The so-called Athenian democracy was built on the backs of slaves and was strongly hierarchical and aristocratic.[4] And the

infrastructure of the Roman Empire heavily depended on the system of slavery—
unlike ancient Israel. As we'll see, non-Hebrews in Israel had it much better legally
than did slaves in Greco-Roman slave systems.[5]

We've noted in chapter 8 the common ancient Near Eastern divide between
the *exploiter* and the *exploited*: the political elite or nobility who *demanded
and extracted tribute*—monetary payment that expressed allegiance, loyalty, and
honor—and those who *paid* it (workers, slaves, the producers of surplus from
their fields and flocks). Joshua Berman observes that a chasm existed between
"the *dominant tribute-imposing class* and the *dominated tribute-bearing class*."[6]
By contrast, the moral and social vision behind the Mosaic law was "more egalitarian," repudiating that standard rigid social division elsewhere in the ancient
Near East.[7] Underlying this "egalitarian" vision was the conviction that all human
beings have intrinsic worth (Gen. 1:26–28).[8]

Although I have discussed the topic of servitude in Israel in *Moral Monster*,[9]
I (a) summarize *Moral Monster*'s points on key provisions for servants in Israel
in the next section, (b) discuss new material on servitude in Israel, and (c) delve
more deeply into Leviticus 25:44–46—the servitude text that raises the most perplexing and troubling questions for readers.[10]

The Mosaic Law: A Repudiation of Southern Slavery

During colonial times, a "Slave Bible" (1807) had been printed for African slaves
in the British West Indies (including Jamaica, Barbados, and the Bahamas) in
order to prevent rebellion or any pursuit of freedom. The official book title was
*Parts of the Holy Bible, Selected for the Use of the Negro Slaves, in the British
West-India Islands*.[11] Ninety percent of the Old Testament was missing and half
of the New Testament. That "Bible" *included* Joseph's enslavement in Egypt and
omitted Israel's liberation from Pharaoh and the Egyptians.

Today, the word "slave" conjures up all kinds of emotions, and when it appears
in Scripture, it seems doubly troubling. Our modern association with the terms
"slave" and "slavery" has been shaped by colonialism and life in the antebellum
(pre–Civil War) American South. Some uninformed Bible readers may associate its use of "slave" with race-based slavery, the slave having no rights, and the
master's "freedom" to inflict any physical harm he wishes.

We may be familiar with critics who make much of this bogus association that
Old Testament "slavery" was "just like" the horrific institution of Southern slavery.[12] Yet the basic biblical recognition of the image of God in all persons would
go a long way to undercutting that abhorrent idea (Gen. 1:26–28).

Now, some may claim that the laws in the antebellum South technically offered
protections for slaves, even if those laws weren't carried out. They assume that
same could be true about ancient servants in Israel—laws prohibited abuses but
were not upheld in practice.[13]

This claim isn't accurate, however. It is true that *overseers* on a plantation could be punished for excessively harsh treatment of Black slaves; but Southern laws, legislators, and judges ignored common law practice in its application to slaves, and they didn't hold slave owners and slave hirers to the same strict standard as the overseers. Ultimately, the two-tiered laws reinforced the slave owner's absolute despotism over the slave. Southern slave laws routinely accommodated the slave owners and were essentially a compact or arrangement that pertained only to the slave owner and his slave.[14]

In *Moral Monster* I noted that if the provisions of the Mosaic law had been heeded in the modern world, there would have been no institution of slavery.[15] We'll see just how accurate is Christopher Wright's observation that the servant in Old Testament law "was given human and legal rights unheard of in contemporary societies."[16] Let's briefly review and elaborate on some of these.

Provision 1: Harsh physical treatment of Israelites or aliens was forbidden. Because the Israelites were once aliens in Egypt, they should not mistreat *fellow Israelites* or *aliens* (that is, immigrants)[17] living in Israel. If an employer (master) gouged out an indentured servant's eye or knocked out a servant's tooth (Exod. 21:27), the servant would be freed without any remaining debt. The clear implication is that *the servant had legal recourse to press for his freedom* due to his injury (cf. Job. 31:13–15): "Thus it is another indication of Old Testament law treating marginal people as human beings, with many of the rights accorded to full members of the covenant community."[18]

Along these lines, a common—and rather absurd—argument from Exodus 21:21 is that an employer (master) could physically abuse his—in this case, Israelite— servant as much as he wanted, just as long as the servant didn't die immediately. But this isn't a realistic or charitable reading of the text. After all, judges could certainly see through *that* charade. These servants did have rights, and the employer who struck a servant and killed him would be liable to the death penalty—"avenged" (v. 20 ESV).

We should note two things about this passage on accidental injury/death. First, even if the employer wasn't to be put to death (which is what "avenged" typically suggests), *that didn't mean he still wasn't liable to some penalty (e.g., payment)*. He would have to make payment for what was deemed an accidental death. After all, simply gouging out an eye or knocking out a tooth of a servant released that servant from servitude and debt, which the employer who struck him would have to absorb (Exod. 21:26–27).

Second, *the immediate context of this verse involves making payment for a person's recovering after having caused an accidental injury* (vv. 18–19: "He . . . shall take care of him until he is completely healed"). As documented in *Moral Monster*,[19] the employer was given leniency if he had shown goodwill by helping to pay the injured servant's medical bills before he died a few days later. In this light, Hittitologist Harry Hoffner rendered Exodus 21:21 as "That [medical payment] is his silver."[20]

Provision 2: Kidnapping, which was the means of establishing colonial slavery, was prohibited in Israelite law—and throughout the ancient Near East. Incidentally, this prohibition against kidnapping was true of Babylonian and Hittite laws as well.[21] Exodus 21:16 gives a more *generic* prohibition against kidnapping: "He who kidnaps [*ganab*] a man [*ish*]." Deuteronomy 24:7 focuses on kidnapping a fellow Israelite. But even there, "the absence of a prohibition does not amount to permission. The exhortations concerning the rights of resident aliens indicate that this would also be considered wrong."[22] Kidnapping would have been not a *property* offense in Israel but rather a *person* offense—as with Joseph, who "was . . . kidnapped [*ganab*] from the land of the Hebrews" (Gen. 40:15). The reason for this difference is rooted in the distinction between the "law of persons" (Mosaic law) and the "law of things" (other ancient Near Eastern law collections), as we discussed in chapter 8.

Provision 3: Foreign runaway slaves who came to Israel seeking refuge were protected from harsh masters (Deut. 23:15–16). Foreign slaves were not to be sent back to their masters. By contrast, the Code of Hammurabi called for the death penalty for those harboring runaway slaves: "If any one receive into his house a runaway male or female slave of the court . . . , the master of the house shall be put to death" (§16; also §19).[23] Various ancient Near Eastern nations (Egyptians, Hittites, Amurru) had extradition treaties to return foreign fugitive slaves to their masters, agreements akin to America's Fugitive Slave Act (1850). And Hittite, Mari (Syria), and Nuzi (Mesopotamia) documents indicate that severe penalties were threatened for fugitive slaves who were caught and returned (e.g., gouging out eyes).[24]

Provision 4: Israel had fixed six-year term limits on servitude (i.e., indentured servitude). In addition to the Year of Jubilee in Leviticus 25 (see chap. 9), this mandated term limit (Exod. 21:2) was unlike legislation in other ancient Near Eastern nations. If they offered freedom to slaves at all, it was left up to the whims of whoever happened to be in power. Israel's law was "a fundamental departure from the norms of the ancient Near East," Berman writes. Israel's law *decoupled* release of servants from the political order.[25] Also, in Israel, the ideal would be that Israelite servants were so well cared for that, rather than return to freedom and normal life when their contract expired, they would continue in lifelong service (Exod. 21:6: "serve him permanently [*olam*]").

As an aside, unlike the common colonialist mindset, servitude in Israel was *not based on some notion of racial inferiority*: "No form of slavery mentioned in the Hebrew Bible was the same as the race-based slavery most familiar to us from eighteenth- and nineteenth-century American history."[26] Yet, surprisingly, the main—and really bad—argument to justify slavery in the antebellum South was the inferiority of "Hamitic" (i.e., African) people.[27] But nothing in the biblical text indicates this.

Not only is every human being a divine image-bearer, but *Israelites had once been aliens in Egypt, which prompts Mosaic exhortations to Israelites—three dozen times—to take special care of the alien* (ger) *in their midst.*[28]

The next two chapters examine a challenging text—Leviticus 25:45, which mentions "the sojourners who live as aliens [*hagarim*] among you" being taken on as servants in Israel. *Given thirty-six admonitions to the contrary—including within Leviticus itself (19:34)—we don't suddenly have here justification for mistreatment of aliens!* That would be a most uncharitable reading. Indeed, Israel's *failure* to take special care of aliens in their midst would result in God's *judgment* on them (Deut. 24:14–15).

"Slave" or "Servant"? Persons in a Dynamic Dependency Relationship

An Aversion to Modern Translations

According to the *Concise Oxford English Dictionary*, a "slave" is "a person who is the legal property of another or others and is bound to absolute obedience, human chattel [i.e., property]."[29] That's the modern dictionary definition. More important than using modern dictionaries is how Old Testament authorities understand the term *ebed*. As we note shortly, this is a neutral term rather than an inherently negative one.

Did you know that in the King James Version of 1611, the word "slave" occurs only *once* in the Old Testament?[30] And that word "slave" isn't actually found in the Hebrew text itself but was inserted by a translator: "Is Israel a servant? is he a homeborn slave?" (Jer. 2:14 KJV). But consider all that has happened since 1611: oppressive slavery in the colonial West, England's abolition of slavery (1833), and specifically in the US, the Civil War (1861–65), a troubled period of Southern Reconstruction, federally initiated segregated housing in the 1930s, Jim Crow laws, horrific mistreatment of Blacks, and eventually the Civil Rights Act of 1964.

Given such a history, why then have *modern* Bible translations used such *emotional trigger words* as "slave" or "slavery" in the Old Testament? For example, the 1982 New King James Version uses the word "slave" forty-two times and "slavery" once. The 1984 New International Version (NIV) has "slave" 104 times and "slavery" seventeen times. Along with a Jewish translation into English (JPS—Jewish Publication Society), more recent German, Spanish, and Dutch translations have followed the same pattern of using stronger "slave" language than their earlier versions.[31] Given the emotion-laden term "slave" and also the adequate translation of *ebed* as "servant" or even "worker," it's strange that newer translations have latched on to the term "slave." Yet to take a neutral Hebrew term that meant "worker" or "servant" and render it "slave" *virtually guarantees a negative association*.

Trying to Remain Neutral

As just noted, the word "servant" (*ebed*) *is not inherently negative*. (Incidentally, the rendering for a *female* servant is "handmaid" [*amah*, e.g., Ps. 86:16], as there was no female equivalent to *ebed*.)[32] The term doesn't assume adjectives like "degrading," "oppressive," or "owned."[33] The context must make clear any positive, negative, or neutral association. A term like "bitter" (Exod. 1:14) or "hard labor" (Exod. 1:11, 14) or an association with an "iron furnace" (Deut. 4:20) makes obvious that this particular experience of servitude is negative. But "servant" can likewise be an honorific title: "the servant [*ebed*] of the LORD" (Moses: Deut. 34:5; Joshua: Josh. 1:1; 24:29).

This neutral term has the basic meaning of "worker" and is related to the verb *abad*—"work" or "serve" or even "worship" (e.g., Exod. 8:1; 20:5; Josh. 24:15). There is a *range* of uses for *the very same term* "servant" (*ebed*):

- *non-Israelites who are lifelong servants*, though they may become persons "of means" in Israel (Lev. 25:47)
- those who are *temporary servants for debt*
- *those who serve God* ("servant of the LORD")

In the words of one scholar: "To render the term [*ebed*] sometimes as 'slave' and at other times as 'servant' fails to represent the fact that there really is no clear distinction between the various occurrences of the word."[34] That is, we shouldn't slap the translation "slave" onto the word *ebed*, because of two dangers: (a) *this infuses each usage with negativity*, conjuring up associations with modern slavery; (b) *this also creates a false binary*: you're either "slave" *or* "free."

The same is true about using the corresponding translation of "master" for *adon*: (a) *the term provokes similar negative association with Southern slavery*; (b) *it creates another binary*—"master" versus "slave": that is, a mere temporary employer entering into a six-year contract with a worker takes on the appearance of an absolute owner or despot.

In the end, the term "servant" is a better translation overall for *ebed*. Keeping to this will help prevent drawing inappropriate negative associations and imposing our own modern societal outlook on what "really" counts as slavery and what doesn't: "The word 'servant' . . . has less definite associations, and a great deal of flexibility. It may pain modern consciences to use the word 'servant' for any worker whom we regard as having in fact been in slavery, but such consciences may not in fact be the best guides to translation."[35]

So just because a person is in one of the three *ebed* categories listed above— each being *in a subordinate role in a dynamic dependency relationship*—doesn't mean we therefore *must impose* the translation "slave" upon him. This is no more the case than when we render the word "king" (*melek*) as "puppet king" because it is sometimes used to denote one.[36]

Exodus: A Brief Case Study

Consider the book of Exodus. Israelites were called Pharaoh's "servants" (5:15, 16), and they were clearly being oppressed in this context. That said, even *Egyptians* were called Pharaoh's "servants" (5:21).

Yet through Moses, God commanded Pharaoh to let Israel go "that they may serve [*abad*] Me in the wilderness" (7:16). That is, Israel would go from one state of servitude to another (Exod. 4:23; 7:16; 8:1, 20; 9:1, 13; 10:3, 7, 8, 11, 24, 26). While in Egypt, the Israelites were *oppressed* and *in bondage* under Pharaoh. After Israel had passed through the Red Sea, they were *free* under Yahweh's rule. Subjection to Pharaoh meant *bitterness*. Subjection to God meant *liberation*. *Both were states of servitude.*

The same theme is captured in 2 Chronicles 12:8. There, Shemaiah the prophet told the unfaithful king Rehoboam that Judah would become a vassal (servant or subordinate) to the Egyptian king Shishak: "They will become his slaves [(*l*)*ebadim*] so that they may learn the difference between My service [*abodah*] and the service [*abodah*] of the kingdoms of the countries." *Serving God was freeing; serving a foreign king would be oppressive.*

Peter J. Williams observes: "The view that the root [word *ebed*] did not have negative associations is strengthened by the observation that the Exodus is not portrayed in the Hebrew as an escape from what is associated with that root."[37] That is, because the term for "servant" in Exodus can be positive, neutral, or negative, we should not assume the term is inherently negative.

Concluding Remarks

The basic meaning of "servant" (*ebed*) in the Old Testament is *one who is in a dynamic dependency relationship*.[38] This may be good, neutral, or negative. Israel's literature itself takes a predominantly negative attitude toward one human in service to another. Why? David Baker writes, "One of the primary motivations for obedience in the laws on care for the poor and oppressed is the exodus, God's liberation of his people from slavery in Egypt." He adds another relevant factor: "Unlike neighbouring countries, Israel had no social stratification, and all Israelites were considered brothers and sisters (cf. Lev. 25:39–43; Deut. 15:7–11; 17:15, 20)."[39]

Baker goes on to say that the "Hebrew word translated 'slave' means literally a 'worker,' whereas the [ancient Near Eastern] Akkadian equivalent means 'one who has come down' in social position."[40] The important implication is this: "Slavery did not fit well with the ideals of Israelite society, and laws were designed to reduce the number of people in slavery and protect slaves who were not actually freed."[41]

24

The "Acquisition" of "Foreign Slaves" (1)

A Deeper Dive into Leviticus 25

For they [Israelites] are My servants whom I brought out from the land of Egypt; they are not to be sold in a slave sale. You shall not rule over him with severity, but are to revere your God. As for your male and female slaves whom you may have—you may acquire male and female [servants] from the pagan nations that are around you. Then, too, it is out of the sons of the sojourners [ha-toshabim] who live as aliens [ha-garim; sing. ger] among you that you may gain acquisition, and out of their families who are with you, whom they will have produced in your land; they also may become your possession. You may even bequeath them to your sons after you, to receive as a possession; you can use them as permanent [servants]. But in respect to your countrymen, the sons of Israel, you shall not rule with severity over one another.

Now if the means of a stranger [ger] or of a sojourner [toshab] with you becomes sufficient [nasag], and a countryman of yours becomes so poor with regard to him as to sell himself to a stranger [ger] who is sojourning [toshab] with you, or to the descendants of a stranger's family, then he shall have redemption right after he has been sold. One of his brothers may redeem him, or his uncle, or his uncle's son, may redeem him, or one of his blood relatives from his family may redeem him; or if he prospers [nasag], he may redeem himself. He then with his purchaser [qanah] shall calculate from the year when he sold himself [makar] to him up to the year of jubilee; and the price of his sale shall correspond to the number of years. It is like the days of a hired man that he shall be with him. If there are still many years, he shall refund part of his purchase price [miqnah] in proportion to them for his own redemption.

—Leviticus 25:42–51

173

Although *Moral Monster* addressed this passage,[1] most of the subsequent servitude questions I've received have focused on it. So apparently more needs to be said by way of summary and further elaboration.

The Year of Jubilee

Leviticus 25 focuses on the Jubilee Year—an event to take place every fifty years. All debts were to be canceled and lands within tribal territories returned to their original families if they had been forced to lease the land because of debt and poverty. As we saw in chapter 9, kings of other ancient Near Eastern nations—if they so chose—might occasionally proclaim release for those in servitude, but nothing regularly scheduled was "in the books" that required this. By contrast, Israel's law—in addition to the six-year debt-service limit—mandated the Year of Jubilee to clear debt throughout the land.

In Leviticus 25, there are *three* stages of helping Israelites stave off poverty:

Stage 1: A poor Israelite *mortgages his land* (vv. 25–28).

Stage 2: In case the first action fails to bring him out of poverty, he takes advantage of an *interest-free loan* (vv. 35–38).

Stage 3: If the loan fails to resolve matters, then he—perhaps along with his family members—*contracts himself out ("sells himself") to work for a fellow Israelite*, typically within his own tribal and clan territory (v. 41). He is treated as a contracted employee who can eventually return to normal life once the debt problem is resolved.[2]

Note two additional matters about Leviticus 25:

1. *Covenantal land:* The Jubilee focuses on Israel and concerns the covenantal land God "gifted" to the tribes of Israel; non-Israelites could not possess or own portions of it.

2. *Limited options:* Non-Israelites could attach themselves to Israelite households, often as servants, as the situation in the ancient Near East presented very limited options.

What about Foreign "Slaves" (Lev. 25:44–47)?

"Chattel Slavery"?

Runaway slave and abolitionist Frederick Douglass wrote of his deceased master, Captain Thomas Auld: "He had struck down my personality, had subjected me to his will, made property of my body and soul, reduced me to a chattel, hired me out to a noted slave breaker to be worked like a beast and flogged into submission."[3] This depersonalization—not to mention abuse—is commonly what we associate with the word "chattel." And if "chattel" implies "no rights," "free to abuse," or "mere property rather than a dignified person," it flies in the face of the biblical vision we've discussed (Gen. 1:26–27; Job 31:13–15; see chap. 7 above).

Now, some biblical scholars *will* use the term "chattel" for Leviticus 25:44–46, but they carefully qualify this. For example, in the *Dictionary of the Old Testament: Pentateuch*, Gene Haas speaks of foreign servants in Israel as permanent "chattel slaves." But he carefully qualifies this: "These slaves are considered human beings" with all kinds of safeguards and privileges associated with living in Israel.[4] Indeed, *all Mosaic law passages on servitude* assume three basic principles, which he summarizes:

> *Principle 1:* "All humans, even slaves and bondslaves, have rights and privileges under the law and before God."
>
> *Principle 2:* It is better to live in the security and provision that servitude in Israel affords than to live in poverty and destitution, especially when one can come to love his employer/"master" (Exod. 21:5–6).
>
> *Principle 3:* "Family is important and must be maintained even in the condition of poverty and bondservice."[5]

David Baker's book *Tight Fists or Open Hands?* draws out the significant worldview and human-rights differences—and similarities too—between the Mosaic law and other ancient law collections. He too uses the term "chattel slavery" in relation to "buying" servants in Leviticus 25:44–46. But again, it is far from a *humans-as-commodities* view.

First, as Baker notes elsewhere, Leviticus *does not encourage* acquiring foreign servants. The law only *permits* this and also *sets limits* to it when dealing with those outside the covenant community—namely, "residents of other countries and foreign residents in Israel."[6]

Second, Baker encourages us to keep in mind three important items: (a) *kidnapping was forbidden*; (b) "acquiring" foreigner servants *was not forcible*; and (c) these "acquired" persons *were not free people suddenly put into servitude*. Rather, these foreign persons "are already slaves, or are offered by sale by their families."[7]

This brings us to at least three implications:

> *Implication 1: Foreign runaway slaves could flee to Israel and attach themselves to (be "acquired" by) Israelite households.* And since they had no realistic economic options and since an Israelite household provided economic security, food, clothing, and shelter, these *foreigners and their children could have a relatively stable life within these households.*

Implication 2: Presumably out of economic deprivation and having no other options, a foreign family abroad might attempt to get out of debt and poverty by "selling" a family member to an Israelite household.

Implication 3: Given the major worldview differences between Israel's humanizing laws and laws of surrounding nations (see chaps. 7–9), *Israel's laws— and its history of deliverance from harsh servitude in Egypt—provided the most optimal, humanizing context for foreign servants at that time.*

So here's a brief review of what we've discussed concerning those surrounding nations' law collections, which proves quite revealing:

- They assume that the king—not all human beings—was the divine image-bearer.
- These laws showed "relatively little concern" for foreigners.[8]
- Foreigners were rarely mentioned in them.
- They had nothing like gleaning laws for the foreigner or the impoverished (think of the foreigner Ruth gleaning in Israel).
- They enforced hierarchical social structures, unlike a more egalitarian structure in Israel (e.g., the Mosaic law's frequent mention of a fellow Israelite as a "brother").
- They focused on the "rights of property" rather than the "rights of persons."
- They had no weekly rest from work (Sabbath law).

And the list could be expanded further.

Once again, those nations' law collections *had no comparable dramatic history of deliverance from harsh servitude like the Israelites*, who had been foreigners in Egypt. Israel would have proved much more of a haven for "acquired" foreign servants than the surrounding nations. *When biblical scholars use the term "chattel," they have in mind a morally elevated, humanizing context that was worlds apart from any of Israel's neighbors.* And it is certainly a far cry from what Frederick Douglass experienced as "chattel."

Carol Meyers writes: "[These] laws provide significant protection for slaves [or, better translated, "servants"]. For example, masters must not abuse their slaves, fugitive slaves are to be given asylum rather than returned to their masters, and slaves are entitled to holidays. Elsewhere in the ancient Near East slaves are subject to property law, which focuses on the rights of slave-owners over their property. In Israel, slaves themselves have rights, and the laws are concerned with the slave as a person, emphasizing compassion for someone in a vulnerable position."[9]

"Acquiring" Non-Israelite Servants

When readers look at certain terms applied to non-Israelite servants, perhaps most startling is the language of *acquiring* non-Israelite servants or *bequeathing* their children to Israelites as their *possession*. This sounds like these immigrants, "alien" (*ger*) workers,[10] are mere objects to be bought and traded. Is that so?

We've observed that unlike the ideal *vision* of Israel's worldview, a number of Israel's particular *laws* recognize the situation "on the ground" and attempt to set up guardrails to regulate and protect. Certain laws permitted nonideal behavior, but this was due to the Israelites' hardness of heart, as Jesus said (Matt. 19:8).

What's more, as we reflect more closely on this more *legal* or *contractual* language used, we recognize that we use the same kind of terms in our sports language: team "owners" who "buy" or "trade" players. In like manner, the Old Testament used contractual language for *persons*—whether individual Israelites, the Israelite nation, or non-Israelites—for example, "that [or 'he'] is his silver" (Exod. 21:21),[11] "acquire" (*qanah*) (Ruth 4:5), "possession" (*ahuzzah*) (Lev. 25:45), or "sells himself" (*makar*) (Lev. 25:39; cf. Exod. 21:7).

In table 24.1, note that *both* Israelites and non-Israelites are called "sojourner" (*toshab*) and "alien" (*ger*) (Lev. 25:23, 45) and "servant" (*ebed*) (Exod. 21:5; Lev. 25:44). *Both* Israelite and alien may be "acquired" (*qanah*) (Lev. 25:50, 44). *Both* Israelite and non-Israelite servants can improve themselves and "prosper" (*nasag*) (Lev. 25:49 with 47). And *both* the Israelite and non-Israelite may be in service to another "permanently" (*olam*) (Exod. 21:5–6; Lev. 25:46)—which, as we'll see, amounts to no more than one or two generations instead of the modern misreading of the text that assumes the offspring of servants continue within a household generation after generation. Yes, a *foreigner* may be "acquired" as a servant, but the same is true of an *Israelite* (Lev. 25:44, 50). Indeed, an *Israelite* might *sell* himself/be voluntarily "sold" (*makar*) to a resident alien (Lev. 25:47).

"Permanent" Service Due to Lack of Alternatives

In our contemporary setting, we are familiar with government assistance, welfare, Social Security, unemployment checks, bankruptcy, and other federal supports for citizens in the United States. Other Western democracies have similar forms of assistance. We're also aware that a Great Depression, a stock market crash, or a banking crisis of some kind can be debilitating. The result is that affected citizens are left with few options. But in the ancient Near East, a political or economic crisis could prove disastrous. Indeed, regular ravages of famine and war and the migrations they created would have been devastating.

In that setting so culturally removed from ours, what would things have been like for the impoverished immigrant coming to another land? One scholar notes: "Like many employees in the modern world, although legally free, a servant may have nowhere else to go and no alternative but to stay."[12] Because of difficult economic times and the poverty that resulted, Israelites and aliens/immigrants in Israel would have to enter into the service of another to work and sustain themselves.

Table 24.1. Terms Associated with Israelites and
Non-Israelites (Mostly) from Leviticus 25

Term	Used of Israelites	Used of Non-Israelites
"sojourner" (*toshab*) and "alien" (*ger*)	In the land, Israelites are "*aliens* [*gerim*] and *sojourners* [*toshabim*] with [God]" (v. 23).	Non-Israelites are "the *sojourners* [*hatoshabim*] who live as *aliens* [*hagarim*]" in the land (v. 45).
"servant" (*ebed*)	An Israelite can be a "servant" (*ebed*) (Deut. 15:17)—although some scholars think this "Hebrew" servant is a *foreigner*.ᵃ (But for our purposes, we'll assume this refers to an Israelite.)	A non-Israelite "male" servant (*ebed*) and female servant (*amah*) may be acquired (v. 44).
"acquire" (*qanah*)	The Israelite servant "must calculate with the one who bought [*qanah*] him . . ." (v. 50 NET). The Israelites were "purchased" (*qanah*) by God, who brought them out of Egypt (Exod. 15:16). In a legal transaction, Boaz was able to "acquire" (*qanah*) Ruth as his wife (4:5, 10). In Genesis, Eve "acquired" (*qanah*) a son with the Lord's help (Gen. 4:1).	Israelites "may acquire" (*qanah*) servants "from the pagan nations that are around [them]" (v. 44).
"prosper" (*nasag*)	If an Israelite servant "grows rich" (ESV) or "prospers [*nasag*], he may redeem himself" (v. 49; cf. v. 26).	"If a stranger [*ger*] or sojourner [*toshab*] with you [Israelites] becomes rich [*nasag*], and your brother beside him becomes poor and sells himself to the stranger [*ger*] or sojourner [*toshab*] with you or to a member of the stranger's [*ger*] clan . . ." (v. 47 ESV).
"permanently" (*olam*)	If the servant declares his love for his employer (master) and declares that "I will not go out free," then after a formal public ceremony, "he shall serve him forever [*olam*]" (Exod. 21:5–6 NET).	Israelites can have "permanent" (*olam*) non-Israelite servants (v. 46).

a. Some scholars take the term "Hebrew" (e.g., Exod. 21:2) to refer to a nonnative person or foreigner living in a land, with no political or national affiliation. Israelites wouldn't have referred to themselves as "Hebrews" (Mary J. Evans, *1 and 2 Samuel* [Peabody, MA: Hendrickson, 2000], 63). If this is the case, then the foreign servant parallels what we see in Leviticus 25:44–46, and Exodus 21's stipulations and protections concerning servants carry over and apply there as well.

Of course, such an arrangement didn't guarantee that an Israelite employer who took in servants—whether domestic or foreign—would treat them kindly. And sometimes a husband's/father's death would leave children in the family susceptible to working off the debt as indentured servants (e.g., 2 Kings 4:1).

On the other hand, permanent servanthood didn't have to involve harsh treatment (Exod. 21:6). Indeed, the Mosaic law demanded that an *Israelite servant* be treated with respect—as a brother or sister under God's covenant—and *not severely* (Lev. 25:43). And in the same spirit, Israelites were *prohibited from mistreating aliens* since they knew what it was to be aliens in Egypt. So for foreign servants, "their advantage is that as servants they are part of the master's household; they get fed, sheltered and looked after like members of the family. Possibly they also get some sort of wage."[13]

Before continuing, we should add that the notion of foreigners' "permanent" (*olam*) servitude is really just for *one or possibly two generations*. According to Egyptologist James Hoffmeier, Egypt's pharaohs might bring back foreign prisoners of war, who would then work for the state. But within a generation or two, Egyptianization took hold: these foreigners would intermarry, assimilate into the culture, take on Egyptian personal names and social practices, and become full-fledged Egyptians. The same would be true in Israel. The modern idea of one generation after another of slaves—their children, grandchildren, and beyond— just didn't exist in the ancient Near East.[14]

The Security of Lifelong Servitude

An immigrant servant-laborer in Israel could potentially improve his lot and become a "person of means" within Israel and could even hire an Israelite servant to work for him (Lev. 25:47). However, some might find that the security of working for someone who is well-established and takes care of their basic needs to be a *more appealing* alternative than striking out on their own economically.

John Goldingay writes that "perhaps many people would be reasonably happy to settle for being long-term or lifelong servants. Servants do count as part of the family."[15] Indeed, a servant's situation "could be secure and reasonably comfortable, and one can even imagine people who started off as debt servants volunteering to become permanent servants because they love their master and his household, and it is good for them to be with their master (Deut. 15:12–18)."[16]

Conclusions So Far

We've made observations about taking on "sons of the sojourners [*ha-toshabim*] who live as aliens [*ha-garim*] among you" to be lifelong servants (Lev. 25:44–46). First, we have seen that the "acquired" resident alien (*ger/toshab*) isn't necessarily stuck in poverty but can grow rich or prosper (*nasag*) in Israel (vv. 45, 47). Second, poor Israelites may likewise be acquired (*qanah*) by the foreigner (v. 47), to whom they "sell" themselves (*mokar*) as servants, though this isn't ideal (v. 47). Finally, as we've noted, any sense of permanent service wouldn't extend beyond one or two generations.

One scholar observes that this law actually "takes into account the potential prosperity of immigrants ('If a stranger or sojourner with you becomes rich . . . ,' Lev. 25:47)."[17] Of course, "initially an immigrant's life may have been very difficult," which was the situation with the immigrant Ruth from Moab. However, Israel's laws helped make way for improving one's economic lot: "Gleaning laws indicate that what is left in the field, on the vine, or on the tree is to be for the poor and for the sojourner' (Lev. 19:10)."[18] Just like an Israelite who has sold himself in desperation but may climb out of poverty and "prosper" or "get rich" (*nasag*) through his hard work (Lev. 25:49), the "stranger" and "alien" in Israel may likewise improve their lot as they became assimilated within Israel (v. 47; cf. Ruth 1–4; 1 Chron. 2:34–35): "Even a foreigner can do well as a servant."[19]

25

The "Acquisition" of "Foreign Slaves" (2)

Two Objections and the Runaway Option

Two Objections: Treating Foreigners Severely and as "Slave" Laborers?

Severe Treatment of Foreigners

A couple of common objections surface from Leviticus 25. The first is this: *the biblical text seems to imply that one can treat a foreigner "with severity"* (Lev. 25:46). While an Israelite may have foreigners as "permanent" servants, the text goes on to say that "in respect to your countrymen, the sons of Israel, you shall not rule with severity over one another." But does that mean that if you're not allowed to mistreat a fellow Israelite, you can *still* mistreat a *foreign* servant? No, that doesn't follow at all.

For one thing, *to "rule [radah] over [an Israelite servant] with severity [perek]"* (v. 43) *here is the coercive attempt to keep that person in servitude beyond the mandated six-year limit.* The word *radah* can have the sense of *subduing* (e.g., "subdues kings" [Isa. 41:2]) or *ruling* (e.g., "[their enemies] ruled over them" [Neh. 9:28]). This verb parallels the term *kabash* ("subdue") in Genesis 1:28, and they both express the need for humans to exert energy and even force to push back certain tendencies in creation that can disrupt peaceful human existence.

Jeremiah later rebuked the Israelites for taking advantage of impoverished fellow Israelites by extending their time of servitude—in violation of the Mosaic

181

law (Jer. 34:12–16): "You brought them into subjection [*kabash*]" (v. 16). That is, these Israelites ruled over their servants "with severity." Contrary to this, any Israelite servitude beyond the six-year term limit had to be voluntary, not forced.[1]

Second, we've noted that *thirty-six times the Israelites were told to be kind to aliens, since Israelites were once aliens in Egypt—and so there is no sudden justification here for mistreating them.* To do so would place Israelites under God's curse.

Cursed is he who distorts the justice due an alien, orphan, and widow. (Deut. 27:19)

You shall not oppress a hired servant who is poor and needy, *whether he is one of your countrymen or one of your aliens who is in your land in your towns.* (Deut. 24:14)

Third, *Leviticus creates a kind of "instability" in the Israelite/non-Israelite distinction.* How so? Leviticus 19:34 commands the Israelites to treat the *alien* as a *fellow Israelite*, and Leviticus 25:40 tells *Israelites* to treat fellow Israelites as they would the *alien.* After all, Israelites themselves are *aliens* and *sojourners* in the land of Israel (Lev. 25:23).

The "instability" in the Israelite/non-Israelite distinction comes to this: *treat the Israelite as an alien* (with compassion and concern), *and treat an alien as an Israelite* (as under the same covenant laws). Kenneth Bergland observes that this can serve as "an invitation to rethink the relation to the foreigner in light of what is said about the native."[2]

Not Subjecting the Israelite to "Slave Labor"

The second objection is this: by asserting that a fellow Israelite must not be subjected to "slave labor" (v. 39 CSB), the biblical text seems to imply that the most difficult, exhausting tasks be given to the foreigner.

Some might think that this "slave labor" relates to the *type* of service—perhaps giving the most difficult, exhausting tasks to the foreigner—as we've seen with the Gibeonites (Josh. 9:27). And as Samuel warned, an Israelite king would press citizens into forced labor, which was severe (1 Kings 12:3–4, 13–14; cf. 1 Sam. 8:11–17). That said, a common—and tiring—task involved working in the fields all day—something a foreigner like Ruth undertook when she was gleaning (Ruth 2:2–3; cf. Matt. 20:12, which speaks of burdensome work in a vineyard during "the scorching heat of the day").

The focus here, however, is the *length* of service: *an Israelite servant had "term limits" of six years, but for an alien servant, those restrictions didn't apply.* So an employer (master) could not force fellow Israelites into permanent service; that had to be voluntary (Exod. 21:6). *Because aliens couldn't own land but could attach themselves to Israelite families, their permanent service was assumed.* But, as we've seen, even these aliens could "grow rich" and improve their lot—to the point of even hiring ("acquiring" [*qanah*]) an Israelite servant; however, it was preferable that an Israelite relative redeem him out of servitude.

The Runaway Option

One other consideration is relevant: just as foreign slaves *outside* Israel could flee from harsh masters to Israel's cities to find refuge (Deut. 23:15–16), so foreign servants *within* Israel could do the same if their conditions of service turned harsh or severe.

Various biblical scholars maintain that the command not to hand over "to his master a slave who has escaped from his master to you" (Deut. 23:15) applies to *both* foreign runaway slaves and Israelite servants who might run away from a harsh Israelite employer.[3] Indeed, we have examples of such runaways within Israel (e.g., 1 Sam. 25:10). The law clearly states, "You shall not mistreat" the foreign runaway slave (Deut. 23:16). So those who claim that the Old Testament justifies harsh treatment of foreign servants haven't read the biblical text with proper care and attention. As one scholar notes, the steady drumbeat of the Mosaic law is to protect the weaker, more vulnerable party rather than to favor the stronger.[4]

Indeed, Old Testament scholar David Clines makes a "deconstructing" observation about this extraordinary provision for runaway slaves, which ultimately undermines the institution of servitude altogether. "What is amazing about the law of the fugitive slave is that it enables a slave to acquire his or her own freedom—by the relatively simple expedient of runaway. A slave can choose not to be a slave."[5] He adds: "If a slave can choose not to be a slave," then "the concept of slavery does not exist as it once was thought to exist."[6]

Clines notes something similar about Exodus 21:6, where a servant *loves* his employer (master) and *freely chooses* to attach himself *permanently* to that household: "Slavery is in a sense abolished when it ceases to be a state that a person is forced into against his will."[7] With this blurring of the lines between *freedom* and "servant" (or "slave"), the institution has "lost its conceptual force."[8]

Summary Comments

Our two-chapter discussion of servitude related to Leviticus 25 makes this clear: *Israel's law forbids the dehumanization of servants, whether Israelite or foreign.* Indeed, the Mosaic law seeks to humanize conditions for all in the thick of the challenges and realties of the ancient Near East, and Leviticus 25 doesn't suddenly remove all protections for vulnerable foreigners.

David Baker writes that those from foreign countries who are willing to live by Israelite laws "are integrated into the covenant community, and are to be loved like Israelites, imitating God's love for vulnerable people."[9] Runaway foreign slaves were *protected* in Israel (Deut. 23:15), and God repeatedly commanded

Israel to look out for the alien in their midst. When we encounter this unusual passage in Leviticus 25:44–46, *our sure guide should be the oft-repeated default principle*: "The stranger [*ger*] who resides with you shall be to you as the native among you, and you shall love him as yourself, for you were aliens [*gerim*] in the land of Egypt" (Lev. 19:34).

Also, because non-Israelites couldn't own land in Israel, *they had a greater sense of dependency on Israelite generosity and hospitality*. Aliens would have to attach themselves to households: "Whether and how an immigrant could acquire real property is not clear. Obviously they had no inheritance when they first settled in Israel and would have been completely dependent on some landowner even for a place to live."[10] But we also noted in the previous chapter how the Egyptian servant Jarha came to improve his lot in Israel (1 Chron. 2:34–35).

We've not claimed that such laws are perfect and can be universalized for modern Western societies. But the vision behind Israel's law presents a significant redemptive, incremental shift forward. In his *Guide for the Perplexed*, medieval rabbi, doctor, and philosopher Moses Maimonides recognized that "utopian" ideals could not be implemented all at once: "It is impossible to go suddenly from one extreme to the other. It is therefore, according to the nature of man, impossible for him suddenly to discontinue everything to which he has been accustomed."[11]

Concerning the Mosaic law on servitude, Baker makes this same point that "the Old Testament is simply being realistic": "Rather than outlawing the institution of [servitude] completely, it establishes various principles to ameliorate the condition of the poor and needy, emphasizing the individual worth of every human being and treating slaves as persons rather than property. If all these principles had been practiced consistently, slavery would probably have disappeared many centuries before [British slave abolitionist William] Wilberforce."[12]

Noted Jewish scholar Jacob Milgrom observes that the "utopian ideals" articulated in Leviticus "are far ahead of their time" even though "it is, at the same time, attempting to solve certain socioeconomic problems."[13] This ideal is expressed in the concern to protect the most vulnerable in Israel. And even though strangers and sojourners are typically the recipients of "charity," Baker observes, they "occasionally may prosper (Lev. 25:47; cf. Deut. 28:43)."[14]

A New Testament Postscript

When we get to the New Testament, Rome is the world power with slavery embedded within its social structure—a very different system, culture, and mindset than ancient Israel. *The earliest Christians lacked any power to abolish slavery within the empire.*[15] Yet the gospel *undermines* the spirit of the Roman Empire that pretty much regarded slaves as transferable property—"furniture with a soul"[16]—as opposed to their having intrinsic dignity, worth, and rights. People became slaves for various reasons (being prisoners of war or kidnapped by slave traders or becoming a slave to avoid starvation, say), and what a slave did was up to his master, but the slave could sometimes be released by a ransom payment or by the master's granting this.[17]

The claim that Jesus never denounced slavery misses the point of his very mission: Jesus came to set free all who are oppressed (Luke 4:18–19). So obviously he would oppose any institution that dehumanizes and objectifies humans.

Likewise, Paul affirmed that in Christ there is "neither slave nor free" (Gal. 3:28)—all social and class distinctions that once divided lose their power at the foot of the cross. Paul urged slaves to find freedom if possible (1 Cor. 7:21). And if Onesimus was truly a runaway slave from Philemon (although some dispute this, as this epistle contains no flight verbs, for example), Paul pressed for *reconciliation* in a very direct manner. This was all the more fitting since they were brothers in Christ—a more fundamental and defining relationship and a radical revision to the Roman way of treating slaves. Though Paul had greater status than Philemon, he appealed to him as a brother and even as a prisoner.[18] *While Paul had no political power to bring about the abolition of slavery in the empire, he began at the level of the household and of the church.*[19]

In the Greco-Roman world, household codes were directed at persons having different roles within a household, but these attempted to reinforce the powerful and to keep the powerless in their place. Paul's Christianized household code is subversive. In Ephesians and Colossians, Paul first addresses those who have less power in a household (women, children, slaves) and offers instruction to them to help minimize conflict and tensions with those toward the top of the hierarchy (e.g., for slaves to do their work as to Christ [Col. 3:24]). Keep in mind that the head of the household may not necessarily be a believer (1 Cor. 7:13–15).

Then he addresses those with greater power in the household (fathers, parents, masters). He urges husbands to do something radical: not only to love their wives but to do so as Christ loved the church (Eph. 5:25, 28–31, 33) and not to be harsh with them (Col. 3:19). He tells fathers not to exasperate children and not to be harsh with them (Eph. 6:4; Col. 3:21). He urges the master to treat slaves fairly and justly since he is accountable to a "Master in heaven" (Col. 4:1; cf. Eph. 6:9). This was the best Paul could do to address attitudes within the hierarchy—from loving and being just and not abusing power (at the top) to showing honor and respect and working hard (at the bottom). For slaves, Paul also urged them to get freedom if they could (1 Cor. 7:21). But for these household codes, rather than reinforcing power structures, the radical and subversive Paul emphasizes love, fairness, and kindness directed from the powerful to the powerless.[20] That was the most strategic way to affect change then and to sow the seeds of slavery's destruction. This is much like the famous slave and later abolitionist Frederick Douglass's realization that getting educated was a subversive act to undermine the institution of slavery.

Furthermore, by urging masters and slaves within his congregations to "greet one another with a holy kiss," Paul calls on them to live according to the reality of *familial equality* (Rom. 16:16; 1 Cor. 16:20; 2 Cor. 13:12; 1 Thess. 5:26). In addition, Romans 16 indicates that Prisca and Aquila were wealthy, with a church meeting in their home (vv. 3–5). Yet within that same congregation were *Andronicus* and *Urbanus*—two typical slave names—and they shared in doing gospel work with Paul as fellow workers and fellow prisoners (vv. 7, 9). Yes, the wealthy Christians and "lowly" slaves in the same congregation were to greet one another with a holy kiss (v. 16). Furthermore, believing masters and slaves *shared in the Lord's Supper together*—a radical picture of equality that further expressed the loving bonds of belonging to a spiritual family.

And we have extrabiblical evidence that attests to the elevated treatment of slaves in the early church. For example, the Roman writer Pliny the Younger expressed in his letter to Emperor Trajan (ca. AD 111–113): "Accordingly, I judged it all the more necessary to find out what the truth was by torturing two female slaves who were called deaconesses."[21]

Finally, the New Testament issues condemnation of "slave traders" (1 Tim. 1:9–10 NIV). Of course, Paul condemned slave trading (a form of kidnapping) in the ancient world, and he would have condemned that same practice in the modern world. And harking back to Ezekiel 27:13 and ancient Tyre's slave trading, John also condemned the slave trade of the anti-God system of Babylon—a trafficking in humans as commodities and cargo ("bodies")—like spices, oil, and cattle (Rev. 18:11–13). However, John adds after "bodies" a humanizing phrase "that is, the souls of humans" (NIV).[22]

The spirit of both testaments reveals a press toward the implementation of structures that supported the dignity of all persons—including those in servitude. Even so, both testaments reveal less-than-ideal circumstances that required taking realistic, incremental, redemptive steps in the face of larger, fixed historical realities.

PART 6

Warfare and Violence in the Old
Testament (and the New)

26

Jesus Loves Canaanites—
and Israelites Too

"Jesus 101" and the Old Testament's "Dark Texts"

When it comes to the Old Testament warfare texts, theologian Roger Olson confesses that he doesn't understand them and that they don't speak God's voice to him: "They are dark and obscure and frightening. I run to Jesus. . . . Jesus is God for us and all we need when contemplating the character of God."[1] To him, these texts display a mindset contrary to that of Jesus, who commanded us to turn the other cheek and not resist evildoers (Matt. 5:39). Isn't Jesus kind, loving, and compassionate? Doesn't Jesus reveal the heart of God? After all, to see Jesus is to see the Father (John 14:9; cf. Col. 2:9; Heb. 1:3). And we can appreciate Olson's concern. After all, Israelite warfare is indeed frightful and a departure from the ideal. Divine wrath and judgment are a reluctant, last-resort departure from God's own loving desires, but these don't stand in contradiction to each other. To be agnostic about what to do with these texts is certainly intellectually and theologically appropriate. And we should all run to Jesus: after all, "a bruised reed he will not break, and a smoldering wick he will not quench," but his kingdom will be established, and he will bring "justice to victory" (Matt. 12:20 ESV)—and his sovereign rule is associated with "a rod of iron" (Rev. 12:5).

However, we run into trouble when we create two radical portrayals of God in Scripture. One of our critics from within, Peter Enns, tells us that the New Testament "leaves behind the violent, tribal, insider-outsider, rhetoric of a significant portion" of the Old Testament. Indeed, "the character of the people of God—now made up of Jew and Gentile—is dominated by such behaviors as faith in Christ working itself out in love, self-sacrifice, praying for one's enemies and persecutors. You know, Jesus 101." He tells us that "the Old and New Testaments . . . give us, rather, different portrayals of God."[2] The ancient Israelites simply "saw the world and their God in tribal ways."[3]

Another critic from within, Randal Rauser, asks us to consider Jesus's parable of the good Samaritan (Samaritans had been long despised by the Jews) and also Jesus's encounter with the Canaanite woman in Matthew 15. In his book *Jesus Loves Canaanites* he comments: "The lesson is not simply that the Canaanites can, at long last, be included as part of God's plan. Rather, I would submit the real revelation is that the Canaanites have always been a people who were part of God's benevolent care. The lesson is that Jesus truly loves all people: Jews, Gentiles, Samaritans, and yes, Canaanites too. So perhaps the next question is this: who are the Canaanites in our time and place? And how can we begin to read from the margins with them?"[4] We'll return to such considerations later in the chapter.

To our critics from within, the problem is that the Old Testament has way too much of the "textual" God; so any synthesis with the "actual" God is an exercise in futility—especially when it comes to the Canaanites.[5]

We can acknowledge that these "dark texts" present a moral challenge to us modern-day Westerners. Four distinctive responses to these texts stand out. (a) Some will claim that this *God should be rejected* (e.g., the atheist Richard Dawkins). (b) Our critics from within will claim that *the Old Testament must be reevaluated* because it isn't a faithful record. (c) Still others take the view that the killing of the Canaanites *could be called genocide but that it was only permitted during this one point in history* (e.g., the theologian John Calvin).[6] (d) Another group, of which I am a part, takes the view that the Old Testament doesn't describe anything like genocide and that *this interpretation of the Old Testament should be reevaluated*.[7] We want to grapple with these texts and discern how best to interpret them.

Since Jesus is the full and final revelation of God, *I want to adopt the viewpoint of Jesus and his designated authorities in the New Testament to put these severe texts into proper perspective*. As it turns out, *neither* testament finds this Canaanite warfare troubling. We've already seen that the New Testament presents us with both a *loving* and *severe* Jesus. He says of his enemies, "Father, forgive them," but he drives out money changers from the temple, "curses" and pronounces judgment on Israel, and destroys Israelites who didn't believe. *That* is "Jesus 101." He's good but not safe.

The Canaanites: *Ethically*—Not *Ethnically*—Problematic

According to some thinkers, the Old Testament allegedly promotes segregation, fear, and hostility toward different races and religions.[8] And it's not unusual to hear charges of genocide and ethnic cleansing from critics like Richard Dawkins.[9]

How do we respond to this claim? The modern term "genocide" is often used loosely, but, for a number of reasons, even the more technical United Nations definitions involving this term don't easily fit with ancient Near Eastern practices—that is, acts committed with the intent to destroy (wholly or partially) a national, ethnic, racial, or religious group.[10] But let's examine the matter more closely.

"Simply Because They Were Pagans"?

Kenton Sparks, another of our critics from within, wonders: "Is it only in Israel's case that divine sanction legitimizes the extermination of pagans?" Did the Israelites drive out the Canaanites "simply because they were pagans"?[11]

In response, first, the real issue *wasn't* that the Canaanites were the *Israelites'* enemy but that they were *God's* enemy.[12] And *Israel* could also become God's enemy if they broke covenant with him: "I will act with wrathful hostility against you" (Lev. 26:28). God threatened to "drive out" Israel for the same reasons he drove out the Canaanites (Lev. 20:23). Was *God himself* promoting the "ethnic cleansing" of Judah when he had many of his own people removed from the land to Babylon? Of course not.

Second, the term "extermination" is grossly inaccurate, as we'll see. The language applied to Canaanites was likewise applied to Israel, and it could simply mean "exile" or "defeat"—not extermination.

Third, as noted in *Moral Monster, the Canaanites were not the worst specimens of humanity in the ancient Near East.* That said, they engaged in acts that would be considered criminal in today's world: *incest, bestiality, infant sacrifice,* and *ritual prostitution.*[13]

Fourth, *Canaanites weren't the only group singled out for divine judgment.* Nations surrounding Israel and Judah were threatened because of their atrocities and the stifling of compassion (e.g., Amos 1–2). Throughout the Old Testament, God brings—or promises to bring—judgment on plenty of wicked cities and nations.

Fifth, *divine judgment repeatedly falls on Israel in both testaments.* Jesus, who loved Jerusalem and wept over it, also *cursed* the nation, symbolized by the withering of the fig tree: "May no one ever eat fruit from you again!" (Mark 11:14). Judgment fell in AD 70 on Jesus's Israelite *neighbors*—whom he loved and over whom he wept—after his preaching and teaching, performing miracles, and warning about judgment. Also, *Jesus* "destroyed" unbelieving Israelites in the wilderness (Jude 5). *Love* and *wrath* are not opposed—and Jesus demonstrates both this enemy-love and enemy-wrath.

The Irrelevance of Canaanite Ethnicity or Tribal Identity

From all appearances, Israelites and Canaanites were virtually indistinguishable. Furthermore, a genetic test would reveal they came from the same "pool"—even if the Canaanites and Israelites weren't an identical genetic match. (Indeed, DNA analysis has revealed that modern-day Lebanese are the descendants of the ancient Canaanites.)[14] The Lord reminded Israel of the pagan roots of their hallowed Jerusalem: born in Canaan of an Amorite father and a Hittite mother (Ezek. 16:3). Their distant heritage is as pagan as their neighbors'.

And what about all of those people groups God mentions to Abram (Gen. 15:18–21)? They are the Kenites, Kenizzites, Canaanites, Hittites, Amorites, and Jebusites. Even the hostile Amalekites were descendants of Abraham (Gen. 36:12). Early on, the patriarchs had friendly relations with them, and along the way they were readily included within the life of Israel:

- Caleb the Kenizzite (Num. 32:11–12)
- Rahab the Canaanite (Josh. 2:1–11)
- Canaanite "strangers"—*not* ethnic Israelites—in the region of Shechem who had "joined themselves to Yahweh"[15] in a covenant-renewal ceremony for Israelites (Josh. 8:33–35)
- Moses's father-in-law the Kenite (Judg. 1:16)
- the Amorites with whom Israel was at peace under Samuel's ministry (1 Sam. 7:14)
- Ahimelech the Hittite (1 Sam. 26:6) and Uriah the Hittite (2 Sam. 11:3; 23:39)
- an Amalekite—"the son of an alien [*ger*]" in the "camp of Israel" (2 Sam. 1:3, 13)
- Araunah the Jebusite (2 Sam. 24:16–18)
- Kenite scribes in Israel (1 Chron. 2:55)
- Ishmaiah the Gibeonite (1 Chron. 12:4; cf. Neh. 3:7)
- the Maacathites, a lesser-known Canaanite tribe that Joshua attempted to drive out (Josh. 13:13); they were later represented in the list of David's mighty men (2 Sam. 23:34), and one appeared as a commander in Judah, "Jezaniah son of the Maacathite" (Jer. 40:8)
- "Obed-Edom the Gittite" (i.e., someone from Gath in Philistia), whom God blessed because the ark of the covenant remained at his home (2 Sam. 6:10–11)[16]

When it comes to the Canaanites, certain facts are quite telling:

1. Rahab's rescue and incorporation into Israel (Josh. 6)
2. The presence of the Canaanites ("strangers" from Shechem) at a covenant-renewal ceremony (Josh. 8)
3. The treaty with the Gibeonites (Josh. 9)
4. No Canaanite cities even attempted to make peace with Israel (Josh. 11)

For the first two, we have no indication of divine disapproval.[17] For the third, we have every reason to think that if the Gibeonites had approached Israel with directness rather than trickery, they would have come to find the same acceptance as Rahab and the strangers from Shechem. This is implied by the fourth observation: no other Canaanites bothered to try making peace with Israel (Josh. 11:19). God is willing to welcome the Canaanites as neighbors. But, as Jesus said, there are circumstances in which people may be a pernicious influence and lead his disciples into sin such that it would be better for them to be removed from the scene altogether—drowning them in the sea with a millstone hung around their neck (Matt. 18:6)—Jesus's words, not mine.

Repeatedly, the biblical text indicates that driving out Canaanites has to do with *ethics* rather than *ethnics*. One commentator notes that the "permeability of any barrier between insider and outsider is a consistent theme in Joshua" and that "entry into the covenant is possible regardless of ethnic or geographic identity"—which anticipates the gospel message of salvation's availability to all.[18]

Were the Canaanites Being Judged for Wickedness?

. . . for the iniquity [*avon*] of the Amorite is not yet complete [*shalem*].

—Genesis 15:16

Some scholars have claimed that the Canaanites weren't really being judged for wickedness. After all, they weren't under Israel's covenant. And according to their best "guess" and "tentative interpretation," they reject that Genesis 15:16 refers to a future judgment on the Canaanites once their sinfulness reached full measure.[19] The Canaanites simply weren't deserving of punishment because they rebelled against God's moral order. They were being portrayed as subhuman "chaos monsters"—"invincible barbarians" who brought disorder.[20]

In his even-handed assessment of such claims, Old Testament scholar Tremper Longman nevertheless calls these views "eccentric." They are rejected by most commentators, which should at least prompt caution. And this "subhuman" understanding of the Canaanites is an "eccentric" one that conflicts with a picture of a righteous God who judges people according to what they deserve.[21] The Canaanites were humans whom God would judge. Beyond this, let's examine the larger point.

First, even if this were nowhere explicitly stated, *Scripture takes for granted Canaanite sinfulness and judgment-worthiness*: "While [Joshua] never specifically names Canaanite sin as the reason Israel received the land, this understanding lies fully behind the text," Lissa Wray Beal notes.[22]

The Canaanites were no exception to God's holding the nations accountable for their actions and thus rendering to all according to their deeds (Rom. 2:6). And the New Testament clearly affirms that the inhabitants of Jericho "were disobedient" (*tois apeithēsasin*) and thus perished (Heb. 11:31). The concept of *disobedience* presupposes violating moral standards and assumes the Canaanites should have known better (cf. *"unclean"* Canaan's *"abominations"*/*"impurity"* [Ezra 9:11]).

Second, *in the Old Testament, God repeatedly threatened judgment on wicked non-Israelite nations.* In Genesis, for instance, the "Judge of all the earth" rained down judgment on Sodom and Gomorrah (Gen. 18:25; 19:1–29). In Amos 1–2, God threatened judgment ("I will send fire") not only on his own people but on Israelite neighbors for their atrocities and for stifling their conscience. God was well aware that they should have known not to violate basic moral laws. Though his chosen people are the primary focus of judgment for covenant breaking, God threatened to act in judgment against other wicked nations as well.

Third, *the language from Genesis 15:16 is found elsewhere in the Old Testament and is applied to all humanity.* The words "iniquity" (*avon*) and "complete" (*shalem*) found in Genesis 15:16 occur together in Jeremiah—an important occurrence not noted by Walton and Walton. First, Jeremiah 16:18 refers to God's judgment on Israel: "I will first doubly *repay* [*shalem*] their *iniquity* [*avon*]." Later in the book, God *universalizes* this judgment against all humans who violate God's law. Following the Sinai covenant language, the text emphasizes how God "shows lovingkindness to thousands, but *repays* [*shalem*] the *iniquity* [*avon*] of fathers" (Jer. 32:18). Then it broadens to *all humanity*: God's "eyes are open to all the ways of mortals, rewarding all according to their ways and according to the fruit of their doings" (32:19 NRSV). God holds all human beings—including Canaanites— accountable for violating the moral law God has placed within human hearts. God's judgment for sin isn't just on Israelites who violate the covenant.

We could add similar-sounding language from Amos 2:9–10 that harks back to Genesis 15:16. Speaking through Amos, God says: "It was I who destroyed the Amorite before them. . . . It was I who brought you up from the land of Egypt . . . that you might take possession of the land of the Amorite."

In addition, *the Old Testament uses sin-laden language in association with the Canaanite inhabitants.* For example, "[Ahab] acted very abominably following idols, according to all that the Amorites had done, whom the LORD cast out before the sons of Israel" (1 Kings 21:26). Canaanite actions were "detestable" (Deut. 18:9) "abominable" (Lev. 18:30), "evil" (Deut. 13:5), and land-defiling. Indeed, Israel imitated the Canaanites, and so they too would be expelled from the land (Deut. 18:10; 2 Kings 16:3; 17:17; 21:6; 2 Chron. 33:6; cf. Ps. 106:35–39; see also Lev. 18:27–28; 20:22–24). God condemned infant sacrifice in Judah, expressing this with horror and shock: "It did not come into My mind" (Jer. 7:31; cf. 19:5; 32:35). Certainly, God considered this practice by the Canaanites an abhorrent, unimaginable immoral practice even for those outside the Israelite community.

No, God had waited patiently for the sin of the Canaanites to reach full measure—well over half a millennium from the time of Abraham to Joshua. By that point, the time was right to drive out the Canaanites in judgment. As John Goldingay aptly comments, "Yahweh cannot simply throw out the current inhabitants of the country in favor of Abraham's offspring whom he wishes to favor, even for the sake of his own purpose for the world as a whole. The Amorites must and will have lots of time to turn from their waywardness before Yahweh will be able to say, 'That's it.'"[23]

Imagine World Peace: Fighting in the Short Run, Blessing in the Long Run

You may be familiar with the distinction between "strategy" and "tactics." "Strategy" refers to the long-range goal while the "tactics" are the necessary steps to achieve that ultimate goal. In the same way, God's long-term *strategy* to bring blessing to humanity through Abraham (Gen. 12:1–3) includes short-term *tactics* to get there. Certain tactics were necessary to remove hostile opposition that hindered or interfered with the achievement of that divinely commissioned final goal.

First, though Israel needed to preserve its own identity, fulfill its mission, and bring blessing to the world, *it faced a real, pernicious, and immediate Canaanite threat.*

Second, *God's gracious saving plan had to begin somewhere, sometime—and what a messy world it was.* To say it again: "God gets his hands dirty to a certain point" in that "he works within a fallen world though not the original product of his own pure hands."[24]

Third, God's character is gracious and compassionate (Exod. 34:6–7), which means *he is ready and eager to withdraw any threat of judgment at any time—* whether for Sodom and Gomorrah (Gen. 18:32), Nineveh (Jon. 3:10–4:2), the Canaanites (Josh. 2:8–14; 8:33, 35; 9:24–25; 11:19), or indeed *any* nation (Jer. 18:7–8).

Fourth, yes, Jesus loves Canaanites, as Randal Rauser's book title rightly affirms,[25] but that doesn't exempt them from judgment. And *that same Jesus, who loves Israelites too, acted in judgment against them as well.* With a christological lens that reminds us of the triune God's involvement in ancient Israel, the New Testament—with our best manuscripts—also tells us, "*Jesus*, having saved the people out of the land of Egypt, later destroyed those who did not believe" (Jude 5 NET). Another version puts it this way: "*Jesus*, who saved a people out of the land of Egypt, afterward destroyed those who did not believe" (ESV). Whether Canaanite or Israelite, the "wrath of the Lamb" will come against those who defy him and his good purposes (Rev. 6:16); those are also Jesus's "neighbors."

Fifth, despite the messiness of working with fallen humans and earthly kingdoms, *God's severe commands for the short term had the long view in mind*: "The fate of Canaan is subordinate to the promise of Israel. But the promise to Israel is in turn subordinate to the fate of the whole world. A temporary unfairness that discriminates for Israel and against Canaan is designed to give way to a broader fairness. Election is exclusive in the short term, but it is designed in due course to benefit others [beyond] its short-term beneficiaries."[26] As we saw in chapter 19, Isaiah 19 presents a long-term vision of Assyria and Egypt—Israel's ancient enemies—as joined together with Israel as the people of God; Psalm 87:4 includes people from Egypt ("Rahab"), Babylon, Philistia, Tyre, and Ethiopia as God's chosen people. And Zechariah 9:2–7 affirms that Tyre, Philistia, Syria, and the Philistines will be a "remnant for our God, and be like a clan in Judah." Even though divine judgment fell on all of these nations—and Israel too—God's ultimate goal was to incorporate them into a "chosen race" (1 Pet. 2:9).

Sixth, though God hates violence (1 Chron. 22:8; Ps. 11:5; Prov. 6:16–17) and is not described as "violent" (*hamas*), *he reluctantly enters a violent world to set things right.* That's not all: *God himself is personally touched and affected as he involves himself deeply in the world's messy affairs, working to bring humans to a place of flourishing in a renewed creation.* The biblical story "tells what this decision costs God."[27] God's "counterviolent" judgment is his reluctant response to *human violence*; it is testimony to his *hatred* of violence: "If God commands violence, it is part of a whole concessionary scheme of operation, an accommodation to the fact of rampant evil which he detests but has not abolished."[28]

Seventh, *this means that both the exodus and the conquest—and the divine counterviolence involved—are necessary for Israel's very existence.* Writes Daniel Hawk, "Israel would not exist apart from the application of divine power and the execution of divine violence to liberate and conquer. No exodus, no conquest. No violence, no Israel."[29] In the exodus, God demonstrated his power and grace by liberating Israelite slaves from the leading superpower of the day and humbling an arrogant Pharaoh. In the conquest, God's power and grace were once again evident as a fledgling, poorly equipped nation eventually established itself in a land of far more numerous Canaanites who possessed superior weaponry in their well-fortified citadels.

In the end, *it was "no Israel, no salvation."* As Goldingay comments: "God had made the destiny of the entire world depend on Israel—not on what Israel would do but on what God would do through Israel. This might seem a weird action on God's part, but it is an action affirmed by both Old and New Testaments. As Jesus put it in John 4, salvation is from the Jews. Therefore, no Jews, no salvation. One can see why this is so: Jesus is Jewish. No Jews, no Jesus."[30]

High-Stakes Fighting: Israel's Battles as Spiritual Warfare

"How would you like it if another nation invaded yours?" Perhaps you've encountered this question in the context of Israel's battles with Canaan. One biblical scholar—a critic from within (Eric Seibert)—suggests we read the Bible *with the Canaanites*—from *their* perspective. He says that too often we read with an *"us versus them"* or *"good guys versus bad guys"* mindset. But what about the feelings of the Canaanites?[31]

First, *God repeatedly reminded the Israelites they were entering the land by the grace of God and not their own righteousness* (e.g., Deut. 9:6). The land was not a right but a gracious gift.

Second, *we actually do get a report providing the divine perspective on the Canaanites in Joshua.* When the Canaanites heard of Israel's Red Sea crossing and the defeat of Kings Sihon and Og, Rahab said the Canaanites' "hearts melted" and "no courage remained" in anyone (Josh. 2:10–11). Similarly, Canaanite kings heard reports about the Jordan crossing, and "there was no spirit in them any longer" (5:1). The Gibeonites gave a similar report: they had heard "the fame of the LORD your God" and the wonders he had done (9:9–10). The Canaanites were well informed about Yahweh, and some of them even turned to the God of Israel. As for the rest of the Canaanites, they didn't attempt to make peace with Israel despite the overwhelming evidence they had of Yahweh's supremacy (11:19).

Third, *we ought to give priority to the author of Joshua over our critic from within about a proper perspective on the Canaanites.* What if we are actually *reading with God*—reading from his perspective—about what he had revealed to Israel? While we should read the Scriptures carefully and ethically, as Seibert recommends, the Old Testament proclaims—and the New Testament affirms— that ancient Israel was like no other nation; *God chose Abraham and his offspring for a unique task in salvation history.*

So, this "How would you like it if another nation invaded yours?" question takes an incorrect stance: it assumes *Israel was "just like any other nation," which ultimately guts the biblical narrative of its truth and power by removing key features of the story.* This is like removing Gandalf and Samwise Gamgee from *The Lord of the Rings.* You just don't have a compelling, coherent story any longer. And remember the New Testament's affirmation that *Jesus* "destroyed" unbelieving Israelites (Jude 5). Jude was reading the Old Testament from a Jesus-shaped perspective, and even if it's rough and uncomfortable, we too should adopt that Jesus-shaped stance.

Fourth, *Israel's battles weren't just earthly clashes between nations, but God the "warrior" was engaging in a cosmic battle with dark powers* (Exod. 15:3). Through Israel, *God was at war with the false gods of the nations* (cf. Exod. 12:12). In so doing, God was building toward the time that Jesus the Messiah would come in the fullness of time to cast down "the ruler of this world" (John 12:31).

Fifth, *in this battling, Israel's identity and mission as a light to the nations were at stake.* The Canaanite influence was strong, and Israel could be—and often was—easily derailed from carrying forward the plan of redemption to the world (Exod. 32; Lev. 17:7; Num. 25:1, 3; 31:16; Josh. 24:23; Amos 5:26; cf. Acts 7:43). No wonder the language of Deuteronomy is so strongly opposed to the Canaanites: it "was only being realistic in recognizing the power of Canaanite temptation when Israelite faith in Yahweh was a newly budded flower."[32] Consider the following:

> If Eve and Adam are portrayed as having transgressed under the most favorable conditions imaginable and the solemn covenant at Sinai was quickly followed by the

worship of the golden calf, was it to be expected that the level of Israelite godliness would suffice to absorb and overcome the remnants of idolatry in a subdued and captive population?

And if idolatry wins out in Canaan, then where in the world is Yahweh to be known and worshiped? Further, the hypothetical sharing of the land by some sort of treaty arrangement would have kept the Canaanite gods in place.[33]

Summary Remarks

So we've seen that God's judgment on the Canaanites wasn't because of their ethnicity—because "they were pagans." Rather, it was because the Canaanites acted wickedly, even if they weren't the most wicked people in the ancient Near East. (God meted out judgments to other nations too.) The Canaanites "were disobedient" to the moral law within and suppressed their conscience (Heb. 11:31; cf. Amos 1–2). And the Canaanites' immoral actions threatened the identity and mission of Israel. It was difficult enough for Israel to maintain its own identity given the nation's continued pattern of idolatry, starting back in the wilderness wanderings and extending into the Babylonian captivity.

So yes, Jesus/God does love Canaanites in the following ways:

1. *God was always willing to relent, even when judgment seemed inevitable*—as with Sodom and Gomorrah (Gen. 18:32), Rahab (Josh. 2), Canaanite strangers (Josh. 8:33, 35), and so on.

2. *God patiently waited over half a millennium before judgment would fall on the Canaanites.*

3. *The Canaanites had ample warning with divine signs and wonders*, which started while Israel was under the dominant empire of Egypt forty years earlier.

4. *The Canaanites had opportunity to align themselves with the God of the Israelites*, which some did, or simply flee.

5. *God had the long-range blessing of all nations, including Canaanites, in mind*—though Canaanite religious practices and immorality presented an obstacle to blessing those nations.

6. The fact that there "was not a city which made peace with the sons of Israel" except the Gibeonites (Josh. 11:19) suggests *the possibility of a negotiated peace with any willing Canaanites.*[34]

God was willing to be neighborly toward the Canaanites—and *any* nation that was willing to be neighborly toward God, as it were. But if they acted wickedly, then God would judge such a nation (Jer. 18:7–8; Jon. 4:2). Indeed, Jesus proclaimed that same message of judgment to the Jewish nation of his own day—his own neighbors whom he loved and for whom he died. He was willing to embrace them, but they refused him. And this refusal met with divine wrath (Matt. 23:37–38).

Also, while Jesus commanded us to love our neighbor (*kindness*), Jesus drove his money-changing "neighbors" out of the temple (John 2:14–17) and "destroyed" his Israelite "neighbors" (Jude 5) because of their disobedience (*severity*). Jesus threatened to cast a false prophetess—his "neighbor"—on a bed of sickness (Rev. 2:20–21). At the judgment, Jesus will consign his religious hypocrite "neighbors" to separation from him (Matt. 7:23). God/Jesus deals with people differently, depending on their stance toward him: "To the pure you show yourself pure, but to the devious you show yourself shrewd" (Ps. 18:26 NIV).

So once again, "If there is a contradiction between loving your enemies and being peacemakers, on one hand, and Joshua's undertaking this task at God's command, on the other, the New Testament does not see it."[35] The "love principle" that summarizes the Law and the Prophets (Matt. 7:12) is not contrary to the divine "vengeance principle" (Rev. 6:9–11).

27

"We Left No Survivors"

Exaggeration Rhetoric in Israel's War Texts

When the LORD your God gives it into your hand, you shall strike all the men in it with the edge of the sword. Only the women and the children and the animals and all that is in the city, all its spoil, you shall take as booty for yourself; and you shall use the spoil of your enemies which the LORD your God has given you. Thus you shall do to all the cities that are very far from you, which are not of the cities of these nations nearby. Only in the cities of these peoples that the LORD your God is giving you as an inheritance, you shall not leave alive anything that breathes. But you shall utterly destroy [haram] them, the Hittite and the Amorite, the Canaanite and the Perizzite, the Hivite and the Jebusite, as the LORD your God has commanded you, so that they may not teach you to do according to all their detestable things which they have done for their gods, so that you would sin against the LORD your God.

—Deuteronomy 20:13–18

Exaggeration: Ancient Near Eastern "Trash Talk"

Ancient Near Eastern Examples

As the *Moral Monster* and (especially) *Genocide* books point out, ancient Near Eastern war texts used heavy hyperbole along with stereotypical words or phrases like "leave alive nothing that breathes"; "man and woman, young and old"; "no survivors"; "utterly destroyed"; "perished."[1] It's an ancient version of modern-day "trash talk" in sports: "We totally destroyed that team," we say today. No one takes such an expression literally. These and other literary devices were used to express that one side was victorious—even if that side barely won.

In the next chapter, we'll look at the often-mistranslated term *haram*— sometimes translated "utterly destroy" or "utterly annihilate." But some extrabiblical examples of this hyperbole reveal strong language even though the historical reality was quite muted in comparison (see table 27.1).

Battle accounts of Assyria, Susa, and Egypt mention taking lands or cities in a "single day"—hyperbole to "heighten the victor's grandeur and prove they have their god's support."[2] Likewise, Joshua 10:13 reflects this ancient Near Eastern language of a great battle taking place in a "single day" or "whole day."

Biblical Examples

Not surprisingly, the biblical text itself reflects this same war-text genre, which its original audience readily understood. But unlike many ancient Near Eastern war texts, the Old Testament accounts actually portray Israel's warfare *more realistically* by mentioning the many survivors in the thick of total-destruction language (see table 27.2).

Table 27.1. Ancient "Trash Talk" and Historical Reality

Ancient Near Eastern "Trash Talk" (Exaggeration)	The Historical Reality
Egypt's Thutmose III (late fifteenth century BC) proclaimed he had overthrown Mitanni's "great army" in "the twinkling of an eye"; it had "perished completely, as though they never existed, like the ashes."[a]	Mitanni's forces lived to fight beyond this in the fifteenth and fourteenth centuries.[b]
The Bulletin of Rameses II reads: "His majesty slew the entire force . . . as well as all the chiefs of all the countries that had come with him. . . . His majesty slaughtered and slew them in their places . . . ; and his majesty was alone, none other with him."[c]	Rameses II exaggerated Egypt's less-than-decisive victory at Kadesh against Syria (1274/3 BC). It was far from an overwhelming victory.
Pharaoh Rameses III boasted about the Battle of the Delta and the invading Sea Peoples (1175 BC): "I slew the Denyen in their islands, while the Tjeker and Philistines were made ashes. The Sherden and the Washesh of the sea were made nonexistent."[d]	This "victory" actually led to Egypt's economic devastation and to its eventual decline. In fact, Philistia would later colonize eastern Egypt—despite the pharaoh's boast.
King Mesha of Moab (840/830 BC) claimed that "Israel has utterly perished for always."[e]	This was a premature judgment—by one hundred years! The Assyrian invasion in 722 BC devastated the Northern Kingdom of Israel.

a. Kenneth A. Kitchen, *On the Reliability of the Old Testament* (Grand Rapids: Eerdmans, 2006), 174.

b. K. Lawson Younger, *Ancient Conquest Accounts: A Study in Ancient Near Eastern and Biblical History Writing*, Journal for the Study of the Old Testament Supplement Series 98 (Sheffield: Sheffield Academic, 2009), 190–92.

c. Younger, *Ancient Conquest Accounts*, 245.

d. James B. Pritchard, ed., *Ancient Near Eastern Texts Relating to the Old Testament*, 3rd ed. (Princeton: Princeton University Press, 1969), 262.

e. Kitchen, *Reliability*, 174.

Table 27.2. "Annihilation" in Biblical Warfare Accounts

"Annihilation" Rhetoric	"No Annihilation" (i.e., many survivors)
Joshua 10:20a: "Joshua and [the Israelites] had finished slaying them with a very great slaughter until they were destroyed."	Joshua 10:20b: "And the survivors [or better, 'the remnant' (ESV) or 'a portion of a larger unit']ª who remained of them had entered the fortified cities."
Joshua 10:33: Joshua "defeated" the king of Gezer and "left him no survivor."	Judges 1:29: "Ephraim did not drive out the Canaanites who were living in Gezer; so the Canaanites lived in Gezer among them." King Solomon would eventually capture Gezer (1 Kings 9:16).
Joshua 10:39: All the inhabitants of Debir were "utterly destroyed."	Joshua 11:21: Then Joshua "utterly destroyed" Anakites in Debir.
Joshua 11:11: At Hazor, Joshua left alive "no one who breathed"; he "burned Hazor with fire." Cities like Hazor were "utterly destroyed."	Judges 4:3: Jabin the king of Hazor fights against Israel with nine hundred chariots. This and other Canaanite cities were cleared out and then reinhabited.ᵇ
Joshua 11:21 (cf. 10:36, 39): The Anakites in Hebron were "cut off" and "utterly destroyed"; there were "no Anakim left in the land" (v. 22).	Joshua 15:13–14: Then five years later,ᶜ Caleb "drove out" the Anakites from Hebron (cf. Judg. 1:20).
Joshua 11:23: Joshua conquered "the whole land."	Joshua 13:1: The Lord told Joshua that "very much of the land remains to be possessed."
Joshua 11:23: "Thus the land had rest from war." Joshua 23:5, 12: "The LORD . . . will thrust them out from before you and *drive them from before you*" unless "you cling to the rest of these nations." Joshua 24:11: "Thus *I gave them into your hand*."	Judges 2:21, 23: "*I also will no longer drive out before them any of the nations* which Joshua left when he died. . . . So the LORD allowed those nations to remain, not driving them out quickly; and *He did not give them into the hand of Joshua*."
Joshua 12:7–8, 21, 23: The cities of Taanach, Megiddo, and Dor were "defeated."	Judges 1:27: "But Manasseh did not take possession of Taanach . . . Dor . . . or . . . Megiddo . . . ; so the Canaanites persisted in living in that land."
Joshua 12:14: Joshua defeated the king of Hormah (cf. 15:30; 19:4).	Judges 1:17: The tribes of Judah and Simeon struck and "utterly destroyed" the Canaanites in Hormah (also called "Zephath").
Judges 1:8: "Then the sons of Judah fought against Jerusalem and captured it and struck it with the edge of the sword and set the city on fire."	Judges 1:21: "But [the Benjamites] did not drive out the Jebusites who lived in Jerusalem; so the Jebusites have lived with [them] in Jerusalem to this day." Even after King David took Jerusalem, the Jebusites still remained during Solomon's time—even beyond the Babylonian exile (2 Sam. 5:6–8; 1 Kings 9:20–21; cf. Ezra 9:1).

a. David G. Firth, *Joshua* (Bellingham, WA: Lexham, 2021), 202.
b. For further elaboration on the hyperbole in these war texts, see chapters 8–12 in William J. Webb and Gordon K. Oeste, *Bloody, Brutal, and Barbaric? Wrestling with Troubling War Texts* (Downers Grove, IL: IVP Academic, 2019).
c. Firth, *Joshua*, 207–8.

As David Firth argues, the term "utter destruction" should be understood along the lines of "comprehensive victory."[3] So no wonder at the end of Joshua, Israel's commander reminded them not to "cling to the remnant of these nations" and make covenantal alliances with them (Josh. 23:12 ESV). Rather, they were to remove their foreign gods from their midst and to serve the Lord (24:1–28). *This threat of idolatry and breaking covenantal allegiance to God was the overriding concern.* It *wasn't* simply the fact of mere Canaanite "strangers who were living among them" who could likewise be open to aligning themselves with Yahweh (cf. Josh. 8:33, 35). In fact, *even while the Canaanites were in the land with the Israelites, God's directives were toward the Israelites destroying Canaanite religious items and not imitating their immoral practices,* as we note in chapter 29.

Gradual Occupation

The occupation of Canaan was gradual, since the Israelites merely engaged in *"disabling raids,"* as leading Egyptologist Kenneth Kitchen asserts. The Israelites raided cities, killed the local kings (military leaders), and, for instance, moved on and returned to their base camp at Gilgal without holding those places (Josh. 10:15, 43). Kitchen concludes: "So there was no sweeping take over and occupation of this region at this point. And no total destruction of the towns attacked."[4]

We have a two-stage operation:

1. *Driving out Canaanites from their cities through disabling raids* ("driving out" assumes Canaanites survived)
2. *The threat of death* if those "set-apart" (*herem*) cities were to be reoccupied, many of which were, a short time afterward

The main objective was to disable Canaanite cities (Deut. 20:16), which were military forts with a military commander or "king" (especially Jericho and Ai). Richard Hess argues that civilians generally lived in hamlets and would flee for the hills if these nearby citadels were attacked.[5] Lissa Wray Beal likewise argues: "Warfare in Joshua, even with the *herem* command, does not empty the land completely or destroy all the inhabitants. God went ahead of Israel to drive out the inhabitants, and Israelite action was directed against the cities. Not all the inhabitants were killed, and even in the face of 'utter destruction' of cities, survivors remained. Israel's possession of the land was accomplished over several years while Israel dwelt in the midst of the remaining Canaanite inhabitants."[6]

At any rate, only three cities—Jericho, Ai, and Hazor—were destroyed by fire (Josh. 6:24; 8:19; 11:11). Even though other cities were "utterly destroyed" or "put under the ban" (*haram*), they were left intact—that is, not literally "utterly destroyed." So no wonder the Israelites were told they would inhabit cities and homes "which you did not build" (Deut. 6:10–11; cf. Josh. 23:13).

Wray Beal observes: "Entry into the land did not envision total destruction of all the population."[7] Many texts refer to "driving out" or the land "vomiting out"

(NIV) the Canaanites (Exod. 23:27–31; 33:2; 34:11; Lev. 18:24–28; 20:22–23; Num. 33:51–56; Deut. 4:37–38; 6:18–19; 7:1, 20–23). Moreover, God would instill fear into the Canaanites (Josh. 2:9–11; cf. Exod. 23:20–23). But occupation would be slow and gradual, or else the land would become desolate and full of wild animals (Exod. 23:29–30). Egyptologist James Hoffmeier points out how Joshua's language portrays a small-scale, "limited conquest of key sites in strategic areas, which enabled the Israelites to settle in their long-promised land."[8] He adds, "Clearly the Bible does not claim a maximal conquest and demolition of Canaan."[9] This eventual takeover would happen only during David's time (ca. 1000 BC).

So when we see language of "no survivors" and "destruction," we can infer that a military campaign took place and that there was some semblance of victory, but the details of "destruction" are "likely couched in rhetorical hyperbole."[10] Firth concludes: "Many [Canaanites] were killed, though not as many as the popular imagination seems to believe, and their deaths occurred because they had chosen to place themselves under God's judgment."[11] He concludes that emotive terms such as "ethnic cleansing" or "genocide" are "inappropriate" because "only combatants are killed and an alternative way was always available."[12] Elsewhere he notes the problem of using modern definitions of "genocide"—not to mention all of their emotion-laden connotations—to describe events in Joshua, which "do not fit with the concept."[13]

An Abundance of Canaanite Inhabitants

As we move from Joshua to Judges 1, the text repeats that, in city after city, Israel "did not drive out" the Canaanites. And so the Canaanites continued to live among the Israelites. Old Testament scholar Iain Provan comments: "There are clearly many Canaanites still living in the land in the *aftermath* of Joshua's victories who are not ultimately even *expelled* from the land, much less killed."[14] They endured well into the reigns of David and Solomon (cf. Josh. 17:13; 23:3, 7; Judg. 3:5; 10:8; 2 Sam. 24:6–7; 1 Kings 9:15–21). He observes that all of this is "very strange" language,[15] and so we ought to be careful about drawing quick conclusions about casualties and the degree of devastation. As Daniel Hawk writes: "To read Joshua as extermination is to misread the text."[16]

Joshua's faithfully carrying out Moses's "utterly destroy" commands (Deut. 7:1–6; 20:16–18) and Joshua's leaving plenty of survivors (Josh. 11:12, 15, 20) were clearly not incompatible. Firth observes that "we have to conclude that the fact that [Joshua] did *not* devote many Canaanites to destruction was actually an expression of obedience."[17]

Another Rhetorical Device: Lesser, Localized Battle Plus "Universal Conquest"

Saul came to the city of Amalek and set an ambush in the valley.
—1 Samuel 15:5

So Saul defeated the Amalekites, from Havilah as you go to Shur, which is east of Egypt.

—1 Samuel 15:7

Besides the "annihilation" or "total-kill" language, another literary device of exaggeration used in ancient Near Eastern war texts involved two components: (1) *a lesser, localized battle* and (2) *a clearly exaggerated representation of a "universal conquest."* This rhetorical device further calls into question the massive extent of war casualties as well as civilian killings. In 1 Samuel 15, the battle with the Amalekites reveals this pairing. Let's unpack this.

First, *the prophet Samuel gave Saul this command using sweeping rhetorical language*: "Now go and strike Amalek and utterly destroy all that he has, and do not spare him; but put to death both man and woman, child and infant, ox and sheep, camel and donkey" (1 Sam. 15:3). This language—reference to "man and woman" or "young and old" (e.g., Josh. 6:21)—is called a *merism.* It uses *two contrasting parts to express totality.* For example, God creating "the heavens and the earth" (Gen. 1:1) refers to all physical reality. Or the phrase "from Dan to Beersheba" (e.g., Judg. 20:1)—that is, the northernmost key city and the southernmost key city in Israel, which turn out to be about 160 miles apart—refers to *the entire land of Israel.*

Second, as we'll see later, *this stereotypical language follows the highly exaggerated rhetoric of Joshua and also Deuteronomy.* Later, we'll compare the account of the campaign against Sihon and Og in Numbers 21 with its recounting in Deuteronomy 3. This reveals quite clearly that the "women and children" mentioned in the recounting were *not* present at the actual battle in Numbers 21. This was a common rhetorical device: the merism "women and children" could be inserted into a war account to contribute to the sweeping exaggerated language without their actually being present.[18] This pattern continues in 1 Samuel 15.

Third, *Amalekite standard operating procedure was to show continued hostility against Israel.* Leading up to Saul's battle was an Amalekite raid on the Israelites (1 Sam. 14:48). But beginning in Exodus 17, the Amalekites attacked the vulnerable and exhausted Israelites, who had just crossed the Red Sea. They were cruel to Israel, attacking Israel generation after generation. Ironically, Amalekites were the offspring of Isaac—through his son Esau (Gen. 36:12). And they lingered on into the time of Esther with Haman the Agagite (Esther 3), who worked to destroy the Jews. (Agag was the king of the Amalekites mentioned in 1 Samuel 15.) As David Lamb says, *feeling sorry for the Amalekites is like feeling sorry for the Nazis.*[19]

Fourth, *1 Samuel 15 uses a clear rhetorical device expressing exaggeration.* Let's explore this in more detail:

Lesser localized battle (v. 5): Saul fought at a "city of Amalek." Before battle, he told Kenites who were at this citadel that he had no interest in fighting against them. After all, the Kenites had been friendly with the Israelites. So "the Kenites departed" (v. 6). Clearly, women and children wouldn't have been hanging out there at the site of an anticipated pitched battle.

Universal conquest (v. 7): The text states that Saul fought against the Amalekites over a massive territory—from Havilah to Shur east of Egypt—that is, from Arabia to Egypt.[20] This big-time exaggeration added to the earlier straightforward account of a local battle.

James Hoffmeier states that "lofty assertions of universal conquest side by side with sober statements about taking individual cities"[21] is a sign of hyperbole in these ancient war texts. Another scholar observes this pairing too, noting that "it is impossible to imagine the battle actually traversed the enormous distance from Arabia almost to Egypt."[22] A third describes Saul as fighting at a semipermanent Amalekite encampment (v. 5), and the massive geographical scope of the "universal" battle (v. 7) would preclude a literal understanding of Saul's wiping out the Amalekites.[23]

To make this clear, *the narrator himself* (v. 8), not just the unreliable Saul (v. 20), reports Saul had "utterly destroyed" (*haram*)—or however *haram* should be translated—the Amalekites. Saul kept animals from the local battle, and he kept alive the king, who represented Amalekite identity. Ultimately, Saul's major fighting was against a smaller contingent of Amalekites, chiefly at this "city of Amalek."[24]

Fifth, *to make the hyperbole perfectly clear, we have an additional indicator in the same book: David fought a local battle against the Amalekites followed by "universal conquest."* After the initial fighting, David was said to have fought in the same vast (exaggerated) territory as Saul did. David—in similar language—"did not leave a man or a woman alive" (1 Sam. 27:8–9). Yet the Amalekites then raided David's camp, and he and his four hundred men "slaughtered" them, and "not a man of them escaped," except four hundred Amalekites (30:10, 17).

These 1 Samuel war texts reveal triple-decker hyperbole: *exaggeration* ("man and woman, child and infant") upon *exaggeration* ("utterly destroyed") upon *exaggeration* (local battle plus universal conquest).

In the next chapter we focus on the language of "utter destruction" (*herem*) or its verb form "utterly destroy" (*haram*), which a number of scholars consider a *mis*translation.

28

Revisiting the Translation of *Herem*

"Utter Destruction," "Consecration," "Identity Removal," "Removal from Ordinary Use"?

As a follow-up from our last chapter on hyperbole, this and the next chapters take a closer look at the term perhaps most commonly associated with the charge of "genocide": *haram/herem* (verb: "utterly destroy"; noun: "utter destruction"). For those who might think this suggests "annihilation,"[1] the biblical text gives evidence that *something else is going on here.*

John Walton and Harvey Walton assert that the word *herem* is "commonly mistranslated"—for example, "utter destruction."[2] So let's explore what a more accurate translation looks like.

"Comprehensive Victory" or "Decisive Victory" in Joshua

David Firth notes that while death was involved in Israel's driving out the Canaanites, "the actual levels of destruction described are considerably less than many people imagine because of the distance between the language of the text and how we might use similar language today."[3] Markus Zehnder makes a similar comment after his analysis of the word *nashal*—sometimes translated "destroy," though it can also have the sense of "dislodging" or "clearing out" (e.g., 2 Kings 16:6). He concludes: "The use of the word *nāšal* implies that the conquest of the land of Canaan will be accomplished with little violence."[4]

According to Firth, routine hyperbole in such narratives was a "standard element."[5] He concludes that "totally destroy" and such renderings of *haram* don't really fit well within the war-text genre of Joshua. He suggests that "defeat comprehensively" more precisely captures its meaning.[6]

Likewise, Lissa Wray Beal states that *Joshua's primary emphasis is on victory*, but "that victory has only initially subdued the land. It has not destroyed all kings and peoples, nor resulted in Israel's immediate and complete habitation of the land."[7]

"Consecrated"—but Remaining Alive

In Leviticus 27:21–28, a *servant*, an *animal*, or a *field* is "set apart" (*haram*). But they are not destroyed. Parallel terms indicate that they are "consecrated" (*qadash*) and are "most holy" (*qodesh qodeshim*) to the Lord. That is, they are *"set apart" for priestly use and cannot be released from this new status*. So, a servant may be *haram*—set apart to serve in the sanctuary—but not killed. We could add that in Joshua 6:17 the entire city of Jericho was "under the ban [*herem*]," but articles of gold, silver, bronze, and iron were not destroyed but put into the treasury of the Lord's house (6:24).

John Goldingay points out that the verb "devote" (*haram*) involves "giving something over to God" without having to involve death at all: "So the word doesn't simply mean slaughtering people."[8] Walter Moberly states that in Deuteronomy specifically, *herem* is used as "a metaphor for unqualified allegiance to [Yahweh]."[9]

In addition, after Achan had disobeyed divine orders by taking spoils from Jericho, the Israelites attacked Ai. But because of this compromised situation, the Israelite soldiers were called *herem* at Ai: "They have become accursed [*herem*]. I will not be with you anymore unless you destroy [*shamad*] the things under the ban [*herem*] from your midst" (Josh. 7:12). But just before this, only thirty-six Israelite soldiers were killed in battle (Josh. 7:5). As Firth notes, it doesn't appear that the Israelite soldiers were targeted for death. All that is meant here is that they wouldn't succeed at Ai and that some of them might lose their lives if they attempted to fight without correcting the Achan situation.[10]

Haram as Exile

> Like the nations that the LORD makes to perish before you, so shall you perish, because you would not obey the voice of the LORD your God.
>
> —Deuteronomy 8:20 ESV

Sometimes the term *haram* refers to *being in exile*. In Jeremiah, God declared that he would bring the Babylonians "against this land [of Judah] and against its inhabitants," and "I will utterly destroy [*haram*] them and make them a horror and a hissing, and an everlasting desolation" (Jer. 25:9 ESV). How long would this "everlasting desolation" last? Oh, about "seventy years" (v. 11). And *then* God would go ahead and make Babylon "an everlasting desolation" (v. 12).

Notice that the Southern Kingdom of Judah was not at all exterminated. But *the Babylonians disabled its social, religious, economic, military, and political structures.* Certainly, Judahites were killed. But the nation survived.

This "*haram* as exile" language was actually anticipated in Deuteronomy 8:20.[11] There, God threatened that Israel would "perish" (*abad*) just "like the nations" of Canaan. Notice this: Israel's "destruction" of the Canaanites parallels the predicted exile under Babylon (sixth century BC). Just as the Canaanites were "spewed out" of the land (*without genocide*) so God's people would be spewed out (*without genocide*) (Lev. 18:24–28). What is indisputable is that Israel's (Judah's) exile was certainly not genocide.

On top of all this, Deuteronomy 32:25, which anticipates the same eventual exile, suggests something similar: "Outside the sword will bereave, and inside terror—both young man and virgin, the nursling with the man of gray hair." And to take hyperbolic language one step further, God would even "remove the memory" of Israel from history (v. 26).

What we have here is sweeping language—namely, the merisms of *young man / virgin* and *nursling / man of gray hair*—that makes the future exile look like *total destruction*. But the reality is that this is just *military defeat*. Yes, the defeat and exile of Judah affected everyone—young and old, male and female. The Chronicler used *this very language* when speaking of God's judgment on Judah: "God gave them *all* into the hands of Nebuchadnezzar" (2 Chron. 36:17; cf. Jer. 6:11; 44:7; Lam. 2:21; Ezek. 9:6). To call this "genocide" is utter mislabeling.

Haram as Identity Removal

Walton and Walton, who say that "utter destruction" is a mistranslation, suggest that *herem* means "removal of identity or removal from use."[12] They illustrate with the analogy of Nazi Germany:

> After World War II, when the Allies destroyed the Third Reich, they did not kill every individual German soldier and citizen, they killed the leaders specifically and deliberately (compare to the litany of kings put to the sword in Josh 10–13) and also burned the flags, toppled monuments, dismantled the government and the chain of command, disarmed the military, occupied the cities, banned the symbols, vilified the ideology, and persecuted any attempt to resurrect it—but most of the people were left alone, and most of those who weren't were casualties of war. This is what it means to *herem* an identity.[13]

The same is true of the *non*–"utter destruction" of the Canaanites. As noted, Joshua literally "utterly destroyed" only three cities: Jericho, Ai, and Hazor (burned with fire). The other *herem* cities are simply "removed from use" though still intact. This means that everyone who lived there had to go away—that is, be "driven out": "Killing them is one way to make them go away, of course, but it is not the only way and probably not the preferred way (especially if they are fighting back). The terror that goes before the Israelite army (e.g., Ex 23:27; also Deut 2:23; 11:25) is probably intended to encourage [the Canaanites] to flee rather than fight. Nowhere in the conquest account does the army systematically hunt down fleeing refugees; nowhere are urban citizens trapped in protracted sieges."[14]

Firth points out something similar. The issue of "devotion to destruction" (*herem*) is directed at those who "engaged in armed resistance, since later chapters will show many alive and well in these regions"—for example, the "destroyed" Hebron and Debir (Josh. 10:36–39) were retaken five years later when the land was apportioned to Caleb (15:13–15). The actual "destruction" was aimed at "those who continued to oppose what God was doing and would themselves have chosen to destroy Israel." So this was not random violence; those who did not set themselves against Israel, and who probably fled their towns during battle, were not destroyed or hunted down. Indeed, "only combatants are killed and an alternative way was always available."[15]

Some definitions of "genocide" include the destruction of the *religion* or the *identity* of a people. But if we think in terms of the Allies', forced dismantling of Nazi *ideology* ("religion") and *identity* in post–World War II Germany, we see clearly that Nazism ideology is distinct from the German people themselves. The German people survived the shedding of their Nazi ideology and identity. The same could be said about Canaanites: they could continue to live in the land if they shed their pernicious, immoral practices that were inspired by their deities, religious objects, and rituals.

We see, then, that the term *haram* as "utterly destroy" needs to be revisited. It can convey "decisive defeat," "consecration/removal from ordinary use," "exile," or "identity removal." In the next chapter, we build on this *haram* theme, looking at how the book of Deuteronomy appropriates and dramatically intensifies this rhetorical language.

29

Deuteronomy's Intensified Rhetoric and the Use of *Haram*

Deuteronomy 7: "Destruction" Followed by No Covenant Making or Intermarriage

> When the LORD your God brings you into the land that you are entering to take possession of it, and clears away many nations before you, . . . and when the LORD your God gives them over to you, and you defeat them, then you must devote them to complete destruction [*haram*]. You shall make no covenant with them and show no mercy to them. You shall not intermarry with them, giving your daughters to their sons or taking their daughters for your sons, for they would turn away your sons from following me, to serve other gods. Then the anger of the LORD would be kindled against you, and he would destroy you quickly. But thus shall you deal with them: you shall break down their altars and dash in pieces their pillars and chop down their Asherim and burn their carved images with fire.
>
> —Deuteronomy 7:1–5 ESV

The first thing to notice about the text is this: *if taken literally, the piled-up verbs here contradict one another.* There is no attention to sequence—"clearing away," "defeating," "devoting to destruction"—and this is followed by the commands: "You shall make no covenant with them," and "You shall not intermarry with them." If taken literally, these verbs would contradict each other. If the Canaanites had already been "driven out" or "cleared away," then "destruction" would have been unnecessary.

Beyond this, *what would be the point of this added prohibition against intermarrying with the Canaanites and making alliances with them?* Iain Provan

211

comments: "All of this, already, raises real questions about the proper under-standing of [*haram*], long before we get to the matter of the typical language of ancient Near Eastern conquest accounts."[1]

Second, *the focus is less on Canaanite individuals; the essential issue is the removal of identity markers of Canaanite religion and morality*: "But thus shall you deal with them: you shall break down their altars and dash in pieces their pillars and chop down their Asherim and burn their carved images with fire" (v. 5 ESV). If Canaanites continued to dwell in the land but their identity markers were removed, then the threat to Israel would be defanged—just as the removal of Nazi identity markers in Germany removed the destructive, pernicious threat without killing German civilians.[2]

As we saw in chapter 27, the dominant command or goal to "drive out" or "dispossess" the Canaanites[3] presupposes Canaanite survival. Had Israel's en-emies simply been removed from the land without one Canaanite death, Israel's mission would have been achieved. Since the "total-kill" language is *hyperbolic* and the "driving out" language presupposes *survival*, the real problem wasn't simply Canaanite inhabitants. As with the Nazi scenario, Israel needed to curb Canaanite influence through identity removal—that is, destroying their idols and shrines and not breaking covenant with the Lord. *That* would have been sufficient.

Consider that, at the beginning of Judges, the angel of the Lord rebuked the nation of Israel. He reminded them of this command from Deuteronomy 7: "You shall make no covenant with the inhabitants of this land; you shall tear down their altars." Then he added: "But you have not obeyed Me" (Judg. 2:2). *The problem wasn't failure to exterminate the Canaanites; rather, their gods had become a snare to Israel.*[4] And later in Israel's history, when Israel controlled the land *and* many Canaanites still lived therein, *the lingering divine directive was simply to destroy their idols and high places rather than to kill the Canaanites* (2 Kings 18:4–5; 23:5, 8, 13, 19–20; 2 Chron. 14:3; 17:6; 32:12; 34:3).[5] Once again, the issue was the Israelite identity and mission.

This brings us to a point made by my good friend Tremper Longman. He thinks that my (and Matt Flannagan's) work on Old Testament warfare attempts to "soften the blow" of those harsh texts. Though we are in basic agreement, he says of me: "He works overtime to diminish the level of violence presented in Scripture. . . . I think he overplays [his insights] in order to minimize the role of divine violence."[6]

He then quotes from Psalm 106:[7]

[The Israelites] did not destroy [*shamad*] the peoples, as the Lord commanded them, but they mixed with the nations and learned to do as they did. They served their idols, which became a snare to them. They sacrificed their sons and their daughters to the demons; they poured out innocent blood, the blood of their sons and daughters, whom they sacrificed to the idols of Canaan, and the land was pol-luted with blood. (106:34–38)

Longman makes a fair point, and it appears that Israel should have done a better job of getting rid of the Canaanites. But perhaps certain considerations are worth noting.

1. *Even here in this psalm, though, the emphasis is on compromised Israelite covenant identity and mission.* They had embraced the Canaanite way of life rather than eliminating the Canaanite religious identity markers. As I read literature on this subject, I see a growing number of commentators who are "softening the blow" on these themes in Israelite warfare.[8] "Driving out" the Canaanites certainly involved bloodshed but, as David Firth reminds us, "not as much as many are led to believe."[9]

2. *As we look at the bigger picture about Canaanite warfare, we see some "strange language" and certain complexities of language that, if taken literally, would be contradictory, as Deuteronomy 7 illustrates.* Provan points out that the reader of Deuteronomy—which strongly emphasizes the Canaanite wars—will find the following strange:

   a. The same book mentions that children were not to be held guilty for the sins of their parents and are not to be caught up in their parents' sin either (Deut. 1:39; 24:16).

   b. The reader will also know from previous Scripture of *the distinction between combatants and noncombatants* (cf. Exod. 22:24; Num. 14:3).

If this isn't strange enough, Provan goes on to say that the idea of not intermarrying or making covenant with the Canaanites makes no sense after being told about "driving out" the Canaanites and then the command to "destroy them totally"—on top of the fact that plenty of Canaanites survive into Joshua and Judges. And that's before we get to standard hyperbole in the ancient Near Eastern war text literature.[10]

John Walton and Harvey Walton likewise note that "the prohibition . . . against intermarriage would be unnecessary."[11] Gordon Wenham notes, what we have here appears "more rhetoric than literal demand. . . . It is evident that destruction of Canaanite religion is more important than destroying the people."[12]

Deuteronomy 20:10–20: "Cities at a Distance" and "Cities Nearby"

When the LORD your God delivers [the city] into your hand, put to the sword all the men in it. As for the women, the children, the livestock and everything else in the city, you may take these as plunder for yourselves. And you may use the plunder the LORD your God gives you from your enemies. This is how you are to treat all the cities that are at a distance from you and do not belong to the nations nearby. However, in the cities of the nations the LORD your God is giving you as an inheritance, do not leave alive anything that breathes.

—Deuteronomy 20:13–16 NIV

Perhaps Deuteronomy 20's distinction between the prescribed treatment of cities *outside* of Canaan and the cities *within* Canaan supports the idea that God wanted all the Canaanite people themselves obliterated.[13] We now explore that charge.

This chapter gives instructions regarding warfare with two groups:

1. Surrounding nations "very far from you" (vv. 10–15)—*outside* the land— which involves killing "all the males" (v. 13)
2. Canaanite cities "nearby"—that is, *within* the promised land (vv. 16–20)— and the warfare language sounds more severe: "Do not leave alive anything that breathes"

In response, first, as we've noted, *the Canaanite warfare in Joshua reveals extensive hyperbole concerning cities within Canaan*, the holy land, which God was giving to Israel. This region is the central focus of fighting in Deuteronomy and Joshua. Despite Joshua's language of "no survivors," "no mercy," "utter destruction," and the like, *many Canaanites survived these disabling raids and continued to dwell in Israel in large numbers.*

Second, *if hyperbole is clearly found in the section about warfare inside the "sacred space" of Canaan designated for God's covenant people, then how much more would hyperbole pertain to those cities outside the land—with a far lesser goal to achieve?*[14] So reference to "killing all the men" in cities outside the land would be another instance of exaggeration. As William Webb and Gordon Oeste write, "If this hyperbole is clear about those who dwell within the land of Canaan, clearly we have reason to think this is the case for cities outside the land where the threat of idolatry and covenant-breaking is removed from the Israelite nation."[15]

Third, *the actual cases in Scripture of warfare "outside the land" where "all the adult males" would purportedly be killed if they didn't surrender reveal a fairly tame picture*: in most cases, the males from territories outside Canaan were left alive. They typically submitted themselves to forced labor or paid tribute to the Israelites.[16]

So with cities both inside and outside the land, we have ample hyperbole. Again, if there is vast hyperbole concerning the cities in Canaan—the major theological focal point of the biblical narrative—then we're justified in seeing the cities outside the land of Canaan as being subject to the same sorts of rhetorical devices.

Fighting against Kings Sihon and Og

"Do to [Og] what you did to Sihon king of the Amorites, who reigned in Heshbon." So they struck him down, together with his sons and his whole army, leaving them no survivors. And they took possession of his land.

—Numbers 21:34–35 NIV

We completely destroyed them, as we had done with Sihon king of Heshbon, destroying every city—men, women and children.

—Deuteronomy 3:6 NIV

The More Realistic Battle Scene in Numbers 21

During Israel's wilderness wanderings, Moses sent messengers to Sihon (Amorite king of Heshbon) and Og (king of Bashan). He requested permission to peacefully pass through their territories, but these kings refused and even took up arms against the Israelites. Each took "all his people" to fight against Israel (Num. 21:23; cf. v. 33). By "all his people" is obviously meant "his entire army" (NIV) or "all his men" (RSV). Verse 35 makes clear that we just have Og, his sons, and his whole army in view, with the added hyperbole, "leaving them no survivors" (NIV). The armies that came to fight against Israel were defeated. Numbers 21 mentions *only* soldiers, the kings, and their sons as having been killed: "Do to him . . ."; "his sons and his whole army" (vv. 34–35 NIV).

On top of this, King Sihon had to march *twenty miles* with his army—and all their military gear—"from the Arnon [River] to the Jabbok [River]" up to Ammonite territory (vv. 23–24 NIV). *That clearly rules out women, children, and the elderly, who wouldn't have been part of this excursion*—a journey sufficiently exhausting for the sturdiest of male soldiers. Furthermore, though Numbers 21 gives a more realistic account of the battle scene, the mention of the *entire army* being wiped out is itself likely hyperbolic.[17]

Extreme Hyperbole Added in the Retelling (Deut. 3)

Something happens when we get to Deuteronomy 3:6 (see also 2:31–35), where the Sihon and Og story is retold. This time, the *totalistic rhetoric* of *women* and *children* (v. 6) has been added to a passage of piled-up merisms (3:1–13 NIV): "no survivors" (v. 3), "all his cities" (v. 4), "not one of the sixty cities" (v. 4), "the whole region" (v. 4), "completely destroyed" (v. 6), and so on.

In Numbers 21, we saw that the killing of all adult males (the king, his sons, his army) was itself hyperbolic. But now in Deuteronomy 3:6, the description includes *women* and *children*. *This indicates that "man and woman" and "young and old" can appear in the text without women, children, and the elderly having been present in the actual battle scene.* And as we observed in chapter 27, later narratives such as Joshua and 1 Samuel 15:3 *adopt Deuteronomy's totalizing language of women and children.*

We've already looked at 1 Samuel 15:3. Likewise, Joshua 6:21 uses this sweeping language of men and women, young and old, cattle, sheep, and donkeys, which is hyperbolic. We've seen clearly that Joshua left many survivors, yet the narrator declares that he carried out "all that Moses commanded" (Josh. 9:24; 11:12, 15,

23).[18] So Moses himself was using that same ancient Near Eastern hyperbole—not commanding annihilation or "genocide."

EXCURSUS:
"Have You Spared All the Women?" A Note on Numbers 31

> They fought against Midian, as the LORD commanded Moses, and killed every man.
>
> —Numbers 31:7 NIV

This text relates to what we have been saying as it pertains to women and children. We have two possible scenarios here. In both cases, we see unique elements.

Scenario 1: Complete Counterattack for Deliberate Midianite Seduction

The Midianites—a nomadic people who lived in modern-day Arabia—would eventually become a thorn in the side of Israel in the book of Judges. In one case, the pagan prophet Balaam—under pressure from Moab's king—enlisted Midianites to maliciously conspire against Israel (Num. 31:16).

Though Moses had married a Midianite (Exod. 2:15–21) and there had been no previous hostility with Israel, now the Midianite women deliberately attempted to seduce the Israelite men into sexual immorality and into covenant-breaking with the Lord and joining themselves to the god Baal (Num. 25:1–3). In this way, Midianite seduction and Israelite treachery would come under God's curse. Israel's mission and identity were in grave danger of derailment. In response to this defiance, God brought death and plague *to the Israelites* for their treasonous activity.

This challenging text involves not only Yahweh's command to fight against the Midianite *men* but also Moses's additional command to strike down *women* and *boys*. The traditional understanding is that this seduction was a particularly malevolent act—a defiant assault on Yahweh and Israel's covenantal integrity and thus a threat to Israel's mission to bring blessing to the world. This called for severe judgment against Midian, including the women involved in the seduction. Why the boys? This would prohibit their rising up in the next generation to attempt Israel's overthrow.[19]

This seduction was *tantamount to an unprovoked attack of war against Israel*—like the Amalekites (Exod. 17) and Kings Sihon and Og (Num. 21). And *it was also tantamount to bringing a curse on Israel* as the Moabite king Balak just solicited the pagan prophet Balaam to do (Num. 22–24). The Israelites weren't the aggressors. *So this particular command, which was not routine, had the very strong element of justice behind it.*

But let's assume for the moment that we should take this in a straightforward manner—that the men, women, and boys were wiped out and that the young girls/women not involved in the subterfuge against Israel assimilated into Israelite households. *We apparently have no more Midianites left over.*

If so, this scenario brings some questions with it—yes, more indications of hyperbole. First, a generation or so later, "innumerable" Midianite soldiers on their camels *rose up to fight against Israel* (Judg. 6:5). John Goldingay notes: "Midian's appearing in strength later in the Old Testament . . . would be odd if they were annihilated in the wilderness."[20]

Second, a *further indication of exaggeration is that every Midianite man was killed without one Israelite fatality* (Num. 31:49). This seems to be the reverse of the ancient Near Eastern trash talk of "There were no survivors." In the case of the Israelite army, the equivalent trash talk was "Everybody on our side survived!"

Scenario 2: Maybe Not So Complete a Counterassault

In my estimation, scenario 2 makes better sense in light of the biblical text. As retribution against the Midianites for intentionally seducing Israel away from the Lord, he "commanded" (*tsavah*) Moses that Israel's army fight against Midian men: "[Israel] fought against Midian, as the LORD commanded Moses, and killed every man" (Num. 31:7 NIV). But after all of this, Moses *added his own command*—to kill the women (nonvirgins) and young boys too (vv. 15–18). What are we to make of these two commands? Is Moses's command simply an extension of what God commanded, or is something more going on? Though I can't go into detail here, I will list a few considerations that have prompted various scholars to take this second alternative seriously.[21]

First, *the Israelite army had already completed their task*, "as the LORD commanded Moses" (v. 7). Apparently, once they carried out the Lord's order, that was it—mission accomplished.

Second, *this appears to be Moses's command and not the Lord's*. After all, the Israelite army had *already done* what the Lord commanded. Moses's additional command seems to be an instance of giving a nonauthoritative judgment. This is comparable to the prophet Nathan telling David to build the temple (2 Sam. 7:3). But the Lord told Nathan that David would *not* build it, but rather Solomon. We have another instance of this in 1 Kings 13:7–26, where one prophet clearly has a word from God and another prophet tests the first prophet with a merely contrived word from the Lord (v. 18: "He lied to him"; cf. vv. 21–22). As with Moses, Nathan, and the deceptive prophet, we have indications within these narrative texts that these prophets are going beyond what God has said. These are instances of occasional off-the-cuff, nonauthoritative prophetic assertions. As we'll see, Moses is *going beyond* what God commanded rather than *fulfilling* what God commanded. Moses is *reformulating* what divine "vengeance" (*neqamah*) calls for (Num. 31:2, 3).

Third, *nothing happened after Moses's command was issued*. The focus at the end of the chapter is on the distribution of material spoils and permission for Israelite men to take Midianite wives for themselves if they chose to (cf. Deut. 21:10–14). But *there was no actual implementation of those orders*. As we saw with Achan and his family (Josh. 7), the Old Testament certainly doesn't recoil from mentioning such things if they actually happened—including potential or actual judgments against women (e.g., Num. 5:20–22; 2 Kings 11:20)—but we just don't see any mention of follow-through in this particular Numbers 31 passage.[22]

Fourth, we've already seen how *this kind of "total-kill" language doesn't appear to apply in case after case*. For one thing, the affirmation that "all" of the Midianite men were killed is *itself* simply another hyperbolic statement. And as we've noted, if all Midianite *men, women*, and *boys* were literally eradicated (with the rest assimilated into Israel), *that pretty much eliminates the entire Midianite nation*. But "elimination" clearly didn't happen. The Midianites lived on for generations, including getting a mention in the apocryphal book of Judith (2:25–26), whose events took place in the fourth century BC.

Fifth, *with Moses's anticipated death* (*Num. 31:2*), *in this one final act he appears to play a more transitional and secondary role here—in contrast to the increased role of the priesthood* (cf. 25:7–8; 27:19–22; 31:6, 21–24, 25, 31, 41, 47, 51–54). This fact is borne out as we look at the literary framework of Numbers 31. The key point is that *the structure of Numbers 31 presents Moses's command* (*v. 16*) *as an outlier—an add-on to what God had already commanded*.[23] The basic literary arrangement of Numbers 31 focuses on two sets of divine commands, two

acts of obedience, and two nonauthoritative extensions of those commands. Between the two
sets of divine commands is the singular section on purification, which emphasizes the central
role of the priesthood:[24]

> *First divine command (31:1–4):* (1) The Lord commands Moses to avenge the people
> of Israel against the Midianites (vv. 1–2), and (2) so Moses commands Israel to "ex-
> ecute the LORD's vengeance on Midian" (v. 3).
>
> *First obedient response (31:5–12):* Phinehas the son of Eleazar the high priest
> goes—or perhaps even leads Israel—into battle with holy vessels from the tabernacle
> and trumpets in hand to sound the alarm (v. 6). Remember that Phinehas had been
> instrumental in bringing an end to the plague God had brought against the Israelites,
> who had sinned at Baal-Peor (Num. 25:6–11). This Midianite seduction and Israelite
> treachery led to the command here to fight against the Midianites, and the priestly
> Phinehas played a central role in both events. And the Israelite army faithfully carried
> out what the Lord commanded (31:7).
>
> *First extension beyond the divine command (31:13–18):* Here Moses went beyond the
> Lord's command, telling the *officers* and *captains* to kill the women and boys too (vv.
> 14, 17). This Mosaic "extension" isn't attributed to the Lord, and there is no indica-
> tion that the command was even carried out. In fact, Moses immediately shifts to the
> matter of purification (vv. 19–20). Also, in this "extension" section of the narrative,
> Phinehas the priest drops out of the picture.
>
> *Purification (31:19–24):* We noted that Moses suddenly turns from his call for addi-
> tional action against the Midianites to purification regulations. Then Eleazar the high
> priest addresses the army that his son had led into battle about the matter of puri-
> fication. He notes that this is what "the LORD commanded Moses" (v. 21)—and he
> elaborates on what is required (vv. 21–24).
>
> *Second divine command (31:25–30):* The Lord commands Moses to count and divide
> the plunder from the battle, and Eleazar is to work alongside Moses in executing this
> command (v. 25).
>
> *Second obedient response (31:31–47):* Both Moses and Eleazar carry out the com-
> mand to count and divide the plunder. Together "Moses and Eleazar the priest did
> just as the LORD had commanded Moses" (vv. 31, 41, 47).
>
> *Second extension beyond the divine command (31:48–54):* The *commanders* and
> *captains* bring an additional gift to Moses—an act that wasn't commanded by the
> Lord (v. 48; cf. vv. 52, 54). This parallels Moses's "extension" *beyond* what God
> commanded and that was *not* explicitly carried out. By contrast, the officers' gift
> that went beyond the Lord's command *was* accepted by Moses. Then *both* Moses
> and Eleazar receive the gifts and bring them into the tent of meeting (vv. 51–54).
> Notice that throughout verses 25–54, Eleazar plays a prominent role. As Ken Brown
> observes concerning the first and second extensions of two divine commands here,
> "Whereas Moses alone spoke and acted in 31:14–18 (despite Eleazar's presence in
> 31:13), Moses and Eleazar are *together* addressed by YHWH in 31:26, *together* fulfill
> YHWH's command in 31:31, 41, and *together* accept the officers' gift in 31:51, 54."[25]

The first of these two scenarios is a bit more murky and less straightforward, involving the
standard hyperbole we've come to see in other war texts. The second scenario seems better
grounded from a literary and theological point of view.

Exodus and Deuteronomy Parallels

As we've seen, Deuteronomy uses sweeping, highly intense warfare language. It tends to take earlier Pentateuchal language about the Canaanites and heighten it to a fever pitch. A clear example can be seen by a comparison of Deuteronomy 7:1–26 with Exodus 23:23–33 along with 34:11–16, which cover the same content. Both relate the divine driving out of the Amorites, prohibitions against making covenants and intermarrying with the Canaanites, the promise to send the "hornet," and commands to tear down Canaanite altars and smash their pillars. But despite the similar content, *Deuteronomy 7 intensifies the language with "utterly destroy" commands, showing no mercy, and the like.* (See table 29.1.)

We could add that in Exodus, *God* promised that *he himself / the angel of the Lord* would drive out the Canaanites. But Deuteronomy 7 (along with chapter 20) emphasizes *divine commands to Israel to "utterly destroy,"* while including language of God's assistance in this effort. Even so, Deuteronomy exhibits hyperbole and strong emotive rhetoric not found in the earlier material.

In personal correspondence, the British ancient Near East scholar Alan Millard firmly agrees with the "intensified rhetoric" I have outlined here. He adds that the structure and context of Deuteronomy are a *public speech*, which utilizes "appropriate exaggeration to make its points." He observes that if we listen to speeches of modern Near Eastern rulers, we will note the "same elements."[26]

Table 29.1. Deuteronomic Intensification of Earlier Pentateuchal Material

Exodus 23:23–33	Exodus 34:11–16	Deuteronomy 7:1–26
"I will drive out / wipe out"	"I will drive out"	"You must destroy"
"My angel will go ahead of you and bring you into the land of the Amorites. . . , and I will wipe them out" (v. 23 NIV). "I will . . . drive out" (vv. 29, 30 NIV); etc. "I will give into your hands the people who live in the land, and you will drive them out before you" (v. 31 NIV).	"I will drive out before you the Amorites . . ." (v. 11 NIV).	"When the LORD . . . drives out before you many nations . . . , *then you must destroy them totally*" (vv. 1–2 NIV). "*You must destroy* all the peoples the LORD your God gives over to you. *Do not look on them with pity*" (v. 16 NIV). "*You will destroy them*" (v. 24 NIV).
No treaty	No treaty	No treaty
"Do not make a covenant with them or with their gods" (v. 32 NIV).	"Be careful not to make a treaty with those who live in the land where you are going, or they will be a snare among you" (v. 12; cf. v. 14 NIV).	"Make no treaty with them, *and show them no mercy*" (v. 2 NIV).

Exodus 23:23–33	Exodus 34:11–16	Deuteronomy 7:1–26
	No intermarriage	No intermarriage
	"And when you choose some of their daughters as wives for your sons and those daughters prostitute themselves to their gods, they will lead your sons to do the same" (v. 16 NIV).	"Do not intermarry with them. Do not give your daughters to their sons or take their daughters for your sons, for they will turn your sons away from following me to serve other gods" (vv. 3–4 NIV).
Destroy their religious objects	Destroy their religious objects	Destroy their religious objects
"Do not bow down before their gods. . . . You must demolish them and break their sacred stones to pieces" (v. 24 NIV).	"Break down their altars, smash their sacred stones and cut down their Asherah poles" (v. 13 NIV).	"This is what you are to do to them: Break down their altars, smash their sacred stones, cut down their Asherah poles and burn their idols in the fire" (v. 5 NIV). "Do not bring a *detestable thing* into your house or you, like it, will be set apart for destruction. *Regard it as vile and detest it, for it is set apart for destruction*" (v. 26).
Sending the hornet, driving out little by little		Sending the hornet, driving out little by little
"I will send the hornet" (v. 28 NIV). "Little by little I will drive them out before you, until you have increased enough to take possession of the land" (v. 30 NIV).		"The LORD your God will send the hornet among them" (v. 20 NIV). "The LORD your God will drive out those nations before you, little by little" (v. 22 NIV).

EXCURSUS:
"The Hornet"

Interestingly, Boyd claims that God himself would send a plague of hornets to displace the Canaanites so that Israel could peacefully enter the land without lifting a military finger (cf. Exod. 23:28; Lev. 18:28). But God's original intentions weren't carried out, Boyd claims. Moses and Joshua distorted this command because of their culturally conditioned, violence-prone mindset, promoting Israelite warfare instead.[27] In response, we can point out that in the same "hornets" passage, God says that the *Israelites* would be involved with him in the process: "For I will deliver the inhabitants of the land into your hand, and you will drive them out before you"

(Exod. 23:31). The parallel passage in Exodus 34:11 likewise indicates that God will "drive out" the Canaanites (v. 11). But he warns that the Israelites should not make any covenant with "the inhabitants of the land" (v. 12) and that they should destroy their religious objects (v. 13), which would make no sense if God had peacefully driven out the Canaanites.

Furthermore, the theme of Israel's military cooperation with God's activity as "hornets" is reinforced by two other "hornet" passages: these include clear references to Israelite warfare (Deut. 7:20) and the Israelites' victory over Kings Sihon and Og and their armies with the Lord's help, since the Israelites' military might ("sword" and "bow") was inadequate to achieve victory (Josh. 24:12).

As we look back on the last three chapters, we've observed that much murky language and hyped-up rhetoric surround Israel's warfare. A realistic picture presents something more nuanced than what our critics from within—and from without—typically present. And it's certainly nothing approaching "genocide" or "ethnic cleansing." In the next chapter, we look at some final themes related to warfare that assist in more accurately representing Israel's engagement with the Canaanites.

30

Did the Israelites "Cruelly Invade" the Land of Canaan?

Some critics from within charge that the Israelites cruelly invaded the cities of the hapless Canaanites. One critic (Eric Seibert) makes the "but today we know better" argument: today we know that victory in battle doesn't take place because God is assisting in the victory but because of an army's superior military force, including troop size and sophisticated weaponry. This critic claims that ancient Israelites made assumptions that "people of faith today should no longer accept."[1] Thus, "we all know" that military victory *doesn't* come about because God is on someone's side.

In this chapter, we'll explore this and several other related issues concerning this charge.

Israel's Need to Trust in God

In the film *Saving Private Ryan*,[2] Daniel Jackson—a sniper from West Fork, Tennessee, and a devout Catholic—was involved in the June 6, 1944, Normandy invasion in an effort to end the Nazi occupation in Europe. While engaged in gun battles, he is portrayed in the film as praying these Scriptures as he fired upon Nazi soldiers:

> But be not thou far from me, O LORD: O my strength, haste thee to help me. (Ps. 22:19 KJV)

Blessed be the LORD my strength which teacheth my hands to war, and my fingers to fight. (Ps. 144:1 KJV)

My goodness, and my fortress; my high tower, and my deliverer; my shield, and he in whom I trust; who subdueth my people under me. (Ps. 144:2 KJV)

These passages certainly illustrate trust in the Lord in resisting evil and in loving one's neighbor in Nazi-occupied Europe to free people from oppression.

All the more, the Israelites' entry into the promised land would require profound trust in God. Indeed, for a number of reasons, the view that Israel "cruelly invaded" Canaan misrepresents what the biblical text repeatedly affirms. For one thing, the *Lord commanded Joshua not to "tremble or be dismayed" but to be "strong and courageous"* (Josh. 1:9). Filling Moses's sandals was a daunting task for Joshua, and the idea of warfare could naturally arouse fear and faintheartedness for Israelites (cf. Deut. 20:1–4).

Second, *Israel had no comparable military personnel or sufficient martial might and weaponry; fighting required remarkable trust in the Lord.* Israelites who fought were not professional soldiers. It was by the Lord's "great power" that Israel could drive out "nations greater and mightier than you" (Deut. 4:37–39; cf. Num. 13:28; Deut. 20:1). In Deuteronomy 7, the "seven nations" of the Canaanites are described as "greater and stronger than you" (v. 1). Israel was right to wonder: "How can I dispossess" these nations that are "greater and stronger" than I am? Moses told the nation not to be fearful but to remember how the Lord had delivered them from Egypt (vv. 17–21). Two chapters later, Moses reminded Israel that these nations were "greater and mightier than you, great cities fortified to heaven, a people great and tall." However, God would work with Israel to "destroy," "subdue," and "drive them out" (9:1–3).

As John Goldingay writes, "Attacking the Canaanites required extraordinary trust in Yahweh, because the Canaanites were more numerous and their weaponry was more sophisticated. And trust in Yahweh is a key ethical principle in the Old Testament and a key principle when you are waging war or thinking about waging war."[3]

Even God's command to hamstring horses and burn chariots after victory reinforces this point (Josh. 11:6). Horses and chariots were like modern-day tanks, and they represented military power and domination. God warned any king of Israel not to accumulate horses (Deut. 17:16), as God wanted Israel dependent on his power rather than on military might (Exod. 15:3; Ps. 20:7).[4]

Third, according to Richard Hess, "The major wars Israel fought were defensive." Hess adds: "Either Israel had to fight or it faced extinction."[5]

Consider the Amalekite attack on Israel (Exod. 17)—and the Amalekites' persistent attacks against Israel throughout its history (e.g., Judg. 3:13; 6:3, 33; 7:12; 10:12; 1 Sam. 14:48; etc.). No wonder the Lord vowed that he "will be at war against the Amalekites from generation to generation" (Exod. 17:16 NIV).

In addition, during the "wilderness campaign," Israel was attacked by the kings Sihon and Og (Num. 21). And as Israel entered the land, Canaanite kings rose up to fight against them (Josh. 10:1–5, 35; 11:1–5). As with Pharaoh in Exodus, these Canaanite "kings" were similarly hard-hearted and "disobedient" (cf. Heb. 11:31), and they never attempted to make peace with Israel (Josh. 11:19). So God withdrew his gracious influences—that is, he "hardened their hearts" (Josh. 11:20)—and Israel was able to successfully engage in their disabling raids.

Fourth, *Israel's wars against the Canaanites focused on well-fortified citadels*. Israel's attacks on Jericho and Ai were against military forts, and we see similar action throughout the cities of Canaan, as is solidly supported by archaeological evidence.[6] Cities—rather than hamlets and rural areas where noncombatants generally lived—were to be the target of Israel's disabling raids (e.g., Deut. 20:16). As Hess notes:

> The detailed description of Joshua 10:28–42, where "city" after "city" is destroyed, should be understood in the context of the "city" as primarily a fort for the king, the temple, and the army. Understood in this way there is no reason to assume that noncombatant innocents were slaughtered in these forts. Even if the common people of Canaan chose not to join Israel as did Rahab and her family, they probably did not station themselves in these forts, as they had been emptied of their armies who went to fight Israel (and faced defeat). Knowing that the Israelites were on their way to attack these forts, the average Canaanite most likely fled to the hills [cf. Jer. 4:29] where they hid until the Israelite army had passed. The biblical evidence for this is that the book of Judges knows of no Canaanite extermination. It only knows that there were plenty of Canaanites around in the next generation to lead Israel astray (e.g., Judg. 2:10–13).[7]

In all of this, keep in mind that just as God could fight *with* Israel, God could also fight *against* Israel (Judg. 2:15; Jer. 21:5). That doesn't sound like the tribalistic, "insider-outsider," "good guys versus bad guys" rhetoric of the "textual" God that our critics from within talk about.

Trusting in Large Troop Numbers?

Some critics from within (e.g., Greg Boyd) will latch onto the alleged massive troop numbers as well as casualty lists given in the Old Testament. They will treat gargantuan numbers as literal. Of course, this reinforces the "slaughter" imagery they tend to highlight.[8] That's not to say that fighting wasn't bloody; nor does it mean that the biblical text celebrates warfare and violence. For example, David could not build the temple because he had been a man of war and bloodshed (1 Chron. 22:8; 28:3).

However, *when we read about tens of thousands of troops in battle*—or 210,000 troops who fight under Saul against the Amalekites (1 Sam. 15:4)—*we must be cautious*. While one can make a case for "numerical hyperbole,"[9] more probable is that the term "thousand" (*eleph*) is inaccurately translated. Rather than dealing with elephantine numbers, something more modest is in view. This word can mean "division," "squad," "(military) unit," "clan," "family," and the like. To assume *eleph* must mean literally "one thousand" would be a misreading of the text. Keep in mind that when David is said to have slain his "ten thousands" (1 Sam. 18:7), up to that point he had only slain Goliath!

Second, *we should consider scholarly efforts at recalculation.* We've already observed that twenty thousand Israelites leaving Egypt is a more sensible number than two million.[10] According to Colin Humphreys, in 1 Samuel 15, there are two hundred fighting units/squads from Israel plus ten fighting units from Judah—probably nine to ten in each unit (i.e., 2,100 soldiers).[11] That's a huge drop from 210,000. And this would be strange when compared to the mere six hundred troops Saul mustered to fight against the Philistines in the previous chapter (14:2).

And when Ai defeated Israel by striking down "thirty-six" men (Josh. 7:3–5), this was a fairly small number, even though it seemed like this was a humiliating defeat for Israel. That's especially the case even if we take literally that "two or three thousand men" were required to fight against Ai.[12]

Third, *to reinforce this point, consider the census in the book of Numbers.* The entire book begins with a census of the people. We read in 3:39: "The total number of Levites counted at the LORD's command by Moses and Aaron according to their clans, including every male a month old or more, was 22,000" (NIV). But then a few verses later we read of a mere "273 firstborn Israelites," but these "exceed the number of the Levites" (3:46 NIV). So those massive numbers need significant readjustment.

Fourth, *no wonder Moses warned the Israelites about gradual occupation since their numbers were small*: "The LORD your God will clear away these nations before you little by little; you will not be able to put an end to them quickly, for the wild beasts would grow too numerous for you" (Deut. 7:22). If the number of Israelites coming into Canaan was two million, the "little by little" would seem far less daunting than twenty thousand coming into a land the size of New Jersey.

All of this certainly fits the rest of the Pentateuch's observations—that the Israelites were going into a land whose inhabitants far outnumbered the Israelites. They would have to trust in God's power to fight—just as God used Gideon's small army of three hundred men to deliver Israel from the Midianite oppression (Judg. 7:1–8). As Saul's son Jonathan told his armor bearer: "The Lord is not restrained to save by many or by few" (1 Sam. 14:6).

Reason to Trust in God's Command: Divine Confirmation through Signs and Wonders

As detailed in the *Genocide* book, any Israelite soldier wondering whether the actual God was behind the command to drive out the Canaanites could plainly see divine confirmation through signs and wonders.[13] These weren't like private "rev-elations" to Muhammad in a cave or Joseph Smith in the woods. No, the highly public ten plagues of Egypt, the Red Sea crossing, the daily manna, the parting of the Jordan, and the constant presence of God manifested in the pillar of cloud by day and fire by night over Israel's camp should have persuaded all Israelites.

We've noted that the Canaanites were already well aware of the power of Israel's God. Indeed, all of the Canaanites had a forty-year "heads-up" about Israel's God. Rahab told the Israelite spies: "I know that the LORD has given you the land, and that the fear of you has fallen upon us, and that all the inhab-itants of the land melt away before you" (Josh. 2:9 ESV; see also 5:1; 9:9–10; cf. 1 Sam. 4:7–8). And the Canaanites could have fled—driving themselves out, as it were—or, of course, recognize the greatness of Israel's God over other gods and made peace with Israel, as other Canaanites had done.

31

The "Actual" God in
Old Testament Warfare

As we draw some strands together in this final chapter on Old Testament warfare, we acknowledge that whatever view we take will not completely resolve all the moral and interpretive challenges. I do believe that the view presented here is more faithful to what both testaments affirm.

Now, our critics from within at first appear to have a tidy and more morally appealing solution—*just pin all the difficulties on the "textual" God and not the "actual" God*. But not only do we seem to catch a glimpse of Marcion in this move, with a huge gap between two "Gods"; we also can't forget that the problem of divine coercive force carries over into the New Testament—and Jesus is actually in the thick of it too. Of course, God's participation in such counterviolence involves his deep anguish of heart and great reluctance. God desires to bless and not curse, to save and not judge, to help rather than afflict, to love his enemies rather than judge them.

Before we review where we've been on Old Testament warfare, let's look at a final example from a critic from within (Boyd).

Does Nehemiah 9:24 Illustrate or Undermine the Critic's Point?

So their sons entered and possessed the land.
And You subdued before them the inhabitants of the land, the
    Canaanites,
and You gave them into their hand, with their kings and the peoples of
    the land,
to do with them as they desired [*kiratsonam*].

—Nehemiah 9:24

According to our critic from within, this passage shows that Israel "resisted Yahweh's nonviolent will," and so God withdrew to "allow his stiff-necked people to
carry out their violent proclivities."[1] The actual God *didn't subdue* the Canaanites.
Rather the text indicates that *Israel's* "doing as they desired" must be negative.
But this is a misreading of the text.

A Premature Negativity

A more careful reading of the text of Nehemiah's prayer reveals that *the negativity has not yet begun, and the narrative continues in a very positive tone after
verse 24*:

> They captured fortified cities and a fertile land.
> They took possession of houses full of every good thing,
> hewn cisterns, vineyards, olive groves,
> fruit trees in abundance.
> So they ate, were filled and grew fat,
> and reveled in Your great goodness. (9:25)

All of that sounds wonderful and divinely approved. But finally we get to the
negative turn in verses 26–27:

> But they became disobedient and rebelled against You,
> and cast Your law behind their backs
> and killed Your prophets who had admonished them
> so that they might return to You,
> and they committed great blasphemies.
> Therefore You delivered them into the hand of their oppressors who
>   oppressed them.

What's more, the premature judgment about verse 24's negativity ("doing
as they desired") is further preempted in verse 22. There, *Nehemiah made another positive statement about God's giving Israel the land*: the Lord "also gave
them kingdoms and peoples, and allotted them to them as a boundary. They
took possession of the land of Sihon the king of Heshbon and the land of Og
the king of Bashan" (v. 22). The Lord himself *gave* them these lands, and it all
sounds positive.

"Doing as They Desired" Isn't Necessarily a Bad Thing

On top of all this, *it is incorrect to assume that "[doing] with them as they
desired" must be negative.* There are a couple of reasons why:

1. *The context makes clear that our critic's interpretation is incorrect, as
   many commentators recognize.*[2] Gordon McConville observes: "*The Lord*

is said to have sent the ancient people of Israel into the land of Canaan to do with its inhabitants 'as they would.' There is no question *there* about where the people's authority came from."[3] H. G. M. Williamson comments that this passage (vv. 22–25) "speaks entirely of God's goodness in providing for his people," which includes "[doing] with them as they desired."[4]

2. *The word translated "as they desired"* (ratson) *is neutral and doesn't in itself suggest moral blameworthiness.* This word group (v. 24: "as they desired") may be used *negatively* in some contexts (Dan. 8:4; 11:3, 16, 36), or it may be used *positively*: "All Judah . . . had sought him *with their whole desire*, and he was found by them, and the LORD gave them rest all around" (2 Chron. 15:15 ESV); God satisfies "the *desire* of every living thing" (Ps. 145:16), "the *desire* of those who fear him" (145:19).

In Esther 9:5, when the Jews did "as they pleased," the meaning there is that they were "given a free hand without official interference."[5] Doing "as they pleased" still included restraint: "They did not lay their hands on the plunder" (Esther 9:10, 15, 16). When it came to Canaanite warfare, the Israelites had various divine commands and restraints to attend: not removing fruit trees, not taking plunder that was *herem* or "removed from use," and not raping women. That is, it is possible to do "what one pleases" but within the parameters of the law, whether divine or human.[6]

A Similar Pattern in Parallels to Nehemiah 9:24–27

Giving further support to the positive tone of verse 24, *a number of biblical parallels to Nehemiah 9:24–27 display the divine blessing associated with Israel's taking the land; these texts are then followed by mention of Israel's falling into disobedience and idolatry, as depicted in Judges.* Jeremiah 32:21–23 presents a parallel to the Nehemiah text. Israel takes the land—without a hint of negativity—and then Israel disobeys once in the land:

> You brought Your people Israel out of the land of Egypt with signs and with wonders, and with a strong hand and with an outstretched arm and with great terror; and gave them this land, which You swore to their forefathers to give them, a land flowing with milk and honey. They came in and took possession of it, but they did not obey Your voice or walk in Your law; they have done nothing of all that You commanded them to do; therefore You have made all this calamity come upon them. (Jer. 32:21–23)

Psalm 78:53–56 depicts the same pattern:

> He guided them safely, so they were unafraid;
> but the sea engulfed their enemies.

> And so he brought them to the border of his holy land,
>   to the hill country his right hand had taken.
> He drove out nations before them
>   and allotted their lands to them as an inheritance [a reference to
>   Josh.18:6, where lands were allocated by casting lots];
>   he settled the tribes of Israel in their homes.
>
> But they put God to the test
>   and rebelled against the Most High;
>   they did not keep his statutes. (NIV)

We could add other texts as well that indicate that God fulfilled his word by bringing Israel into the land (e.g., Judg. 2:1–13).

The Real Problem Is Idolatry, Not Warfare

Crucial to this discussion is putting our finger on what the *actual* problem is in these texts. Contrary to what Boyd contends—that "fallen, violence-prone" prophets issued these commands—*none of these texts portrays Israel's rebellion or deviation in terms of resorting to violence*. The problem is that *Israel has been engaging in idolatry*. Israel's inability to drive out the Canaanites was *due not to an alleged proneness to violence that overrode God's intentions but rather to the snare of idolatry*. But our critic from within has misdiagnosed the problem. The ancient Israelites were less *violence* prone than they were *idol* prone. That is a huge oversight by various critics from within. And even if the Israelites were violence prone, it still would have been insane for them to attack the militarily superior and more numerous Canaanites with their walled cities. This is why God had to remind the Israelites—and Joshua in particular—not to fear them.

The New Testament's Affirmations of Divinely Endorsed Wars

Just as those Old Testament texts we've just reviewed speak positively about Israel's entering the promised land and God's giving them victory in battle, so does the New Testament. It speaks in a unified voice with those Old Testament texts we've just reviewed about driving out the Canaanites and receiving the land as a gift from God. Our critics from within give the impression that the "more enlightened" New Testament voices should condemn Moses and Joshua as examples of immorality. After all, the New Testament provides a robust critique of ancient Israel's disobedience—for example, 1 Corinthians 10. There Paul even mentions Israel's grumbling against the Lord (v. 10). But if we follow the reasoning from our critics from within, surely being violence prone toward the Canaanites is far worse than complaining. But the New Testament itself is only favorable about Israel's taking the land:

> And having received [the portable tabernacle] in their turn, our fathers brought it in with Joshua upon dispossessing the nations whom God drove out before our fathers, until the time of David. (Acts 7:45)

> When He had destroyed seven nations in the land of Canaan, He distributed their land as an inheritance—all of which took about four hundred and fifty years. (Acts 13:19)

In keeping with this pattern, Hebrews 11:30–34 treats Israel's divinely commanded warfare favorably:

> By faith the walls of Jericho fell down after they had been encircled for seven days. By faith Rahab the harlot did not perish along with those who were disobedient, after she had welcomed the spies in peace.

Notice again that this act is seen as just divine judgment on Canaanite *disobedience*. Also, the text goes on to say that "by faith [they] conquered kingdoms, . . . became mighty in war, put foreign armies to flight." Finally, James 2:25 commends Rahab for rescuing the Israelite spies and siding with the God of Israel, who had delivered his people out of Egypt. To again cite John Goldingay, "If there is a contradiction between loving your enemies and being peacemakers, on one hand, and Joshua's undertaking this task at God's command, on the other, the New Testament does not see it."[7] Indeed, rather than any assumption of being violence prone, both testaments give Moses unwavering, glowing commendation (Num. 12:7; Deut. 34:10–12; Matt. 23:2–3; Mark 7:9; Heb. 3:2, 5).[8] Consider Matthew 23:2–3, where Jesus doesn't shrink from promoting Moses's teaching: "The scribes and the Pharisees have seated themselves in the chair of Moses; therefore all that they tell you, do and observe, but do not do according to their deeds; for they say things and do not do them." This undermines Boyd's claim that Jesus is "refuting" Moses.

Now Jesus has authority over the Torah, and he relaxes certain Mosaic commands like circumcision, the Sabbath, and food laws—subjects that would eventually figure in to the incorporation of the Gentiles into the new covenant community Jesus established. But Jesus's command in Matthew 23:2–3 flies in the face of Boyd's claim that Jesus refuted the Mosaic law. Tellingly, Boyd's two-volume tome ignores this passage, though Boyd mentions surrounding verses (vv. 1, 4, and 8–12). The same is true of Paul's statement that the Mosaic law is "holy," "just," and "good" (Rom. 7:12 NRSV). Once again, Boyd doesn't discuss this text, though he mentions surrounding verses (vv. 4–11 and 13)! As I note elsewhere, Boyd's work reveals a glaring selectivity.[9]

We could add that if Moses *were* so violence prone, then why was he pleading with God *not* to obliterate Israel after its covenant-breaking, golden-calf incident while still at Mount Sinai (Exod. 32)? If anything, we have in that story a *reversal* of what our critic from within says: it looks like *God* is more violence prone than the compassionate Moses!

Now, some of our critics claim that such "violent texts" could be (and have been) used as *carte blanche* justification to kill "outsiders." This is a misinterpretation of God's unique activity in salvation history. So this unique slice of salvation history—the time of "Yahweh wars"—was basically limited to Joshua's generation and restricted to a unique land mass the size of New Jersey. Thus "any use of these texts to justify massacre, injustice and oppression is not a reading that is pleasing to God, but blasphemous."[10] As Roy Gane puts it, "In the case of the Canaanites, during a certain phase of history, [God] *uniquely* delegated a *carefully restricted part* of his destructive work to his chosen nation of ancient Israel, *which he highly controlled and held accountable under theocratic rule.*"[11]

And as we noted in chapter 2 with the Crusades, these were largely a defensive, protective measure against the assault of Islamic hordes. And the biblical texts medieval authorities called on to inspire fighting in the Crusades and pushing back those forces were *not* Deuteronomy and Joshua. Rather, they were quotations from Jesus's lips—loving one's neighbor, laying down one's life for one's friends.

Finally, *the New Testament doesn't eliminate all divine counterviolence.* Though it *continues* the Old Testament's message of loving one's personal enemies and not taking personal vengeance, it leaves room for the state as vehicle for the *just* administration of the sword (Acts 23:12–25; Rom. 13:1–6). Furthermore, Jesus was at times an agent of wrath and forceful physical judgment (John 2:14–17; Acts 9:3–9; 12:23; 13:8–11; Jude 5; Rev. 2:20–23).

The Bigger Picture of Divine Counterviolence

Here is a brief summary of the biblical picture of God's reluctant, grieved counterviolent response to oppression, dehumanization, and other wickedness in the world.[12]

1. *The Old Testament associates the term "violence" (*hamas*) with wicked humans, not with God or those using justified coercive force.* In this book, we've referred to "divine counterviolence"—or quoted scholars speaking of "divine violence"—but this is by way of concession. In the Old Testament, violence isn't merely any kind of physical force—whether just or not, whether from God or from humans—as many readers themselves might think. *The Old Testament speaks of "violence" (*hamas*) with reference to humans engaged in criminal or wicked activity* (verb: eight times; noun: sixty times). As Old Testament scholar Jerry Shepherd points out, the Hebrew Bible does not associate God with the word "violence"—nor does it associate with violence "those who are involved in the use of force against law-breakers" or "persons or nations that are engaged in legitimately authorized military activity." This word never characterizes God's actions against persons. It is only attributed to the wicked and to those who oppress the righteous. Though scholars will refer to "divine violence" in a conventional

way, from a strictly biblical viewpoint "it would be oxymoronic to call God violent," as that would be "the equivalent of referring to him as wicked or unholy."[13]

2. *God is actively involved in renewing the world.* God is deeply engaged with a world gone bad. All along, God has been doing his renewing work to restore people. For example, he brings about a kind of re-creation after the Noahic flood, putting in place measures for societal rule to protect his human image-bearers against violence. In this process of renewal, he uses the flawed, fragile nation of Israel.

3. *God's judgment is principled and not capricious.* The removal of the Canaanites from the land was not without justification (Canaanites were disobedient); it was not due to ethnicity or tribalism. Nor was it extermination; it was more like disabling raids. Many Canaanites remained in the land. Indeed, the biblical text commonly uses exaggerated or hyperbolic language to express defeat: "To read Joshua as extermination is to misread the text."[14] Even so, divine severity leaves us with some lingering or only partially resolved questions.

4. *God helps Israel in battle though he desires to show compassion to all.* Both testaments portray the sovereign God as the one who helps bring victory to Israel in battle. And even where there is fighting, God greatly favors showing grace and compassion to Israel's opponents over bringing judgment to them (Exod. 34:6; Num. 14:18; Jon. 4:2). God "utters no word of rebuke when peoples of the land are spared, acclaim Yahweh's supremacy, and become members of the covenant people."[15]

5. *God becomes increasingly involved with Israel and its earthly power structures.* With each successive step in Israel's development, God remains bound to this nation and its earthly involvements. In order to accomplish the fulfillment of Israel's mission, God connects himself to the structures of ancient Near Eastern covenant making, nationhood, monarchy, empires, and warfare. Though not ideal, God enters into this messy arrangement in order to prepare for the coming renewal and redemption through his Messiah.

6. *God's reentry into the world begins at the margins of power, not the center.* After an intertestamental hiatus, God circles back to take a different tack in his engagement with the world. Daniel Hawk writes: "To simplify, the Old Testament presents God at work primarily at the center of society, while the New Testament presents God at work primarily at the margins."[16] Whereas earlier, God directly challenged the Egyptian superpower and its leader—and other boastful rulers (e.g., Dan. 4:1–37)—*he later shifts to the edges of earthly power and political structures.* The birth of a new kind of king in Bethlehem signaled a new vision and a new order. The ministry of King Jesus orients adherents to "justice, self-giving, and love for others, and steadfastly rejects entanglement with the world and the retaliatory violence that infuses it."[17]

Through his death and resurrection, Jesus triumphs over the powers of death and destruction: "At the cross, God receives the full force and malevolence of human violence without retaliating whatsoever. Unfettered by tethers to human systems of power, the cross displays the love of the Creator in its purest form."[18] As a result, Jesus brings renewal by gathering a new humanity to be "agents of God's saving activity in the world."[19]

7. *The New Testament does not fully abandon earthly power and the use of divine physical coercive force ("violence").* Some Christians will claim that God totally rejects earthly power and physical force. A more consistent picture in both testaments reflects God's interaction with a messy, fallen world and that earthly social realities and power structures cannot be tidily cordoned off and easily ignored by God's people. Though God works primarily outside the margins of power, he still works within human societies and political structures, including the use of just coercive physical force. These include Christian involvement and influence within these structures.

Boyd considers "just soldiering" opposed to the gospel and that positive attitudes toward soldiers in the New Testament are just an argument from silence.[20] Jesus isn't affirming soldiering when he proclaims the great faith of a centurion (Matt. 8:8–10; cf. Acts 10:1–2). After all, Jesus also ate with prostitutes, but he didn't affirm their line of work. But are soldiers or police morally equivalent to prostitutes? The pacifist New Testament scholar Richard Hays has claimed this.[21] To the contrary, philosopher Elizabeth Anscombe once wrote that, to the pacifist's mind, Jesus's praise of the centurion "must be much as if a madam in a brothel had said: 'I know what authority is, I tell this girl to do this, and she does it . . .' and Christ had commended her faith."[22]

If soldiering was so heinous, why didn't John the Baptist command Roman soldiers to "sin no more" by leaving the military life? Surely, this is far worse than extortion or discontentment about wages or falsely accusing a citizen (Luke 3:14). John would have told prostitutes to leave their lives of sin. Indeed, he wasn't afraid to confront pagan unbelievers about their immoral lifestyles: "It is not lawful for you [Herod] to have your brother's wife" (Mark 6:18).

We've noted Paul's reliance on Roman military protection from mob attack (Acts 23). And Paul took for granted that some basic soldiering or policing is necessary for keeping order and preventing anarchy; that is a basic good in society (cf. 1 Tim. 2:1–2). Unlike prostitution, soldiering is portrayed positively by Paul in his analogies for the Christian life (1 Cor. 9:7; 2 Tim. 2:4; Paul would *not* have said, "Who at any time serves as a prostitute at her own expense?" or "No harlot in a prostitution ring entangles herself in the affairs of everyday life, so that she may please the pimp who enlisted her").

Jesus himself uses this matter-of-fact example of a king first counting the cost before engaging in battle (Luke 14:31). Jesus would *not* say, "Or what pimp, when he sets out to start a prostitution ring, does not first sit down and consider whether he can afford to open such a business?" All of these positive military examples fit very well with the general understanding that, in this fallen world, there is a time for war and a time for peace (Eccles. 3:8; Prov. 20:18; 24:6, 11–12).

Indeed, God/Jesus is portrayed as acting with coercive physical force in the New Testament as well. God can work in a variety of ways both within and outside of these earthly systems, which includes forceful physical activity. The Old Testament "testifies that even God had to adapt ideals to reality and participate in violent systems in order to accomplish redemptive purposes."[23] But the New Testament, though operating with different rules of engagement, hints that "Yahweh has not altogether abandoned violence as a means of dealing with human defiance."[24] As the late Old Testament scholar and pacifist Peter Craigie rightly observed, God "acts in the world as it is, for if the prerequisite for divine action were sinless men and sinless societies, God could not act through human beings and human institutions at all."[25]

Even Jürgen Moltmann—the noted "cruciform" theologian[26] and author of *The Crucified God* (1973)—acknowledges that certain forceful acts in a fallen world may be unavoidable. A bus driver suddenly goes mad and drives toward the precipice. What to do? Moltmann claims that it may be "unavoidable" not only to disable but perhaps to kill the bus driver since "doing nothing would have meant being responsible for the deaths of many people."[27] In a world where "the just struggle of the oppressed for identity and dignity cannot be achieved" and where a "redistribution of power presupposes participation in power" that is "notoriously and violently refused, counterviolence is often the only remedy."[28] Even this "theologian of the cross" still leaves room for necessary coercive physical force under certain conditions.

That said, the issue of whether Christians should today practice pacifism or nonviolence is a *secondary* one. Though I am not a Christian pacifist, my argument about divinely sanctioned warfare in the Old Testament can be and is actually held by various Christian pacifists who disagree with how our critics from within handle the Old Testament war texts and other passages concerning divine severity.[29] And God himself is clearly not a pacifist, as the final judgment involves just, severe, coercive force. And the wrath of Jesus inspires fear in the hearts of his enemies (Rev. 6:16–17). In his wrath, God doesn't always withdraw his presence so that evil forces may rush in to do damage. No, God may *directly punish* those who defy him and attempt to thwart his workings in the world— perhaps through sickness, blindness, or even death—as the New Testament amply affirms. This is a tragedy that God does not celebrate, however. He would rather show grace and mercy.

Concluding Remarks

Back in 1963, the skeptic John Beversluis wondered what C. S. Lewis thought about these harsh warfare texts in Joshua. He was not thinking of these texts in terms of ancient Near Eastern hyperbole. But Lewis pointed out that we must firmly believe in God's goodness and that his commands are not arbitrary. Rather,

God's good character is the source of his commands. However, a good God, who is also the Cosmic Authority, may command something *difficult*, even though he will not command what is *intrinsically evil*.

In the end, this is what Lewis wrote:

> The ultimate question is whether the doctrine of the goodness of God or that of the inerrancy of Scriptures is to prevail when they conflict. I think the doctrine of the goodness of God is the more certain of the two. Indeed, only that doctrine renders this worship of Him obligatory or even permissible.[30]

Lewis qualified this, though:

> But of course having said all this, we must apply it with fear and trembling. Some things which seem to us bad may be good. But we must not consult our consciences by trying to feel a thing good when it seems to us totally evil. We can only pray that if there is an invisible goodness hidden in such things, God, in His own good time will enable us to see it. If we need to. For perhaps sometimes God's answer might be "What is that to thee?" The passage may not be "addressed to our (your or my) condition" at all.[31]

Likewise, the Christian philosopher Eleonore Stump presents an illustration about difficult divine commands and conditions. She asks us to imagine "an intelligent being Max from a far-distant world" in which all sentient beings never get seriously sick and none ever dies. Max is then enabled to view a video of "events inside a large city hospital on earth where the Chief of Staff is a surgeon." Upon seeing the video, "Max is filled with moral indignation at the doctors," who plunge sharp objects into human beings first to render them helpless and then to slice them open with sharp knives."[32] The patients appear to leave the hospital in far worse shape than when they came in.

Stump compares this to the Canaanite question we've been discussing. Throwing out terms like "genocide" or "torture" without qualification or reference to intent or motivation is sure to be misleading. What looks like "torture" to Max has the ultimate aim of healing, even if this seems counterintuitive on the surface. And what if warfare against the Canaanites is actually motivated by "providential care"?[33]

Even if we find biblical texts that don't make sense, and even as honest doubts linger, perhaps some material in this volume will better enable us to see that divine goodness more clearly.

PART 7

The Heart of
the Matter

*The Summing Up of All
Things in Christ*

32

"God Is Christlike, and in Him There Is No Un-Christlikeness at All"

Our Critics from Within

Michael Ramsey, the one hundredth archbishop of Canterbury, famously said, "God is Christlike, and in Him there is no un-Christlikeness at all."[1] If this line sounds familiar, it's because he was echoing 1 John 1:5: "God is Light, and in Him there is no darkness at all." We can certainly agree with Ramsey. However, all too often those who quote this line tend to emphasize a strong *dis*continuity between the testaments because of their apparently different portrayals of God. In our case, these critics from within affirm a seemingly unbridgeable chasm between the textual and the actual God.

Throughout this book, *we've mostly engaged with our critics from within.* As we've observed, these critics would and do repudiate the idea that they follow in the path of the ancient heretic Marcion. We want to be careful about affixing labels and pronouncing heresy just because we find ourselves disagreeing with others within Christendom.

With some exceptions,[2] these critics from within *don't* reject the Old Testament as inspired Scripture. But they *do* think the Old Testament prophets and narrators got a lot wrong and misspoke when they said "Thus says the LORD." *Nor* do they accept the idea of two deities—the (evil) God of the Old Testament and the (good) God of the New. But on closer examination, their "deity distinction" centers on the radically different portrayals of the *textual* God and the *actual* God—a similar "two Gods" view. We've also seen that Boyd puts the Mosaic law against Jesus, but in a wholly inaccurate fashion. The end result is the unwarranted creation of a deep chasm between Moses and Jesus, which is further exacerbated by claiming that Moses issued "demonic" commands. Boyd even calls the textual God "a blasphemous lie" and "a diabolical violent warrior god."[3] Are such critics from within, as Tremper Longman has put it, "practical Marcionites"?[4]

If these things don't sound troubling enough, consider how very much aligned our critics from within are with the atheist Richard Dawkins's description about "the Old Testament God"—or the "textual" God. He is "arguably the most unpleasant character in all of fiction."[5] He is allegedly unlike the (*actual*) "God" of forgiveness, enemy-love, compassion, nonviolence, and so on—"Jesus 101," as Peter Enns puts it.[6] *But this textual-God position looks nothing like Jesus's or any other New Testament authority's view of the Old Testament portrayal of God.*

I believe that our critics from within do present troubling views. In their earnestness to present a tidier "cruciform" picture of the "actual" God as revealed in Jesus, their approach doesn't do justice to the actual interpretation of the Old Testament taken by Jesus and the New Testament authorities. And as we'll see, they leave out or water down a number of clarifying texts about "the actual God" presented in the New Testament itself.

In the remainder of this chapter, we try to put things into focus for the critic from within—and then, in the final chapters, the critic from without.

Qualifying the Textual-Actual Distinction

Some might ask the question: But doesn't the *actual* God do some accommodating to human sin and fallenness? Doesn't he work with hard-hearted Israelites (Matt. 19:8), giving them less-than-ideal legislation in places? Isn't this an example of the *textual* God then? Up to a point, we can accept a *mild* textual-actual distinction. Let's explore this a bit more.

> God *portrayed as physical:* Sometimes God may be portrayed as physical, having hands or eyes (the literary or textual portrayal of God) whereas he is spirit and invisible, as other Scriptures clearly indicate.
>
> God *as ignorant of the future—and present:* God is sometimes *literarily* portrayed as not knowing something even in the *present*, let alone the *future*. To Adam in the garden, God calls "Where are you?" (Gen. 3:9). And concerning God's investigating the wickedness of Sodom and Gomorrah, he says, "I will go down and see if what they have done is as bad as the outcry that has reached me. If not, I will know" (Gen. 18:21 NIV). This is a literary device. *Other Scriptures make clear that God fully knows the present.*
>
> He also knows the *future*—like Jesus's prediction of Peter's three denials or Judas's betrayal. But what about certain Old Testament texts? For instance, as Abraham is lifting the knife to slay Isaac during this test, the

angel of the Lord says, "Do not lay your hand on the boy or do anything to him, for now I know that you fear God, seeing you have not withheld your son, your only son, from me" (Gen. 22:12 ESV). *Did God really just find out at the final moment that Abraham feared God?* Not at all—no more so than God would find out whether or not Sodom and Gomorrah were really wicked ("If not, I will know").

In fact, just prior to this Abraham himself expressed confidence to his servants: "*We* will worship and then *we* will come back to you" (v. 5 NIV). No wonder Hebrews 11:19 states that Abraham reasoned that God could raise the dead. Abraham was confident that Isaac—the miracle child of promise—would *somehow* accompany him on his return trip. God clearly knows the future free actions of human agents.

Divine permission versus direct action: In both testaments, God's sovereignty is sometimes expressed as God *causing* something to happen—like David's census, which we noted in chapter 13. But even the Old Testament itself affirms that God creates all things good (Gen. 1:31) and that he cannot be the source of evil (e.g., Jer. 7:31; Hab. 1:13). God may cause or make "disaster" or "calamity" (*ra*)—though the King James Version incorrectly translates this as "evil" in Isaiah 45:7, falsely suggesting that God is the author of evil (cf. Matt. 7:11; James 1:13, 17).

So as to the question of *which* agent incited David's census—*God* (1 Sam. 24:1) or *some malign adversary* (1 Chron. 21:1), we can affirm the following: creaturely sin is carried out with God's *permission* even if, at first glance, God may appear to be the agent involved (God "incited" David). On the other hand, when prophets like Moses or Jeremiah are saying "This is what the LORD says/commands," then this should be taken as the gist of the actual God's message, not the product of a mere textual God.

While we may have some *marginal* textual God / actual God distinctions, they are nothing like what our critics from within claim, as we'll now clearly see.

Why the Textual God Is Strikingly Like the Actual God

It would be most instructive to undertake a comparison between our critics' official "this is the *textual* God" pronouncements and their *actual match-up* to the biblical evidence. As we'll see, *the "textual" God repeatedly closely resembles the "actual" God.* To add to the damage, *our critics' attempts to widen the textual-actual gap only diminish their credibility (e.g., pitting Moses against Jesus).* A further problem is that one of our leading critics from within—Greg Boyd—*repeatedly ignores many crucial texts that would undermine his case.*[7] Indeed, the critics from within tend to read the Scriptures selectively, as we have seen and as table 32.1 shows.

Table 32.1. The Textual God as the Actual God

TEXTUALITY	CRUCIFORMITY	IDENTICALITY
The presentation of the "textual" God (the *fallen, distorted* perspective of the ancient authority)	The alleged cruciform "correction" (the "actual" God as revealed in Jesus on the cross)	The "textual" God turns out to be identical to the "actual" God in this case
The textual God commanded the death penalty in various instances.	The actual God could not have commanded this violent punishment. Boyd: "Everyone who carried out any of the executions demanded in the OT were not justified in doing so."[a]	Jesus and other New Testament authorities affirmed that the death penalty was divinely mandated or permissible under certain conditions in the Old Testament (Matt. 15:1–7: "word of God" and "commandment of God"; Acts 3:23; Heb. 2:2–3; 10:28; cf. 10:29; 12:25).
The textual God commanded vows and oaths (Deut. 6:13).	Jesus prohibited all oaths (Matt. 5:34); only a straight "yes" or "no" will do. All else is from the evil one. Boyd: "Any kind of oath-taking, such as those that Leviticus 19:12 (and, we could add, Deuteronomy 23:21) allows, is from the devil."[b]	Jesus actually prohibited the common practice of *misusing* oaths to avoid truth telling (casuistry). But Jesus places himself under oath at his trial (Matt. 26:63–64). God himself swears, as do other New Testament authorities (Luke 1:73; Acts 2:30; 18:18; 21:23; Rom. 1:9; 9:1; 1 Thess. 2:5; 1 Tim. 2:7; Heb. 6:17; 7:21, 28; Rev. 10:6).
The textual God commanded an "eye-for-an-eye" (*lex talionis*) form of punishment (Exod. 21:23–25).	Jesus rejected *lex talionis* and all vengeance (Luke 4:18–19); he commanded turning the other cheek, not resisting evil persons (Matt. 5:38–42). Boyd: "Jesus explicitly repudiated the *lex talionis*."[c]	The "eye for an eye" was simply an expression for judicial proportionality (rendering to each person according to what he has done). Jesus proclaimed that severe retribution is fitting for those who lead disciples into sin (Matt. 18:6). God will bring vengeance (Rom. 12:19; Heb. 11:31; Rev. 19:2). Though Paul rejected personal retaliation (Rom. 12:17–21), he stated that God will bring vengeance upon persecutors (2 Thess. 1:6–9; cf. 2 Tim. 4:14). God will render to each according to what he has done (Rom. 2:6)—the "eye-for-an-eye" principle. Even heavenly martyrs call for *vengeance* (Rev. 6:9–11). God's final retribution is a cause for rejoicing (Rev. 18:20). Also, Jesus didn't literally turn the other cheek when struck (John 18:23); cheek striking was an *insult*, not an act of *violence*.

a. Gregory Boyd, *Crucifixion of the Warrior God: Violent Portraits of God in Light of the Cross*, 2 vols. (Minneapolis: Fortress, 2017), 1:318.

b. Greg Boyd, "Jesus Repudiates OT Commands on Oath-Taking: A Response to Paul Copan (#9)," *ReKnew*, January 2, 2018, https://reknew.org/2018/01/jesus-repudiates-ot-commands-oath-taking-response-paul-copan-9/.

c. Boyd, *Crucifixion*, 1:318.

EXTUALITY	CRUCIFORMITY	IDENTICALITY
he textual God nreatened curses pon humans, in-luding Israel (Gen. 2:2–3; Lev. 26:1–46;)eut. 27:15–29).	Jesus commanded blessing and not cursing (Luke 6:28); one should not call someone a "fool" (Matt. 5:22). In that spirit, Paul calls for blessing and not cursing (Rom. 12:14). Boyd: "[Paul's] language ["dogs" in Phil. 3:2] was inconsistent with Jesus' own teaching to never apply slanderous labels to people (Matt 5:22)."d	Though God prefers blessing to curse and woe, and though this language is lessened in the New Testament, it is still present (Matt. 23; 25:41; Mark 11:13–14, 21; Gal. 1:8–9; 1 Cor. 16:22). Jesus himself labels hypocritical religious leaders "fools" and a "brood of vipers" (Matt. 23:17, 33), refers to certain persons as "swine" and "dogs" (Matt. 7:6), and tells his opponents of "your father the devil" (John 8:44).
he textual God ommanded warfare gainst the Canaan-:es (Deut. 7:1–5).	Such "demonic" commands were not from the actual God, but from fallen, violence-prone prophets like Moses and Joshua. Jesus repudiated all such actions as contrary to a loving Father and to the cruci-fied Jesus's cry of enemy-love, "Father, forgive them" (Luke 23:34). Boyd: Regarding "the 'show no mercy' command that Moses allegedly received from Yahweh," we "should rather place it 'under God's curse.'"e	The New Testament indicates that God granted victory over the Canaanites and helped Israel in battle (Acts 7:45; 13:19; Heb. 11:31, 33; cf. James 2:25). We see absolutely no hint of qualification or any distancing from the Old Testament "warrior God" portrayal.
The textual God gave he law to Moses .t Mount Sinai. Moses was God's aithful messenger .nd authoritative epresentative.	Jesus repeatedly repudiated and contradicted the Mosaic law, especially in Matthew 5:21–48. Moses's legislation was deeply flawed because he was fallen, violence prone, and culturally conditioned. Boyd: "Jesus repudiated commands of the OT."f	Both testaments affirm the authority of Moses as God's faithful representative and authoritative spokesman. More than any other Old Testament prophet, Moses knew God as a friend and spoke with him face-to-face (Num. 12:7; Deut. 34:10–12; cf. Matt. 8:4; 23:2–3; Luke 16:31; John 5:45–46; 7:19; Heb. 3:5). Also, Jesus said that the *Israelites* were hard-hearted, *not* Moses (Matt. 19:8). Finally, Paul also calls the Mosaic law "good" and "spiritual" and "holy" (Rom. 7:12, 14), though not ulti-mate or final.

d. Boyd, *Crucifixion*, 1:590.   f. Boyd, *Crucifixion*, 1:72.
e. Boyd, *Crucifixion*, 2:926.

TEXTUALITY	CRUCIFORMITY	IDENTICALITY
Regarding the Davidic census, the author of 2 Samuel claimed that *God* incited David to sin (2 Sam. 24:1).	The Chronicler (1 Chron. 21:1) had a more "enlightened" perspective than did the author of 2 Samuel (24:1). It was "Satan" rather than "God" who incited David. Boyd: "The Chronicler . . . understandably found this theology [in 1 Sam. 24:1] objectionable and so changed the reference from God to Satan."[g]	The claim that the Chronicler was "more enlightened" is misleading. The *same* Chronicler used "textual God" language by claiming that *the Lord* "killed" Saul "and turned the kingdom to David the son of Jesse" (1 Chron. 10:14). By the same standard, the author of *Samuel* would have been "more enlightened" than the Chronicler by declaring that "Saul"—not God—"took his sword and fell on it" (1 Sam. 31:4). See also the "deceiving spirit" passage (1 Kings 22:22–23) that is identical to the later "uncorrected" Chronicles parallel (2 Chron. 18:21–22).
The imprecatory psalms are vindictive "prayer-curses" against the psalmists' enemies to bring vengeance and calamity.	These imprecatory psalms are in "direct contradiction to Jesus" (Boyd).[h] These anti-gospel psalms are the product of the fallen ancient Near Eastern psalmists' mindset.	The New Testament appropriates various imprecatory psalms. Paul cites Psalm 69:22[23] in Romans 11:8–10 ("Let their table become a snare and a trap"). Peter cited imprecatory psalms (69:25 and 109:8) in Acts 1:20. See also Luke 18:7–8 and Revelation 6:10, where God's righteous people call on God to bring justice / to avenge.
The textual God acted violently and commanded violence.	The actual God does not act violently. He does not strike people dead or harm them (human and demonic agents do this when God withdraws his influence). The cruciform picture of Jesus praying for his enemies makes this clear. Boyd: "God judges sin and defeats evil simply by withdrawing his merciful hand."[i]	Jesus acted with coercive force ("violently") when he drove money changers out of the temple and prevented people from entering. Jesus "destroyed" unbelieving Israelites (Jude 5). After threatening to cast the false prophetess "Jezebel" on a bed of sickness, Jesus threatened to "strike dead" her followers (Rev. 2:20–23). We have other instances of "the hand of the Lord" or "the angel of the Lord" afflicting or striking down people in the New Testament.
The textual God allowed the Israelites "to do with [the Canaanites] as they desired" (Neh. 9:24).	Although God didn't like the violence-prone tendencies of the Israelites, he allowed Moses, Joshua, and the Israelites to have their own violent way with the Canaanites. Boyd: Because Israel "resisted Yahweh's non-violent will," God allowed them to do "what they 'pleased'"—namely, to "destroy" the Canaanites.[j]	The flow of the Nehemiah passage indicates that Israel's taking the land was *positive*. (This is already clear from v. 22.) The *negativity* enters in at vv. 26–27. Various parallel passages have the same positive "entering of the land" followed by the negative "falling into idolatry" pattern (Jer. 32:21–23; Ps. 78:53–56). Also, the Canaanites were a daunting, superior foe, and the natural inclination would have been to *fear*, not to attack. Furthermore, the real issue was not Israel's "*violence*" but rather its *idolatry*, which these passages make abundantly clear.

g. Boyd, *Crucifixion*, 2:888. i. Boyd, *Crucifixion*, 2:849.
h. Boyd, *Crucifixion*, 1:328. j. Boyd, *Crucifixion*, 2:982.

TEXTUALITY	CRUCIFORMITY	IDENTICALITY
The textual God called for a future day of vengeance of our God" (Isa. 61:2).	According to Boyd, in Luke 4, when "Jesus read this passage, he stopped just before" the reference to Isaiah's mention of "vengeance."[k] The actual God does not engage in taking vengeance. The apostle Paul was wrong to say that God will "repay" those who afflicted the Thessalonians (2 Thess. 1:6–9); Paul "seems to be satisfying the Thessalonians' and/or his own fallen thirst for vengeance to come upon their enemies."[l]	Jesus came to save rather than to judge (John 3:16–17), but vengeance still remains for those who reject him and persecute his people (Rev. 6:9–11; 18:20; 19:2; cf. Rom. 12:19; Heb. 10:30). Paul repudiated *personal* revenge (Rom. 12:19), but that is different from divine vengeance. Jesus said being drowned with a millstone would be fitting judgment for some (Matt. 18:6). In addition, Jesus *also omitted "to bind up the brokenhearted"* from Isaiah 61:1.
The textual God visits the sins of the parents on the third and fourth generations (Exod. 20:5; 34:7).	The prophet Ezekiel is *more morally and spiritually enlightened* than Moses. Boyd: "In Ezekiel 18:1–4, [Ezekiel's] insight arguably corrects the earlier Israelite conception of Yahweh's 'punishing the children for the sin of the parents'" (Exod. 20:5).[m]	Aside from our critics' misunderstanding of the Exodus passages, prophets just before or during Ezekiel's time refer back to these Exodus texts and use the same language—God is "avenging" and "takes vengeance" (Nah. 1:2) and also "repays the iniquity of fathers into the bosom of their children after them" (Jer. 32:18). But notice too that in the preceding chapter, Jeremiah also *affirms* what Ezekiel said: "Everyone will die for his own iniquity" (Jer. 31:30). Even Deuteronomy uses this language of not punishing children for their parents' sin (Deut. 24:16). There is no shift from the "textual" God of Exodus to the "actual" God of Ezekiel (or Jeremiah).

k. Boyd, *Crucifixion*, 1:88.   m. Boyd, *Crucifixion*, 2:838n58.
l. Boyd, *Crucifixion*, 1:589.

Are our critics from within—particularly Boyd—correct about their "textual God" label? No. *Something else must be going on.* Contrary to their attempt to pit the "textual" God against the "actual" God, the Scriptures repeatedly affirm that the *textual-God* and the *actual-God* representations converge upon closer examination. Whatever the correct balance is between kindness and severity, our critics from within certainly have not "nailed it," as the table clearly reveals.

Behold, the Kindness and Severity of Jesus

We know that wrath, punishment, and judgment aren't God's "heart language." Rather, love is the central characteristic of the mutually loving triune God.

Consider this parallel: if God had freely chosen *not* to create anything, then being "Creator" wouldn't have been a divine characteristic. You can't have a Creator without a creation. The same is true about wrath: if God had freely chosen not to make creatures who could defy him, he would never have become wrathful. We could call wrath an "emergent property" of God; that is, wrath is a *nonessential attribute* that arises only when God's moral creatures rebel against him and when they degrade and dehumanize each other.

The centrality of God's love is evident in the Old Testament (Exod. 34:6–7a), although Israel was constantly straying from its covenant relationship with God and provoking God to wrath (Exod. 34:7b). Yet God was constantly pleading with Israel to return to him, and he was constantly renewing his covenant with wayward Israel and working toward renewal and re-creation.

The triune God is *reluctantly* wrathful. In the Old Testament, he grieves that he finally must judge (Gen. 6:6; Ps. 78:41; Isa. 16:9–11; Jer. 9:1, 10, 17–24; 48:29–33; Lam. 3:32–33). God laments over Israel, "How I have been hurt by their adulterous hearts" (Ezek. 6:9). And Jesus weeps over Jerusalem yet reluctantly pronounces judgment against it (Matt. 23:1–24:34). In both testaments, God doesn't desire that any should perish (cf. Jer. 18:7–8; 1 Tim. 2:4; 2 Pet. 3:9).

Through God's revelation in Jesus, *we see a greater emphasis on blessing over cursing, kindness over severity, mercy over judgment, and God as an intimate, loving Father—indeed, triunity of love—and not simply a sovereign Lord. In his own self-sacrifice, Jesus shows us that God's "heart language" is love and forgiveness.* But, as we've seen, the severity and even coercive physical force ("violence") of the Old Testament do not disappear in the New (Rom. 11:22).

We earlier noted theologian Roger Olson, who said that those warfare texts don't speak God's voice to him.[8] And we can see why that is so. *Love is the central attribute of God; wrath is not.* Furthermore, as we look at the New Testament and the interethnic people of God, who no longer have an earthly kingdom with national boundaries, the emphasis on physical warfare and divine counterviolence is diminished. Even so, Jesus clearly exhibits both astonishing love and wrathful severity. In fact, if creatures repudiate God's self-giving love clearly manifested in Jesus Christ, then there are *even more severe consequences for this than under the Mosaic law* (as Heb. 2, 10, and 12 remind us). Jesus said it would be more tolerable for ancient cities like Sodom, Tyre, and Sidon that were divinely judged than for Jesus's own contemporaries who rejected him (Luke 10:10–15). The book of Revelation further emphasizes this greater severity of judgment (e.g., Rev. 14:14–20; 19:11–21), even if some interpreters want to blunt this message by treating it as metaphorical. Metaphor doesn't blunt severity.

The Croatian theologian Miroslav Volf concluded—after seeing the ravages of war in the former Yugoslavia—that God is wrathful *because* God is love.[9] Or to quote N. T. Wright again: "No, evil is real, and some people are so wicked that we simply must wish judgment upon them."[10] God's wrath is an expression of God's care for the world he has made (e.g., Luke 18:7; Rev. 6:9–11).

Thomas Cahill reminds us that God is no Hallmark greeting card: "If God is to be God the Creator of all, he must be utterly beyond our comprehension—and therefore, *awfully scary*."[11] Or we can recall C. S. Lewis's description of the Jesus-figure Aslan in *The Lion, the Witch and the Wardrobe*: "'Course he isn't safe. But he's good."[12]

So we can certainly agree with Ramsey that "God is Christlike, and in Him there is no un-Christlikeness at all." But let us not forget that Christ, who in *love* poured out his very life for us on the cross, is also the *severe*, wrathful judge who stands against those who resist his loving, gracious initiative. Behold, the kindness and severity of Jesus.

33

Our Critics from Without (1)

Two Important Questions

At the outset of this book, I mentioned critics from without like atheists Richard Dawkins or A. A. Milne. Perhaps atheists and others who don't embrace the biblical worldview may see much of this discussion as more of an in-house debate between Christians who don't see eye to eye on Old Testament ethical challenges. But maybe this and the final chapter would be the place to take a peek and see more of the big-picture issues as we try to put all of these things in a proper framework and context. We'll do this in a step-by-step fashion here. In these two chapters, I direct my focus to the atheist or agnostic, although much of the discussion is relevant to any who hold a non-biblical worldview.

Addressing the "Secularist" Critic

At the 2014 Hay Festival, New Atheist Richard Dawkins confessed he could describe himself as a "secular Christian." He has a "feeling of nostalgia" for certain Christian ceremonies and traditions.[1] And despite his earlier claim that "religion" is "the root of all evil,"[2] apparently he prefers certain "religions" over others—like the Christian faith: "There are no Christians, as far as I know, blowing up buildings. I am not aware of any Christian suicide bombers. I am not aware of any major Christian denomination that believes the penalty for apostasy is death. I have mixed feelings about the decline of Christianity, insofar as Christianity might be a bulwark against something worse."[3] As I've written elsewhere,[4] I don't think the term "religion" is very helpful in our modern discourse. It's vague and defined in at least seventeen different ways, according to University of Chicago religion expert Martin Marty.[5] Furthermore, a lot of secularists just presume they hold the intellectually superior, default view that rejects religion.

The problem is this: *How do secularists defend their own deeply held views when they conflict with each other?* For example, certain secularists claim that humans have intrinsic dignity and worth, that individual human rights are a reality, that we have moral duties, and so on. But other secularists reject all of this as nonsense. Intrinsic human dignity is an illusion. So then, which is the *secularist* default view? There isn't a self-justifying secular worldview.

The fact is *all* of us hold to a worldview—a philosophy of life that we believe has the power to explain

- what's really real (metaphysics),
- how or whether we can know (epistemology),
- the nature of right and wrong, moral duties, and virtues (ethics), and
- what makes for the good life or genuine human flourishing, if that is possible.

Furthermore, every worldview claim must be *justified* rather than *assumed*. An atheist (who believes that God doesn't exist) isn't making a self-justifying, neutral statement. That's a knowledge claim ("I know that God does not exist"). But what are the *reasons* for that stance?

We don't have space to get into the details here,[6] but the real question is, *Which worldview has the best resources to make sense of the basic features of the universe as well as of our own human experience?*

Question 1: Theism versus Naturalism—How Do They Compare?

In table 33.1, I compare two competing worldviews, though this could be done with others as well:

Theism: a personal, all-good, all-powerful, all-knowing Creator exists who makes humans with dignity and worth

Naturalism: a view with three tenets—the physical universe is all the reality that exists (*materialism*); all events are the product of blind, nonconscious, valueless, nonrational, physical forces (*determinism*); and science is the source of knowledge (*scientism*)

As table 33.1 shows, if God exists, the basic features of the universe and human experience are highly probable. If naturalism is true, all of these basic features are highly improbable or even impossible. If you're a betting person, go with theism.

Table 33.1. Theism versus Naturalism

Phenomena We Observe, Assume, or Recognize	Theistic Context	Naturalistic Context
Things exist. (Yet why does anything exist at all?)	God's very nature requires his existence. God necessarily exists.	The physical universe's parts are all contingent and thus cannot be self-existent.
Consciousness exists.	God is supremely self-aware/self-conscious.	Consciousness was produced by mindless, nonconscious processes.
Personal beings exist.	God is a personal being.	The universe was produced by impersonal processes.
We believe we make free personal decisions; the fact that choices are up to us assumes we are accountable for our actions.	God is spirit and a free being who can freely choose to act (e.g., to create or not).	We have emerged by materialistic, deterministic processes beyond our control.
We trust our senses and rational faculties as generally reliable in producing true beliefs. The world is knowable.	A God of truth and rationality exists.	Naturalistic evolution is interested only in survival and reproduction, not truth. So, many beliefs would help us survive (e.g., the belief that humans have dignity and worth) but be completely false.
Human beings have intrinsic value/dignity and rights.	God is the supremely valuable being.	Human beings were produced by valueless processes.
Objective moral values/duties exist.	God's character is the source of goodness/moral values, and his commands constitute human duties ("ought").	The universe was produced by nonmoral processes. Things just are what they are.
The universe began to exist a finite time ago—without previously existing matter, energy, space, or time.	A powerful, previously existing God brought the universe into being without any pre-existing material. (On theism, something emerges from something.)	The universe came into existence from nothing by nothing. (Here, something comes from nothing.)
First life emerged.	God is a living, active being capable of bringing contingent life into existence.	Life somehow emerged from nonliving matter.

Phenomena We Observe, Assume, or Recognize	Theistic Context	Naturalistic Context
The universe is finely tuned for human life (known as "the Goldilocks effect"—the universe delicately balanced on a razor's edge of conditions that are "just right" for life).	God is a wise, intelligent Designer.	All the cosmic constants just happened to be right; given enough time and/or many possible worlds, a finely tuned world could have eventually emerged.
Beauty exists—not only in landscapes and sunsets but in "elegant" or "beautiful" scientific theories.	God is creative and capable of creating beautiful things according to his pleasure.	Beauty in the natural world is superabundant and, in many cases, superfluous (often not linked to survival).
We (tend to) believe that life has purpose and meaning. Most of us believe that life is worth living.	God has created/designed us for certain purposes (to love him, others, etc.); when we live them out, our lives find their true meaning and greater enrichment.	There is no cosmic purpose, blueprint, or goal for human existence.
Real evils—both moral and natural—exist and take place in the world.	Evil's definition assumes a design plan (how things ought to be) or standard of goodness by which we judge something to be evil. God is a good Designer; his existence supplies the crucial moral context to make sense of evil.	Atrocities, pain, and suffering just happen. This is just how things are—with no design plan or ultimate or objective standard of goodness to which things ought to conform.
We have deep longings for security (relationship), significance (purpose), forgiveness and relief from guilt, and freedom from fear of death.	God has created us to find our satisfaction in him.	These longings are merely biological, being hardwired into us by naturalistic processes to enhance survival and reproduction.

Source: Paul Copan, *Loving Wisdom: A Guide to Philosophy and Christian Faith*, 2nd ed. (Grand Rapids: Eerdmans, 2020), 142–44.

In light of the comparison in the table, we should be alert to two things:

Keep the main thing the main thing. We are asking, Which worldview has the *best* or most robust resources available and makes the *best* sense of *the basic features of the universe and human experience*? The question is *not* about whether the worldview answers *all* of our questions. For example, *all* worldviews—not just the biblical one—must grapple with the problem of evil. As we'll see shortly, the biblical faith actually gives to us robust resources on this topic, even if we have remaining questions about it.

What are the alternatives? It's a lot easier to tear down or criticize another worldview. But if I've rejected another worldview, what improved alternative do I put up in its place? A person may reject the Christian faith, say, but may offer only a flimsy alternative that doesn't explain a whole lot. And those who call themselves "freethinkers" still limit themselves within a particular worldview: they're not "free" to consider the possibility of God's existence or miracles or life after death.

Question 2: Has This God Done Anything to Help Us?

Our next consideration is this: If a personal, good God exists, we should ask: Has this God done anything to help us out of our miserable plight of evil and suffering? Has God stepped into our world to show us the way? It's not enough to say that evil is a problem. Evil is a problem for *all* of us. But in the Christian faith, rich resources exist that aren't available in other worldviews:

- *Standard of goodness.* God is the standard of goodness (and evil is a deviation from this standard). It's like counterfeit money: you can have real currency without counterfeit money, but not counterfeit money without real currency.
- *Human worth.* God makes human beings with dignity and worth. Our value has a transcendent source. It isn't the result of valueless, material, deterministic processes.
- *Identification with humanity.* As God incarnate (John 1:14), Jesus identifies with us in our human condition, entering into our world of suffering, human weakness, temptation, and injustice, and even dying on a cross.
- *Compassion and concern for the marginalized.* Jesus expressed the love and acceptance of God for the outcast and the marginalized while speaking out against injustices. He also challenged and denounced many of the hypocritical "religious" elites of his day.
- *Redemption made available.* Christ's death paves the way for our redemption and reconciliation with our Creator and Designer. The possibility of being properly aligned with this personal Ultimate Reality is confirmed by Jesus's historical bodily resurrection from the dead.
- *A renewed humanity that transforms communities and cultures.* When believers have faithfully followed Christ, this renewed humanity has been at the forefront of alleviating suffering and helping fellow humans in deep crisis throughout church history.
- *Guaranteed cosmic justice.* While a "secular" worldview simply *cannot guarantee* that cosmic justice will be done, the existence of a just God absolutely

ensures that the unrepentant Hitlers and Stalins of this world will not "get away with murder" millions of times over. And the dedicated Mother Teresas of this world will experience a full happiness not experienced during their mortal days. Happiness and virtue will coincide when God finally puts the world to rights.

The Christian philosopher Alvin Plantinga has written: "As the Christian sees things, God does not stand idly by, coolly observing the suffering of his creatures. He enters into and shares our suffering. He endures the anguish of seeing his Son, the second person of the Trinity, consigned to the bitterly cruel and shameful death of the cross. Some theologians claim that God cannot suffer. I believe they are wrong. God's capacity for suffering, I believe, is proportional to his greatness."[7] Given all of this, it is no wonder C. S. Lewis said: "I believe in Christianity as I believe that the sun has risen, not only because I see it, but because by it I see everything else."[8]

This brings us to the historical sequence of God's involvement with a broken, messy world—to move a fallen humanity toward renewal and restoration. We look at this in the final chapter.

34

Our Critics from Without (2)

Five Big Steps

In five big steps, we trace the trajectory of God's activity in the world and hope for a world in chaos, brokenness, and confusion. We begin with a *loving* and, when necessary, *severe* God who made himself known in the messiness of the ancient Near East and then in Jesus of Nazareth. That same Jesus who more clearly reveals the *kindness* and *severity* of God has propelled forward a new humanity to bring the spirit of Christ to their communities and spheres of influence and into individual lives.

1. Israel: God Engages the Powers of the Ancient Near East

From the garden in Eden and beyond, God would meet with human beings. The creation in Genesis 1 is a picture of God's creating an earthly temple where the divine and the human converged in conversation and friendship (e.g., Gen. 3:9). This humanity-engaging God is quite unlike the one "out there" and completely removed from us (*deism*) and unlike the impersonal "God" that is identical to his creation (*pantheism*)—a God that "just is" and nothing more.

Despite human sin and rebellion against the Creator's intentions, God took initiative to rescue a fallen humanity. In the setting of the ancient Near East, God called Abram, through whom blessing would eventually come to the whole earth (Gen. 12:1–3).

And *God stepped into the center of political might*. He confronted the superpower of the day—Egypt and its pharaoh—to deliver his enslaved people from this oppressive condition. He made a binding covenant with this flawed and rebellious nation, aligning and identifying himself with this fledgling society and its political fortunes. His people had an *identity* to preserve and a *mission* to carry out to benefit all the peoples of the world.

So God gave them the Mosaic law, which was like a booster rocket intended to get Israel moving forward, to help shape its identity and calling. Yet more would be necessary once the law's purpose has been achieved (Rom. 10:4). But in the meantime, *Israel's redemptive story and its humanizing, democratizing worldview far outshone that of the surrounding nations* (Deut. 4:6). As we've seen, scholars like Christopher Wright, Joshua Berman, and David Baker have documented just how radical Israel's democratizing, nonhierarchical law collection was.[1]

In the ancient Near East, God stepped into—and continued to work with—the messy world of Israelite idolatry and rebellion in the thick of nationhood, warfare, rising and falling empires, judgment, exile, and more. *God didn't wait for humanity to become more finely developed. Exhibiting both love and severity, God began where Israel was in order to move them—and all of history—in a redemptive direction.*

2. Jesus: God Steps In at the Margins of Political Power

The incarnate Christ appeared not at the center of political power but *at its very edges*. He came as the fulfillment and climax of Israel's mission. The interethnic promise to Abram to bless all nations was realized in this faithful Israelite from Nazareth.

What should be stunning to Gospel readers—as it was to Jesus's first-century audience—is this: Jesus assumed and spoke with an unheard-of authority that astonished his hearers. He claimed that entrance into God's kingdom—rightly living under divine rule—depended on *personally embracing him*: "Come to Me, all who are weary and heavy-laden, and *I* will give you rest" (Matt. 11:28; cf. 11:27–31). And as he wept over Jerusalem, Jesus spoke in authoritative terms reminiscent of Yahweh's words to Israel: "Therefore *I* send you prophets and wise men and scribes" (23:37). Also, his first-century hearers recognized that *only God* could rightfully forgive sins, but here was Jesus proclaiming that very authority to do so (Mark 2:7). Unlike the religious leaders of his day, Jesus spoke with unheard-of power and authority (Matt. 7:29; 26:53–55; Mark 4:41). Even officers sent to arrest Jesus came back empty-handed. Their reason? "No one ever spoke like this man!" (John 7:46 ESV).

With his authority came a severity—to drive money changers out of the temple, to pronounce woes (curses) on hostile religious leaders, and, as necessary, to strike down the *hostile* persecutor of the church who then became a Christ-follower (Acts 9:1–9), the *haughty* (Acts 12:23; cf. Jude 5), and the *heretic* (Rev. 2:20–23). Jesus is both *gentle* and *fierce*. The tender Jesus would not snuff out a smoldering wick or break a bruised reed, but he took a whip to drive crass, nationalistic religionists from the temple. But at the cross, Jesus does not take the path of severity or forcefulness; rather, he willingly faces violence by surrendering himself to malicious religious leaders and brutal Roman soldiers for the sake of our salvation. As we note below, that unique deity—Jesus of Nazareth—did not come into the world to punish rebellious humans, as the gods of antiquity did; rather, he came to take on himself the punishment they deserved. Gospel readers find themselves confronted with an incomparable, compelling character that simply couldn't be made up. The Gospels tell a story that is "too good to be false."[2]

Instead of expounding on this further, I'll defer to the noted biblical scholar Michael Bird, who grew up as an atheist but was drawn to this compelling Jesus of the Gospels. He tells of his own deconversion story from atheism:

> Some have great confidence in skeptical scholarship, and I once did, perhaps more than anyone else. If anyone thinks they are assured in their unbelief, I was more committed: born of unbelieving parents, never baptized or dedicated; on scholarly credentials, a PhD from a secular university; as to zeal, mocking the church; as to ideological righteousness, totally radicalized.
>
> But whatever intellectual superiority I thought I had over Christians, I now count it as sheer ignorance. Indeed, I count everything in my former life as loss because of the surpassing worth of knowing the historical Jesus who is also the risen Lord. . . .
>
> Many years later . . . I read the New Testament for myself. The Jesus I encountered was far different from the deluded radical, even mythical character described to me. This Jesus—the Jesus of history—was real. He touched upon things that cut close to my heart, especially as I pondered the meaning of human existence. I was struck by the church's testimony to Jesus: In Christ's death God has vanquished evil, and by his resurrection he has brought life and hope to all.
>
> When I crossed from unbelief to belief, all the pieces suddenly began to fit together. I had always felt a strange unease about my disbelief. I had an acute suspicion that there might be something more, something transcendent, but I also knew that I was told not to think that. I "knew" that ethics were nothing more than aesthetics, a mere word game for things I liked and disliked. I felt conflicted when my heart ached over the injustice and cruelty in the world.
>
> Faith grew from seeds of doubt, and I came upon a whole new world that, for the first time, actually made sense to me. To this day, I do not find faith stifling or constricting. Rather, faith has been liberating and transformative for me. It has opened a constellation of meaning, beauty, hope, and life that I had been indoctrinated to deny. And so began a lifelong quest to know, study, and teach about the one whom Christians called Lord.[3]

The God who called the nation of Israel into existence was making himself known in the flesh—through his saving agent Jesus of Nazareth.

3. The Cross of Christ: How the Love of God Reshaped History

The impact Jesus had on history is reflected in our calendars: BC = before Christ; AD = *anno Domini* ("in the year of the Lord"). In a more pluralistic, less-Christianized setting, we have (Before) the Common Era: BCE/CE. But there's much more: what Jesus's self-sacrificial death by crucifixion meant in the Mediterranean world has powerfully shaped key values of Western civilization. Again, rather than describe this, I quote at length the agnostic British historian Tom Holland's story about why he was wrong about Christianity.

Having been enamored of the Greco-Roman (classical) world, Holland came to change his mind about its values:

> The longer I spent immersed in the study of classical antiquity, the more alien and unsettling I came to find it. It was not just the extremes of callousness that I came to find shocking, but the lack of a sense that the poor or the weak might have any intrinsic value. As such, the founding conviction of the Enlightenment—that it owed nothing to the faith into which most of its greatest figures had been born—increasingly came to seem to me unsustainable.
>
> "Every sensible man," Voltaire wrote, "every honourable man, must hold the Christian sect in horror." Yet Voltaire, in his concern for the weak and oppressed, was marked more enduringly by the stamp of biblical ethics than he cared to admit.
>
> "We preach Christ crucified," St Paul declared, "unto the Jews a stumbling block, and unto the Greeks foolishness." He was right. Nothing could have run more counter to the most profoundly held assumptions of Paul's contemporaries—Jews, or Greeks, or Romans.
>
> The notion that a god might have suffered torture and death on a cross was so shocking as to appear repulsive. Familiarity with the biblical narrative of the Crucifixion has dulled our sense of just how completely novel a deity Christ was. In the ancient world, it was the role of gods who laid claim to ruling the universe to uphold its order by inflicting punishment—not to suffer it themselves.
>
> Today, even as belief in God fades across the West, the countries that were once collectively known as Christendom continue to bear the stamp of the two-millennia-old revolution that Christianity represents. It is the principal reason why, by and large, most of us who live in post-Christian societies still take for granted that it is nobler to suffer than to inflict suffering.
>
> It is why we generally assume that every human life is of equal value. In my morals and ethics, I have learned to accept that I am not Greek or Roman at all, but thoroughly and proudly Christian.[4]

The strong value we attach to human beings, who are made in God's image, is reinforced by God's love for the world demonstrated in Christ. The Son of God stooped to humiliating depths of a naked death on a barbaric Roman cross to pay the penalty for a lost, undeserving humanity. Rather than dealing out punishment to us, he bore it himself.

Keep in mind that Holland is not a professing Christian. But his mindset—as well as the rest of us in the West and other places the gospel has penetrated—has been profoundly shaped by the crucifixion of Jesus. Other "secular" scholars like Niall Ferguson, Douglas Murray, Jordan Peterson are recognizing the hope, power, and intellectual resonance of the gospel, especially in light of the ideological failures of modernity.[5] That Christ-event that shook the ancient world and reshaped the world of its day has ongoing relevance.

4. Faithful Followers of Christ: The Ongoing Impact of the Gospel

Back in December 2011, I had written to the noted sociologist Rodney Stark at Baylor University. He had earlier identified himself as an agnostic, and since he had written so affirmatively about the positive historical impact the Christian faith has had over two millennia, I thought I would inquire concerning where he was in his pilgrimage. Stark replied that after researching the historical impact of the Christian faith during his career, it began to dawn on him that the Christian faith was actually true: "I basically wrote myself into the Christian faith."[6]

This was also the experience of Canadian Broadcasting Corporation journalist Brian Stewart. Despite his skepticism and dislike of "institutional religion," he became convinced of the truth of the Christian faith when he saw it in action. As a journalist, he reported himself into the Christian faith, as it were. Once again, you can read his testimony here:

> I've found there is no movement, or force, closer to the raw truth of war, famines, crises and the vast human predicament, than organized Christianity in action. And there is no alliance more determined and dogged in action than church workers, ordained and lay members, when mobilized for a common good. It is these Christians who are right "on the front lines" of committed humanity today and when I want to find that front, I follow their trail.
>
> It is a vast front, stretching from the most impoverished reaches of the developing world to the hectic struggle to preserve caring values in our own towns and cities. I have never been able to reach these front lines without finding Christian volunteers already in the thick of it, mobilizing congregations that care, and being a faithful witness to truth, the primary light in the darkness, and so often the only light.
>
> Now I came to this admiring view slowly and reluctantly. At the start of my career, I'd largely abandoned religion for I, too, regarded the church as a rather tiresome irrelevance. What ultimately persuaded me otherwise—and I took a lot of persuading—was the reality of Christianity's mission, physically and in spirit, before my very eyes.[7]

The historians I cited above—Tom Holland and Rodney Stark—have written about Jesus-shaped cultures. I myself have done so as well, noting how many non-Christian authors readily acknowledge the singular, profoundly humanizing, democratizing influence the Christian faith has had in history.[8]

5. The Personal Step: The Present Relevance of Jesus

In this final segment, we come to the personal appropriation of the biblical story in the present. That *kind* and *severe* God began to work with a stubborn, rebellious nation in the thick of a messy and broken ancient Near Eastern setting. A *kind* and *severe* Jesus came into this broken world *not to punish but to voluntarily and freely take our punishment—to pay the legal penalty that we were unable to pay so that his righteous record could be imputed to our account and place us in right standing with God.*

Here I arrive at a final testimony—that of Francis Spufford, a former atheist. He wrote a book after his conversion—*Unapologetic: Why, Despite Everything, Christianity Can Still Make Surprising Emotional Sense.*[9] Spufford's pilgrimage brought him to the profound realization of how humans are deeply morally deficient and flawed; we all have a real knack for messing things up. He observed that in our default state, we are restless and not at peace with ourselves. Of course, we can attempt to evade our deficiencies and our moral shortcomings by easily distracting ourselves with technology, social media, and sports. But the philosopher Blaise Pascal observed that humanity's problems are rooted in a person's inability to sit alone quietly in a room.[10]

The more we scrutinize our lives, we see how our lives are characterized by unsightly smudges, deep cracks, and profound brokenness. We carry guilt with us in the face of our moral failure—falling far short of the people we desire to be and the very standards we profess.

The theologian John Calvin rightly observed that "there is not one man who is not covered with infinite pollutions."[11] He challenged the most perfect person to descend into his conscience and examine himself. Calvin asked: Will that person feel calm and at peace with God? No, but "will he not rather be strong with dire torment, when he sees the ground of condemnation within him if he be estimated by his works?"[12]

Even if we reject a transcendent law or norm for all people, we can't even live up to the this-worldly standards or values we profess. We fail to live up to the moral ideal even of our own making, and we feel the burden of falling short and feeling deeply inadequate.

Even so, guilt and shame can lead to genuine self-discovery. If we allow it, we can find a solution—something to bridge the moral gap between the *ideal* we know and the *reality* of our failed performance. In an interview, Spufford spoke about why he left atheism:

> It turned out not to contain what my soul needed for nourishment in bad times. It was not any kind of philosophical process that led me out from disbelief. I had made a mess of things in my life, and I needed mercy, and to my astonishment, mercy was there. An experience of mercy, rather than an idea of it. And the rest followed from there. I felt my way back to Christianity, discovering through many surprises that the religion I remembered from my childhood looked different if you came to

it as an adult with adult needs: not pretty, not small, not ridiculous, but tough and gigantic and marvellous.[13]

Final Thought

In this book, we have addressed puzzles and challenges. We have looked a bit more closely at the morally broken, messy, and foreign ancient Near Eastern setting into which God stepped and spoke and worked to redeem. Then, in Jesus, God physically entered into *another* context of damaged humanity, claiming to represent and embody that God who began that process of renewal. The voluntary death of Jesus on the cross to ransom humanity (Mark 10:45) involved incredible love—an innocent man, betrayed by a friend, unjustly arrested and accused, beaten, stripped naked, and crucified in a public place where he was subjected to mockery and scorn. *That is how low God is willing to go for our salvation.* The power of his life, his voluntary substitutionary death, and his bodily resurrection have remained with us and influenced history in profound ways. Indeed, he represents hope for a broken, sinful humanity in the present.

We have approached untidy and unsettling (and perhaps some still unsettled) questions. Nevertheless, we see a generally coherent picture of a God who has made a path for reconciling a broken humanity to himself. *Could it be that this biblical story—as former skeptics have discovered—is true and offers a better explanation than the alternative worldviews?* In the Scriptures and in Jesus himself, we find a *better* explanation than any other. That is why we look in that direction rather than elsewhere.[14]

When people abandon belief in the God of Scripture—for whatever reason—the alternatives look far more problematic. They have far less explanatory power and coherence. In John's Gospel, a number of Jesus's followers walked away after hearing something severe: "This is a hard teaching. Who can accept it?" (John 6:60 NIV). Jesus then asked his own band of disciples if they would also walk away. But Peter replied, "Lord, to whom shall we go? You have the words of eternal life" (v. 68 NIV).

Questions for Small Groups

Due to reasons of space, these are *general questions* that can be asked for any of the chapters in the book, although some may be more relevant for one chapter than for another. You may want to tackle two chapters at a time for your discussion.

1. What are the key issues or questions raised in this chapter?

2. Which ones had you thought of before, and which ones were new to you?

3. How does our modern culture influence the way you think about these issues? In what way might our culture distort a biblical understanding on these topics?

4. How does our understanding of the Old Testament context help resolve some of these issues?

5. Did you find that the chapter offered some insight about one or more of these questions? If so, how?

6. Were there murky or unresolved issues to explore or ponder?

7. What further questions did this chapter raise for you?

8. In what ways is the *kindness* of God/Jesus evident in this chapter? Divine *severity*?

9. Have you gained a greater understanding of the character of God as you have delved into this chapter?

10. How do the themes you have discussed touch on your everyday life? In what ways were the themes in this chapter profitable and instructive for you as a follower of Christ (cf. 2 Tim. 3:16)?

Notes

Preface

1. Paul Copan, *Is God a Moral Monster? Making Sense of the Old Testament God* (Grand Rapids: Baker Books, 2011).

2. Paul Copan and Matthew Flannagan, *Did God Really Command Genocide? Coming to Terms with the Justice of God* (Grand Rapids: Baker Books, 2014).

3. See the excursus "A Quick Word on God and Violence" in chap. 1. For a traditional Jewish perspective on Old Testament difficulties, see Michoel Stern, *Is the Good Book Bad? A Traditional Jewish Response to the Moral Indictments of the Bible* (Los Angeles: Mosaica, 2022).

Chapter 1 The Old Testament God

1. Cited in David Mills, *The Atheist Universe* (Berkeley: Ulysses, 2006), 54.

2. Richard Dawkins, *The God Delusion* (Boston: Houghton Mifflin, 2006), 51.

3. See Paul Copan and William Lane Craig, eds., *Contending with Christianity's Critics: Answering New Atheists & Other Objectors* (Nashville: B&H Academic, 2009).

4. P. Z. Myers, "The Train Wreck That Was the New Atheism," *Freethoughtblogs.com*, January 25, 2019, https://freethoughtblogs.com/pharyngula/2019/01/25/the-train-wreck-that-was-the-new-atheism/.

5. Gregory Boyd, *Crucifixion of the Warrior God: Violent Portraits of God in Light of the Cross*, 2 vols. (Minneapolis: Fortress, 2017); Eric Seibert, *The Violence of Scripture: Overcoming the Old Testament's Troubling Legacy*

(Minneapolis: Fortress, 2012); Eric Seibert, "When the 'Good Book' Is Bad: Challenging the Bible's Violent Portrayals of God," guest post on *Pete Enns* (blog), accessed October 1, 2021, https://peteenns.com/when-the-good-book-is-bad-challenging-the-bibles-violent-portrayals-of-god/.

6. Boyd, *Crucifixion*, 2:1261.

7. Brian Zahnd, *Sinners in the Hands of a Loving God: The Scandalous Truth of the Very Good News* (Wheaton, IL: Waterbrook, 2015). Boyd also rejects penal substitution.

8. I summarize this doctrine in my book *Loving Wisdom: A Guide to Philosophy and Christian Faith*, 2nd ed. (Grand Rapids: Eerdmans, 2020). See especially William Lane Craig, *Atonement and the Death of Christ* (Waco: Baylor University Press, 2020).

9. Zahnd, *Sinners*, 30.

10. N. T. Wright, "The Word of the Cross," NTWrightPage.com, accessed December 14, 2021, https://ntwrightpage.com/2016/03/30/the-word-of-the-cross/.

11. Bruce C. Birch, "Old Testament Ethics," in *The Blackwell Companion to the Hebrew Bible*, ed. Leo G. Purdue (Oxford: Blackwell, 2001), 297.

12. On this, see Matthew Richard Schlimm, *This Strange and Sacred Scripture: Wrestling with the Old Testament and Its Oddities* (Grand Rapids: Baker Academic, 2015).

13. Stanley Hauerwas, *Wilderness Wanderings: Probing Twentieth-Century Theology and Philosophy* (repr., New York: Routledge, 2018), 29.

14. Garret Keizer, *The Enigma of Anger: Essays on a Sometimes Deadly Sin* (San Francisco: Jossey-Bass, 2002), 10.

15. Karen Armstrong, *A History of God: The 4,000-Year Quest of Judaism, Christianity and Islam* (repr., New York: Random House, 2011), 378.

16. Conor Cunningham, *Darwin's Pious Idea: Why the Ultra-Darwinists and Creationists Both Got It Wrong* (Grand Rapids: Eerdmans, 2010), 235. I came across this and the immediately prior Armstrong citation in Schlimm, *Strange and Sacred Scripture*, 193.

17. Thanks to Jerry Shepherd on this point. See an overview in Terrence E. Fretheim, "God and Violence in the Old Testament," *Word & World* 24, no. 1 (Dec. 2004): 18–28.

18. William J. Webb, *Slaves, Women & Homosexuals: Exploring the Hermeneutics of Cultural Analysis* (Downers Grove, IL: InterVarsity, 2001), 66.

19. Webb, *Slaves, Women & Homosexuals*, 73.

20. Kenton Sparks, Defenders Conference (September 2018), at which both of us spoke: https://apologetics315.com/2018/09/the-defenders-conference-2018/.

21. Boyd, *Crucifixion*, 2:1292–95.

22. Randal Rauser, "The Mutilation of Isaac," Randal Rauser (website), January 25, 2011, https://randalrauser.com/2011/01/the-mutilation-of-isaac/.

23. See Matthew Flannagan and Paul Copan, "Does the Bible Condone Genocide?" in *In Defense of the Bible*, ed. Steven Cowan and Terry Wilder (Nashville: B&H Academic, 2012), 297–334; also, Paul Copan and Matthew Flannagan, *Did God Really Command Genocide? Coming to Terms with the Justice of God* (Grand Rapids: Baker Books, 2014), 194–209.

24. Randal Rauser, *Jesus Loves Canaanites: Biblical Genocide in the Light of Moral Intuition* (Canada: 2 Cup Press, 2021), 64–67.

25. J. Budziszewski, *Commentary on Thomas Aquinas's "Treatise on Law"* (Cambridge: Cambridge University Press, 2014), 287. Thanks to J. Budziszewski for his email correspondence on this topic (Jan. 1, 2022).

26. J. Budziszewski, *Commentary on Thomas Aquinas's "Treatise on Law,"* 287–88.

27. Noted in Michael Mears Bruner, *A Subversive Gospel: Flannery O'Connor and the Reimagining of Beauty, Goodness, and Truth* (Downers Grove, IL: IVP Academic, 2021), 123. Thanks to my wife, Jacqueline, for pointing this out to me.

28. See Copan, *Loving Wisdom*; Paul Copan and Charles Taliaferro, eds., *The Naturalness of Belief: New Essays on Theism's Rationality* (Lanham, MD: Lexington Books, 2017). See other books of mine that address these issues at www.paulcopan.com.

Chapter 2 Is the God of the Old Testament the Same as the God of the New? (1)

1. Andy Stanley, *Irresistible: Reclaiming the New That Jesus Unleashed for the World* (Grand Rapids: Zondervan, 2018), 158.

2. Stanley, *Irresistible*, 278, 280. For a reply, see Michael Kruger, "Why We Can't Unhitch from the Old Testament," *Gospel Coalition*, October 22, 2018, https://www.thegospelcoalition.org/reviews/irresistible-andy-stanley/.

3. Paul Copan and Matthew Flannagan, *Did God Really Command Genocide? Coming to Terms with the Justice of God* (Grand Rapids: Baker Books, 2014), 203–7, 287–98.

4. Jaroslav Pelikan, *Jesus through the Centuries* (New York: Harper & Row, 1987), 20.

5. Fleming Rutledge, *And God Spoke to Abraham: Preaching from the Old Testament* (Grand Rapids: Eerdmans, 2011), quoted in Brent Strawn, *The Old Testament Is Dying* (Grand Rapids: Baker Academic, 2017), 129.

6. Tremper Longman III, *Confronting Old Testament Controversies: Pressing Questions about Evolution, Sexuality, History, and Violence* (Grand Rapids: Baker Books, 2019), 164. See chap. 3, which summarizes the views of Seibert, Enns, and Boyd.

7. See Daryl Charles's review of Boyd in "The Lion *and* the Lamb," *Providence Journal* 13 (Winter 2019): https://providencemag.com/wp-content/uploads/J_Daryl_Charles_-_The_Lamb_and_the_Lion.pdf.

8. Boyd makes this claim in conversation with me and Justin Brierley, *Unbelievable?*, January 19, 2018, http://unbelievable.podbean.com/e/greg-boyd-paul-copan-debate-old-testament-violence-and-boyds-new-theology-in-crucifixion-of-the-warrior-god/. Seibert attempts a definition of violence, however: "*physical, emotional, or psychological harm done to a person by an individual (or individuals), institution, or structure that results in injury, oppression, or death.*" Eric Seibert, *The Violence of Scripture: Overcoming the Old Testament's Troubling Legacy* (Minneapolis: Fortress, 2012), 9 (emphasis in original).

9. When God *said*, "I want you to enter the land of Canaan," the culturally conditioned ears of the violence-prone Moses *heard*, "You must mercilessly slaughter the indigenous population" (Boyd, *Crucifixion*, 2:979).

10. Boyd, *Crucifixion*, 1:84.

11. Boyd, *Crucifixion*, 2:926.

12. Gordon J. Wenham, *Story as Torah: Reading Old Testament Narrative Ethically* (Grand Rapids: Baker Academic, 2000), 80.

13. John Goldingay, *Approaches to Old Testament Interpretation* (Downers Grove, IL: InterVarsity, 1981), 59.

14. N. T. Wright, *Galatians*, Commentary for Christian Formation (Grand Rapids: Eerdmans, 2021), 231.

15. See Patrick Miller, *The Ten Commandments* (Louisville: Westminster John Knox, 2009).

16. See my comments in Robertson McQuilkin and Paul Copan, *An Introduction to Biblical Ethics* (Downers Grove, IL: IVP Academic, 2014), 205–16.

17. Darian Lockett, "The Use of Leviticus 19 in James and 1 Peter: A Neglected Parallel," *Catholic Biblical Quarterly* 82, no. 3 (2020): 456–72. Both letters quote Leviticus 19 (19:18b in James 2:8; 19:2 in 1 Pet. 1:16); additional allusions from Lev. 19:15 are found in James 2:1, 9 and 1 Pet. 1:17. See also Lev. 19:18b in 1 Pet. 1:22.

18. Gordon Graham, *Evil and Christian Ethics* (Cambridge: Cambridge University Press, 2001), 14 (emphasis added).

19. Graham, *Evil and Christian Ethics*, 30.

20. Millar Burrows, "Old Testament Ethics and the Ethics of Jesus," in *Essays in Old Testament Ethics*, ed. J. L. Crenshaw and J. T. Willis (New York: Ktav, 1974), 242. On the significant moral carryover from the Old Testament, see Christopher J. H. Wright, *Old Testament Ethics for the People of God* (Downers Grove, IL: InterVarsity, 2004); Wright, *Walking in the Ways of the Lord: The Ethical Authority of the Old Testament* (Downers Grove, IL: InterVarsity, 1995); Roy E. Gane, *Old Testament Law for Christians: Original Context and Enduring Application* (Grand Rapids: Baker Academic, 2017).

21. C. S. Lewis, "On Ethics," in *Christian Reflections*, ed. Walter Hooper (Grand Rapids: Eerdmans, 1967), 46.

Chapter 3 Is the God of the Old Testament the Same as the God of the New? (2)

1. For a fuller treatment on this kind of selectivity, see Paul Copan, "Not Cruciform Enough: Getting Our Hermeneutical Bearings in the Wake of a Boydian Reinterpretation," in *Hermeneutics of Biblical Violence*, ed. Trevor Laurence and Helen Paynter (Sheffield: Sheffield Phoenix Press, forthcoming).

2. For example, see Greg Boyd, "Jesus Refuted Old Testament Laws," *ReKnew*, January 25, 2017, https://reknew.org/2017/01/jesus-refuted-old-testament-laws/. See Jerry Shepherd's thorough response to Boyd: "No, Jesus Did Not Refute Old Testament Laws," *The Recapitulator*, January 30, 2017, http://www.therecapitulator.com/no-jesus-did-not-refute-old-testament-laws/.

3. Boyd, "Jesus Refuted Old Testament Laws."

4. For more details on Jesus's affirmation of the Mosaic law, see Paul Copan, "Greg Boyd's Misunderstandings of the 'Warrior God,'" *The Gospel Coalition*, January 26, 2018, https://www.thegospelcoalition.org/reviews/crucifixion-warrior-god-greg-boyd/. Additional responses to Boyd are at Paul Lucas's YouTube channel, https://www.youtube.com/channel/UCWVplItQfUkicTYAC0mXoeA.

5. In one of his posts, Boyd completely ignores biblical texts that refer to divine swearing as well as apostolic swearing. Greg Boyd, "Jesus Repudiates OT Commands on Oath-Taking: A Response to Paul Copan (#9)," *ReKnew*, January 2, 2018, https://reknew.org/2018/01/jesus-repudiates-ot-commands-oath-taking-response-paul-copan-9/.

6. Gregory Boyd, *Crucifixion of the Warrior God: Violent Portraits of God in Light of the Cross*, 2 vols. (Minneapolis: Fortress, 2017), 1:577.

7. Boyd, *Crucifixion*, 2:783.

8. John Goldingay, *Numbers and Deuteronomy for Everyone* (Louisville: Westminster John Knox, 2010), 86.

9. See Paul Copan, *Is God a Moral Monster? Making Sense of the Old Testament God* (Grand Rapids: Baker Books, 2011), chap. 9.

10. See Glen H. Stassen and David P. Gushee, *Kingdom Ethics: Following Jesus in Contemporary Context* (Downers Grove, IL: IVP Academic, 2003), 167.

11. Boyd, *Crucifixion*, 1:577.

12. For example, see Greg Boyd, "Who Killed Ananias and Sapphira? A Response to Paul Copan (#6)," *ReKnew*, December 17, 2017, https://reknew.org/2017/12/killed-ananias-sapphira-response-paul-copan-6/.

13. Susan E. Hylen, "Metaphor Matters: Violence and Ethics in Revelation," *Catholic Biblical Quarterly* 73 (2011): 777–96.

Chapter 4 Is the God of the Old Testament the Same as the God of the New? (3)

1. Gregory Boyd, *Crucifixion of the Warrior God: Violent Portraits of God in Light of the Cross*, 2 vols. (Minneapolis: Fortress, 2017), 1:88.

2. Boyd, *Crucifixion*, 1:589.

3. Boyd, *Crucifixion*, 2:799.

4. Boyd, *Crucifixion*, 2:798, 799.

5. In AD 70, the Roman emperor Titus led the siege against Jerusalem after a Jewish insurgency, culminating in the city's ultimate destruction.

6. See Edmund Neufeld, "Vulnerable Bodies and Volunteer Slaves: Slave Parable Violence in the Rest of Matthew," *Bulletin for Biblical Research* 30, no. 1 (2020): 41–63. I would disagree, however, that all of divine violence is eschatological and doesn't include the temporal.

7. Robert H. Gundry, *Commentary on the New Testament* (Peabody, MA: Hendrickson, 2010), 1006.

8. L. Daniel Hawk, *The Violence of the Biblical God: Canonical Narrative and Christian Faith* (Grand Rapids: Eerdmans, 2019), 186–87.

9. Hawk, *Violence*, 221.

10. Miroslav Volf, *Exclusion and Embrace: A Theological Exploration of Identity, Otherness, and Reconciliation* (Nashville: Abingdon, 1996), 301.

11. Hawk, *Violence*, 15.

12. John Goldingay, *Old Testament Ethics: A Guided Tour* (Downers Grove, IL: IVP Academic, 2019), 2.

13. Gordon Wenham, *Story as Torah: Reading Old Testament Narrative Ethically* (Grand Rapids: Baker Academic, 2000), 154.

14. Greg Boyd, "Jesus Refuted Old Testament Laws," *ReKnew*, January 25, 2017, https://reknew.org/2017/01/jesus-refuted-old-testament-laws/.

15. Graeme Goldsworthy, *Preaching the Whole Bible as Christian Scripture* (Grand Rapids: Eerdmans, 2000), 154. Thanks to Jerry Shepherd on this point ("No, Jesus Did Not Refute Old Testament Laws," *The Recapitulator*, January 30, 2017, http://www.therecapitulator.com/no-jesus-did-not-refute-old-testament-laws/).

16. See Andrew Wilson, "The Jesus Lens, or the Jesus Tea-Strainer," *Think Theology* (blog), February 26, 2014, https://thinktheology.co.uk/blog/article/the_jesus_lens_or_the_jesus_tea_strainer.

Chapter 5 "From Heaven or from Human Origin?"

1. Tremper Longman III, *Proverbs* (Grand Rapids: Baker Academic, 2006), 45–58.

2. Term used in Nicholas Wolterstorff, *Divine Discourse: Philosophical Reflection on the Claim That God Speaks* (Cambridge: Cambridge University Press, 1995).

3. See C. S. Lewis, "Myth Became Fact," in *God in the Dock*, ed. Walter Hooper (Grand Rapids: Eerdmans, 1970), 63–67; J. R. R. Tolkien, "On Fairy Stories," in *Essays Presented to Charles Williams*, ed. C. S. Lewis (Oxford: Oxford University Press, 1947), 38–89 (Tolkien's essay is also available at various places on the internet).

4. The heading ("The Extraordinary in the Ordinary") is taken from Kevin Vanhoozer, "The Sufficiency of Scripture," *Worldview Bulletin*, April 25, 2021, https://worldviewbulletin.substack.com/p/the-sufficiency-of-scripture-from.

5. David Baker, *Tight Fists or Open Hands? Wealth and Poverty in Old Testament Law* (Grand Rapids: Eerdmans, 2009), 3–5.

6. Roy E. Gane, *Old Testament Law for Christians: Original Context and Enduring Application* (Grand Rapids: Baker Academic, 2017), 43 (emphasis added). See also John Goldingay, *Old Testament Theology*, vol. 3, *Israel's Life* (Downers Grove, IL: IVP Academic, 2009), 38.

7. All quotations from the Code of Hammurabi are taken from "The Hammurabi Code," https://history.hanover.edu/courses/excerpts/211ham.html, which utilizes the electronic text from Virginia Tech's Eris database.

8. Alan Millard, personal correspondence, January 20, 2022. See Gil Davis, "The Rise of Silver Coinage in the Ancient Mediterranean," *Ancient Near East Today* 9, no. 12 (December 2021), https://www.asor.org/anetoday/2021/12/rise-of-silver-coinage.

9. Gane, *Old Testament Law for Christians*, 125–26.

10. Goldingay, *Old Testament Theology*, 3:38–39; Gane, *Old Testament Law for Christians*, 37–38.

11. For example, D. P. Wright, "The Laws of Hammurabi as a Source for the Covenant Collection (Exodus 20:23–23:19)," *Maarav* 10 (2003): 11–87.

12. For example, Bruce Wells, "The Covenant Code and Near Eastern Legal Traditions: A Response to David P. Wright," *Maarav* 13 (2006): 85–118.

Chapter 6 Multiple Sources and Late Dates?

1. Gordon Wenham, *Exploring the Old Testament*, vol. 1, *A Guide to the Pentateuch* (Downers Grove, IL: InterVarsity, 2003), 173. For fuller discussion on this topic, see 159–85. For an early

critique, see Umberto Cassuto, *The Documentary Hypothesis and the Composition of the Pentateuch*, trans. Israel Abrahams (Jerusalem: Magnes, 1961); see also Wenham, "Genesis: An Authorship Study and Current Pentateuchal Criticism," *Journal for the Study of the Old Testament* 42 (1988): 3–18.

2. The comparison can be found at "The Documentary Hypothesis in Detail—Genesis," *Three Jews, Four Opinions* (blog), July 27, 2008, http://www.threejews.net/2008/07/documentary -hypothesis-in-detail.html. On disagreement in Exodus, see T. Desmond Alexander, *Exodus* (Downers Grove, IL: IVP Academic, 2019), 102.

3. David Clines, "New Directions in Pooh Studies: *Überlieferungs- und religionsgeschichtliche Studien zum Pu-Buch*," in *On the Way to the Postmodern: Old Testament Essays, 1967–1998*, 2 vols. (Sheffield: Sheffield Academic Press, 1992), 2:830–39; see article also at *Union*, https://www .uniontheology.org/resources/bible/biblical-theology/new-directions-in-pooh-studies.

4. On this, see John Sailhamer, *The Meaning of the Pentateuch: Revelation, Composition and Interpretation* (Downers Grove, IL: IVP Academic, 2009).

5. Matthew Richard Schlimm, *This Strange and Sacred Scripture: Wrestling with the Old Testament and Its Oddities* (Grand Rapids: Baker Academic, 2015), 121–38.

6. This section on supersessionism and complementarity summarizes themes and insights from Joshua Berman, "Supersessionist or Complementary? Reassessing the Nature of Legal Revision in the Pentateuchal Law Collections," *Journal of Biblical Literature* 135, no. 2 (Summer 2016): 201–22.

7. Adrian Schenker, "The Biblical Legislation on the Release of Slaves: The Road from Exodus to Leviticus," *Journal for the Study of the Old Testament* 78 (1998): 23–24.

8. For specifics, see Berman, "Supersessionist."

9. Christopher Wright, "Response to Gordon McConville," in *Canon and Biblical Interpretation*, ed. Craig G. Bartholomew, Scott Hahn, Robin Parry, Christopher Seitz, and Al Wolters, Scripture and Hermeneutics Series 7 (Grand Rapids: Zondervan, 2006), 283.

10. Bruce Wells says they were motivated by priestly and ceremonial considerations (Priestly Code), by legal concerns mixed with ceremonial ones (Holiness Code), or by deeper theological and legal concerns (Deuteronomic Code). Wells,

"The Interpretation of Legal Traditions in Ancient Israel," *The Hebrew Bible and Ancient Israel* 4 (2015): 234–66.

11. Randal Rauser, *Jesus Loves Canaanites: Biblical Genocide in the Light of Moral Intuition* (Canada: 2 Cup Press, 2021), 259–63.

12. Kenneth Kitchen, *On the Reliability of the Old Testament*, 465, 466. See 464–68 for further elaboration on *The Bible Unearthed*.

13. Kitchen, *Reliability*, 159–239, 480–82.

14. On the conquest, see Tremper Longman III, *Confronting Old Testament Controversies: Pressing Questions about Evolution, Sexuality, History, and Violence* (Grand Rapids: Baker Books, 2019), 79–121; also, chapter 5 in Kenneth A. Kitchen, *On the Reliability of the Old Testament* (Grand Rapids: Eerdmans, 2006).

15. See David G. Firth, *Joshua* (Bellingham, WA: Lexham, 2021), 85, 128–31, 146–49. See also Lorenzo Nigro, "The Italian-Palestinian Expedition to Tell es-Sultan, Ancient Jericho (1997–2015): Archaeology and Valorisation of Material and Immaterial Heritage," in *Digging Up Jericho Past, Present and Future*, ed. Rachael Thyrza Sparks, Bill Finlayson, and Josef Mario Briffa (Oxford: Oxford University Press, 2020), 175–214, esp. 203–4.

16. Douglas S. Earl, *The Joshua Delusion? Rethinking Genocide in the Bible* (Eugene, OR: Cascade, 2011); Jerome F. D. Creach, *Violence in Scripture* (Louisville: Westminster John Knox, 2013); Kenton Sparks, *God's Word in Human Words: An Evangelical Appropriation of Critical Biblical Scholarship* (Grand Rapids: Baker Academic, 2008); Rauser, *Jesus Loves Canaanites*.

17. David Firth notes this in David Firth, William Ford, and Paul Copan, "The Conquest of Canaan: Round-table Discussion," in *Hermeneutics of Biblical Violence*, ed. Trevor Laurence and Helen Paynter (Sheffield: Sheffield Phoenix Press, forthcoming).

18. Hawk, *Violence*, 14.

19. See K. A. Kitchen, *Ancient Orient and Old Testament* (Downers Grove, IL: InterVarsity, 1975).

20. Kitchen, *Reliability*, 287–88.

21. K. Lawson Younger Jr., *Ancient Conquest Accounts: A Study in Ancient Near Eastern and Biblical History Writing*, Journal for the Study of the Old Testament Supplement Series 98 (Sheffield: JSOT Press, 1990).

22. From J. G. McConville, *Law and Theology in Deuteronomy* (Sheffield: JSOT Press, 1985).

23. Cooper Smith, "The 'Wilderness' in Hosea and Deuteronomy: A Case of Thematic Reappropriation," *Bulletin for Biblical Research* 28, no. 2 (2018): 240–60.

24. Bill T. Arnold, "Deuteronomy as the *Ipsissima Vox* of Moses," *Journal of Theological Interpretation* 4, no. 1 (2010): 53–74.

25. On Paul's Athens speech, see Paul Copan and Kenneth Litwak, *The Gospel in the Marketplace of Ideas: Paul's Mars Hill Experience for Our Pluralistic World* (Downers Grove, IL: IVP Academic, 2014).

26. On the Pentateuch's literary unity, see Sailhamer, *Meaning of the Pentateuch.*

Chapter 7 Differences between the Law of Moses and Ancient Near Eastern Laws (1)

1. John Goldingay, *Old Testament Ethics: A Guided Tour* (Downers Grove, IL: IVP Academic, 2019), 151.

2. John H. Walton and J. Harvey Walton, *The Lost World of the Torah: Laws as Covenant and Wisdom in Ancient Context* (Downers Grove, IL: IVP Academic, 2019), 44, 210.

3. Walton and Walton, *Lost World of the Torah*, 212 (emphasis added).

4. Walton and Walton, *Lost World of the Torah*, 212.

5. For a fuller response to Walton and Walton's *Lost World of the Torah*, see Paul Copan, "Interpreting the Law of Moses: Relative, Normative, or Something In-Between? A Review of *The Lost World of the Torah*, by John H. Walton and J. Harvey Walton," *Christian Research Journal*, December 2, 2019, https://www.equip.org/article/interpreting-the-law-of-moses-relative-norma tive-or-something-in-between-a-review-of-the -lost-world-of-the-torah-by-john-h-walton-and -j-harvey-walton/.

6. Shalom M. Paul, *Studies in the Book of the Covenant in the Light of Cuneiform and Biblical Law*, Supplements to Vetus Testamentum 18 (Leiden: Brill, 1970), 37, 43.

7. John Goldingay, *Old Testament Theology*, vol. 3, *Israel's Life* (Downers Grove, IL: IVP Academic, 2009), 38.

8. As argued by Walton and Walton, *Lost World of Torah*, 100.

9. Using the Greek rendering of Leviticus 18:22 and 20:13, Paul coins a new term—*arsenokoitai*—meaning "[practicing] homosexuals" (1 Cor. 6:9; 1 Tim. 1:10), from the words *arsenikos* ("male") and *koitē* ("bed"). See also Jay Sklar, "The Prohibitions against Homosexual Sex

in Leviticus 18:22 and 20:13: Are They Relevant Today?," *Bulletin for Biblical Research* 28, no. 2 (2018): 165–98.

10. Gordon J. Wenham, *Story as Torah: Reading Old Testament Narrative Ethically* (Grand Rapids: Baker Academic, 2000), 3.

11. Matthew Richard Schlimm, *This Strange and Sacred Scripture: Wrestling with the Old Testament and Its Oddities* (Grand Rapids: Baker Academic, 2015), 69.

12. Wenham, *Story as Torah*, 15.

13. Wenham, *Story as Torah*, 107.

14. See Meir Sternberg, *The Poetics of Biblical Narrative: Ideological Literature and the Drama of Reading* (Bloomington: Indiana University Press, 1987).

15. Jon D. Levinson, "The Shema and the Commandment to Love God in Its Ancient Contexts," The Torah.com, accessed December 15, 2021, https://www.thetorah.com/article/the-shema-and -the-commandment-to-love-god-in-its-ancient -contexts.

Chapter 8 Differences between the Law of Moses and Ancient Near Eastern Laws (2)

1. Peter Enns, *Inspiration and Incarnation: Evangelicals and the Problem of the Old Testament* (Grand Rapids: Baker Academic, 2008), 32.

2. John Goldingay, "Justice and Salvation for Israel in Canaan," in *Reading the Hebrew Bible for a New Millennium: Form, Concept, and Theological Perspective*, vol. 1, *Theological and Hermeneutical Studies*, ed. Deborah L. Ellens, Michael Floyd, Wonil Kim, and Marvin A. Sweeney (Harrisburg, PA: Trinity Press International, 2000), 184.

3. Iain Provan makes this point in his *Seriously Dangerous Religion: What the Old Testament Really Says and Why It Matters* (Waco: Baylor University Press, 2014).

4. See Russell Hittinger, *A Critique of the New Natural Law Theory* (Notre Dame, IN: University of Notre Dame Press, 1987), 44–45.

5. As will be evident in this and the following chapter, I am indebted to the work of Daisy Yulin Tsai, *Human Rights in Deuteronomy* (Berlin: de Gruyter, 2014), 165–82; David Baker, *Tight Fists or Open Hands? Wealth and Poverty in Old Testament Law* (Grand Rapids: Eerdmans, 2009); and Christopher J. H. Wright, *Old Testament Ethics for the People of God* (Downers Grove, IL: InterVarsity, 2004); Wright, *God's People in God's Land: Family, Land, and Property in the Old Testament* (Downers Grove, IL: InterVarsity,

1990). Baker's and Wright's books in particular offer an impressive examination of both similarities and differences between the Mosaic law and other ancient Near Eastern law collections.

6. Walter Brueggemann, *Genesis* (Louisville: Westminster John Knox, 1982), 32.

7. Tsai, *Human Rights*, 2.

8. Tsai, *Human Rights*, 174.

9. Jean Louis Ska, review of *Understanding the Pentateuch as a Scripture*, by James W. Watts, *Review of Biblical Literature*, July 16, 2020, https://www.sblcentral.org/home/bookDetails /13090.

10. Mark S. Smith, trans., *Ugaritic Narrative Poetry*, ed. Simon B. Parker (Atlanta: Society of Biblical Literature, 1997), 148; Albrecht Goetze, trans., "El, Ashertu and the Storm-god," in *The Ancient Near East: Supplementary Texts and Pictures Relating to the Old Testament*, ed. James B. Pritchard (Princeton: Princeton University Press, 1969), 519.

11. L. Daniel Hawk, *The Violence of the Biblical God: Canonical Narrative and Christian Faith* (Grand Rapids: Eerdmans, 2019), 71, 83–85.

12. This is from the Babylonian account of creation Enuma Elish (5.139).

13. John H. Walton and J. Harvey Walton, *The Lost World of the Torah: Laws as Covenant and Wisdom in Ancient Context* (Downers Grove, IL: IVP Academic, 2019), 65–69.

14. Paul Copan and Matthew Flannagan, *Did God Really Command Genocide? Coming to Terms with the Justice of God* (Grand Rapids: Baker Books, 2014), 246–56, esp. 252–53.

15. John Walton, *Ancient Near Eastern Thought and the Old Testament* (Grand Rapids: Baker Academic, 2006), 267.

16. See James K. Hoffmeier, "Egyptian Religious Influences on the Early Hebrews," in *Did I Not Bring Israel Out of Egypt? Biblical, Archaeological, and Egyptological Perspectives on the Exodus Narratives*, ed. James K. Hoffmeier, Alan R. Millard, and Gary A. Rendsberg (Winona Lake, IN: Eisenbrauns, 2016), 27–31.

17. Walton, *Ancient Near Eastern Thought*, 271, 273. Walton notes Scripture's historical *uniqueness* when "Moses performs signs to establish his credibility" (274); see also, Jeffrey Niehaus, *Ancient Near Eastern Themes in Biblical Theology* (Grand Rapids: Kregel, 2008), 56, 82.

18. John H. Walton, "Interpreting the Bible as an Ancient Near Eastern Document," in *Israel:*

Ancient Kingdom or Late Invention?, ed. Daniel I. Block (Nashville: B&H Academic, 2008), 321–22.

19. Walton and Walton, *Lost World of the Torah*, 249–50; William W. Hallo, *The Ancient Near Eastern Background of Some Modern Institutions* (Leiden: Brill, 1996), 127–35.

20. Baker, *Tight Fists*, 295–96.

21. Baker, *Tight Fists*, 307.

22. Baker, *Tight Fists*, 307.

23. Baker, *Tight Fists*, 307.

24. Tsai, *Human Rights*, 179.

25. Gordon McConville, "Old Testament Laws and Canonical Intentionality," in *Canon and Biblical Interpretation*, ed. Craig Bartholomew, Scott Hahn, Robin Parry, Christopher Seitz, and Al Wolters, Scripture and Hermeneutics Series 7 (Grand Rapids: Zondervan, 2006), 263.

26. Tsai, *Human Rights*, 168, 182.

27. Norman Gottwald, "Social Class as an Analytic and Hermeneutical Category in Biblical Studies," *Journal of Biblical Literature* 112 (1993): 6.

28. Baker, *Tight Fists*, 111–12.

29. Baker, *Tight Fists*, 135.

30. Baker, *Tight Fists*, 295–96.

31. Joshua Berman, "In Conversation with Joshua A. Berman, *Created Equal: How the Bible Broke with Ancient Political Thought* (Oxford University Press, 2008)," *Journal of Hebrew Scriptures* 10 (2010): 46.

32. For example, the late critic Hector Avalos made such claims in his *Slavery, Abolitionism, and the Ethics of Biblical Scholarship* (Sheffield: University of Sheffield Press, 2011).

Chapter 9 Differences between the Law of Moses and Ancient Near Eastern Laws (3)

1. David Baker, *Tight Fists or Open Hands? Wealth and Poverty in Old Testament Law* (Grand Rapids: Eerdmans, 2009), 106–7.

2. Baker, *Tight Fists*, 177.

3. Roy E. Gane, *Old Testament Law for Christians: Original Context and Enduring Application* (Grand Rapids: Baker Academic, 2017), 111.

4. Baker, *Tight Fists*, 220, 221.

5. Baker, *Tight Fists*, 314.

6. Baker, *Tight Fists*, 315.

7. John H. Walton, "Interpreting the Bible as an Ancient Near Eastern Document," in *Israel: Ancient Kingdom or Late Invention?*, ed. Daniel I. Block (Nashville: B&H Academic, 2008), 321–22.

8. On this passage, see Christopher J. H. Wright, *Deuteronomy* (Peabody, MA: Hendrickson, 1996), 258–59, 262. Wright notes that, unlike those who tended to be "fairly permanent residential employees"—strangers (*gerim*) and resident aliens (*toashabim*)—the hired laborer in v. 14 (*sakir*) didn't have this kind of security but survived on short-term employment for certain types of labor and skills (262).

9. Baker, *Tight Fists*, 238.

10. Baker, *Tight Fists*, 237; cf. 249.

11. Baker, *Tight Fists*, 248.

12. Baker, *Tight Fists*, 253–54.

13. Baker, *Tight Fists*, 263–65.

14. Wright, *Deuteronomy*, 187–88.

15. John L. Hartley, *Leviticus* (Dallas: Word, 1992), 246.

16. Baker, *Tight Fists*, 276.

17. Baker, *Tight Fists*, 284; see also 276–78.

18. Baker, *Tight Fists*, 284.

19. See summary in John H. Walton and J. Harvey Walton, *The Lost World of the Torah: Laws as Covenant and Wisdom in Ancient Context* (Downers Grove, IL: IVP Academic, 2019), 133–53.

Chapter 10 A Bit of Ancient Near Eastern Context

1. Ted Landphair, "Outmoded Laws Still on US Books," *Voice of America*, August 28, 2011, https://www.voanews.com/a/outdated-laws-still -books-in-us-states--128590038/162753.html.

2. For example, Gregory Boyd, *Crucifixion of the Warrior God: Violent Portraits of God in Light of the Cross*, 2 vols. (Minneapolis: Fortress, 2017), 1:577.

3. Walter C. Kaiser, *Toward Old Testament Ethics* (Grand Rapids: Zondervan, 1983), 91–92; and Kaiser, "God's Promise Plan and His Gracious Law," *Journal for the Evangelical Theological Society* 33, no. 3 (Sept. 1990): 293.

4. Craig Keener, "The Sin of Achan," Craig-Keener.org, June 6, 2018, https://craigkeener.org /the-sin-of-achan-2-minutes/.

5. Joe M. Sprinkle, *Biblical Law and Its Relevance* (Lanham, MD: University Press of America, 2006), 76–77. Thanks to Matt Flannagan for various insights on punishments: "Stoning Adulterers," *Christian Research Journal* 34, no. 6 (2011), https://www.equip.org/article/stoning -adulterers/; also, note Flannagan's responses to the late critic Hector Avalos: "A Reply to Hector Avalos' 'Why Flannagan Fails History,'" MandM, June 28, 2011, http://www.mandm.org.nz/2011

/06/a-reply-to-hector-avalos-why-flannagan-fails -at-history.html.

6. J. J. Finkelstein, "The Ox That Gored," *Transactions of the American Philosophical Society* 71, no. 2 (1981): 34–35.

7. Finkelstein, "Ox That Gored," 35.

8. In this paragraph I am summarizing Finkelstein, "Ox That Gored," 35.

9. Raymond Westbrook, "The Character of Ancient Near Eastern Law," in *A History of Ancient Near Eastern Law*, vol. 1, ed. Raymond Westbrook (Boston: Brill, 2003), 774.

10. Joe M. Sprinkle, "The Interpretation of Exodus 21:22–25 (*Lex Talionis*) and Abortion," *Westminster Theological Journal* 55 (1993): 241–42; also, Raymond Westbrook, "The Character of Ancient Near Eastern Law," in *A History of Ancient Near Eastern Law*, vol. 1, ed. Raymond Westbrook (Boston: Brill, 2003), 774.

Chapter 11 Israel's Punishments as Nonliteral in the Pentateuch

1. John Goldingay, *Old Testament Theology*, vol. 3, *Israel's Life* (Downers Grove, IL: IVP Academic, 2009), 38.

2. John Goldingay, *Old Testament Ethics: A Guided Tour* (Downers Grove, IL: IVP Academic, 2019), 89; cf. 91.

3. Goldingay, *Old Testament Theology*, 3:38.

4. Note that the treatment of this passage is a slight revision of what I wrote in *Moral Monster*: see Paul Copan, *Is God a Moral Monster? Making Sense of the Old Testament God* (Grand Rapids: Baker Books, 2011), chap. 9.

5. Joe M. Sprinkle, "Interpretation of Exodus 21:22–25 (*Lex Talionis*) and Abortion," *Westminster Theological Journal* 55 (1993): 243.

6. See Matthew Flannagan, "Slavery and the Old Testament," MandM, April 3, 2010, http:// www.mandm.org.nz/2010/04/contra-mundum -slavery-and-the-old-testament.html.

7. Victor P. Hamilton, *Exodus: An Exegetical Commentary* (Grand Rapids: Baker Academic, 2011), 392.

8. Hamilton, *Exodus*, 393. For a discussion of John 8, the passage to which this quote alludes, see chap. 12.

9. J. J. Finkelstein, "The Ox That Gored," *Transactions of the American Philosophical Society* 71, no. 2 (1981): 21.

10. Finkelstein, "Ox That Gored," 21.

11. T. Desmond Alexander, *Exodus* (Downers Grove, IL: IVP Academic, 2019), 491. According to Leviticus 27:2–8, there was a sliding payment

scale for a contracted servant depending on the servant's age, skills, and sex (which also suggests physical strength). This wasn't a matter of intrinsic worth. Gordon J. Wenham, "Leviticus 27:2–8 and the Price of Slaves," *Zeitschrift für die Alttestamentliche Wissenschaft* 90 (1978): 264–65.

12. Sprinkle, "Interpretation," 242.

13. Copan, *Is God a Moral Monster?*, chap. 11.

14. Gordon J. Wenham, "*Betûlāh*: 'A Girl of Marriageable Age,'" *Vetus Testamentum* 22, no. 3 (July 1972): 330.

15. Roy E. Gane, *Old Testament Law for Christians: Original Context and Enduring Application* (Grand Rapids: Baker Academic, 2017), 274.

16. Joseph Fleishman, "Spreading the Cloth in Deuteronomy 22:17b: Conclusive Evidence or the Beginning of the Evidential Procedure?," *Zeitschrift für altorientalische und biblische Rechtsgeschichte* 18 (2012): 295–308.

17. Wenham, "*Betûlāh*," 332.

18. Sprinkle, "Interpretation," 243.

19. Raymond Westbrook and Bruce Wells, *Everyday Life in Biblical Israel* (Louisville: Westminster John Knox, 2009), 79.

20. Westbrook and Wells, *Everyday Life*, 79.

21. Bruce Wells, personal email, July 6, 2011.

22. Christopher J. H. Wright, *Old Testament Ethics for the People of God* (Downers Grove, IL: InterVarsity, 2004), 54–56.

Chapter 12 Israel's Punishments as Nonliteral in Old Testament History

1. This is noted by the late Westbrook's coauthor Bruce Wells (they cowrote *Everyday Law in Biblical Life: An Introduction* [Louisville: Westminster John Knox, 2009]). Wells offered this comment (July 10, 2011) on Paul Copan, "Deuteronomy 25:11–12, an Eye for an Eye, and Raymond Westbrook: A Reply to Hector Avalos," July 8, 2011, https://credohouse.org/blog/deuteronomy-2511-12-an-eye-for-an-eye-and-raymond-westbrook-a-reply-to-hector-avalos#_ftn5. By the way, in this blog post, I expound on my *Moral Monster* treatment of Deuteronomy 25:11–12 (punishment as depilation rather than amputation for a woman who grabs a man's genitals): Paul Copan, *Is God a Moral Monster? Making Sense of the Old Testament God* (Grand Rapids: Baker Books, 2011). Bruce Wells commented on the blog posting that he found this "quite convincing," although he said—and I agree—that monetary compensation would have been an option in such situations.

2. Joe M. Sprinkle, "The Interpretation of Exodus 21:22–25 (*Lex Talionis*) and Abortion," *Westminster Theological Journal* 55 (1993): 239. Sprinkle mentions King Adoni-Bezek (Judg. 1:6–7), who had cut off the thumbs and big toes of seventy kings. When Judah defeated his forces, Adoni-Bezek's own thumbs and big toes were cut off. This is more "poetic justice" than literally applying the eye-for-eye principle (242).

3. Gordon J. Wenham, "*Betûlāh*: 'A Girl of Marriageable Age,'" *Vetus Testamentum* 22, no. 3 (1972): 333.

4. Greg Boyd, "Jesus Refuted Old Testament Laws," ReKnew, January 25, 2017, https://reknew.org/2017/01/jesus-refuted-old-testament-laws/.

5. Jerry Shepherd, "No, Jesus Did Not Refute Old Testament Laws," *The Recapitulator*, January 30, 2017, http://www.therecapitulator.com/no-jesus-did-not-refute-old-testament-laws/.

6. Elias J. Bickerman, "The Warning Inscriptions of Herod's Temple," *Jewish Quarterly Review* 37, no. 4 (April 1947): 387–405. Josephus mentions this in *Jewish Wars* 6.2.4.

7. See Henry Keating, "Sanctions against Adultery in Ancient Israelite Society, with Some Reflections on Methodology in the Study of Old Testament Ethics," *Journal for the Study of the Old Testament* 11 (1979): 57–72.

8. Keating, "Sanctions," 69.

9. Jay Sklar, *Leviticus* (Downers Grove, IL: IVP Academic, 2014), 248–49.

10. Sklar, *Leviticus*, 249.

11. Keating, "Sanctions," 58.

12. John Goldingay, *Old Testament Ethics: A Guided Tour* (Downers Grove, IL: IVP Academic, 2019), 148–49.

13. See Copan, *Is God a Moral Monster?*, chap. 9.

14. Herbert C. Brichto, *The Problem of "Curse" in the Hebrew Bible*, rev. ed. (Philadelphia: Society of Biblical Literature, 1968), 132–35.

15. Keating, "Sanctions," 67.

16. T. Desmond Alexander, *Exodus* (Downers Grove, IL: IVP Academic, 2019), 505 (emphasis added).

17. Alexander, *Exodus*, 505.

18. Goldingay, *Old Testament Ethics*, 93.

19. John Goldingay, *Exodus and Leviticus for Everyone* (Louisville: Westminster John Knox, 2010), 85.

20. John Goldingay, *Old Testament Theology*, vol. 3, *Israel's Life* (Downers Grove, IL: IVP Academic, 2009), 38.

Chapter 13 How Was David "a Man after God's Own Heart"?

1. Pierre Bayle, *An Historical and Critical Dictionary*, vol. 1 (London: Hunt and Clark, 1826), 363. Thanks to my former church history professor John Woodbridge for pointing this out in his Enlightenment class at Trinity Evangelical Divinity School (1987)—and for his helpful correspondence on this topic more recently (June 11, 2021).

2. Bayle, *Historical and Critical Dictionary*, 369. These "offending" comments can be found in Elisabeth Labrousse, *Bayle*, Past Masters, trans. Denys Potts (Oxford: Oxford University Press, 1983), 42.

3. Bayle, *Historical and Critical Dictionary*, 383.

4. Bayle, *Historical and Critical Dictionary*, 384.

5. On the "man after God's own heart" discussion, I am following the work of John Goldingay, *Old Testament Ethics: A Guided Tour* (Downers Grove, IL: IVP Academic, 2019), 250–51; and Goldingay, *Men Behaving Badly* (Carlisle, UK: Paternoster, 2000), 115–16.

6. Goldingay, *Men Behaving Badly*, 115.

7. David G. Firth, *1 & 2 Samuel* (Downers Grove, IL: IVP Academic, 2009), 156.

8. Gregory Boyd, *Crucifixion of the Warrior God: Violent Portraits of God in Light of the Cross*, 2 vols. (Minneapolis: Fortress, 2017), 2:888.

9. Boyd, *Crucifixion*, 1:320.

10. See Paul Copan, *Is God a Moral Monster? Making Sense of the Old Testament God* (Grand Rapids: Baker Books, 2011), chap. 6.

11. For example, Walter Brueggemann, *First and Second Samuel*, Interpretation (Louisville: Westminster John Knox, 1990).

12. See Firth, *1 & 2 Samuel*, 177–78.

13. David G. Firth, *Including the Stranger: Foreigners in the Former Prophets* (Downers Grove, IL: IVP Academic, 2019), 101.

14. John H. Walton and J. Harvey Walton, *The Lost World of the Israelite Conquest: Covenant, Retribution, and the Fate of the Canaanites* (Downers Grove, IL: IVP Academic, 2017), 217.

15. Walton and Walton, *Lost World of the Israelite Conquest*, 222.

16. Walton and Walton, *Lost World of the Israelite Conquest*, 218.

17. Firth, *Including the Stranger*, 104.

Chapter 14 Why Does God Harden People's Hearts?

1. T. Desmond Alexander, *Exodus* (Downers Grove, IL: IVP Academic, 2019), 105, 163–71.

2. On the hardening of Pharaoh's heart, see Victor P. Hamilton, *Exodus: An Exegetical Commentary* (Grand Rapids: Baker Academic, 2011), 170–74; Douglas K. Stuart, *Exodus* (Nashville: Holman, 2006), 146–50.

3. From Hamilton, *Exodus*, 173–74.

4. Alexander, *Exodus*, 130.

5. For insights in this "Challenging the Egyptian Superpower" section, I follow L. Daniel Hawk, *The Violence of the Biblical God: Canonical Narrative and Christian Faith* (Grand Rapids: Eerdmans, 2019), 82–85.

6. Lissa M. Wray Beal, *Joshua* (Grand Rapids: Zondervan, 2019), 254; David G. Firth, *Joshua* (Bellingham, WA: Lexham, 2021), 228.

7. For example, theologian Abraham Kuyper made this point in *The Work of the Holy Spirit* (New York: Funk and Wagnalls, 1900), 594–97.

8. John Goldingay, *Old Testament Theology*, vol. 1, *Israel's Gospel* (Downers Grove, IL: IVP Academic, 2003), 351; see also Hawk, *Violence*, 85.

9. Douglas K. Stuart, *Exodus* (Nashville: Holman, 2006), 149–51.

10. Isaiah 63:17 reads: "Why, O LORD, do You cause us to stray from Your ways and harden our heart from fearing You?" As noted in chapter 17 below, not every plea and prayer in Scripture is theologically accurate (e.g., Jer. 20:7), and in the same vicinity of Isaiah 63 are indicators of Israel's refusing God's gracious initiative (Isa. 65:2, 12; 66:4).

11. See William Klein, *The New Chosen People: A Corporate View of Election*, rev. and exp. ed. (Eugene, OR: Wipf & Stock, 2015); I. Howard Marshall, *Jesus the Savior: Studies in New Testament Theology* (Downers Grove, IL: InterVarsity, 1991); Robert Shank, *Elect in the Son: A Study of the Doctrine of Election* (Minneapolis: Bethany House, 1989).

Chapter 15 Divine Smitings (1)

1. For an overview, see Paul Copan and Douglas Jacoby, *Origins: The Ancient Impact and Modern Implications of Genesis 1–11* (New York: Morgan James, 2019), chaps. 12–13; in more detail, see Tremper Longman III and John H. Walton, *The Lost World of the Flood: Mythology, Theology, and the Deluge Debate* (Downers Grove, IL: IVP

Academic, 2017); also see flood-related articles in Paul Copan, Tremper Longman III, Christopher L. Reese, and Michael G. Strauss, eds., *The Zondervan Dictionary of Christianity and Science* (Grand Rapids: Zondervan, 2017).

2. Gordon Wenham, *Exploring the Old Testament*, vol. 1, *A Guide to the Pentateuch* (Downers Grove, IL: InterVarsity, 2003), 30.

3. L. Daniel Hawk, *Violence of the Biblical God: Canonical Narrative and Christian Faith* (Grand Rapids: Eerdmans, 2019), 31.

4. See Hawk, *Violence*, 31–37.

5. See Walter Brueggemann, *Genesis* (Louisville: Westminster John Knox, 1982), 77.

6. Matthew J. Lynch, *Portraying Violence in the Hebrew Bible: A Literary and Cultural Study* (Cambridge: Cambridge University Press, 2020), 68–69.

7. Richard Swinburne, *The Existence of God*, 2nd ed. (Oxford: Clarendon, 2004), 257.

8. These sources are cited in Mordechai Gilula, "The Smiting of the First-Born—An Egyptian Myth?," *Tel Aviv* 4, nos. 1–2 (1977): 94.

9. Gilula, "Smiting of the First-Born," 94–95.

10. Seibert attempts to evade the historical grounding for certain biblical events because of their association with God's severe ("violent") actions. He makes the startling claim that only in a "few cases"—such as Jesus's bodily resurrection—does the historicity of a biblical event really matter. Eric Seibert, *Disturbing Divine Behavior: Troubling Old Testament Images of God* (Minneapolis: Fortress, 2009), 120.

11. See Egyptologist James K. Hoffmeier's work on these questions: "The Exodus and Wilderness Narratives," in *Ancient Israel's History: An Introduction to Issues and Sources*, eds. Bill T. Arnold and Richard S. Hess (Grand Rapids: Baker Academic, 2014), 46–90; Hoffmeier, *Israel in Egypt: The Evidence for the Authenticity of the Exodus Tradition* (Oxford: Oxford University Press, 1999); and Hoffmeier, *Ancient Israel in Sinai: The Evidence for the Authenticity of the Wilderness Tradition* (Oxford: Oxford University Press, 2005). See also Mark D. Janzen, ed., *Five Views on the Exodus: Historicity, Chronology, and Theological Implications* (Grand Rapids: Zondervan, 2021); Benjamin J. Noonan, *Non-Semitic Loanwords in the Hebrew Bible: A Lexicon of Language Contact* (Winona Lake, IN: Eisenbrauns, 2019); and Egyptologist Kenneth Kitchen's *On the Historical Reliability of the Old Testament* (Grand Rapids: Eerdmans, 2006).

12. Douglas Stuart claims that *Gershom's* life was under threat (Stuart, *Exodus* [Nashville: Holman, 2006], 152–56). However, T. Desmond Alexander observes that, given "God's concern for Israelite firstborn males," *Moses's* life is more likely the one under threat (Alexander, *Exodus* [Downers Grove, IL: IVP Academic, 2017], 104–8).

13. Christopher J. H. Wright, *Exodus* (Grand Rapids: Zondervan, 2021), 152.

14. Stuart, *Exodus*, 292–93.

15. Stuart, *Exodus*, 163n.

16. Gregory Boyd, *Crucifixion of the Warrior God: Violent Portraits of God in Light of the Cross*, 2 vols. (Minneapolis: Fortress, 2017), 2:1241–45.

17. *Raiders of the Lost Ark*, directed by Steven Spielberg (Paramount Pictures, 1981).

18. Boyd, *Crucifixion*, 2:1257.

Chapter 16 Divine Smitings (2)

1. Gregory Boyd, *Crucifixion of the Warrior God: Violent Portraits of God in Light of the Cross*, 2 vols. (Minneapolis: Fortress, 2017), 2:1223.

2. Boyd, *Crucifixion*, 2:791.

3. Boyd, *Crucifixion*, 2:1223.

4. Joel S. Burnett, "'Going Down' to Bethel: Elijah and Elisha in the Theological Geography of the Deuteronomistic History," *Journal of Biblical Literature* 129, no. 2 (2010): 295.

5. Burnett, "'Going Down' to Bethel," 295.

6. Burnett, "'Going Down' to Bethel," 296.

7. Burnett, "'Going Down' to Bethel," 296. On the symbolic significance of forty-two, see Joel S. Burnett's fascinating article, "Forty-Two Songs for Elohim: An Ancient Near Eastern Organizing Principle in the Shaping of the Elohistic Psalter," *Journal for the Study of the Old Testament* 31 (2006): 81–102.

8. See Keith Bodner, *The Theology of the Book of Kings* (Cambridge: Cambridge University Press, 2019), 133–35.

9. See Brian P. Irwin, "The Curious Incident of the Boys and the Bears: 2 Kings 2 and the Prophetic Authority of Elisha," *Tyndale Bulletin* 67, no. 1 (2016): 23–35.

10. Daniel I. Block, *The Book of Ezekiel: Chapters 1–24* (Grand Rapids: Eerdmans, 1997), 639–41.

11. Some scholars see these "not good" commands as less than ideal—though not evil—but relating to consecrated animals ("firstlings") used in offerings, not humans. Scott Walker Hahn and John Sietze Bergsma, "What Laws Were 'Not

Good'? A Canonical Approach to the Theological Problem of Ezekiel 20:25–26," *Journal of Biblical Literature* 123, no. 2 (Summer 2004): 201–18.

Contrary to some scholars claiming God was admitting here that "bad laws" included child sacrifice to Yahweh, Christopher Wright challenges this misinterpretation: it "ignore[s] the fact that Ezekiel is being horrendously controversial in this whole chapter, creating a rhetorical parody of Israel's history," using "sarcasm and irony." So we cannot "suddenly take a verse like this as a face-value doctrinal or historical affirmation" (Wright, *The Message of Ezekiel* [Downers Grove, IL: InterVarsity, 2001], 160). Indeed, it is "impossible to imagine, in light of the overwhelming emphasis on the goodness and importance of God's law [e.g., Deut. 4:6] and on the horrific act of child sacrifice, that Ezekiel could have seriously meant that Yahweh himself gave bad laws and commanded human sacrifice" (Wright, *Message of Ezekiel*, 160). John Goldingay makes a similar point, commenting on Micah 6:6–8, that the offerings move from the strange to the outrageous. Human sacrifice—to the Lord or foreign gods—was strictly forbidden (Goldingay, *Hosea–Micah* [Grand Rapids: Baker Academic, 2021], 474–75). Indeed, the context of dedicating or giving one's firstborn to the Lord (Exod. 22:29–30) is not infant sacrifice. Earlier in Exodus, Israel's dedicated firstborn are not killed; they are redeemed (Exod. 13:2, 13, 15). But a firstborn can be given to the Lord even without mention of redemption: Hannah *gave* her firstborn Samuel to serve the Lord all his days (1 Sam. 1:11)—as did Mary and Joseph with Jesus (Luke 2:23–25)—and the Levites were "wholly given" to the Lord (Num. 8:16). This is dedication, not sacrifice. Victor P. Hamilton, *Exodus: An Exegetical Commentary* (Grand Rapids: Baker Academic, 2011), 418–19.

For a critique of this "infant sacrifice to Yahweh" view articulated by Jon Levenson, see Frederick E. Greenspahn, review of *The Death and Resurrection of the Beloved Son: The Transformation of Child Sacrifice in Judaism and Christianity*, by Jon D. Levenson, *Association for Jewish Studies Review* 21, no. 1 (1996): 129–32.

12. See Paul Copan, *Is God a Moral Monster? Making Sense of the Old Testament God* (Grand Rapids: Baker Books, 2011), chap. 9.

13. John H. Walton and J. Harvey Walton, *The Lost World of the Torah: Laws as Covenant and Wisdom in Ancient Context* (Downers Grove, IL: IVP Academic, 2019), 138.

14. For example, Boyd, *Crucifixion*, 2:1260.

15. Stephen Williams, "The Transfiguration of Jesus Christ (Part 2): Approaching Sonship," *Themelios* 28, no. 2 (Spring 2003): 23.

16. Other relevant Pentateuchal texts are Numbers 14:18–19 and Deuteronomy 5:9–10 (which Boyd doesn't discuss). Other Old Testament texts referring back to Exodus 34 are abundant: Neh. 9:17; Pss. 86:15; 103:8; 145:8; Jer. 32:19; Joel 2:13; Jon. 4:2; Nah. 1:2–3.

17. Boyd, *Crucifixion*, 2:838n58.

18. Claude Mariottini, "Greg Boyd and the Character of God," Dr. Claude Mariottini (blog), April 22, 2019, https://claudemariottini.com/2019/04/22/greg-boyd-and-the-character-of-god-part-3-exodus-205-the-second-commandment/. See also Claude Mariottini, *Divine Violence and the Character of God* (Eugene, OR: Wipf & Stock, 2022), as well as Mariottini's blog, which contains an extensive treatment of Boyd's *Crucifixion* book: https://claudemariottini.com/.

19. Mariottini, "Greg Boyd and the Character of God."

20. Carol Meyers, *Exodus* (Cambridge: Cambridge University Press, 2005), 172.

21. Barnabas Lindars, "Ezekiel and Individual Responsibility," *Vetus Testamentum* 15, no. 4 (1965): 458.

22. Douglas Stuart, *Exodus* (Nashville: B&H, 2006), 454.

23. Stuart, *Exodus*, 454.

24. Thanks to Jerry Shepherd on this—and for a number of other insights and suggestions.

25. Boyd, *Crucifixion*, 2:883.

26. N. T. Wright, "The Word of the Cross," NTWrightPage.com, accessed December 14, 2021, https://ntwrightpage.com/2016/03/30/the-word-of-the-cross/. See discussion above, "God's Kindness, God's Severity, and Human Honesty" in chap. 1.

Chapter 17 "Bashing Babies against the Rock"?

1. Walter C. Kaiser, *Toward Old Testament Ethics* (Grand Rapids: Zondervan, 1983), 293.

2. See appendix A in John N. Day, "Imprecatory Psalms and Christian Ethics" (PhD diss., Dallas Theological Seminary, 2000).

3. Gregory Boyd, *Crucifixion of the Warrior God: Violent Portraits of God in Light of the Cross*, 2 vols. (Minneapolis: Fortress, 2017), 1:328.

4. James Crenshaw, *An Introduction to the Psalms* (Grand Rapids: Eerdmans, 2001), 67–68.

5. C. S. Lewis, *Reflections on the Psalms* (New York: Harcourt Brace Jovanovich, 1958), 20–33, 12.

6. Lewis, *Reflections on the Psalms*, 118.

7. Dietrich Bonhoeffer, "A Bonhoeffer Sermon," trans. Daniel Bloesch, ed. F. Burton Nelson, *Theology Today* 38 (1982): 467.

8. Lewis, *Reflections on the Psalms*, 30–31.

9. D. J. Wiseman, *The Vassal-Treaties of Esarhaddon* (London: British School of Archeology in Iraq, 1958), 60–78.

10. Day, "Imprecatory Psalms," chap. 3.

11. Erich Zenger, *A God of Vengeance? Understanding the Psalms of Divine Wrath*, trans. Linda M. Maloney (Louisville: Westminster John Knox, 1996), 50.

12. Zenger, *God of Vengeance?*, 91.

13. James Watt, review of *A God of Vengeance? Understanding the Psalms of Divine Wrath*, by Erich Zenger, *Hebrew Studies* 39 (1998): 238.

14. Knut Heim, "How and Why We Should Read the Poetry of the Old Testament for Public Life Today," *Comment*, November 14, 2011, https://www.cardus.ca/comment/article/how-and-why-we-should-read-the-poetry-of-the-old-testament-for-public-life-today/. Noted in Helen Paynter, *God of Violence Yesterday, God of Love Today?* (Abingdon, UK: BRF, 2019), 79.

15. Zenger, *God of Vengeance?*, 91.

16. Othmar Keel, *The Symbolism of the Biblical World: Ancient Near Eastern Iconography and the Book of Psalms*, trans. Timothy J. Hallett (Winona Lake, IN: Eisenbrauns, 1997), 9, quoted in John Goldingay, *Psalms*, vol. 3, *Psalms 90–150* (Grand Rapids: Baker Academic, 2008), 610.

17. Edwin M. Yamauchi, *Persia and the Bible* (Grand Rapids: Baker, 1990), 87.

18. John H. Sailhamer, *The NIV Compact Bible Commentary* (Grand Rapids: Zondervan, 1994), 346.

19. G. B. Caird, *The Language and Imagery of the Bible* (London: Duckworth, 1980), 110.

20. For examples of this view, see citations in Hans-Joachim Kraus, *Psalms 60–150*, trans. Hilton C. Oswald (Minneapolis: Augsburg, 1989), 341–42.

21. Eugene H. Peterson, *Answering God: The Psalms as Tools for Prayer* (New York: HarperCollins, 1989), 100.

22. Derek Kidner, *Psalms 73–150* (Downers Grove, IL: InterVarsity, 1975), 460–61.

23. Sailhamer, *NIV Compact Bible Commentary*, 340.

24. While the two purported "voices" in Psalm 109 make sense, in the end (given v. 20), this doesn't ultimately change the issue. See David G. Firth, "Prayer and Violence in the Psalms," in *Wrestling with the Violence of God: Soundings in the Old Testament*, ed. M. Daniel Carroll R. and J. Blair Wilgus, Bulletin for Biblical Research Supplement 10 (Winona Lake, IN: Eisenbrauns, 2015), 83.

25. Craig C. Broyles, *Psalms* (Peabody, MA: Hendrickson, 1999), 480.

26. Kraus, *Psalms 60–150*, 342.

27. Edmund Hill, *Prayer, Praise and Politics* (London: Sheed and Ward, 1973), 99.

28. Broyles, *Psalms*, 480.

29. The principles listed here are from Day, "Imprecatory Psalms," 3.

Chapter 18 "Let His Homestead Be Made Desolate"

1. Eugene H. Peterson uses this term in *Answering God: The Psalms as Tools for Prayer* (New York: HarperCollins, 1989).

2. See "The Imprecatory Psalms and Their Critics" in chap. 17.

3. See John N. Day, "The Imprecatory Psalms and Christian Ethics," *Bibliotheca Sacra* 159 (April–June 2002): 166–86.

4. Gregory Boyd, *Crucifixion of the Warrior God: Violent Portraits of God in Light of the Cross*, 2 vols. (Minneapolis: Fortress, 2017), 1:589.

5. Boyd, *Crucifixion*, 1:218.

6. Boyd, *Crucifixion*, 1:590, 217.

7. Boyd, *Crucifixion*, 1:328.

8. John Goldingay, *Reading Jesus's Bible* (Grand Rapids: Eerdmans, 2017), 87.

9. C. S. Lewis, *Reflections on the Psalms* (New York: Harcourt Brace Jovanovich, 1958), 12. See "The Imprecatory Psalms and Their Critics" in chap. 17.

10. Such stories are found at websites like the Barnabas Fund (https://barnabasfund.org/us), Voice of the Martyrs (www.vomcanada.org), and Help the Persecuted (www.htp.org).

11. See the website "Abolish!" for documentation of these international horrors: https://www.iabolish.org/.

12. Miriam Adeney, *Kingdom without Borders: The Untold Story of Global Christianity* (Downers Grove, IL: InterVarsity, 2015), 258. This rendering of Psalm 27:1–2 is taken from the story about Elizabeth documented by Adeney.

13. Goldingay, *Reading Jesus's Bible*, 87.

14. John Goldingay, *Psalms*, vol. 3, *Psalms 90–150* (Grand Rapids: Baker Academic, 2008), 289.

15. See a discussion on this at the Witchcraft Project at Trinity Evangelical Divinity School's Henry Center: https://henrycenter.tiu.edu/witchcraft-accusations/nairobi-colloquium/.

16. John Goldingay, *Psalms*, 3:611.

17. David G. Firth, "Prayer and Violence in the Psalms," in *Wrestling with the Violence of God: Soundings in the Old Testament*, ed. M. Daniel Carroll R. and J. Blair Wilgus, Bulletin for Biblical Research Supplement 10 (Winona Lake, IN: Eisenbrauns, 2015), 81.

18. Goldingay, *Reading Jesus's Bible*, 189.

19. Interview with N. T. Wright, "N. T. Wright Wants to Save the Best Worship Songs," *Christianity Today*, August 29, 2013, http://www.christianitytoday.com/ct/2013/september/nt-wright-saving-psalms.html?start=2.

20. Gordon J. Wenham, *Psalms as Torah: Reading Biblical Song Ethically* (Grand Rapids: Baker Academic, 2012), 177.

21. Erich Zenger, *A God of Vengeance? Understanding the Psalms of Divine Wrath*, trans. Linda M. Maloney (Louisville: Westminster John Knox, 1996), 12.

22. This 2021 figure is from Open Doors USA: https://www.opendoorsusa.org/christian-persecution/.

23. In this section, I follow both Zenger (*God of Vengeance?*, 25, 63, 73–79), and Gordon Wenham, *The Psalms Reclaimed: Praying and Praising with the Psalms* (Wheaton, IL: Crossway, 2013), 49.

24. John N. Day, "The Imprecatory Psalms and Christian Ethics" (PhD diss., Dallas Theological Seminary, 2000), 3; for a summary, see Day, "The Imprecatory Psalms and Christian Ethics," *Bibliotheca Sacra* 159 (April–June 2002): 166–86.

Chapter 19 Loving Jacob, Hating Esau?

1. See Douglas Stuart, "Malachi," in *The Minor Prophets*, vol. 3, ed. Thomas E. McComiskey (Grand Rapids: Baker, 1998), 1282–84.

2. Christopher J. H. Wright, *The God I Don't Understand: Reflections on Tough Questions of Faith* (Grand Rapids: Zondervan, 2008), 102.

3. Victor P. Hamilton, *Exodus: An Exegetical Commentary* (Grand Rapids: Baker Academic, 2011), 57.

4. Jon D. Levinson, "The Shema and the Commandment to Love God in Its Ancient Contexts," TheTorah.com, accessed December 15, 2021, https://www.thetorah.com/article/the-shema-and-the-commandment-to-love-god-in-its-ancient-contexts.

5. Levinson, "The Shema and the Commandment to Love."

6. John Goldingay, *Psalms*, vol. 1, *Psalms 1–41* (Grand Rapids: Baker Academic, 2006), 128–29, 192.

7. John Goldingay, *Psalms*, vol. 3, *Psalms 90–150* (Grand Rapids: Baker Academic, 2008), 638.

8. Craig C. Broyles, *Psalms* (Peabody, MA: Hendrickson, 1999), 486.

9. Goldingay, *Psalms*, 3:289.

10. John Stott, *Favorite Psalms* (Chicago: Moody, 1988), 121.

11. Stott, *Favorite Psalms*, 121.

12. David G. Firth, "Prayer and Violence in the Psalms," in *Wrestling with the Violence of God: Soundings in the Old Testament*, ed. M. Daniel Carroll R. and J. Blair Wilgus, Bulletin for Biblical Research Supplement 10 (Winona Lake, IN: Eisenbrauns, 2015), 811.

Chapter 20 Is the Old Testament Really Misogynistic and Patriarchal?

1. Andy Stanley, *Irresistible: Reclaiming the New That Jesus Unleashed for the World* (Grand Rapids: Zondervan, 2018), 290, 214, 215.

2. Rosemary R. Ruether, "Feminist Interpretation: A Method of Correlation," in *Feminist Interpretations of the Bible*, ed. Letty M. Russell (Philadelphia: Westminster, 1985), 119.

3. See Paul Copan, *Is God a Moral Monster? Making Sense of the Old Testament God* (Grand Rapids: Baker Books, 2011), chap. 10.

4. Matthew J. Lynch, *Portraying Violence in the Hebrew Bible: A Literary and Cultural Study* (Cambridge: Cambridge University Press, 2020), 126.

5. Carol Meyers "Was Ancient Israel a Patriarchal Society?," *Journal of Biblical Literature* 133, no. 1 (Spring 2014): 8–27. The first part of this chapter draws on this article.

6. Meyers, "Was Ancient Israel a Patriarchal Society?," 27.

7. Meyers, "Was Ancient Israel a Patriarchal Society?," 27.

8. See Carol Meyers, *Rediscovering Eve: Ancient Israelite Women in Context* (New York: Oxford University Press, 2012).

9. Meyers, *Rediscovering Eve*, 27.

10. Carol Meyers, "Hierarchy or Heterarchy? Archaeology and the Theorizing of Israelite Society," in *Confronting the Past: Archaeological and*

Historical Essays on Ancient Israel in Honor of
William G. Dever, ed. Seymour Gitin, J. Edward
Wright, and J. P. Dessel (Winona Lake, IN: Eisen-
brauns, 2006), 245.

11. Meyers, "Was Ancient Israel a Patriarchal
Society?," 27.

12. Lynch, Portraying Violence, 126.

13. John Goldingay, Old Testament Theology,
vol. 2, Israel's Faith (Downers Grove, IL: IVP Academic, 2006), 546, 547.

14. Meyers, "Was Ancient Israel a Patriarchal
Society?," 27.

15. Paul Copan, Is God a Moral Monster?
Making Sense of the Old Testament God (Grand
Rapids: Baker Books, 2011), chap. 7.

16. See Paul Copan and Wes Jamison, eds.,
What Would Jesus Really Eat? A Biblical Defense
of Eating Meat (Toronto: Castle Quay, 2019).
This book discusses kosher foods, the sacrifi-
cial system, the legitimacy of eating meat, and
problems with an allegedly biblically mandated
veganism.

17. S. Tamar Kamionkowski, Leviticus (Col-
legeville, MN: Liturgical Press, 2018), 96.

18. Sarah Shectman makes this point in her review of Kamionkowski's Leviticus commentary
in the Review of Biblical Literature (May 2020),
available through subscription: https://www
.sblcentral.org/API/Reviews/12768_14241.pdf.

19. For a brief overview, see "Jewish Food:
Eating in Historical Jerusalem" Jewish Virtual
Library, accessed February 15, 2022, https://www
.jewishvirtuallibrary.org/eating-in-historical
-jerusalem.

20. Meyers, "Was Ancient Israel a Patriarchal
Society?," 21–22.

21. Meyers, "Was Ancient Israel a Patriarchal
Society?," 22.

22. Meyers, "Was Ancient Israel a Patriarchal
Society?," 27.

23. The Shunammite woman persuaded her
husband to have an "upper chamber" built for
Elisha so that he could stay with them when
passing through (2 Kings 4:9–11). And when
the woman's son died, she told her husband,
"Please send me one of the servants and one of
the donkeys, that I may run to the man of God
and return" (v. 22). She found Elisha and refused
to return home without him. He agreed—and
brought her son back from the dead. A few chapters later, Elisha warned this same woman that a
massive seven-year famine was coming. He urged
her to sojourn in another land. So she mobilized
her entire household to leave for Philistia. Then

when she returned, her property had been taken
over by squatters. To resolve the matter, she appealed to the king in order to get back her property, which he granted her (8:1–6).

24. These lists are found in Meyers, "Was
Ancient Israel a Patriarchal Society?"

25. Meyers, "Hierarchy," 248.

26. Carol Meyers, Exodus (Cambridge: Cambridge University Press, 2005), 118.

27. Ada Taggar-Cohen, "Why Are There No
Israelite Priestesses?," TheTorah.com, accessed
January 20, 2022, https://www.thetorah.com
/article/why-are-there-no-israelite-priestesses.

Chapter 21 Espousing Multiple Wives?

1. Jennifer Wright Knust, Unprotected Texts:
The Bible's Surprising Contradictions about Sex
and Desire (New York: HarperOne, 2012).

2. Jennifer Wright Knust, interview with
Terri Gross, Fresh Air, National Public Radio,
March 10, 2011, https://www.npr.org/2011/03/10
/133245874/unprotected-texts-the-bible-on-sex
-and-marriage.

3. See Robertson McQuilkin and Paul Copan,
An Introduction to Biblical Ethics: Walking in the
Way of Wisdom, 3rd ed. (Downers Grove, IL: IVP
Academic, 2014), part 7.

4. L. Daniel Hawk, The Violence of the Biblical God: Canonical Narrative and Christian
Faith (Grand Rapids: Eerdmans, 2019), 204.

5. Thanks to Greg Koukl for this formula-
tion at a gathering of Christian apologists in San
Antonio, Texas, in November 2016.

6. John H. Walton and J. Harvey Walton, The
Lost World of the Torah: Laws as Covenant and
Wisdom in Ancient Context (Downers Grove, IL:
IVP Academic, 2019), 36.

7. See Paul Copan, Is God a Moral Monster?
Making Sense of the Old Testament God (Grand
Rapids: Baker Books, 2011), chaps. 10–11.

8. See Copan, Is God a Moral Monster?,
chap. 11.

9. For a summary of this view, see Richard
Davidson, "Condemnation and Grace: Polygamy
and Concubinage," Christian Research Journal
38, no. 5 (2015): 34–37, https://www.equip.org
/PDF/JAF4385.pdf. In personal correspondence
(July 3, 2021), Davidson reported that Roy Gane
(author of the 2017 book Old Testament Law
for Christians) "has recently informed me that
since the publication of his book, he has become
convinced that my position [i.e., that the Mosaic
law prohibits polygamy] is the correct one!"

10. For example, Tremper Longman III, *Confronting Old Testament Controversies: Pressing Questions about Evolution, Sexuality, History, and Violence* (Grand Rapids: Baker Books, 2019), 229–31; also, David Lamb, *Prostitutes and Polygamists: A Look at Love, Old Testament Style* (Grand Rapids: Zondervan, 2015).

11. David Lamb, *Prostitutes and Polygamists*, 67.

12. E.g., Richard Davidson, *Flame of Yahweh* (Peabody, MA: Hendrickson, 2007), 191–97. Gordon P. Hugenberger, *Marriage as a Covenant: Biblical Law and Ethics as Developed from Malachi* (Grand Rapids: Baker, 1998), 118.

13. See Angelo Tosato's thorough linguistic analysis of the Leviticus 18 text: "The Law of Leviticus 18:18: A Reexamination," *Catholic Biblical Quarterly* 46 (1984): 199–214.

14. In Leviticus 18:17, one should not uncover the nakedness of "a woman *and* her daughter" (not "in addition to her daughter"). The phrase "a woman in addition to her sister" isn't referring specifically to a *biological* sister. Otherwise, the text could more easily have said "a woman *and* her sister." If this phrase ever refers to relatives, it's *by coincidence*, but in itself, this phrase doesn't refer to relatives. And the Old Testament narratives tell us plenty about the problems of a "rival wife," especially 1 Samuel 1:2, which harks back to the *rival* wife in Leviticus 18:18. See Jay Sklar, *Leviticus* (Downers Grove, IL: IVP Academic, 2014), 234–36; he considers the prohibition against polygamy to be a more plausible—though not absolutely decisive—reading of the text.

15. "He shall not take another wife in addition to [the first], for she alone shall be with him all the time of her life" (11QT 57:17–18).

16. John Goldingay, *Old Testament Theology*, 2:547.

17. Gregory Boyd, *Crucifixion of the Warrior God: Violent Portraits of God in Light of the Cross*, 2 vols. (Minneapolis: Fortress, 2017), 2:718–19.

18. On this, see Davidson, "Condemnation and Grace." Davidson notes that David himself returned to monogamy (with Bathsheba) toward the end of his life (2 Sam. 20:3; 1 Kings 1:1–4).

19. Mary J. Evans, *1 and 2 Samuel* (Peabody, MA: Hendrickson, 2000), 189 (boldfacing removed).

20. Lamb, *Prostitutes and Polygamists*, 85.

21. Lamb, *Prostitutes and Polygamists*, 85.

Chapter 22 Other Troubling Texts about Women

1. In this section on the "nameless concubine," I have benefited from the insights of Bekah Legg, "Judges 19: Does the Bible Victim-Blame the Woman with No Name?" The paper was presented at "In the Cross-Hairs"—a student symposium sponsored by the Bristol Baptist College's Center for the Study of Bible and Violence (May 2020). It is published in *In the Cross-Hairs: Bible and Violence in Focus*, ed. Michael Spalione and Helen Paynter (Sheffield: Sheffield Phoenix Press, 2022), 109–22.

2. For example, the late atheist philosopher Michael Martin, "Atheism, Christian Theism, and Rape," *Internet Infidels*, accessed January 25, 2022, http://www.infidels.org/library/modern/michael_martin/rape.html.

3. Greg Boyd, "A History of Violence," interview by Bonnie Kristian, *Relevant*, August 1, 2017, https://relevantmagazine.com/god/a-history-of-violence/.

4. Jennifer Wright Knust, *Unprotected Texts: The Bible's Surprising Contradictions about Sex and Desire* (New York: HarperOne, 2012).

5. The major points in this section on war rape are taken from William J. Webb and Gordon K. Oeste, "War Rape, Part Two: The Redemptive Side," in *Bloody, Brutal, and Barbaric? Wrestling with Troubling War Texts* (Downers Grove, IL: IVP Academic, 2019), 99–127.

6. See the summary of these ideas in Webb and Oeste, *Bloody, Brutal, and Barbaric?*, 363–66.

7. For documentation of such depictions, see Webb and Oeste, *Bloody, Brutal, and Barbaric?*, 109–12.

8. Benjamin R. Foster, *Before the Muses: An Anthology of Akkadian Literature*, 3rd ed. (Bethesda, MD: CDL Press, 2005), 678, quoted by Webb and Oeste, *Bloody, Brutal, and Barbaric?*, 118.

Chapter 23 "Servants" in Israel

1. Aristotle, *Politics* 1.3–6.

2. Aristotle, *Politics* 1.2.8–14.

3. Aristotle, *Nicomachean Ethics* 8.11.

4. Joshua Berman, *Created Equal: How the Bible Broke with Ancient Political Thought* (Oxford: Oxford University Press, 2008), 160; Luc Ferry, *A Brief History of Thought: A Philosophical Guide to Living* (New York: Harper Perennial, 2011), 72–73.

5. Benjamin J. Wright III, "*'Ebed/Doulos* Terms and Social Status in the Meeting of Hebrew Biblical and Hellenistic Roman Culture," *Semeia* 83/84 (1998): 83, 84n.

6. Berman, *Created Equal*, 4 (emphasis in original).

7. Berman, *Created Equal*, 5.

8. Berman, *Created Equal*, 168.

9. See Paul Copan, *Is God a Moral Monster? Making Sense of the Old Testament God* (Grand Rapids: Baker Books, 2011), chaps. 12–14.

10. A particularly helpful essay on Old Testament servitude is Peter J. Williams, "'Slaves' in Biblical Narrative and in Translation," in *On Stone and Scroll: Essays in Honour of Graham Ivor Davies*, ed. James K. Aitken, Katharine J. Dell, and Brian A. Mastin (Berlin: de Gruyter, 2011), 441–52.

11. "Slave Bible from the 1800s Omitted Key Passages That Could Incite Rebellion," NPR.org, December 9, 2018, https://www.npr.org/2018/12/09/674995075/slave-bible-from-the-1800s-omitted-key-passages-that-could-incite-rebellion.

12. Hector Avalos, *Slavery, Abolitionism, and the Ethics of Biblical Scholarship* (Sheffield: University of Sheffield Press, 2011).

13. Assyriologist Joshua Bowen raised this in a conversation with me back in 2019.

14. For careful documentation on this matter, see Andrew Fede, "Legitimized Violent Slave Abuse in the American South, 1619–1865: A Case Study of Law and Social Change in Six Southern States," *The American Journal of Legal History* 29, no. 2 (April 1985): 93–150.

15. Copan, *Is God a Moral Monster?*, chap. 12.

16. Christopher J. H. Wright, *Walking in the Ways of the Lord* (Downers Grove, IL: InterVarsity, 1995), 124.

17. "Immigrant" is an appropriate translation of the Hebrew word *ger* ("sojourner" or "alien") according to Donald E. Gowan, "Wealth and Poverty in the Old Testament: The Case of the Widow, the Orphan, and the Sojourner," *Interpretation* 41 (Oct. 1987): 345.

18. David Baker, *Tight Fists or Open Hands? Wealth and Poverty in Old Testament Law* (Grand Rapids: Eerdmans, 2009), 129.

19. Copan, *Is God a Moral Monster?*, chap. 13.

20. Harry A. Hoffner Jr., "Slavery and Slave Laws in Ancient Hatti and Israel," in *Israel: Ancient Kingdom or Late Invention?*, ed. Daniel I. Block (Nashville: B&H Academic, 2008), 150–51.

21. Babylonian: Code of Hammurabi §14; Hittite: §§19–21.

22. Baker, *Tight Fists*, 117.

23. Quotation is from "The Hammurabi Code," https://history.hanover.edu/courses/excerpts/211ham.html, which utilizes the electronic text from Virginia Tech's Eris database.

24. Baker, *Tight Fists*, 132.

25. Berman, *Created Equal*, 99.

26. Carol Meyers, *Exodus* (Cambridge: Cambridge University Press, 2005), 35.

27. Williams, "'Slaves' in Biblical Narrative and in Translation," 444.

28. Baker, *Tight Fists*, 188.

29. *Concise Oxford English Dictionary*, 12th ed. (Oxford: Oxford University Press, 2011), s.v. "slave."

30. On this, see Peter Williams's helpful essay "'Slaves' in Biblical Narrative and in Translation."

31. Williams, "'Slaves' in Biblical Narrative and in Translation," 444.

32. Wright, "*'Ebed/Doulos*," 85n.

33. Helmut Ringgrenn, "*'abad*," *Theological Dictionary of the Old Testament*, vol. 10, ed. G. Johannes Botterweck (Grand Rapids: Eerdmans, 2000), 383–85, 390.

34. Williams, "'Slaves' in Biblical Narrative and in Translation," 451.

35. Williams, "'Slaves' in Biblical Narrative and in Translation," 451.

36. Williams, "'Slaves' in Biblical Narrative and in Translation," 452.

37. Williams, "'Slaves' in Biblical Narrative and in Translation," 452.

38. Ingrid Riesener, *Der Stamm ['Abad] im Alten Testament: Eine Wortuntersuchung unter Berücksichtigung neuerer sprachwissenschaftlicher Methoden*, Beihefte zur Zeitschrift für die alttestamentliche Wissenschaft 149 (Berlin: de Gruyter, 1979), 268–69. She writes that the "basic meaning" ("*Grundbedeutung*") of *ebed* is "a dynamic concept of relations" ("ein *dynamischer Relationsbegriff*") that involves being "dependent" ("*abhängig*") (emphasis in original).

39. David L. Baker, "The Humanisation of Slavery in Old Testament Law," in *The Humanisation of Slavery in the Old Testament*, ed. Thomas Schirrmacher (Bonn: Verlag für Kultur und Wissenschaft, 2015), 14.

40. Baker, "Humanisation," 14.

41. Baker, "Humanisation," 14.

Chapter 24 The "Acquisition" of "Foreign Slaves" (1)

1. See Paul Copan, *Is God a Moral Monster? Making Sense of the Old Testament God* (Grand Rapids: Baker Books, 2011), chap. 13.

2. David Baker, *Tight Fists or Open Hands? Wealth and Poverty in Old Testament Law* (Grand Rapids: Eerdmans, 2009), 162.

3. Quoted in Ta-Nehisi Coates, "'I Have Since Heard of His Death,'" *The Atlantic*, November 18, 2011, https://www.theatlantic.com/personal /archive/2011/11/i-have-since-heard-of-his-death /248728/. See also Douglass's September 1848 letter to his former master: "Read This Moving Letter Frederick Douglass Wrote to His Slave Master 10 Years after Escaping from Him," *Watch the Yard*, accessed January 28, 2022, https://www .watchtheyard.com/history/fredrick-douglas -letter-to-slave-master-auld/.

4. G. H. Haas, "Slave, Slavery," *Dictionary of the Old Testament: Pentateuch* (Downers Grove, IL: InterVarsity, 2003), 781.

5. Haas, "Slave, Slavery," 782.

6. David L. Baker, "The Humanisation of Slavery in Old Testament Law," in *The Humanisation of Slavery in the Old Testament*, ed. Thomas Schirrmacher (Bonn: Verlag für Kultur und Wissenschaft, 2015), 14n.

7. Baker, "Humanisation," 14n.

8. Baker, *Tight Fists*, 177.

9. Carol Meyers, *Exodus* (Cambridge: Cambridge University Press, 2005), 308.

10. As noted above, "immigrant" is an appropriate translation of the Hebrew word *ger* ("sojourner" or "alien") according to Donald E. Gowan, "Wealth and Poverty in the Old Testament: The Case of the Widow, the Orphan, and the Sojourner," *Interpretation* 41 (October 1987): 345.

11. Again, this rendering is from Harry A. Hoffner Jr., "Slavery and Slave Laws in Ancient Hatti and Israel," in *Israel: Ancient Kingdom or Late Invention?*, ed. Daniel I. Block (Nashville: B&H Academic, 2008), 150–51.

12. John Goldingay, *Old Testament Theology*, vol. 3, *Israel's Life* (Downers Grove, IL: IVP Academic, 2009), 465.

13. Goldingay, *Old Testament Theology*, 3:465.

14. James Hoffmeier, "Slavery and the Bible," panel discussion at Lanier Theological Library, Houston, Texas, October 30, 2015, https://vimeo .com/144318832, 9:15 to 22:00. In personal correspondence with Hoffmeier (Feb. 9, 2022), he noted the work of anthropologist and Egyptologist Stuart Tyson Smith on this assimilation question. See James K. Hoffmeier, "Egyptian Religious Influences on the Early Hebrews," in *Did I Not Bring Israel Out of Egypt? Biblical,* *Archaeological, and Egyptological Perspectives on the Exodus Narratives*, ed. James K. Hoffmeier, Alan R. Millard, and Gary A. Rendsberg (Winona Lake, IN: Eisenbrauns, 2016), 3–35. In this work, Hoffmeier engages with Smith's scholarship, especially on pages 7–17. I am grateful for Hoffmeier's resourcefulness in providing material on this topic.

15. Goldingay, *Old Testament Theology*, 3:465.

16. Goldingay, *Old Testament Theology*, 3:465–66.

17. Gowan, "Wealth and Poverty," 345.

18. Gowan, "Wealth and Poverty," 345.

19. Goldingay, *Old Testament Theology*, 3:467. For another perspective on the topic of servitude, see Assyriologist Joshua Bowen's *Did the Old Testament Endorse Slavery?* (n.p.: Digital Hammurabi Press, 2021). See also the debate between Jewish-Christian scholar Michael Brown and Bowen, "Was Slavery in the OT Morally Permissible?," https://youtu.be/32y7rbiiR0s.

Chapter 25 The "Acquisition" of "Foreign Slaves" (2)

1. Jay Sklar, *Leviticus* (Downers Grove, IL: IVP Academic, 2014), 306.

2. From Kenneth Bergland, *Reading as a Disclosure of the Thoughts of the Heart: Proto-Halakhic Reuse and Appropriation Between Torah and the Prophets*, Beihefte zur Zeitschrift für altorientalische und biblische Rechtsgeschichte 23 (Wiesbaden: Harrassowitz Verlag, 2019), 257. On this point, see also Jacob Milgrom, *Leviticus 23–27*, Anchor Yale Biblical Commentary (New Haven: Yale University Press, 2001), 2206–8. Thanks to Richard Davidson for directing me to Bergland's work.

3. For example, Gordon McConville holds that this law pertains to a foreign runaway slave (McConville, *Deuteronomy* [Downers Grove, IL: IVP Academic, 2002], 351). But Christopher Wright holds that this can also apply to Israelite servants who are treated harshly (Christopher J. H. Wright, *Deuteronomy* [Peabody, MA: Hendrickson, 1996], 249–50).

4. Wright, *Deuteronomy*, 250.

5. D. J. A. Clines, "Ethics as Deconstruction, and, the Ethics of Deconstruction," in *The Bible in Ethics: The Second Sheffield Colloquium*, ed. J. W. Rogerson, Margaret Davies, and M. Daniel Carroll R., Journal for the Study of the Old Testament Supplement Series 207 (Sheffield: Sheffield Academic Press, 1995), 78.

6. Clines, "Ethics as Deconstruction," 79.

7. Clines, "Ethics as Deconstruction," 81.

8. Clines, "Ethics as Deconstruction," 81.

9. David Baker, *Tight Fists or Open Hands? Wealth and Poverty in Old Testament Law* (Grand Rapids: Eerdmans, 2009), 312.

10. Donald E. Gowan, "Wealth and Poverty in the Old Testament: The Case of the Widow, the Orphan, and the Sojourner," *Interpretation* 41 (Oct. 1987): 345.

11. Cited in Jonathan Sacks, *Covenant and Conversation: Leviticus* (Jerusalem: Koren, 2015), 370.

12. Baker, *Tight Fists*, 312.

13. Milgrom, *Leviticus 23–27*, 2207.

14. Baker, *Tight Fists*, 188.

15. Roy E. Gane, *Old Testament Law for Christians: Original Context and Enduring Application* (Grand Rapids: Baker Academic, 2017), 213.

16. N. T. Wright and Michael Bird, *The New Testament in Its World: An Introduction to the History, Literature, and Theology of the First Christians* (Grand Rapids: Zondervan Academic, 2019), 467.

17. Wright and Bird, *New Testament*, 148–49.

18. Wright and Bird, *New Testament*, 467.

19. See Scot McKnight, *The Letter to Philemon* (Grand Rapids: Eerdmans, 2017).

20. For an accessible summary on Paul's use of household codes, see Margaret Mowczko, "The Household Codes Are about Power, not Gender," *Marg Mowczko* (blog), February 27, 2019, https://margmowczko.com/household-codes-power-not-gender/. See also Philip B. Payne and Vince Huffaker, *Why Can't Women Do That? Breaking Down the Reasons Churches Put Men in Charge* (n.p.: Vinati Press, 2021), 121–37.

21. Pliny the Younger, *Letters* 10.96–97. Quoted in Rebecca Denova, "Pliny the Younger on Christianity," *World History Encyclopedia*, October 6, 2021, https://www.worldhistory.org/article/1846/pliny-the-younger-on-christianity/.

22. For an elaboration on this, see Craig R. Koester, "Roman Slave Trade and the Critique of Babylon in Revelation," *Catholic Biblical Quarterly* 70, no. 4 (Oct. 2008): 766–86.

Chapter 26 Jesus Loves Canaanites—and Israelites Too

1. Roger E. Olson, "What about Those Old Testament 'Texts of Terror?' (A Review of an Almost New Book by Philip Jenkins)," *Roger E. Olson* (blog), October 29, 2012, https://www.patheos.com/blogs/rogereolson/201q12/10/what-about-those-old-testament-texts-of-terror-a-review-of-an-almost-new-book-by-philip-jenkins/.

2. Peter Enns, "Is Peter Enns a Marcionite?," *Peter Enns: Rethinking Biblical Christianity* (blog), January 17, 2014, https://www.patheos.com/blogs/peterenns/2014/01/is-pete-enns-a-marcionite/. See also Peter Enns, *The Bible Tells Me So* (New York: HarperOne, 2015).

3. Enns, *Bible Tells Me So*, 61.

4. Randal Rauser, *Jesus Loves Canaanites: Biblical Genocide in the Light of Moral Intuition* (Canada: 2 Cup Press, 2021), 312.

5. For an overview of some of these themes on Old Testament warfare discussed in this book, see Paul Copan, "Some Bright Spots Concerning Old Testament Violence," in *In the Cross-Hairs: Bible and Violence in Focus*, ed. Michael Spalione and Helen Paynter (Sheffield: Sheffield Phoenix, 2022), 13–36.

6. John Calvin, *Commentaries on the Book of Joshua*, trans. Henry Beveridge (Edinburgh: Calvin Translation Society, 1854), 97.

7. These positions are laid out by Charlie Trimm, *The Destruction of the Canaanites: God, Genocide, and Biblical Interpretation* (Grand Rapids: Eerdmans, 2022), 50.

8. As argued in Philip Jenkins, *Laying Down the Sword: Why We Can't Ignore the Bible's Violent Verses* (New York: HarperOne, 2012).

9. Richard Dawkins, *The God Delusion* (Boston: Houghton Mifflin, 2006), 51.

10. In addition to Paul Copan and Matthew Flannagan, *Did God Really Command Genocide? Coming to Terms with the Justice of God* (Grand Rapids: Baker Books, 2014), see Charlie Trimm, who observes about the ancient Near Eastern nations in general: "Upon closer examination it is difficult to find examples of genocide in the ancient Near East due to very different cultural ideas. While mass killing certainly happened, the core element of killing people because of their group identity is missing, especially related to ethnic or religious identities." Trimm, "Causes: Genocide in the Ancient Near East," in *The Cultural History of Genocide*, vol. 1, *The Ancient World*, ed. Tristan Taylor (London: Bloomsbury, 2021), 49.

11. Kenton Sparks, *God's Word in Human Words: An Evangelical Appropriation of Critical Biblical Scholarship* (Grand Rapids: Baker Academic, 2008), 297, 298.

12. John Goldingay, *Old Testament Ethics: A Guided Tour* (Downers Grove, IL: IVP Academic, 2019), 271.

13. See the first section of chap. 15 in Paul Copan, *Is God a Moral Monster? Making Sense of the Old Testament God* (Grand Rapids: Baker Books, 2011).

14. See Marc Haber et al., "Continuity and Admixture in the Last Five Millennia of Levantine History from Ancient Canaanite and Present-Day Lebanese Genome Sequences," *American Journal of Human Genetics* 101, no. 2 (August 3, 2017), https://www.cell.com/ajhg/fulltext/S0002-9297 (17)30276-8.

15. David G. Firth, *Joshua* (Bellingham, WA: Lexham, 2021), 168.

16. Thanks to Matt Bohlman for some of his insights.

17. See L. Daniel Hawk, *Every Promise Fulfilled: Contesting Plots in Joshua* (Louisville: Westminster John Knox, 1991), 73.

18. Lissa Wray Beal, *Joshua* (Grand Rapids: Zondervan, 2019), 46.

19. John H. Walton and J. Harvey Walton, *The Lost World of the Israelite Conquest: Covenant, Retribution, and the Fate of the Canaanites* (Downers Grove, IL: IVP Academic, 2017), 62–63.

20. Walton and Walton, *Lost World of the Israelite Conquest*, 166. Randal Rauser adopts this view in *Jesus Loves Canaanites*, 174.

21. For a fuller discussion, see Tremper Longman III, *Confronting Old Testament Controversies: Pressing Questions about Evolution, Sexuality, History, and Violence* (Grand Rapids: Baker Books, 2019), 172–76.

22. Wray Beal, *Joshua*, 46.

23. John Goldingay, *Genesis* (Grand Rapids: Baker Academic, 2020), 252.

24. John Goldingay, "Justice and Salvation for Israel in Canaan," in *Reading the Hebrew Bible for a New Millennium*, vol. 1, *Theological and Hermeneutical Studies*, ed. Wonil Kim, Deborah Ellens, Michael Floyd, and Marvin A. Sweeney (Harrisburg, PA: Trinity Press International, 2000), 184.

25. See Randal Rauser, *Jesus Loves Canaanites*.

26. Goldingay, "Justice and Salvation," 184.

27. L. Daniel Hawk, *The Violence of the Biblical God: Canonical Narrative and Christian Faith* (Grand Rapids: Eerdmans, 2019), xiv.

28. J. Gordon McConville and Stephen N. Williams, *Joshua* (Grand Rapids: Eerdmans, 2010), 112. Likewise, see M. Daniel Carroll R.,

"Reflections of the Violence of God in Amos," in *Wrestling with the Violence of God: Soundings in the Old Testament*, Bulletin for Biblical Research Supplement 10, ed. M. Daniel Carroll R. and J. Blair Wilgus (Winona Lake, IN: Eisenbrauns, 2015), 120–21.

29. Hawk, *Violence*, 165.

30. John Goldingay, *Numbers and Deuteronomy for Everyone* (Louisville: Westminster John Knox, 2010), 85.

31. Eric Seibert, *The Violence of Scripture: Overcoming the Old Testament's Troubling Legacy* (Minneapolis: Fortress, 2012), 101.

32. Goldingay, "Justice and Salvation," 186.

33. McConville and Williams, *Joshua*, 114.

34. Wray Beal, *Joshua*, 254.

35. John Goldingay, *Joshua, Judges, and Ruth for Everyone* (Louisville: Westminster John Knox, 2011), 3.

Chapter 27 "We Left No Survivors"

1. Paul Copan, *Is God a Moral Monster? Making Sense of the Old Testament God* (Grand Rapids: Baker Books, 2011), chap. 16; Paul Copan and Matthew Flannagan, *Did God Really Command Genocide? Coming to Terms with the Justice of God* (Grand Rapids: Baker Books, 2014), chaps. 7–9; see also K. Lawson Younger, *Ancient Conquest Accounts: A Study in Ancient Near Eastern and Biblical History Writing*, Journal for the Study of the Old Testament Supplement Series 98 (Sheffield: Sheffield Academic, 2009), 253.

2. Lissa Wray Beal, *Joshua* (Grand Rapids: Zondervan, 2019), 225.

3. David G. Firth, *Joshua* (Bellingham, WA: Lexham, 2021), 207–8.

4. Kenneth A. Kitchen, *On the Historical Reliability of the Old Testament* (Grand Rapids: Eerdmans, 2006), 162 (emphasis in original).

5. See Richard Hess's argument in appendix 2 of Douglas Groothuis, *Christian Apologetics*, 2nd ed. (Downers Grove, IL: IVP Academic, 2021).

6. Wray Beal, *Joshua*, 38–39.

7. Wray Beal, *Joshua*, 38.

8. James K. Hoffmeier, *The Archaeology of the Bible* (Oxford: Lion, 2008), 67.

9. Hoffmeier, *The Archaeology of the Bible*, 68.

10. John H. Walton and J. Harvey Walton, *The Lost World of the Israelite Conquest: Covenant, Retribution, and the Fate of the Canaanites* (Downers Grove, IL: IVP Academic, 2017), 178, 193.

11. David G. Firth, *The Message of Joshua* (Downers Grove, IL: IVP Academic, 2015), 21.

12. Firth, *Message of Joshua*, 27.

13. David G. Firth, *Including the Stranger: Foreigners in the Former Prophets* (Downers Grove, IL: IVP Academic, 2019), 14.

14. Iain Provan, *Seriously Dangerous Religion: What the Old Testament Really Says and Why It Matters* (Waco: Baylor University Press, 2014), 421n52.

15. Provan, *Seriously Dangerous Religion*, 420n48.

16. L. Daniel Hawk, *The Violence of the Biblical God: Canonical Narrative and Christian Faith* (Grand Rapids: Eerdmans, 2019), 167.

17. Hawk, *Violence*, 26.

18. Contra Arie Versluis, *The Command to Exterminate the Canaanites: Deuteronomy 7*, Old Testament Studies 71 (Leiden: Brill, 2017).

19. David Lamb, "God Behaving Badly: Part I," interview by Frank Viola, *Beyond Evangelical* (blog), accessed January 28, 2022, https://frankviola.org/2012/05/08/godbehavingbadly1/. See Lamb, *God Behaving Badly: Is the God of the Old Testament Angry, Sexist and Racist?* (Downers Grove, IL: IVP Academic, 2010).

20. The fact that Amalekites were nomads doesn't undermine the hyperbole bound up in the "universal conquest" motif, contra William J. Webb and Gordon K. Oeste, *Bloody, Brutal, and Barbaric? Wrestling with Troubling War Texts* (Downers Grove, IL: IVP Academic, 2019), 210–11.

21. See James K. Hoffmeier, *Israel in Egypt: The Evidence for the Authenticity of the Exodus Tradition* (Oxford: Oxford University Press, 1999), 1–42.

22. Ralph W. Klein, *1 Samuel*, Word Biblical Commentary 10 (Waco: Word, 1983), 150.

23. David G. Firth, *1 & 2 Samuel* (Downers Grove, IL: IVP Academic, 2009), 173.

24. Firth, *1 & 2 Samuel*, 173.

Chapter 28　Revisiting the Translation of *Herem*

1. Critics from within such as Greg Boyd and Randal Rauser make this claim in their aforementioned works.

2. See John H. Walton and J. Harvey Walton, *The Lost World of the Israelite Conquest: Covenant, Retribution, and the Fate of the Canaanites* (Downers Grove, IL: IVP Academic, 2017), 167–94.

3. David G. Firth, *Joshua* (Bellingham, WA: Lexham, 2021), 55.

4. Markus Zehnder. "The Annihilation of the Canaanites: Reassessing the Brutality of the Biblical Witnesses," in *Encountering Violence*

in the Bible, ed. Markus Zehnder and Hallvard Hamelia (Sheffield: Sheffield Phoenix, 2013), 269.

5. Firth, *Joshua*, 22.

6. Firth, *Joshua*, 56.

7. Lissa Wray Beal, *Joshua* (Grand Rapids: Zondervan, 2019), 254.

8. John Goldingay, *Old Testament Ethics: A Guided Tour* (Downers Grove, IL: IVP Academic, 2019), 269.

9. W. L. Moberly, *Old Testament Theology: Reading the Old Testament as Christian Scripture* (Grand Rapids: Baker Academic, 2013), 73–74.

10. David G. Firth, *The Message of Joshua* (Downers Grove, IL: IVP Academic, 2015), 21.

11. See William Ford, "'Dispossessing' the Canaanites in Deuteronomy," in *In the Cross-Hairs: Bible and Violence in Focus*, ed. Michael Spalione and Helen Paynter (Sheffield: Sheffield Phoenix Press, 2022), 57–72.

12. Walton and Walton, *Lost World of the Israelite Conquest*, 167–94.

13. Walton and Walton, *Lost World of the Israelite Conquest*, 177.

14. Walton and Walton, *Lost World of the Israelite Conquest*, 176–77.

15. Firth, *Message of Joshua*, 127.

Chapter 29　Deuteronomy's Intensified Rhetoric and the Use of *Haram*

1. Iain Provan, *Seriously Dangerous Religion: What the Old Testament Really Says and Why It Matters* (Waco: Baylor University Press, 2014), 421n52.

2. See "*Haram* as Identity Removal" in chap. 28.

3. "Drive out" (*garash*): Exod. 23:28; Lev. 18:24; Num. 33:52; Deut. 6:19; 7:1; 9:4; 18:12; "dispossess" (*yarash*): Num. 21:32; Deut. 7:17; 9:1; 11:23; 18:14; 19:1; Josh. 13:6; 14:12; 15:63; 16:10; 17:13, 18; Judg. 1:19; etc.

4. William J. Webb and Gordon K. Oeste, *Bloody, Brutal, and Barbaric? Wrestling with Troubling War Texts* (Downers Grove, IL: IVP Academic, 2019), 248–49.

5. Webb and Oeste, *Bloody, Brutal, and Barbaric?*, 249n.

6. Tremper Longman III, *Confronting Old Testament Controversies: Pressing Questions about Evolution, Sexuality, History, and Violence* (Grand Rapids: Baker Books, 2019), 168.

7. Longman, *Confronting Old Testament Controversies*, 171.

8. This includes Goldingay, Firth, Lamb, Wray Beal, Provan, Walton and Walton, and others.

9. David G. Firth, *The Message of Joshua* (Downers Grove, IL: IVP Academic, 2015), 21.

10. Provan, *Seriously Dangerous Religion*, 421n52.

11. John H. Walton and J. Harvey Walton, *The Lost World of the Israelite Conquest: Covenant, Retribution, and the Fate of the Canaanites* (Downers Grove, IL: IVP Academic, 2017), 193.

12. Gordon Wenham, *Exploring the Old Testament*, vol. 1, *A Guide to the Pentateuch* (Downers Grove, IL: InterVarsity, 2003), 137.

13. Longman, *Confronting Old Testament Controversies*, 171.

14. Webb and Oeste, *Bloody, Brutal, and Barbaric?*, 194–95.

15. Webb and Oeste, *Bloody, Brutal, and Barbaric?*, 194.

16. See Judg. 3:7–11; 2 Sam. 8:2, 11–14; 10:1–14 // 1 Chron. 19:1–15; 2 Sam. 10:15–19 // 1 Chron. 19:16–19; 2 Sam. 12:29–31 // 1 Chron. 20:1–3; 1 Kings 11:15–17; 22:29–40; 2 Kings 3:1–27; 8:20–22 // 2 Chron. 21:8–10; 2 Kings 8:28 // 2 Chron. 22:5–6; 1 Chron. 5:10, 19–22; 18:1–2, 3–9, 12–13; 2 Chron. 20:7; 25:11–12, 14–15 // 2 Kings 14:7; 2 Chron. 27:5; Isa. 11:14. These references come from Webb and Oeste, *Bloody, Brutal, and Barbaric?*, 193n.

17. Webb and Oeste, *Bloody, Brutal, and Barbaric?*, 196–97 (see footnotes also).

18. Some insights in this section drawn from Webb and Oeste, *Bloody, Brutal, and Barbaric?*, 174–230, esp. 196–202. In two explicitly detailed accounts, a literal totalistic language applies: (a) Achan and his family (Josh. 7); (b) the entire priestly family of Ahimelech—save one—killed by an enraged, vindictive Saul (1 Sam. 22). For the other *herem* cases we have contextual and genre reasons for rejecting literal "total-kill" scenarios.

19. For example, Peter John Naylor, "Numbers," in *The New Bible Commentary*, ed. G. J. Wenham, J. A. Motyer, D. A. Carson, and R. T. France (Downers Grove, IL: InterVarsity, 1994), 194. Thanks to David Firth (July 29, 2021) and Lissa Wray Beale (August 2, 2021) for their insights on this question through personal correspondence. In addition, see David G. Firth, *Including the Stranger: Foreigners in the Former Prophets* (Downers Grove, IL: IVP Academic, 2019).

20. John Goldingay, *Numbers and Deuteronomy for Everyone* (Louisville: Westminster John Knox, 2010), 86.

21. See Ken Brown, "Vengeance and Vindication in Numbers 31," *Journal of Biblical Literature* 134, no. 1 (Spring 2015): 65–84; Brown cites other scholars (e.g., Horst Seebass) sympathetic to this second scenario. See also Goldingay, *Numbers and Deuteronomy*, 85–86.

22. Goldingay, *Numbers and Deuteronomy*, 85.

23. Brown, "Vengeance and Vindication," 67.

24. Brown, "Vengeance and Vindication," 69.

25. Brown, "Vengeance and Vindication," 79. See Brown's article for extensive elaboration on scenario 2.

26. Alan Millard, personal correspondence, January 20, 2022.

27. Gregory Boyd, *Crucifixion of the Warrior God: Violent Portraits of God in Light of the Cross*, 2 vols. (Minneapolis: Fortress, 2017), 2:965–68, 979; Randal Rauser follows Boyd to a point in *Jesus Loves Canaanites: Biblical Genocide in the Light of Moral Intuition* (Canada: 2 Cup Press, 2021), 298–99. He disagrees with the literal hornets strategy (302–6).

Chapter 30 Did the Israelites "Cruelly Invade" the Land of Canaan?

1. Eric Seibert, *The Violence of Scripture: Overcoming the Old Testament's Troubling Legacy* (Minneapolis: Fortress, 2012), 117. Seibert believes that these "violent" Old Testament events didn't take place. By contrast, Greg Boyd claims they *did* take place but that the actual God didn't command this: Boyd, *Crucifixion of the Warrior God: Violent Portraits of God in Light of the Cross*, 2 vols. (Minneapolis: Fortress, 2017), 1:343.

2. *Saving Private Ryan*, directed by Steven Spielberg (Dreamworks/Paramount Pictures, 1998).

3. John Goldingay, *Old Testament Ethics: A Guided Tour* (Downers Grove, IL: IVP Academic, 2019), 267.

4. Richard Hess, *Joshua* (Downers Grove, IL: IVP Academic, 2008), 233; J. Gordon McConville, *Deuteronomy* (Downers Grove, IL: IVP Academic, 2002), 212–32.

5. Richard Hess, "Appendix 2," in Douglas Groothuis, *Christian Apologetics* (Downers Grove, IL: IVP Academic, 2021), 731 (emphasis added).

6. Hess responded to some of the criticisms Charlie Trimm directed against his view (Trimm, *The Genocide of the Canaanites* [Grand Rapids: Eerdmans, 2022], 72–73). Hess claimed that Trimm makes claims but doesn't offer substantive archaeological evidence to the contrary. (a) Jericho doesn't reflect that a civilian population lived

there. It was a fort without various classes of people, as "diagnostic," elite-style pottery would attest to this, but it is missing. (b) For Joshua, Jericho is the city in focus. In other cities, no other civilians are specifically mentioned—only kings, agents of the king, and soldiers of the army. Hess writes, "In the end, I have now tested this argument for decades and have yet to find any significant flaws in it or a more reliable model that incorporates the biblical and Late Bronze Age archaeological evidence." In addition to Hess, *Joshua*, see Richard S. Hess, "The Jericho and Ai of the Book of Joshua," in *Critical Issues in Early Israelite History*, ed. Richard S. Hess, Gerald A. Klingbeil, and Paul J. Ray Jr. (Winona Lake, IN: Eisenbrauns, 2008); also, John M. Monson, "Enter Joshua: The 'Mother of Current Debates' in Biblical Archaeology," in *Do Historical Matters Matter to Faith? A Critical Appraisal of Modern and Postmodern Approaches to Scripture*, eds. James K. Hoffmeier and Dennis R. Magary (Wheaton, IL: Crossway, 2012), 427–58; Anson Rainey, *The Sacred Bridge: Carta's Atlas of the Biblical World*, ed. Anson Rainey and R. Steven Notley (Jerusalem: Carta, 2006).

7. Hess, "Appendix 2," 731.

8. Boyd, *Crucifixion*, 2:957.

9. Daniel M. Fouts observes, "If numerical hyperbole was employed, and is especially prevalent in the largest numbers of Scripture, then the problems traditionally ascribed to the large numbers can be reconciled easily." Fouts, "Numbers, Large Numbers," in *Dictionary of Old Testament Historical Books*, ed. Bill Arnold and H. G. M. Williamson (Downers Grove, IL: InterVarsity, 2003), 753.

10. Fouts, "Numbers, Large Numbers," 753.

11. Colin J. Humphreys, "The Number of People in the Exodus from Egypt: Decoding Mathematically the Very Large Numbers in Numbers I and XXVI," *Vetus Testamentum* 48 (1998): 196–213, esp. 203–4. See also David G. Firth, *1 & 2 Samuel* (Downers Grove, IL: IVP Academic, 2009), 173. How does this square with the large number Paul uses in 1 Corinthians 10:8 (where twenty-three thousand fell in one day)? In personal correspondence (June 28, 2019), Humphreys notes that the translators of the Septuagint (the Greek Old Testament) used those large numbers. As the notion that these were much smaller numbers was lost to the scribes, Paul went along with what was translated—namely, the larger number.

12. Humphreys, "Number of People." Also, Colin J. Humphreys, "The Numbers in the

Exodus from Egypt: A Further Appraisal," *Vetus Testamentum* 50, no. 3 (2000): 323–28.

13. See Paul Copan and Matthew Flannagan, *Did God Really Command Genocide? Coming to Terms with the Justice of God* (Grand Rapids: Baker Books, 2014), chap. 19.

Chapter 31　The "Actual" God in Old Testament Warfare

1. Gregory Boyd, *Crucifixion of the Warrior God: Violent Portraits of God in Light of the Cross*, 2 vols. (Minneapolis: Fortress, 2017), 2:928.

2. A representative voice is Joyce Baldwin, *Esther* (Downers Grove, IL: InterVarsity, 1984), 104.

3. J. G. McConville, *Ezra, Nehemiah, and Esther* (Louisville: Westminster John Knox, 1985), 193. See also H. G. M. Williamson, *Ezra, Nehemiah* (Waco: Word, 1985), 316: "These verses [22–25] are . . . bound together by a certain theme (the conquest as fulfillment of God's promise to give the land)."

4. Williamson, *Ezra, Nehemiah*, 315.

5. Baldwin, *Esther*, 104.

6. See L. Allen and T. Laniak, *Ezra, Nehemiah, Esther* (Peabody, MA: Hendrickson, 2003), 256.

7. John Goldingay, *Joshua, Judges, and Ruth for Everyone* (Louisville: Westminster John Knox, 2011), 3. See chap. 26 above.

8. Of course, *both* Moses and Aaron acted faithlessly at Meribah (27:13–14; cf. 20:12, 24). The problem wasn't that Moses struck the rock with his staff. He had done that before at the start of Israel's wilderness wanderings (Exod. 17:6), and in this scenario God told Moses to take his rod (Num. 20:8–9). His unbelief was expressed when he said, "Shall we bring forth water for you from this rock?" (Num. 20:10; cf. Ps. 106:32: "He [Moses] spoke rashly with his lips"). God chastised both Moses and Aaron because they had "not believed" God or "treated [him] as holy" in the sight of Israel (Num. 20:12). The Lord then announced Aaron's death and commanded that he be stripped of his high priestly garments, which were then given to his son Eleazar. And then Aaron died (vv. 23–29). Likewise, God announced that Moses would not enter the promised land and would likewise die (27:13–14). Even so, both testaments fully praise Moses as a divinely guided, authoritative, and trustworthy prophet who spoke with God face-to-face.

9. Paul Copan, "Not Cruciform Enough: Getting Our Hermeneutical Bearings in the Wake of a Boydian Reinterpretation," in *Hermeneutics of Biblical Violence*, ed. Trevor Laurence and

Helen Paynter (Sheffield: Sheffield Phoenix Press, forthcoming).

10. Christian Hofreiter, *Making Sense of Old Testament Genocide: Christian Interpretations of Herem Passages* (Oxford: Oxford University Press, 2018), 251.

11. Roy E. Gane, *Old Testament Law for Christians: Original Context and Enduring Application* (Grand Rapids: Baker Academic, 2017), 335.

12. This is largely pulled together from L. Daniel Hawk, *The Violence of the Biblical God: Canonical Narrative and Christian Faith* (Grand Rapids: Eerdmans, 2019).

13. Jerry Shepherd, personal correspondence, July 26, 2021. Only in Lamentations 2:6 do we see God's action against the temple as *violent*.

14. Hawk, *Violence*, 167.

15. Hawk, *Violence*, 168. Claude Mariottini notes that Boyd virtually ignores the book of Jonah, where God's compassionate character informs the book's events (4:2). More to the point, before Nineveh's repentance after Jonah's preaching, God had threatened to punish Nineveh ("Nineveh will be overthrown" [3:4]). Mariottini, *Divine Violence and the Character of God* (Eugene, OR: Wipf & Stock, 2022), 161–62.

16. Hawk, *Violence*, 199.

17. Hawk, *Violence*, 197.

18. Hawk, *Violence*, 188.

19. Hawk, *Violence*, 188.

20. Boyd, *Crucifixion*, 1:580.

21. I was present when Richard Hays asserted this in a panel discussion that included James Skillen and Keith Pavlischek at the Evangelical Philosophical Society meeting in Nashville, Tennessee (November 2000). He claimed that a Christian who worked as a military recruiter was tantamount to someone running an organization called "Pimps for Jesus."

22. G. E. M. Anscombe, "War and Murder," in *War, Morality, and the Military Profession*, ed. Malham M. Wakin (Boulder, CO: Westview, 1979), 294.

23. Anscombe, "War and Murder," 200.

24. Anscombe, "War and Murder," 197.

25. Peter C. Craigie, *The Problem of War in the Old Testament* (Grand Rapids: Eerdmans, 1979), 96.

26. Moltmann has been a strong influence on Boyd (*Crucifixion*, 1:xxxvii).

27. Jürgen Moltmann, *The Experiment Hope* (1975; repr., Eugene, OR: Wipf & Stock, 2003), 142. Moltmann speaks of this act of love "that is ready to incur guilt in order to save."

28. Moltmann, *Experiment Hope*, 135.

29. For example, M. Daniel Carroll R., "Reflections from a Christotelic Pacifist on Greg Boyd's Christocentric Pacifism" (paper, Evangelical Theological Society, Denver, CO, November 2018); Peter Craigie, *The Problem of War in the Old Testament* (Grand Rapids: Eerdmans, 1979).

30. C. S. Lewis to John Beversluis, July 3, 1963, quoted in John Beversluis, *C. S. Lewis and the Search for Rational Religion* (Grand Rapids: Eerdmans, 1985), 156–57.

31. C. S. Lewis to John Beversluis, July 3, 1963, quoted in Beversluis, *C. S. Lewis*, 157.

32. Eleonore Stump, "Reply to Draper," in *Divine Evil? The Moral Character of the God of Abraham*, ed. Michael Bergmann, Michael J. Murray, and Michael C. Rea (New York: Oxford University Press, 2010), 204.

33. Stump, "Reply to Draper," 207.

Chapter 32 "God Is Christlike, and in Him There Is No Un-Christlikeness at All"

1. Arthur Michael Ramsey, *God, Christ and the World: A Study in Contemporary Theology* (1969; repr., Eugene, OR: Wipf & Stock, 2012), 37.

2. Eric Seibert's "general inspiration" rather than full ("plenary") inspiration of the Old Testament (*Disturbing Divine Behavior: Troubling Old Testament Images of God* [Minneapolis: Fortress, 2009], 273) stands against the New Testament's perspective—including Jesus's (cf. 2 Tim. 3:16; Matt. 5:18: "the smallest letter or stroke").

3. Gregory Boyd, *Crucifixion of the Warrior God: Violent Portraits of God in Light of the Cross*, 2 vols. (Minneapolis: Fortress, 2017), 2:1261.

4. Tremper Longman III, *Confronting Old Testament Controversies: Pressing Questions about Evolution, Sexuality, History, and Violence* (Grand Rapids: Baker Books, 2019), 164.

5. Richard Dawkins, *The God Delusion* (Boston: Houghton Mifflin, 2006), 51.

6. Peter Enns, "Is Peter Enns a Marcionite?," *Peter Enns: Rethinking Biblical Christianity* (blog), January 17, 2014, https://www.patheos.com/blogs/peterenns/2014/01/is-pete-enns-a-marcionite/.

7. For a fuller treatment of Boyd in particular, see Paul Copan, "Not Cruciform Enough: Getting Our Hermeneutical Bearings in the Wake of a Boydian Reinterpretation," in *Hermeneutics of Biblical Violence*, eds. Trevor Laurence and Helen Paynter (Sheffield: Sheffield Phoenix Press, forthcoming).

8. Roger E. Olson, "What about Those Old Testament 'Texts of Terror?' (A Review of an Almost New Book by Philip Jenkins)," *Patheos* (blog), October 29, 2012, https://www.patheos.com/blogs/rogereolson/201q12/10/what-about-those-old-testament-texts-of-terror-a-review-of-an-almost-new-book-by-philip-jenkins/. See chap. 26 above.

9. Miroslav Volf, *Free of Charge: Giving and Forgiving in a Culture Stripped of Grace* (Grand Rapids: Zondervan, 2006), 138–39; see also Volf, *Exclusion and Embrace: A Theological Exploration of Identity, Otherness, and Reconciliation* (Nashville: Abingdon, 1996). See the quotation and discussion in Paul Copan, *Is God a Moral Monster? Making Sense of the Old Testament God* (Grand Rapids: Baker Books, 2011), 192.

10. Interview with N. T. Wright, "N. T. Wright Wants to Save the Best Worship Songs," *Christianity Today*, August 29, 2013, http://www.christianitytoday.com/ct/2013/september/nt-wright-saving-psalms.html?start=2." See chap. 18 above.

11. Thomas Cahill, *Gifts of the Jews: How a Tribe of Desert Nomads Changed the Way Everyone Thinks and Feels* (New York: Anchor, 1999), 245.

12. C. S. Lewis, *The Lion, the Witch and the Wardrobe* (New York: HarperCollins, 1950), chap. 8.

Chapter 33 Our Critics from Without (1)

1. "Richard Dawkins Talks to Joan Bakewell," YouTube video, 57:33, posted by Hay Festival, August 8, 2014, https://youtu.be/daW8Yz3vbUg. Dawkins's comments start at 30:38 in the video.

2. Dawkins's 2006 BBC documentary on religion *The Root of All Evil?* (available at https://youtu.be/YrB1riTURhU) was the basis of his 2008 book: Richard Dawkins, *The God Delusion* (Boston: Houghton Mifflin, 2008).

3. In Ruth Gledhill, "Scandal and Schism Leave Christians Praying For a 'New Reformation,'" *The Times*, April 6, 2010, https://www.thetimes.co.uk/article/scandal-and-schism-leave-christians-praying-for-a-new-reformation-lflgv79r7js.

4. Paul Copan, *Loving Wisdom: A Guide to Philosophy and Christian Faith*, 2nd ed. (Grand Rapids: Eerdmans, 2020). See the first section, "Preliminary Matters."

5. Martin E. Marty, *Politics, Religion, and the Common Good*, with Jonathan Moore (San Francisco: Jossey-Bass, 2000), 10.

6. See chapters 1–6 in Copan, *Loving Wisdom*.

7. Alvin Plantinga, "A Christian Life Partly Lived," in *Philosophers Who Believe: The Spiritual Journeys of 11 Leading Thinkers*, ed. Kelly James Clark (Downers Grove, IL: InterVarsity, 1993), 71.

8. C. S. Lewis, "Is Theology Poetry?," in *The Weight of Glory and Other Addresses* (New York: Macmillan, 1965), 140.

Chapter 34 Our Critics from Without (2)

1. See, e.g., Joshua Berman, *Created Equal: How the Bible Broke with Ancient Political Thought* (Oxford: Oxford University Press, 2008); David Baker, *Tight Fists or Open Hands? Wealth and Poverty in Old Testament Law* (Grand Rapids: Eerdmans, 2009).

2. See Tom Gilson's excellent book, *Too Good to Be False: How Jesus' Incomparable Character Reveals His Reality* (Tampa: DeWard, 2020).

3. Michael F. Bird, "How God Became Jesus—and How I Came to Faith in Him," *Christianity Today*, April 16, 2014, https://www.christianitytoday.com/ct/2014/april-web-only/how-god-became-jesus-and-how-i-came-to-faith-in-him.html.

4. Tom Holland, "Why I Was Wrong About Christianity," *New Statesman*, September 14, 2016, http://www.newstatesman.com/politics/religion/2016/09/tom-holland-why-i-was-wrong-about-christianity. See also Tom Holland's magisterial book *Dominion: How the Christian Revolution Remade the World* (New York: Basic Books, 2019).

5. Jonathon Van Maren, "The Turning Tide of Intellectual Atheism," Mercatornet, June 29, 2021, https://mercatornet.com/the-turning-tide-of-intellectual-atheism/72999/.

6. Rodney Stark, email correspondence, December 12, 2011. For documentation on the impact of the gospel in history, see Alvin J. Schmidt, *How Christianity Changed the World* (Grand Rapids: Zondervan, 2004); Vishal Mangalwadi, *The Book That Made Your World: How the Bible Created the Soul of Western Civilization* (Nashville: Thomas Nelson, 2012).

7. Brian Stewart, "On the Front Lines," Christianity.ca, address at Knox College, Galesburg, IL, May 12, 2004, https://waynenorthey.com/wp-content/uploads/2015/03/On-The-Front-Lines.pdf.

8. Paul Copan, "Grounding Human Rights: Naturalism's Failure and Biblical Theism's Success," in *Legitimizing Human Rights*, ed. Angus Menuge, Applied Legal Philosophy Series (Aldershot, UK: Ashgate, 2013), 11–31; Copan, "The

Biblical Worldview Context for Religious Liberty," in *Religious Liberty: Its Nature, Scope, and Limits*, ed. Angus Menuge (London: Routledge, 2017), 11–33.

9. Francis Spufford, *Unapologetic: Why, Despite Everything, Christianity Can Still Make Surprising Emotional Sense* (New York: HarperOne, 2012).

10. Pascal, *Pensées*, no. 139.

11. John Calvin, *Institutes of the Christian Religion*, trans. Henry Beveridge (Grand Rapids: Eerdmans, 1953), 3.13.3.

12. Calvin, *Institutes* 3.8.3.

13. Luis Rivas with Francis Spufford, "Q&A on 'Impenitente' [*Unapologetic*]," October 11, 2014, http://unapologetic-book.tumblr.com/post /99715799639/qa-about-impenitente-english -version.

14. R. W. L. Moberly, *The Bible in a Disenchanted Age: The Enduring Possibility of Christian Faith* (Grand Rapids: Baker Academic, 2018), 92.

Subject Index

Scripture Index